REVISED EDITION

Public Policymaking in a Globalized World

Some Books from Social Science Press and Aurum Books

Society and Culture in India: A Reader (PB)
EDITED BY SUBAS MOHAPATRA

Labour, State and Society in Rural India: A Class-relational Approach (HB)
JONATHAN PATTENDEN

From 'People' to 'Citizen': Democracy's Must Take Road (HB)
DIPANKAR GUPTA

Much Ado Over Coffee: Indian Coffee House Then and Now
BHASWATI BHATTACHARYA

Gitanjali Reborn: William Radice's Writings on Rabindranath Tagore
Edited by MARTIN KÄMPCHEN

Gandhi: Anti-biography of a Great Soul (HB)
MICHAEL DE SAINT-CHERON

Shades of Difference: Selected Writings of Rabindranath Tagore with Audio Visual Material, *Tagore and His World* (HB)
Edited by RADHA CHAKRAVARTY

Calcutta: The Stormy Decades (HB)
Edited by TANIKA SARKAR AND SEKHAR BANDYOPADHYAY

Dalit Women: Honour and Patriarchy in South India (HB)
CLARINDA STILL

Tamil Brahmans: The Creation of a Middle-Class Caste (HB)
CJ FULLER AND HARIPRIYA NARASIMHAN

Persistence of Poverty in India (HB)
Edited by NANDINI GOOPTU AND JONATHAN PARRY

Savage Attack: Tribal Insurgency in India (HB)
Edited by CRISPIN BATES AND ALPA SHAH

The Year of Blood: Essays on the Revolt of 1857 (HB)
RUDRANGSHU MUKHERJEE

The Autobiography of a Revolutionary in British India (HB)
KALI GHOSH

The Many Worlds of Sarala Devi: A Diary
Translated by SUKHENDU RAY and
The Tagores and Sartorial Styles: A Photo Essay (HB)
MALAVIKA KARLEKAR

Viramma: Life of a Dalit (PB)
VIRAMMA, JOSIANE RACINE, AND JEAN-LUC RACINE

Everyday Nationalism: Women of the Hindu Right (HB)
KALYANI DEVAKI MENON

Marriage, Love, Caste & Kinship Support: Lived Experiences of the Urban Poor in India (HB)
SHALINI GROVER

Religious Division and Social Conflict: The Emergence of Hindu Nationalism in Rural India (PB)
PEGGY FROERER

Literature and Nationalist Ideology: Writing Histories of Indian Languages (PB)
HANS HARDER

The Everyday State and Society in Modern India (PB)
Edited by CJ FULLER AND VERONIQUE BENEI

Economics and Its Stories (HB)
AMAL SANYAL

Telecommunications Industry in India: State Business and Labour in a Global Economy (HB)
DILIP SUBRAMANIAM

Cultural History of Modern India (PB)
Edited by MEENAKSHI KHANNA

Income Poverty and Beyond: Human Development in India
Edited by RAJA J CHELLIAH AND R SUDARSHAN

The Politics of the Pharmaceutical Industry and Access to Medicines: World Pharmacy and India (HB)
Edited by HANS LOGREN

SERIES: EVERYDAY LIFE OF POLITICAL STRUGGLES

Windows into a Revolution: Ethnographies of Maoism in India and Nepal (HB)
Edited by ALPA SHAH AND JUDITH PETTIGREW

Rebels from the Mud Houses: Dalits and the Making of the Maoist Revolution in Bihar (HB)
GEORGE KUNNATH

Unruly Hills: Nature and Nation in India's North-East (HB)
BENGT G. KARLSSON

SERIES: GERMAN WRITINGS ON INDIA AND SOUTH ASIA

'When the war began we heard of several kings': South Asian Prisoners in World War I Germany (HB)
Edited by FRANSIZKA ROY, HEIKE LIEBAU AND RAVI AHUJA

Cultural Encounters in India: The Local Co-Workers of the Tranquebar Mission, 18th-19th Centuries (HB)
HEIKE LIEBAU

'Everwhere is Becoming the Same'? Regulating IT-work between India and Germany (HB)
NICOLE MAYER-AHUJA

SERIES: FRENCH WRITINGS ON INDIA AND SOUTH ASIA

Scholars and Prophets: Sociology of India from France in the 19th and 20th Centuries (HB)
ROLAND LARDINOIS

Tocqueville in India (HB)
JEAN ALPHONSE BERNARD

AURUM BOOKS

Sabotage (PB)
ANITA AGNIHOTRI
Translated by ARUNAVA SINHA

Opium Poppy (PB)
HUBERT HADDAD
Translated by RENUKA GEORGE

REVISED EDITION

Public Policymaking in a Globalized World

Edited by

Robin J. Lewis

SOCIAL SCIENCE PRESS

Published by

Esha Béteille
Social Science Press
69 Jor Bagh, New Delhi 110003

ISBN 978-93-83166-24-4

Set in Plantin Std
Typeset by Manmohan Kumar, Delhi 110035
Printed by Vee Enn Print-O-Pac
A-5, Flatted Factory Complex, Okhla Industrial Estate,
New Delhi - 110020
Email : vnprints@gmail.com

Contents

PART II REFLECTIONS ON POLICYMAKING AND POLICY ANALYSIS

PART III GLOBAL CASE STUDIES: INDIA, CHINA, EGYPT, SOUTH AFRICA AND RWANDA

Graphs, Tables, Figures and Diagrams

Graphs

Tables

Figures

Diagrams

Appendices

Acknowledgements

Many people contributed to the completion of this volume and I am very pleased to acknowledge their efforts here. This volume grew out of a path-breaking conference hosted by Sabancı University and the Istanbul Policy Center (IPC) in November 2014. The conference brought together public policy scholars from around the world with their colleagues at Turkish universities to discuss the challenges of teaching this subject in a globalized policy environment. The conference received generous financial support from the Friedrich Naumann Stiftung and its then Head of Istanbul Office, Hans-Georg Fleck, whom we thank.

Professor Korel Göymen, a distinguished policy scholar and practitioner— and a dear, long-time colleague — and I together edited an earlier version of this volume that was produced by the IPC in 2015. My deep and abiding gratitude goes to Korel for his vision and guidance.

The current volume is published by the Social Science Press in Delhi, under the able direction of Esha Béteille and with the kind mentorship of Sudarshan Ramaswamy of O.P. Jindal Global University.

A very special vote of thanks is due to Radha Béteille, whose immense contribution to its quality cannot be measured. She did her copyediting work with great intelligence and subtlety, qualities not easy to find in today's professional life. I am most grateful to Radha and Social Science Press.

Finally, I am thankful to my brilliant and dedicated colleagues whose papers appear here: their incisive scholarly contributions to global public policy studies speak for themselves.

Contributors

Hüseyin Gül is Dean, Faculty of Economics and Administrative Sciences, Department of Political Science and Public Administration at Süleyman Demirel Üniversitesi, Turkey.

Gökhan Orhan is Professor and Head of Department at the Faculty of Economic and Administrative Sciences, Department of Political Science and Public Administration, Bandırma Onyedi Eylül University, Turkey. He was formerly with Balıkesir University, Turkey.

Raymond Saner is Founder of Centre for Socio-Eco-Nomic Development (CSEND) in Geneva and is Professor in Organization and International Management, University of Basle, Switzerland.

Lichia Yiu is President, Centre for Socio-Eco-Nomic Development (CSEND) in Geneva, Switzerland.

Hubert Heinelt is Professor of Public Administration, Public Policy and Urban Studies at the Institute of Political Science at Technische Universitat Darmstadt, Germany.

Ramaswamy Sudarshan is Dean, Jindal School of Government and Public Policy, O.P. Jindal Global University in Sonepat, India.

Erhard Friedberg is Professor Emeritus of Sociology at Sciences Po, Paris, who completed a 28-month mission at the School of Government and Public Policy, Indonesia.

Sergey Zuev is Dean of the School of Public Policy and a Member of the Academic Council of the Russian Presidential Academy of National Economy and Public Administration (RANEPA), Russia.

Göktuğ Morçöl is Professor of Public Policy and Administration at Pennsylvania State University, USA.

Alexey Verbetsky is Deputy Director, School of Public Policy and Management at the Russian Presidential Academy of National Economy and Public Administration (RANEPA). He also serves as the Executive Director of the International Development and Public Policy Alliance (IDPPA).

Pregala Pillay is Vice-Dean, Social Impact and Transformation in the Faculty of Economic and Management Sciences, Stellenbosch University, South Africa.

Firoz Khan is Senior Lecturer at the School of Public Leadership, Stellenbosch University, South Africa.

Bhuvaneswari Raman is Associate Professor and Assistant Director, Centre for the Study of Urban Transformation, Jindal School of Government and Public Policy, O.P. Jindal Global University in Sonepat, India.

Tian Fangmeng is Assistant Professor at the School of Social Development and Public Policy, Beijing Normal University, China.

Dina Wafa is Director of the Executive Education unit of the School of Global Affairs and Public Policy (GAPP) at The American University in Cairo, Egypt.

İzak Atiyas is Senior Scholar at Istanbul Policy Center and Professor at the Faculty of Arts and Social Sciences, Sabancı University, Turkey.

Muhittin Acar is Professor at the Department of Political Science and Public Administration (ANTICORRP) at Hacettepe University in Ankara, Turkey.

A. Argun Akdoğan is Associate Professor in the Public Administration Institute for Turkey and the Middle East, TODAİE, Turkey.

Mustafa Kemal Bayırbağ is Associate Professor at the Department of Political Science and Public Administration, Middle East Technical University (METU), Turkey.

Mete Yıldız is Professor of Public Administration in the Department of Political Science and Public Administration at Hacettepe University, Turkey.

Can Umut Çiner is Associate Professor, Faculty of Political Science, Department of Political Science and Public Administration, Ankara University, Turkey.

Introduction to the First Edition

Public policy is a contested sphere. From politics to civil society, bureaucracy to academia, many professions have staked a claim on it since the latter half of the 20th century. For most of our known history, the government was the sole proprietor of public policy. Until the civil rights movements that rattled the world in the 1960s, very little outside influence played a role in the government's policies for the greater good of the public. A few non-governmental organizations that had succeeded in affecting public policy in the first half of the 20th century were professional lobbying groups, cartels or unions. They were mostly confined to the Western world and could be counted on one hand. In fact, since these institutions were formed to look after the interests of particular groups, their impact on public policymaking was dubious at best.

However, the tumultuous 1960s brought the curtain down on the post-war stability of the 1950s, and with that the invisible barrier between the public and the government cracked. With the outbreak of the Vietnam War, the civil rights movements, fights for gender equality and women's suffrage, the OPEC crisis and global economic volatility, people all over the world mobilized and staked their claim on policymaking in various shapes and forms. Some used mass protests, some organized around public advocacy groups, and a few built professional public policy research institutes. Especially from the mid-60s to the mid-80s, advocacy groups funded and initiated by the public, monitoring agencies, and think tanks mushroomed in North America and Western Europe. This epoch also corresponded to the increased access granted to public advocates, civil rights representatives and attorneys, as well as to outside policy experts by governments mostly in the aforementioned territories.

By the turn of the last millennium, public policy was no longer confined to the realm of civil society; it had evolved far beyond the perception of a ragtag, concerned citizens' movement which would assemble in world capitals whenever the interests of their constituencies were threatened or ignored. On the contrary, these groups had become much more institutionalized. Many had opened permanent representations in power capitals such as Washington, New York, London, Berlin, Brussels, and even in Ankara and Istanbul towards the end of the millennium. More importantly, they constructed their policy advocacy on sound academic research and legal bases and often confronted governments with irrefutable, fact-based, and powerful alternative policy options.

With the advent of globalization around this time, two important occurrences changed public policymaking once and for all. First, governance as a concept had become more fragmented. The international and local levels of governance for the first time came into the limelight as actors to be reckoned with. On certain occasions, central governments were bypassed; local and international governmental actors were able to engage one another freely. Second, the concept of 'public' left national confines and assumed a more global definition that rallied concerned citizens of different states around common global causes. The coming of the EU as a supranational entity and its power over national competences, the influence of UN programmes on regimes in non-Western part of the world, and the increasing number of multinational corporations, multilateral agreements as well as free trade zones, turned policymaking into a more sophisticated endeavour. This development eventually tampered with the traditional definition of policymaking, as well as the fundamental principles, depth, and breadth of governance.

Therefore, there is a general shift in the understanding of public policymaking in recent years. The changing tenets of public policy also render academics, policy specialists, and decision-makers more flexible in determining the actors, instruments, and influence of public policymaking. The current sophistication of this concept requires thinking about government beyond its primary characteristics as an administration to decide on and look after the best interests of the public. For most academicians, policymaking has evolved to a different level now, and inter-regional relations have had an important impact on this change.

Cognizant of this evolving nature of the tenets of public policymaking in the 21st century, IPC, joined by the Friedrich Naumann Foundation, dedicated the 13th gathering of its time-honoured governance conference series to 'Public Policymaking in a Globalized World', with the participation of Turkish academicians interested in teaching public policy in Turkey, and of member-institutions of the International Development of Public Policy Alliance Network (IDPPA) coming from Brazil, China, Egypt, India, Russia and South Africa. This book is an outcome of the international workshop on public policymaking, structured into theoretical discussions and case studies on public policymaking at both national and international levels. I extend my thanks to each and every IPC research and administrative aide that was involved in the conference organization and preparation of this book.

We are thankful to the Friedrich Naumann Foundation and Hans George Fleck, Resident Representative, and to Belma Bağdat, Programme Director, for their continuous support.

Dr E. Fuat Keyman
Director, Istanbul Policy Center
Professor of International Relations, Sabancı University

Introduction to the Revised Edition

The advent of globalization has created new and complex contexts in which policymakers must operate. Previous norms and benchmarks for determining public policy have had to be discarded, as even the smallest and most seemingly circumscribed local issues now take on significance at the national, regional and global levels. Similarly, multilateral institutions such as the World Bank, International Monetary Fund and World Trade Organization have been compelled to expand their fields of vision to encompass an entirely new set of issues and multiple stakeholders wielding their concerns in increasingly assertive ways.

This, at the same time, has meant that quite a lot of policy seemingly adopted and implemented at the national level has really been a case of 'policy transfer'. The interaction between Brussels and member-states of the European Union attests to this clearly.

The Istanbul Policy Center and the Friedrich Naumann Foundation for Freedom on 28–29 November 2014 in Istanbul assembled scholars and practitioners from nearly a dozen countries to share their insights and to focus on new perspectives from the major emerging economies, whose views of globalization differ significantly in many respects from the foundational concepts of public policy (and of public administration) developed in the US and Europe. This book is an outcome of that initiative.

The contributions from seven member countries (except Malaysia and Thailand) of the International Development and Public Policy Alliance (IDPPA), a consortium of nine graduate schools of public policy from Brazil, China, Egypt, India, Russia, South Africa, Turkey, Malaysia and Thailand that has its headquarters at the Russian Presidential Academy of National Economy and Public Administration (RANEPA), further enrich the book.

The animating concept that run through almost every contribution in this volume, is a sense of urgency as to the need for an effective science (and art) of policymaking. As an academic field, public policy is inherently instrumental rather than intellectual: it seeks to create pathways to solutions of a complex of critical global crisis points – agriculture and global food supply, climate change, economic development, global trade and finance, terrorism and security, global pandemics, natural disasters – that can only be ameliorated by collective initiatives that cut decisively across national borders and traditional conceptual boundaries. While every policy dilemma at any level is mired in its unique economic, social, and political setting, in the end it is only the creation of global policy knowledge and training that can avert the enormous risks our planet faces. Whether explicit or implied in the papers that comprise this volume, it can be said that this is the fundamental objective of this fruitful gathering of all the scholars, practitioners and experts who have contributed to this volume.

Robin J. Lewis
Professor and Director (MGPP), RANEPA
President, IDPPA

PART I

GOVERNANCE AND THE POLICY PROCESS

1 Global Governance and Public Policymaking

Trends, Actors and Values

Hüseyin Gül

Abstract

The world has undergone transformations with important consequences for the way democracy, the state, and public policymaking processes have been structured and have worked. As a market ideology and democratic paradigm, neoliberalism has been the dominant model shaping all these recent changes and reform efforts as well as influencing the functioning of democratic policymaking processes at all levels. Many of the current issues drive actors at all levels to look at such matters from a global perspective in developing solutions. Since globalization implies interdependency in a contradictory world of competition and cooperation, global public policymaking processes involve increasingly learning from one another or monitoring, transferring, and implementing the best practices.

Some scholars continue to argue about what global governance actually means and how it works in practice. Still others dispute its importance. Yet, there is a general shift toward a complex system of governance in the area of global politics and public policymaking. This paper aims at exploring the changing environment and nature and the processes of public policymaking in the context of global governance. It also presents and discusses recent trends, developments, dynamics, and actors influencing the processes of global governance and public policymaking. Moreover, the paper aims to evaluate how these trends and developments influence the values driving or shaping global governance and public policymaking processes, and the interactions among the involved actors in the world. In this respect, this paper presents a critical analysis of how global governance works in practice, with a focus on what is being governed and how challenges to global governance are met.

Introduction

The world has undergone important transformations with profound consequences for the way in which democracy, the state and public policymaking processes have been structured and work. Major transformations and developments taking place globally include, but not limited to, increased and diversified citizen demands and expectations, revolutionary changes in ICTs, democratization, marketization, globalization, regionalization, decentralization, weakened nation states and urbanization. For instance, globalization has made it much easier to move around the globe, and financial assets, capital, labour, goods and services have become more fluid than ever before. In addition, international immigration, human trafficking, human right violations, the regulation of international trade and global commons, economic, environmental, fiscal and social crises, poverty, political conflicts, the protection of intellectual property and patent rights, among others, all drive countries and other related actors to look at such matters from a global perspective in order to develop viable, sustainable and mutual solutions. Many of such policy fields require thinking and developing policies globally but acting locally.

These developments are also accompanied by the proliferation of neoliberalism as a global ideology (Cerny 2008; Karaman and Altay 1997). The market system with competing actors and economic growth as its major goal has become the dominant model. Many developed and developing countries have economies that are globally integrated, technologically advanced and market-driven. Liberal democratic political systems with free competitive elections have proliferated in the world since the 1980s as was the case during the period following the Second World War. The collapse of the Soviet Union, increased diversity due to ethnic and religious revival, international mechanisms to protect human rights, global initiatives to govern the production of global goods and commerce, among others, all have contributed to the enhancement of global standards on democracy, basic human rights and markets.

In other words, neoliberalism as a market ideology and democratic paradigm has been the dominant model shaping all these recent changes and reform efforts as well as influencing the functioning of democratic policy processes globally, nationally, and locally, since the 1980s (Rosow 2000). Gu, Humphrey and Messner (2009: 274) argue that 'most discussions in the 1990s on the future of the world economy and of the global governance architecture turned around the concept of an OECD-led world order, with the United States, Europe, and Japan as the main pillars (the triad)'. Farazmand (1994: 64) states that this new global world order is also associated with the global slogan of democratization, marketization, global privatization and accompanying structural adjustments in political, economic and administrative systems in various countries.

One of the important results of such developments is the reshaping of the role of the state in and its relations with the market and society. Fougner critically states that 'neoliberalism has come to inform multiple practices on the part of state authorities' and 'that states are themselves increasingly subjected to a form of neoliberal governance in the contemporary world political economy... Neoliberals share the view that the market exists, and can only exist, under certain political, legal and institutional conditions that must be actively constructed by government' (2008: 307–08). In addition, that construction ought to be built on 'the ideas of governing society in the name of the economy' and of 're-defining the social sphere as a form of the economic domain'.

To meet the challenges raised by the new neoliberal world order and the new economy and society, the understanding of the state, public administration and public policymaking is also redefined by a neoliberal vision and rationality derived from arranged forms of entrepreneurial and competitive behaviour (namely the New Public Management – the NPM). Accordingly, the new reforms in the public sector have been introduced on the basis of the market rules and principles, competition, entrepreneurship, efficiency, effectiveness, performance, output legitimacy, etc. Along with the new developments and reforms, a hike in the demand for participation, responsiveness, transparency and accountability also seems to have triggered a tendency towards some form of democratic governance not only at the local, regional, and national levels but also at the global level.[1] Yet, this is a big challenge in a global polity of unprecedented size, diversity, and discord, requiring effective governance. But 'effective institutions are difficult to create and maintain and they must also meet standards of accountability and participation, and should foster persuasion rather than rely on coercion and interest-based bargaining' (Keohane 2001: 1).

Globalization implies interdependency binding states and international actors together in a contradictory world ridden with competition and cooperation, and with globalization and localization trends at the same time. Yet, this global web requires and depends on effective governance because 'effective governance is not inevitable. If it occurs, it is more likely to take place through interstate cooperation and transnational networks than through a world state' (Keohane 2001: 1). Thus, global governance also involves global, national and local (glocal) public policymaking processes. Moreover, global governance operates through global public policy processes that increasingly include learning from one another or monitoring, transferring and implementing the best practices. For instance, today countries, public agencies, and/or corporations watch the policies of their competitors carefully to ensure that they do not lag behind or are harmed by disadvantageous developments and regulations. Thus, they try to adopt international standards, transfer policies or implement best practices in order to stay competitive in the global economy. Of course there are cautionary and contradictory views. Keohane (2001: 1) states that not all patterns of globalization would be beneficial, especially one 'controlled by self-serving elites working to depress wages and suppress local political autonomy'. Thus, he argues that there is 'a need for not just effective governance but the

[1] Fraser-Moleketi (2012: 192–93) argues that the business model and market model of governance have failed because both sought to impose on government the methods, standards and values of private enterprise and the rational actor model. This failure has caused a hollowing out of the state and democracy. What is needed today is a restoration of committed public leadership and competent professionalism, institution-building, a restoration of public space and strong sense of community along with a creation of new tools and mechanisms for citizens to participate in the processes of democratic governance.

right kind of governance'. More critically, Webb (2006: 73) sees the present climate as the calm before the storm because 'the loss of democratic legitimacy within nation-states, combined with rising inequality, make the world system quite vulnerable to crisis (even revolutions) in the long run'.

Today, there are still discussions on what global governance actually means and how it works in practice. Yet, one could argue that there is a general shift towards a complex system of governance in the area of global politics and public policymaking. Thus, the main goal of this study is to explore the changing environment and nature of global governance and public policymaking. It also presents and discusses recent trends, developments, dynamics and actors influencing the processes of global governance and public policymaking. Moreover, the paper has the goal of evaluating how these trends and developments influence the values driving or shaping global governance and public policymaking processes and the interactions and collaboration among the involved state and non-state actors. In that respect, this paper presents a critical analysis of how global governance works in practice, with a focus on what is being governed and how challenges to global governance are met. Yet, the vast scope of the subject makes it difficult to cover and discuss all the topics related to the issues of global governance and public policymaking in the space allowed for this study.

Global Trends Shaping the Relations of Global Actors and Governance

An examination of trends regarding global governance and global policymaking processes requires us to have a sense of democratic trends in the world since it influences the way global governance and the policymaking process operates. In this regard, there is a *democratization* trend shaping the public policymaking and governance processes at the global scale as well as local, national and even organizational levels. Democratization refers to the proliferation of neoliberal pluralist democratic regimes in the world and this neoliberal democratic theory has been an integral part of the new world order with implications for public administration and politics since the 1980s (Farazmand 1994: 70). Democracy and democratization as political processes are valued as basic foundations for human freedom and a free and open society (Farazmand 1994: 67). Thus, democracy is seen as 'a set of practices and principles that institutionalize and thus ultimately protect freedom' (EIU 2014: 25).

From the perspective of participatory and deliberative democracy, the scope and form of participation in deliberation, decision making or other political activities are the key concerns. Generally speaking, the more inclusive the deliberation or decision making, the more democratic a political system is. The model of representative democracy stresses formal accountability mechanisms rather than participation. Yet, effective accountability requires mechanisms for information and communication between decision makers and stakeholders as well as mechanisms for imposing penalties. There is a distinction between external accountability of the power wielder to those affected by its activities, and internal accountability to the principles, values, goals, and employees of the organization. From the perspective of participatory democracy, the inclusion of the civic organizations, the public and stakeholders in the process of decision or policymaking is important for external accountability (Bexell, Tallberg and Uhlin 2010: 82). However, in Dingwerth's (2014) view, such notions of democracy are insufficient because they underpin formalistic procedures such as access of civil society organizations to policymaking process, availability of policy-relevant documents online or establishment of global assemblies. Dingwerth (2014) asserts that global institutions are sufficiently democratic in general. Thus, discussions on global democracy should rather focus on such areas as health, education and subsistence. What is needed is not better procedures, but investments that help the weaker members of global society to make effective use of contemporary global democratic institutions.

Before the 1980s, the democratic universe was restricted to Western Europe, North America and a few other scattered locales. During the 1970s and 1980s more than 30 countries shifted from authoritarian to democratic political systems. However, in recent years there has been backsliding on previously attained progress in democratization in some European countries such as Greece and Italy as well as several Eastern European countries. The post-1970s wave of democratization has slowed or reversed in the wake of the 2008–09 global economic crisis (EIU 2014: 2). Besides, there has been a decline in some aspects of governance, political participation, freedom of expression, freedom of press, rule of law and associational rights (Puddington 2014: 3). Public opinion polls indicate that confidence in public institutions in Western Europe, which was already low before 2008 in many countries, has declined further since the 2008 crisis. Only less than 20 per cent of West Europeans trust political parties and around one third trust their governments and parliaments. These ratios are exceptionally low in Eastern Europe where less than 10 per cent of people trust political parties and less than 20 per cent trust their governments and their parliaments (EIU 2014: 16–17).

Yet, democracy as a value retains strong universal appeal worldwide. Despite setbacks and overall stagnation, surveys show that most people in most places still want democracy. Trends such as globalization, increasing education and expanding middle classes tend to favour democracy (EIU 2014: 2–3). According to Freedom House (2014), 76 out of 165 countries in the world (46 per cent) were electoral democracies and 65 countries of 76 (39.4 per cent of the world's independent states) were classified as free in 1990. In 2000, 120 out of 192 countries in the world (62.5 per cent) were

Graph 1.1: Percentage of Countries That Are Electoral Democracies

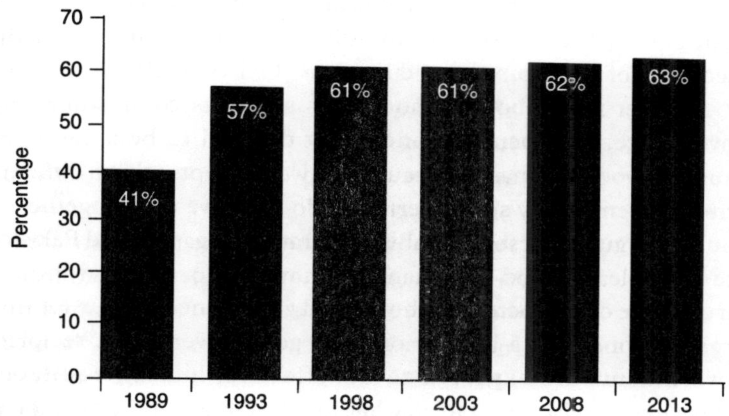

Source: Freedom House (2014).

electoral democracies and 86 of the 120 (44.8) were classified as free. In 2013, 122 out of 195 countries in the world (63 per cent of the total) were electoral democracies and 88 of the 122 (45 per cent of the total) were classified as free. These figures indicate that there seems to be a steady increase in the number of countries that are electoral democracies despite a slowdown in recent years as seen in Graph 1 (Puddington 2014: 6).

Democratic regimes and global governance processes have been adversely affected by the economic and financial crises but globalization itself may also be a threat to democracy (Puddington 2014: 4). Gill argues that 'the emerging world order involves a contradiction between globalization and democratization' and maintains that globalization may destroy democracy due to the dominance of internationally mobile capital and the growth of its power relative to labour (Gill 1996: 207–10). Based on the 'unseen hand' of market competition, a 'business civilization' has grown since the 1980s, accompanied by the spread of formal aspects of liberal democracy. Nonetheless, it has also involved tremendous increases in social inequality and erosion of public social provisions and redistribution (e.g. education, public health, social welfare) and public trust. This means that the social and material basis for greater political equality as the central idea of democracy has been undermined in many countries. The decline of organized labour and the increases in segregation and poverty mostly experienced by marginal groups such as women, children, immigrants, the elderly and disabled are some examples of the inequality of opportunities and burdens (Gill 1996: 215).

Another issue about democracy is about its compliance with governance. Democracy alone is not deemed to be a sufficient cause of good governance because the two concepts rely on different criteria. Democracy and governance do not have to be together. It could be argued that some Arabian Emirates, Singapore and Pakistan are examples of good governance without democracy and India is an example of democracy without good governance. Because donor organizations have a high priority on good governance, recipient governments are expected to be 'effective, honest, equitable, transparent, and accountable', while for UNDP, a 'good government' is also expected to provide for sustainable human development and participation usually of NGOs rather than the public in general (Albritton and Bureekul 2009; Zaidi 2009).

In summary, a short list of global trends and developments influencing global governance and public policymaking processes may be listed as in Table 1.1.

Table 1.1: Global Trends and Developments Influencing Global Governance

Trends/Developments	Consequences / Responses
- Technological change - Informatization - Globalization of business & politics civic culture and - Environmental issues - Flexible production - Liberalization	- Knowledge & technology oriented institutional patterns - E-democracy - Increased use of technology & e-government services - Increased collaboration; global governance & leadership - Increased respect for diversity & basic freedoms - More decentralization/regionalization & innovation - Increased use of market mechanism, tools & principles
- A far more complex and constantly changing world - Blurred lines between public-civic-private sectors	- Establishment of policy networks including diverse groups - Participative new mechanisms of policymaking - Accountability, responsiveness, legitimacy & code of conducts - Need for increased public leadership
- Increased ethnic consciousness - Changed family & labour market - Diverse & educated urban society - Continuing migration	- Democratization, decentralization and increased participation - Continuing need for neutrality with responsiveness to the specific needs of different groups, flexible/mobile jobs - Respecting & maintaining individual rights and diversity together with the common good / public interest
- Redesigned relations between the state, market and society - Changing role for public administration as public governance	- Deregulation and a limited regulatory role for the state - Increased role for civic & market actors - Enhancement of transparency and accountability of the government to the public and the private and civil sectors - Commercialization and marketization of public services - Increased importance of participation & market principles in the public sector

Source: Author.

A Global Trend towards Governance

In the major global trend of the proliferation of neoliberal democratic system and capitalist values, the market has been taken as the basic driver of political, administrative and economic reforms. The EU, IMF, WB, OECD and UN along with some other international or regional organizations have played a significant role in the proliferation of neoliberal capitalist market ideology and governance structures and practices. It is acknowledged that neoliberal view and the new public management (NPM) approach have had an important impact on the new understanding of public administration and public policy in a global scale. Hood (1991: 3) defined the NPM as 'one of the most striking international trends in public administration' during the early 1990s. The supporters of the NPM argue that many people are not satisfied by public services because public sector does not operate like a business. Thus, there is a focus on minimizing the role of the state, increasing efficiency in public service delivery, empowering the market and society to provide goods and services, and adopting the rules, methods and values of the private sector in the public sector (such as self-interest, customer-orientation, efficiency, economy, competition, flexibility and entrepreneurialism) (Peters and Pierre 2006: 36; Cepiku 2013: 17). Besides, the market based liberal democratic model of governing 'provided at a minimum a reasonably clear institutional linkage between elected officials, public policies, and the electorate' (Peters and Pierre 2006: 31).

However, there has always been a debate on the compatibility of the NPM approach with the basic principles and methods of public administration because public administration is considered as something more than business matters. To restore the confidence of citizens in public administration, public institutions must be more responsive, participative, collaborative (Cepiku 2013: 20) and respectful to diversity (Ostrom 2008: 115). People have lost their trust in government because they do not see public administration as being responsive to their needs, accessible, participative, transparent and accountable.

Accordingly, since the late 1990s and particularly the 2000s as Baimyrzaeva (2012) and Güler (2004: 27) assert, the efforts are concentrated on improving competitiveness in the market and the capacity of the public administration or the state as the facilitator of good governance as the market has still continued to be the driving force. Thus, a need for a new paradigm on public administration centred especially on governance capabilities is widely acknowledged (Kooiman and van Vliet 1993; Bao et al. 2012). In fact, Borgonovi (2002 cited in Cepiku 2013: 14) and Morçöl (2013) identify a trend towards governance. Bao et al. (2012) argue that 'concerns with the NPM have spawned a counter movement by both practitioners and academics to place substantive political values more at the centre of the governance debate than has been the case with NPM's narrow instrumental focus'. The authors state that New Public Governance (NPG) movement underline the promotion of the larger common good, not just improved efficiency, effectiveness or responsiveness. Besides, the NPG sees politics as 'the politically mediated expression of collectively determined preferences rather than simply an aggregation of individual preferences', and thus 'emphasizes the importance of creating government processes that facilitate the generation of implementable agreements among wide-ranging stakeholders'. Moreover, the NPG movement considers the provision of the public services as a coproduction process involving the public, private and non-profit sectors. In this model, 'the role of government is not simply to regulate, distribute, or redistribute public benefits but to serve as a catalytic agent to invest private and non-profit stakeholders in shared ownership of the public good' (Bao et al. 2012: 446–47).

Similarly, Peters and Pierre (2006: 29, 38) define governance as a process of defining collective goals, making political priorities, and bringing together resources from a large number of different actors necessary to attain those objectives. In governance, networks composed of autonomous but interdependent actors play a central role, and public, civic and private organizations exchange different kinds of resources and share objectives (Cepiku 2013: 7–8, 11; Rhodes 2000). The state is a crucial actor but its role has shifted to be mobilizing governance resources from different actors, facilitating democratic public governance, and steering the society and economy. The state is considered as an 'enabling state' exercising formal and informal authority and collaboration, with the aim of building consensus on specific decisions in an open system beyond the traditional politics-administration or bureaucracy-democracy dichotomies. Not compulsory requirements but incentives, opportunities and conditions lead the behaviour of the different actors. Rhodes (2000, 2004) considers governance as process involving a transition from a unitary bureaucracy and top-down management to a fragmented service delivery and participatory policymaking context in which different actors (and not a dominant state) share responsibility. Hence, the NPG is seen to offer solutions to the problems of democratic deficit (inadequate participation, deliberation, transparency and legitimacy), majoritarian leanings of democracy, transparency, responsiveness, overloaded public administration, low performance, and, to some degree, ungovernability and public confidence in the liberal democratic state.

According to Stoker (1998), governance ensures collective action by involving actors drawn both from and beyond government in order to reduce and manage complexity and to resolve social and economic issues. In this sense, governance refers to mutual dependence and vigorous exchanges between the institutions through coordination, equilibration, integration and regulation rather than hierarchy or anarchy. However, Stoker (1998) states that public governance based on networks gives rise to new dilemmas, mostly associated with accountability and the fragmentation of institutional frameworks. Besides, public administration scholars, assuming an irreplaceable steering role for public administration, draw attention to a lack of adequate tools for achieving the goals of governance such as real public participation (input legitimacy), governability, accountability and performance (output legitimacy), meaning that the function often tends to remain unexercised (Cepiku 2013: 21).

Morçöl (2013) points out that governance is inevitable but not democratic governance (and free, pluralist and participatory democracy). Since 'governance without democratic politics is dangerous' (van Gunsteren 2006: 94), governance requires an intentional and serious effort for greater democratic and fair participation. In that effort, public administration has the legitimacy and strategic role necessary to steer and coordinate networks and governance process. Thus, a change from classical administration to the new public management with a neoliberal market orientation is not seen to be enough. What is needed is democratic public governance with active public leadership and public participation with an understanding of a new public service, public good, and complex and diverse world involving interdependency, multiple publics, private and civic actors. Such an understanding of public governance would help solve the problem of overloaded public administration by shedding some of its load to the (global, national and local) market and civil society and local and regional administrations while increasing participation, responsiveness, transparency, trust and legitimacy and governability. The new public governance also requires a new type of public leadership and democratic values such as common good or public interest, democratic participation, deliberation, negotiation, collaboration and equity. To the extent we acknowledge global problems such as climate warming, terrorism, global poverty and other forms of human insecurity, 'we will agree that we need global leaders who will adapt and innovate locally and globally to solve or ameliorate our global problems' (Masciulli 2011: 71).

General characteristics of global and glocal governance, based on literature review, are listed below:

- A multi-level and multi-actor process of glocalization of governance and public policymaking process (Benz and Papadopoulos 2006: 11; Cepiku 2013: 7; Teune 1997: 5).
- Increased importance, involvement and influence of private actors in all stages and phases of global politics and policymaking (Benz and Papadopoulos 2006: 20).[2]
- A new functional division of labour and authority between public and non-governmental civic and private actors, developed particularly since the 1980s.
- A changed character of regulation with an increasing number

[2] The involvement of market and civic actors has contributed to the *privatization* of governance systems at all levels. In global governance, private actors are drawn attention to as actors that could improve legitimacy, but in national and subnational arenas these actors are often deemed to cause legitimacy problems. Thus, there is still a need for the mechanisms of wider participation, democratization, legitimatization, accountability, responsiveness and governability.

of voluntary, soft or loose regulations with no compulsory compliance mechanisms attached (de-governmentalization) (Wolf 2006: 200; Stone 2008).

- A growing number of regulations based on market principles, self-interest (pressure group interests) and arbitration (commercialization) (Wolf 2006: 201).
- A proliferation of policy transfers, and autonomous and non-majoritarian regulatory state agencies outside the direct control of the politics for the purpose of increasing the competitiveness and efficiency of the market (marketization).
- Diverse sectoral demands and regulatory efforts by private actors causing some negative externalities and creating a need for inter-sectoral coordination by the state.
- Cooperative steering, rather than rowing, of the governance processes by governments, having easier access to the institutions of international governance,[3] based on effective public leadership at all (local, national, global or organizational) levels (Masciulli 2011).

Despite these general characteristics of global or glocal governance, different constitutional frameworks, national priorities, government attitudes, economic structures, administrative, and political cultures influence how a nation or governments at different (national, regional and local) levels are connected to the global governance system. For example, local 'internationals' have long tended to emphasize international relief assistance, exchange programmes and education (Alger 1999). Yet, for many public, private, or civic international organizations, global security issues, terrorism, and environmental problems as well as the regulation of international economic affairs and trade have become the most important issues in recent years.

The Process of Global Governance and Actors

In the current literature, discussions on the processes of marketization, democratization, and glocalization go in tandem with the processes

[3] 'The state now attempts to capitalize on, and to coordinate, resources controlled by a wide variety of actors, and to employ those resources in the pursuit of goals for the society.' (Peters and Pierre 2006: 38)

of governance on the one hand, and 'hollowing out of the state' on the other. Yet, Stone argues that economic globalization and regional integration have proceeded at a much faster pace than processes of global governance (2008: 23). The result of this disjuncture is the reduced power of the nation-states without a corresponding development of global governance. This is one of the major reasons for the deficiency of public goods at global levels. For example, the regulation of financial flows, environmental protection, or intellectual property safeguards are inadequately provided.

Another process is the 'hollowing out of the state' in which power and functions of the state is delegated, on the one hand, downward vertically to local and regional governments through decentralization, devolution, intergovernmental contracting etc., and upward to international institutions and to the global market; and, on the other hand, horizontally to regulatory authorities, executive agencies, the market, networks, the private and civic sectors through de-governmentalization, decentralization, contracting out or outsourcing, public-private partnerships or even public-private-civic partnerships (Cepiku 2013: 7; Rhodes 2004: 1248). Similarly, focusing more on nations, Benz and Papadopoulos (2006: 11) assert that governance takes place at three different levels from a global perspective: Intra-national (national and subnational level), European (or regional or supra-national) and International, involving vertical and horizontal relations among different types of actors. In much the same way, Teune (1997: 5) argues that: 'The political system of the world is now made up of two conflicting systems, one of cities and political communities within them as well as their organizations and associations, and the other of countries, the new and the old-a global political economy and an international system of states'. Accordingly, governance is multilevel, glocal and complex, and may take place at local, urban, regional, national and supranational levels as well as organizational level.

Despite the important impact of the worldwide economic restructuring process, Stohr (1990: 23) argues that 'local and regional communities have substantial "voluntaristic" room for manoeuver in confronting global change and "making" their own history'. For instance, a city may have such a diversity representing many nations or ethnicities in the world along with the natives, their civic and private organizations and other multinational companies, governmental and local agencies with implication for urban policymaking processes. Yet, the same city may have national and international sister cities and relations and joint projects carried out with them. Early in the 1980s, Cohen (1981: 300) discerned a hierarchy of cities at the top of which are 'a series of global cities which serve as international centres for business decision making and corporate strategy formulation'. However, based on research in the United States, Kirby and Marston (1995: 278) assert that important local actors involved in local-global links are not limited to those in the giant world cities. Many small and medium-sized cities are also active players on the global stage for many different reasons. Peirce (1993: 1) conducted a study on Phoenix, Seattle, Baltimore, Owensboro, Dallas and St. Paul in the United States, and asserted that 'Across America and across the globe, city-states are emerging as a critical focus of economic activity, of governance, of social organization for the 1990s and the century to come'. In addition, Sassen (2004: 649) argues that even those who are geographically immobile, such as NGOs and indigenous peoples, immigrants and refugees, and many others have increasingly become part of global politics.

A dramatic increase in the number of international and regional associations of local governments and of the international offices in municipal governments around the world since the 1990s is an indicator of growing involvement of the local in the global policy domain. Today, most of municipal governments have incorporated 'international affairs policies' into their long-term regional strategy. In fact, international relations divisions of some metropolitan city governments may be larger than foreign ministries of some nation states.

The Council of Local Authorities for International Relations (CLAIR) was established in 1988 by the Japanese Ministry of Home Affairs, some local governments, and others in order to support the internationalization efforts of local governments. (Alger, 1999: 201) In 1995, again with the initiative of the Japanese Ministry of Home Affairs, CLAIR established the Local Authorities Center for International Cooperation, staffed with 15 members in the CLAIR

Tokyo office (Menjiu 1995: 54). There are many other such examples of international or regional associations of local governments, including, but not limited to, the International Union of Local Authorities (IULA),[4] The Summit Conference of Major Cities of the World (SUMMIT), the World Associations of Cities and Local Authorities Coordination (WACLAC), and the UN Centre for Human Settlements (HABITAT) (Alger 1999: 197–98). Similarly, the Congress of Local and Regional Authorities of Europe (CLRAE) has been the key actor in the preparation of the European Charter of Local Self-Government accepted by the Council of Europe, now considered to be the main document by many countries to enhance their local government structures. The ratification of this charter is now required for admission to the Council of Europe.

As documented above, global governance is multilevel and complex, and includes different forms of non-governmental policymaking and implementation, supplemented by negotiated vertical and horizontal inter-governmental cooperation between multiple levels of decisional units (for example, the European Union bodies, national, regional, and local institutions) and extension of the public administration by partnerships and contracts or grants to third parties (Benz and Papadopoulos 2006: 13; Frederickson 2007). More specifically, global actors of global governance include global companies and the organizations representing or regulating global private enterprises, global civil society or non-governmental organizations (NGOs), global public policy networks, global inter-governmental organizations, and an array of nations, states, local, and regional governments.

Global public policy networks are 'transnational public–private partnerships' and have a more mixed character than the 'inter-governmental networks'. Global public policy networks are composed of business, NGOs, and other civil society actors, governments, and international organizations. Of particular interest are global civil society actors, whose participation in policymaking increasingly

[4] The International Union of Local Authorities (IULA) founded in 1913 in Ghent may be the oldest in this category of global organizations. The IULA aims to promote local autonomy, promote the idea of public participation civic affairs, and establish and develop international municipal relations, among others.

is seen as holding the promise of a democratization of global governance. Democracy theorists have advanced blueprints for how global governance arrangements may be reformed to integrate transnational actors and thus meet the standards of democratic decision making (Bexell, Tallberg and Uhlin 2010: 82). Yet, there is still a need for developing new models of democracy tailored for the global level.

Table 1.2: Some Important Actors of Global Governance

Global private enterprises and business-related networks (European Round Table of Industrialists - ERT, the Transatlantic Business Dialogue - TABD, & the Global Business Coalition on HIV/AIDS, etc.)	*Sovereign states, local-regional governments and their delegates* *Global intergovernmental organizations and networks* (Council of Europe, the EU, UN, WTO, OECD, World Bank, OSCE, Global Environment Facility, International Energy Agency, etc.)
Global civil society or international nongovernmental organizations (INGOs)[5] (advocacy groups, coalitions, networks, philanthropic foundations, etc.)	*Global public policy networks or partnerships* composed of business, civil society actors, governments, and international organizations
International civil servants (Employees of international organizations)	*World, global or globally connected cities* (as actors, arenas and forums for global public policymaking)
Transnational policy professionals (consultants, foundation officers, business leaders, knowledge networks, scientific experts, think tanks and NGO executives, etc.	

Source: Author.

Global Public Policymaking

Traditionally, public policy has been closely associated with the 'nation state', 'national governments', and 'national public administrations'. Yet, glocalization along with democratization, marketization and empowered civil society, etc., all have led to the

[5] The term is used by Evans and Newnham (1998: 270) to refer to non-governmental organizations (NGOs) operating internationally, including international non-profit organizations and worldwide companies such as the World Organization of the Scout Movement and International Committee of the Red Cross.

development of globalized and diversified policymaking processes. Thus, global governance takes place in global public space or domain that includes increasingly institutionalized transnational arena of fluid, dynamic, and intermeshed relations, involving plural civic, public and private actors, generated by glocalization and mainly regarding the production of global public goods (Stone 2008: 21; Ruggie 2004: 504).

Thus, the state or other national public institutions no longer serve as the sole organizing centre for public policy. Due to increased marketization, decentralization and globalization trends ongoing at the same time, interactions and cooperation are between not only different levels of national, regional, and local administrations/ governments but also different sectors of public, private and civic actors. (Benz and Papadopoulos 2006: 11) As the state or central government has dispersed some of its powers to the market actors, NGOs, local, and regional public authorities, the involvement and influence of these actors in the process of public policymaking have increased. As a result of the concomitant processes of globalization and decentralization/localization, the influence of global, national, regional and local public, civic, and private actors has grown in public policymaking processes at different levels.

Accordingly, the traditional elements of the 'policy cycle', as understood in domestic contexts, could be conceptually stretched to the global context. Thus, the global policymaking process would also be made of four stages:

1. Problem definition and agenda setting
2. Formal decision making
3. Policy implementation
4. Monitoring and evaluation

The context of global public policymaking is evolving and fast changing. The first stage of the 'policy cycle', global agenda setting, is complex, fragmented, and indeterministic, and characterized by uncertainty and divergent sets of debates and demands. Continuing conflict and power battles are common. Due to vast differences, diversity and complexity, there is no one consistent pattern of global policy processes. Similarly, there is no one dominant global institution, forum or parliament or 'global state' with the authority or legitimacy for mediation or for global decision-making. Nation states make global polices generally through international treaties and conventions, whose effectiveness depends on compliance by the states and other global actors. International organizations such as the UN and World Bank also develop policies to deliver global public goods. International commissions such as those headed by Brandt, Palme, and Brundtland function as venues for official discussion of global public policies. A Brundtland Report titled *Our Common Future* was the official discussion of global public policies on environmental problems and had important impact on global, national and local policies on environment and development. It was the UN document that introduced the concept of 'sustainable development' into the arguments and literature on development and environmental problems. Similarly, the World Bank uses its development grants to fund programmes, public-private partnerships and other initiatives that reach a number over 50.

A major issue in the global policy process is 'policy transfers' that has increased since the 1980s. It is debatable how promoting cross-border policy harmonization works but it is happening in many policy areas such as privatization, mediation (arbitration, ombudsman, etc.), gender mainstreaming, economic cooperation, standard setting, guidelines, and best practices.

Policy implementation is dependent on international cooperation, engineering consensus, joint commitment, diplomatic pressures along with educating and convincing citizens about the real impact of global problems on localities. There are few sanctions that can be employed against disobedient states such as moral pressure from other states, trade sanctions, and, at the extreme, military intervention (Stone 2008: 27).

In the global sphere, evaluation comes from various sources. International financial institutions often have their own evaluation units. Some contract it out to private sector experts and advisers. Unsolicited advice and evaluation comes from NGOs, research institutes, think thanks, and academicians.

Policy Issues and Areas with Involved Actors in Global Governance

What are the issues or problems faced by the global community requiring governance and leadership at the global level in order to develop viable, sustainable and mutual solutions to them? It is almost impossible to make an exclusive list. Yet, one could easily count for such glocal problems or issues as global warming, apocalyptic terrorism and cyber warfare, global poverty and other forms of human insecurity, resource depletion, international immigration, human trafficking, human right violations, the regulation of international trade and global commons, economic, environmental, fiscal and social crises, biotechnological accidents and pathogenic pandemics, political conflicts, the protection of intellectual property and patent rights, among others. (Bernstein and Cashore 2007; Lipschutz 1997: 99; Masciulli 2011: 71) These problems or issues are glocal because they not only have influences at global, national or local levels but also stem from causes at all three levels. Therefore, Biermann et al. (2012: 54–55) urge for the establishment of a global sustainability governance system beyond national governance systems for the management of global environment issues and problems.

Some policy issues and areas for global (or glocal) governance with involved actors are provided below:

- *Global democracy and governance along with local and regional autonomy* (examples of involved actors: Council of Europe; UN; EU; European Council; etc.[6])
- *Environmental problems and global environmental governance system* (examples of involved actors: UNEP, European Environment Agency—EEA; World Wide Fund for Nature—WWF; Greenpeace; Global Commission on Economy and Climate[7]; and

[6] Benz and Papadopoulos (2006: 15) considers EU committee system as a model of network governance since it is a weak and developing institutional framework and, unlike national systems of member states, the EU has no directly elected central government with legitimate constitutional power.

[7] It is a commission established by 7 governments including the ministers of public finance, former prime ministers and corporate CEOs.

UN Convention of the Conservation of Migratory Species of Wild Animals—CMS[8]; Partnerships in Environmental Management for the Seas of East Asia—PEMSEA; Local Governments for Sustainability—ICLEI; etc.)

- *Human rights and freedoms and group rights* (for women, children, consumers, workers, etc.) (examples of involved actors: UN Human Rights Council; United Nations Children's Fund—UNICEF; European Convention of Human Rights; ARTICLE 19; Amnesty International; Walk Free; ILO; Save the Children; CEDAW and Istanbul Convention to Fight Violence Against Women; etc.; as well as nation states)
- *International immigration, human trafficking, crime, peace-making, global aid, regulation of global social-economic issues* (examples of involved actors: UN; UNDP; WHO; EU; the Red Cross; Doctors Without Borders; International Refugee Organization; International Criminal Police Organization—Interpol; International Criminal Court; etc.)
- *Coordination and cooperation of global security affairs* (examples of involved actors: UN Security Council; North Atlantic Treaty Organization—NATO; Organization for Security and Co-operation in Europe—OSCE; etc.)
- *Higher education and research* (examples of involved actors: International Association of Universities—IAU; European University Association—EUA; United Nations Educational; Scientific and Cultural Organization—UNESCO; European

[8] CMS or Bonn Convention aims to conserve terrestrial, marine and avian migratory species across their range. CMS provides a framework within which Parties may act to conserve migratory species and their habitats. CMS met with 900 experts from 120 countries in Quito, Ecuador in November of 2014 and added 31 more species on the protected wildlife list of 176 endangered species. CMS meets every 3 years to discuss this list. It is headquartered in the UN Campus in Bonn, Germany, and works according to an intergovernmental treaty, concluded under the aegis of the UNEP. Parties include signatory states, regional economic integration organizations, UN and UNEP representatives, and involved civic organizations (such as Shark Advocates International, the PEW Charitable Trusts, European Federation of Associations for Hunting and Conservation (FACE) and Humane Society International). (See www.cms.int; http://www.unep-wcmc.org/cms/, http://www.un.org/earthwatch/about/docs/scpCMS.htm)

University Institute; European Research Council; European Organization for Nuclear Research—CERN; etc.)

- *Management of international sports* (examples of involved actors: International Federation of Football Association—FIFA; Union of European Football Associations—UEFA; International Basketball Federation—FIBA; International Olympics Committee—IOC; etc.)
- *Regulation of international trade, coordination of global economic-financial affairs, and the use and provision of global commons* such as oceans, Antarctica, atmosphere, space, etc. (examples of involved actors: Nation states, WTO; OECD; WB; IMF; EU; G8; G20; NAFTA; Association of Southeast Asian Nations—ASEAN; World Economic [Davos] Forum; World Social [Porto Alegre] Forum; Universal Postal Union—UPU[9]; etc.)
- *International arbitration and mediation* (examples of involved actors: International Chamber of Commerce (ICC) International Court of Arbitration; American Arbitration Association—AAA; London Court of International Arbitration—LCIA; Hong Kong International Arbitration Center—HKIAC; Istanbul Arbitration Center; etc.)
- *International standard setting and industry self-regulations* (examples of involved actors: Internet Corporation for Assigned Names and Numbers—ICANN[10]; International Standardization Organization—ISO; European Telecommunications Standards Institute; barcodes for commercial products—U.P.C.; ISBN; ISSN; DOI numbers; etc.[11])

[9] The UPU was established in 1874 and headquartered in Bern. With its 192 member countries, it is the primary forum for cooperation between postal sector players. It is a United Nations specialized agency since 1948. (See, http://www.upu.int/en/the-upu/the-upu.html)

[10] It is an organization that regulates access to the Internet.

[11] Bernstein and Cashore (2007: 348) also include non-state market driven (NSMD) governance systems under this category. NSMD systems, unlike the voluntary nature of most other forms of private authority, are designed to create binding and enforceable rules and defined as 'deliberative and adaptive governance institutions designed to embed social and environmental norms in the global marketplace that derive authority directly from interested audiences, including those they seek to regulate, not from sovereign states. Operationally, they use global supply

- *Cooperation among local and regional governments and administrations* (examples of involved actors: Sister Cities International; Euro Mediterranean Partnership of Local and Regional Authorities; Council of European Municipalities and Regions; Organization of World Heritage Cities, League of Historical Cities; etc.)
- *International public-private partnerships* (examples of involved actors: the Global Alliance for Vaccines and Immunization—GAVI; the Global Water Partnership; etc.)
- *Protecting intellectual property/patent rights* (examples of involved actors: World Intellectual Property Organization—WIPO; European Patent Organization (EPO or EPOrg); Eurasian Patent Organization (EAPO); etc.)

Conclusion

In today's global world, plurality and diversity along with the need for global collaboration to develop mutual solutions to global problems and for the protection and enhancement of human rights and individual freedoms have been increasingly recognized in the processes of governance, global politics, democracy and public

---

chains to recognize, track, and label products and services from environmentally and socially responsible businesses'. NSMD systems derive policymaking ability or authority from the market's supply chain not from states' sovereign authority. NSMD systems possess mechanisms to verify compliance and to create consequences for non-compliance through mandatory standards for those who sign onto the system. The most common compliance mechanism is a third-party audit in which auditors certify firm or producer compliance with the rules or identify improvements required for a successful audit. Examples include the UN Global Compact, the Organisation for Economic Co-operation and Development's (OECD) Guidelines for Multinational Enterprises, the Forest Stewardship Council (FSC) certification programme and the Global Reporting Initiative. In many cases, their interest in competing as a 'legitimate' NSMD system in the global marketplace led them to adapt their systems to transnational market requirements or, as in the case of the Program for Endorsement of Forest Certification (PEFC), to create formal global institutions. Another example is the Fair Trade Labeling Organization (FLO), which coordinates under one system groups that had worked separately on consumer campaigns to improve the conditions of poor and marginalized producers in the developing world. The FLO covers internationally traded commodities and specialized goods including coffee, tea, cocoa, sugar, bananas, rice, nuts, clothing, wine and diamonds, among others. (Bernstein and Cashore 2007: 349–51, 364)

policymaking. Besides, the involvement of private and civic actors has improved legitimacy in global governance. Yet, democratic global governance is still a major goal waiting to be achieved (Bexell, Tallberg and Uhlin 2010: 82). Global governance based on networks and self-organization seems to have led to new dilemmas, mostly associated with real public participation, legitimacy, accountability, performance, and the fragmentation of institutional frameworks in international, national and subnational arenas (Stoker 1998; Cepiku 2013: 21). International institutions and corporations, public-private partnerships, and other global governance arrangements are criticized for suffering from democratic deficits, such as unbalanced, inadequate or lack of participation, legitimacy, and accountability (Bexell, Tallberg and Uhlin 2010: 81). Many developing countries and most ordinary citizens do not have sufficient resources to devote to national or global policy deliberations. In fact, marginalized, poor, or unorganized groups are not generally present in global or other types of governance processes. In addition, some active actors of global governance, especially international corporations, have decision making structures confined to the top management and major stakeholders and thus have very limited capacity of representing broad interests.

In order to avoid such pitfalls in the process of global governance and in order to attain real and sustainable results, governance has to become more democratic, accountable, and participative with more participative and pluralistic mechanisms of responsiveness and democratic governance as opposed to disproportionate influence of the private sector and the influential groups. Greater transnational actor involvement would increase democratizing potential of global governance and enhance democratic legitimacy. The involvement of NGOs, social movements, advocacy networks, etc., can expand participation in global governance 'not only because it broadens the range of actors involved in global policymaking and the provision of global or other public goods, but also because these actors by nature tend to allow for more direct citizen participation. In addition, transnational actor involvement can strengthen accountability in global governance by supplementing existing mechanisms of internal accountability within institutions and organizations with new mechanisms of external accountability through stakeholders and citizens' (Bexell, Tallberg and Uhlin 2010: 91).

In fact, civic organizations can claim legitimacy based on broader participation and act more like quasi representative institutions in the process of governance. However, the weaknesses of global governance calls for representative democratic institutions to exercise 'meta-governance' on the process of local governance and the relations of specific actors or partnerships with public policy and their impact public interest. There is also a need for broader dialogue on global governance as an overarching global good in international relations. Moreover, the theory and implementation of global democracy need to be further developed in order to provide a solid base for the successful implementation of global democracy (Bexell, Tallberg and Uhlin 2010: 91, 96–97). Furthermore, all these matters indicate a need for wider access to public knowledge about global governance processes and local links to the world. Otherwise, globalization may be counterproductive and increase the influence of the groups with disproportionate power and influence in the process of public policymaking.

A final issue is the growing need for the enhancement of global collaborative public leadership and meta-governance by representative democratic institutions (the EU, national governments or metropolitan administrations) to render governance processes more effective and legitimate, to bring together a diverse group of global actors towards global common good, and to steer global/glocal governance. An effective global collaborative public leadership ought to involve: (1) diminishing polarization, teaching diversity, and building community with a focus on democratic participation and common good; and (2) building networks of varied interests through collaboration that can work effectively to develop policies, solve public problems; and establish future directions for the global community.

Meta-governance would require a third way beyond the love and hate of the state, the market, or the corporate sector. They all are indispensable parts of today's world. What is needed is an effective role of representative democratic institutions in the process of governance with the increased democratic involvement of the civic (unions, chambers, think tanks, NGOs, etc.) and public sectors along with market actors in public policy processes. Greater principles guiding public policymaking processes should include common good or public interest, equality of opportunity, justice, freedom, responsiveness, collaboration, respecting and maintaining diversity, just and democratic participation, legitimacy and accountability to the public, and governance should be above tedious level of mere technical details or business of management. Democratic global governance requires a strong establishment of the rule of law, participative policy development and follow-up and evaluation of public policies on the base of robust data, transparency and accountability. In short, since a genuine participative global (and even national) democracy seems to be a difficult aim to achieve, there is a clear and strong need for the advancement of democratic global governance.

References

Albritton, R.B., and T. Bureekul. 2009. *Are Democracy and 'Good Governance' Always Compatible? Competing Values in the Thai Political Arena*. Working Paper Series: No. 47. Chile: International Political Science Association.

Alger, C.F. 1999. 'The Future of Democracy and Global Governance Depends on Widespread Public Knowledge about Local Links to the World.' *Cities*, 16 (3), 195–206.

Baimyrzaeva, M. 2012. *Institutional Reforms in the Public Sector: What did We Learn?* Bingley: Emerald Group Publishing.

Bao, G., X. Wang, G.L. Larsen and D.F. Morgan. 2012. 'Beyond New Public Governance: A Value-Based Global Framework for Performance Management, Governance, and Leadership.' *Administration & Society*, 45 (4), 443–67.

Benz, Arthur and Ioannis Papadopoulos (eds.). 2006. 'Introduction: Governance and Democracy – Concepts and Key Concepts.' In *Governance and Democracy: Comparing National, European and International Experiences* (eds.) A. Benz & I. Papadopoulos. London & New York: Routledge. pp. 1–26.

Bernstein, S., and B. Cashore. 2007. 'Can Non-State Global Governance Be Legitimate? An Analytical Framework.' *Regulation & Governance*, 1, 347–71.

Bexell, M., J. Tallberg and A. Uhlin. 2010. 'Democracy in Global Governance: The Promises and Pitfalls of Transnational Actors.' *Global Governance*, 16, 81–101.

Biermann, F. et al. 2012. 'Transforming Governance and Institutions for Global Sustainability: Key Insights from the Earth System Governance Project'. *Current Opinion in Environmental Sustainability*, 4, 51–60.

Borgonovi, E. 2002. *Principi e Sistemi Aziendali per le Amministrazioni Pubbliche*. Milano: Egea.

Cepiku, D. 2013. 'Unraveling the Concept of Public Governance: A Literature Review of Different traditions.' In *Conceptualizing and Researching Governance in Public and Non Profit Organizations Studies in Public and Non-profit Governance*. L. Gnan, A. Hinna & F. Monteduro (eds.), Volume 1, 3–32. Bingley: Emerald Group Publishing.

Cerny, P.G. 2008. 'Embedded Neoliberalism: The Evolution of a Hegemonic Paradigm.' *Journal of International Trade and Diplomacy*, 2(1), 1–46.

Cohen, R.B. 1981. 'The New International Division of Labor, Multinational Corporations and Urban Hierarchy.' in *Urbanization and Urban Planning in Capitalist Society*, (eds.). M. Dear & A.J. Scott. New York: Methuen.

Dingwerth, K. 2014 'Global Democracy and the Democratic Minimum: Why a Procedural Account Alone is Insufficient.' *European Journal of International Relations*, 20(4), 1124–47.

Economic Intelligence Unit (EIU). 2014. 'Democracy Index 2013 – Democracy in Limbo.'

———. 2014. http://www.eiu.com/Handlers/WhitepaperHandler.ashx?fi=Democracy_Index_2013_WEB2.pdf&mode=wp&campaignid=Democracy0814.

Evans, G., and R. Newnham. 1998. *Penguin Dictionary of International Relations*. Penguin.

Farazmand, A. 1994. 'The New World Order and Global Public Administration.' In *Public Administration in the Global World*. J.C. Garcia-Zamor & R. Khator (eds.). Westport & London: Praeger. pp. 61–81.

Frederickson, H.G. 2007. 'Whatever Happened to Public Administration?: Governance, Governance Everywhere.' In *Oxford Handbook of Public Management*. E. Ferlie, L.E. Lynn & C. Pollitt (eds.). Oxford: Oxford University Press. pp. 282–304.

Freedom House. 2014. *Freedom in the World Percentages by Year*. Freedom House. http://www.freedomhouse.org.

Fougner, T. 2008. 'Neoliberal Governance of States: The Role of Competitiveness Indexing and Country Benchmarking.' *Millennium: Journal of International Studies*, 37(2), 303–26.

Fraser-Moleketi, G.J. 2012. 'Democratic Governance at Times of Crisis: Rebuilding Our Communities and Building on Our Citizens.' *International Review of Administrative Sciences*, 78(2), 191–208.

Gill, S. 1996. 'Globalization, Democratization, and the Politics of Indifference.' In *Globalization: Critical Reflections*. J.H. Mittelman (ed.). Boulder: Lynne Rienner. pp. 205–28.

Gu, J., J. Humphrey and D. Messner. 2009. 'Global Governance and Developing Countries: The Implications of the Rise of China.' *World Development*, 36(2), 274–92.

Güler, B.A. 2004. 'Kamu Yönetimi Temel Kanunu Üzerine.' *Hukuk ve Adalet*, 1(2), 26–61.

Hood, C. 1991. 'A Public Management for All Seasons.' *Public Administration*, 69 (Spring), 3–19.

Karaman, Z.T., and A. Altay. 1997. 'Global Governance Caused by New World Order.' *Marmara Journal of European Studies*, 5(1–2), 61–87.

Keohane, R.O. 2001. 'Governance in a Partially Globalized World.' *American Political Science Review*, 95(1), 1–13.

Kirby, A., and S. Marston. 1995. 'World Cities and Global Communities: The Municipal Foreign Policy Movement and New Roles for Cities.' In *World Cities in a World System*. P. Knox & P.J. Taylor (eds.). Cambridge: Cambridge University Press.

Kooiman, J., and M. van Vliet. 1993. 'Governance and Public Management.' In *Managing Public Organizations: Lessons from Contemporary European Experience*. K.A. Eljassen & J. Kooiman (eds.). London: Sage. pp. 3–32.

Lipschutz, R.D. 1997. 'From Place to Planet: Local Knowledge and Global Environmental Governance.' *Global Governance*, 3, 83–102.

Masciulli, J. 2011. 'Global Public Leadership in a Technological Era.' *Bulletin of Science, Technology & Society*, 31(2), 71–80.

Menjiu, T. 1995. 'Emerging Japanese Initiatives for International Cooperation through Community Exchange.' In *Researchers Seminar on Municipal International Cooperation*. The Hague: Association of Netherlands Municipalities (VNG). pp. 51–56.

Morçöl, G. 2013. *Kamu Politikaları için Karmasıklık Kuramı*. Presentation at the 5.Workshop on Public Policies. Ankara: Yıldırım Beyazıt University. pp. 25–26.

Ostrom, V. 2008. *The Intellectual Crisis in American Public Administration*. Tuscaloosa: University of Alabama Press.

Peters, B.G., and J. Pierre. 2006. 'Governance, Accountability and Democratic Legitimacy.' In *Governance and Democracy: Comparing National, European and International Experiences*. A. Benz & I. Papadopoulos (eds.). London & New York: Routledge. pp. 29–43.

Peirce, N. 1993. *Citistates: How Urban America Can Prosper in a Competitive World*, Washington, DC: Seven Locks Press.

Puddington, A. 2014. *Freedom in the World 2014: The Democratic Leadership Gap*. http://www.freedomhouse.org/report/freedom-world2014/essay-democratic-leadership-gap#.U_3oxDvlpjp.

Rhodes, R.A.W. 2004. 'Governance: Governing without Government.' *Political Studies*, 44 (September), 652–67.

———. 2000. 'Understanding Governance: Ten Years On.' *Organization Studies*, 28(8), 1243–64.

Rosow, S.J. 2000. 'Globalisation as Democratic Theory.' *Millennium Journal of International Studies*, 29(1), 27–45.

Ruggie, J.G. 2004. 'Reconstituting the Global Public Domain – Issues, Actors, and Practices.' *European Journal of International Relations*, 10(4): 499–531.

Sassen, S. 2004. 'Local Actors in Global Politics.' *Current Sociology*, 52(4), 649–70.

Stohr, W.B. 1990. *Global Challenge and Local Response: Initiatives for Economic*, Regeneration in Contemporary Europe. London: Mansell.

Stoker, G. 1998. 'Governance as Theory: Five Propositions.' *International Social Science Journal*, 50(155), 17–28.

Stone, D. 2008. 'Global Public Policy, Transnational Policy Communities, and Their Networks.' *Policy Studies Journal*, 36(1), 19–38.

Teune, H. 1997. 'Why the World Got Big in Thousands of Places.' *International Seminar: Thematic Group #6*. Pultusk: International Sociological Association.

van Gunsteren, H. 2006. 'Resilience through Governance with Democracy.' In *Governance and Democracy: Comparing National, European and International Experiences*. A. Benz & I. Papadopoulos (eds.). London & New York: Routledge. pp. 81–95.

Webb, A.K. 2006. 'The Calm before the Storm? Revolutionary Pressures and Global Governance.' *International Political Science Review*, 27(1), 73–92.

Wolf, K.D. 2006. 'Private Actors and the Legitimacy of Governance beyond the State.' In *Governance and Democracy: Comparing National, European and International Experiences*. A. Benz & I. Papadopoulos (eds.). London & New York: Routledge. pp. 200–27.

Zaidi, S.A. 2009. *The Politics of Democracy and Good Governance in Pakistan*. Islamabad: Pakistan Institute of Legislative Development and Transparency (PILDAT).

2 Dilemmas of Democratization in the Policy Process

The Role of Experts and People Revisited

Gökhan Orhan

Abstract

The practice of public policymaking is a complex process and has been shaped by growing globalization and relations of governance. The mainstream accounts of the policy process have assumed a rather straightforward link between findings of science and the public policy process. From fact finding to problem definition and proposing alternatives to implementation, scientists and experts have contributed to the policy process to a significant extent. However, the authority of science and neutral experts has long been challenged from the 1970s onwards. Interpretive approaches to policy analysis, for instance, have contributed to the development of an understanding of the role of ideas, narratives and discourses in shaping the policy process and policy change. The second wave of science and technology studies also followed suit and highlighted the social character of science and technology, and their embedded assumptions. The most distinctive proposal of the second wave was the participation of stakeholders in the policy process. Yet again, a third wave of criticisms questioned the role of lay people in the policy process and had a more sceptical stance towards 'levelling of the epistemological playing field' with the decline of expertise. A number of high-profile events, such as MMR vaccines and Brent Spar stirred the debate concerning the role of experts and the lay people in the policy process. However, there are a number of objections to third wave arguments as well. At the end of the day, although the role of experts, as in the case of complex models on climate change, is vital, people have made important contributions in the field concerning implementation. Democratization of the policy process is vital, and expertise needs transparency, not blind trust.

Introduction

In recent years, the practice of public policymaking has profoundly been shaped by further globalization and relations of governance. Public policymaking is a complex process where there is a multitude of factors interacting with each other in various ways. As Sabatier pointed out, the policy process is an extremely complex one in which a number of diverse are players involved. Interest groups, governmental agencies and legislatures at different levels of the government, as well as researchers and journalists are engaged in one or more aspects of the process (Sabatier 1999: 3). This interaction has a global quality and there is a well-developed literature on the impact of supranational/international bodies and treaty commitments, as well as the role of transnational policy communities, global policy networks, and epistemic communities on policy processes of individual countries. The impact of international factors has been studied with reference to policy learning, diffusion, transfer, convergence, and divergence and there is well-developed literature in this field.

This paper aims to focus on the role of science and experts in the policy process with reference to democratization and opening of the policy process to the general public. According to mainstream accounts of the policy process, scientists and experts play a major role at almost every stage of the policy process. From fact finding to problem definition and proposing alternatives to implementation, scientists and experts contribute to the policy process to a large extent with their expertise. However, scientists and experts are not alone in this process and each of these actors (either individual or corporate) has potentially different values and interests, perceptions of the situation, and policy preferences. Furthermore, Sabatier argues, most disputes in the policy process involve deeply-held values and interests, large amounts of money, and at some points, authoritative coercion. Given these stakes, policy disputes seldom resemble polite academic debates. Instead, most actors face enormous temptation to present evidence selectively, to misrepresent the position of their opponents, to coerce and discredit opponents, and generally to distort the situation to their advantage (Sabatier 1999: 3). As a result, the policymaking and implementation process is not a straightforward technical process, where we cannot speak of purely technical concerns and objective analyses of problems and alternative solutions. Rather, there is a major political struggle and this struggle starts at the stage of problem definition or what others define as the 'creation of problems'.

In this context, interpretive approaches to policy analysis have contributed to the development of an understanding on the role of ideas, narratives and discourses in shaping the policy process and policy change. If problems and solutions are socially constructed and deeply held values on issues influence the rest of the process, as do experts and scientists, this leads us to question the role of experts in the policy process. Since the policy process is no longer open to solely the guidance of experts and informed by scientists, and there are competing knowledge claims on some policy issues, there are calls for a more democratic and open policy process. This brings us to the issue of experts versus layman in the policy process. Can we take opinions of experts and layman as equals in the policy process? Do some groups of people develop an irrational and emotional attitude to problems, or do they have a more comprehensive and sound conception of rationality with the support of some other experts?

This is an issue discussed earlier in the Turkish context by the author of this chapter with reference to politics of risk perception in the Bergama Gold Mine dispute (Orhan 2006). Indeed, being 'ideological, short-sided, and biased' have been frequently used as accusations in Turkey. These accusations are employed in a variety of contexts, especially for these initiatives standing against top-down decisions of authorities in a variety of occasions. On top of these accusations, being 'irrational and emotional' have also been used in similar contexts by powerful players. Yet again, there is a thin line between expertise and engaged expertise as well as local knowledge on issues and sheer ignorance about the causes and consequences of policies.

This paper aims to contextualize these dilemmas with reference to waves of science studies, a typology developed by Collins, Evans and Weinel (Collins and Evans 2002; Collins, Weinel and Evans 2010) and demonstrate changing conceptions of the role of experts and others in the policy process. In doing so, this paper will analyse the role of experts and expertise through waves of science and technology studies. The paper will go onto analyse and discuss a number of influential cases, including Brent Spar and MMR vaccines, as well as new cases from Turkey.

Indeed, there are competing claims on the authority of experts which calls for a more accountable and democratized version of science-policy interface in the policy process. Yet again, there are some objections to the involvement of lay people in the policy process as it is manifested in a number of cases throughout this chapter. At the end having experts may be inevitable, but their role in the policy process should be open to discussion, as well as that of people who have claims through their local knowledge on policy issues. The socially-embedded nature of experts and scientists as well as lay people requires us to develop a more cautious approach to policy problems.

Experts, Expertise and Democratization of Policy Process: The Evolution of Science and Technology Studies

For mainstream accounts, policy analysis is an interdisciplinary field of study and practice that aims to solve problems of modern societies. There is a very crucial role for knowledge in this process, because policy analysis is supposed to benefit from findings of various disciplines of social and natural sciences. From fact finding to problem definition and proposing alternatives to implementation, scientists and experts are expected to contribute to policy analysis and influence the rest of the process.

In fact, undisputed authority of science in the policy process reflects developments during and in the aftermath of World War II. New methods developed in research in economics, psychology, and operations were used during the war and employed in civilian life in the aftermath of the war. The rise of behaviouralism has also contributed to supremacy of quantitative techniques over others. Overall, quantitative techniques had supremacy over others and in

Harold Lasswell's words 'the battle for method is won' (Lasswell 1965: 7).

In the second half of the twentieth century, boundary organizations linked the scientific community and players of the policy process. Evidence based policy analysis contributed to the authority of science through incorporation of rigorous research evidence into public policy debates and internal public sector processes for policy evaluation and programme improvement, as well as, improvement of the reliability of advice concerning the efficiency and effectiveness of policy settings and possible alternatives (Head 2009).

In this context, we cannot speak of any problem concerning the authority of science and scientists during the 1950s and 1960s. This is what Collins and Evans called the first wave of science studies (Collins and Evans 2002: 239). In this period, science and scientists enjoyed special authority. According to Collins and Evans in this period a good scientific training was seen to put a person in a position to speak with authority and decisiveness in their own field, and often in other fields... Because the sciences were thought of esoteric and authoritative, it was inconceivable that decision-making in matters that involved science and technology could travel in any other direction than from the top down (Collins and Evans 2002: 239).

At the end, there was a straightforward link between the authority of science and the policy process independent of social practices. However, the undisputed positions of science, scientists, and experts did not last much longer. From 1970s onwards, the authority of experts was questioned from a constructivist angle. If problems and solutions are socially constructed, deeply-held values on issues influence the rest of the process, including experts and scientists. That is, scientists and experts cannot act independent of the social processes and institutions surrounding them.

Drawing from BSE crisis, Irwin and Wynne point out to the intrinsically social character of science in framing the public debate. For Irwin and Wynne, science offers a framework which is unavoidably social as well as technical since in public domains scientific knowledge embodies implicit models or assumptions about the social world. In addition, as an intervention in public life, scientific knowledge involves rhetorical claims to the superiority of the scientific worldview but it also builds upon social processes of trust and credibility. Whilst claiming to stand apart from the rest of society, science will reflect social interests and social assumptions (Irwin and Wynne 1996: 2–3).

This is what Collins and Evans called the second wave of science studies. This wave highlighted the social character of scientific research and questioned the neutral image of scientists and experts. In parallel to the conventional wisdom of the era, governance paradigm's policy proposals such as the 'participation of stakeholders' and the 'democratisation of the policy process' were offered as viable alternatives to solve policy problems of modern societies (Orhan 2014). Thus, extending public participation in both politics and science emerged as a solution to problem of technocracy, scientism, and top-down policy style in the second wave of science and technology studies. Leaving aside other critical issues concerning the difficulty of participation (Orhan 2014), the levelling of experts and people was criticized in this third wave. In a number of cases, problems stemming from the ignorance or exaggeration of lay people were highlighted to display problems of the previous wave of science and technology studies.

The Third Wave of Science Studies

The third wave of science and technology studies was introduced by Collins and Evans (Collins and Evans 2002) and later developed by Collins, Evans and Weinel (Collins, Weinel and Evans 2010). In their first article published in 2002, Collins and Evans dealt with what they called 'the problem of extension'. According to Collins and Evans, the need to extend the domain of technical decision-making beyond the technically qualified elite to enhance political legitimacy replaced the Problem of Legitimacy with the Problem of Extension in which there is a tendency towards dissolving the boundary between experts and the public and there are no longer any grounds for limiting the indefinite extension of technical decision-making rights (Collins and Evans 2002: 235).

In this context, they recognize problems concerning the first wave; yet again they do not completely discard arguments of the second wave but would like to reinstate the role of experts in the policy process. They criticize notions of lay experts, stand against technological populism and argue that demands for increased public participation in science have the tendency to lead to a levelling of the epistemological playing field and to a collapse of the concept of expertise (Collins, Weinel and Evans 2010: 186).

Collins, Weinel and Evans also refer to Miller, who argued that there is a knowledge deficit between scientific researchers and members of the general public and problems emerge if there is no gap between them (Miller 2001: 118). For Miller, 'scientists and lay people are not on the same footing where scientific information is concerned, and knowledge, hard won by hours of research, and tried and tested over the years and decades, deserves respect' (Miller 2001: 118).

In this context, Collins, Weinel and Evans aim to recreate a role for science in policy and reproduce the central role of science and scientists, develop a new understanding of expertise, and concentrate their efforts in reclaiming the status of experts. They further try to accomplish this without disregarding the political nature of scientific enterprise, on the one hand, and importance of local knowledge, on the other. Yet again, they keep these hierarchical relations intact.

Collins, Weinel and Evans refer to a number of high profile cases in defending their position concerning the experts and people. At this point, it could be better to remind readers about the original questions posed in the introduction of this chapter on the issue of experts versus laymen in the policy process. Can we take opinions of experts and laymen as equal in the policy process? Do some groups of people develop an irrational and emotional attitude to problems or, do they have a more comprehensive and sound conception of rationality with the support of some other experts?

The rest of this section will discuss the cases of MMR (measles, mumps, and rubella) vaccine revolt and the Brent Spar oilrig. These cases seems to support arguments of the third wave in the sense that opening of the policy process to influence of people has the potential of having unintended consequences. Yet again, these cases also demonstrate that it is not very easy to make overall generalizations concerning experts and people in the policy process.

The MMR vaccine revolt has been a controversial issue concerning the interface between science and society and later created serious public health problems in several parts of the developed world. This controversy surrounding the MMR vaccine first emerged following the publication of a study by Dr Andrew Wakefield in Lancet, on the alleged relationship between combined vaccine MMR and autism in 1998 (Wakefield et al. 1998). Following the publication of the article, the mass media covered the story with enthusiasm and, in the end, these developments contributed to some parents rejecting the vaccination of their children, which decreased the use of the MMR vaccine in Britain, Ireland, United States, among others. Ireland, in particular, experienced measles outbreaks in which there were more than 300 cases, 100 hospitalizations, and three deaths (Poland and Jacobson 2011).

The levels of undervaccination have contributed to a number of outbreaks with substantial human and financial costs. For instance in 2008, an intentionally unvaccinated 7-year-old boy was unknowingly infected with measles after returning from Switzerland, resulting in the largest outbreak in San Diego, California since 1991. In this case, 839 people were exposed, and 11 other unvaccinated children were infected. The high vaccination rate in the rest of the community, absence of vaccine failure, and a vigorous outbreak response helped keep the outbreak from becoming an epidemic. It halted spread beyond the third generation, at a net public sector cost of $10,376 per case (Sugerman et al. 2010).

As was reported in the *Daily Finance* by Melly Alazraki, undervaccination resulted in considerable financial and human costs in several parts of the developed world:

- The total cost of containing one case of measles after an unvaccinated student returned from India in 2004 to Iowa was $142,452.
- A mumps outbreak in 2006 in a hospital in Chicago, caused by poorly immunized employees, cost the institution $262,788, or $29,199 per mumps case.
- Another mumps outbreak in Nova Scotia in 2007 – traced back to an inadequate immunization regimen among a certain age

group of Canadians – cost an estimated total of nearly CDN$2.5 million or $3,511 per case.

- A 2002–03 measles outbreak in Italy, which led to the hospitalizations of more than 5,000 people, had a combined estimated cost between 17.6 million euros and 22.0 million euros. That amount of money could have inoculated between 1.5 million and 1.9 million children with a dose of the MMR vaccine (Alazraki 2011).

Allegations of serious conflicts of interest and the manipulation of samples brought the validity of the study into question. In the meantime, some other co-authors retracted their names and finally Lancet retracted this paper fully from its records. The United Kingdom's General Medical Council charged Dr Wakefield with professional misconduct (*Sunday Times* 2009)

At the moment, NGOs operating in the field of autism clearly state that, 'over the last two decades, extensive research has asked whether there is any link between childhood vaccinations and autism. The results of this research are clear: Vaccines do not cause autism. We urge that all children be fully vaccinated' (Rob Ring, Chief Science Officer, Autism Speaks).

Yet again, antivaccine campaigns still sustain themselves in different forms throughout the world. According to Poland and Jacobson, antivaccinationists come from people who are simply ignorant about science; unable to understand and incorporate concepts of risk and probability into science-grounded decision making; radical fringe elements who use deliberate mistruths, intimidation, falsified data, and threats of violence in efforts to prevent the use of vaccines and to silence critics. They also have a complete mistrust of the government and manufacturers, conspiratorial thinking, denialism, low cognitive complexity in thinking patterns, reasoning flaws, and a habit of substituting emotional anecdotes for data (Poland and Jacobson 2011).

The case of the Brent Spar Oil Rig, which was an oil platform in the North Sea, has been a controversial issue for global environmental politics. After completing its mission, Shell applied to the UK government to be allowed to dump the entire installation in the

Atlantic Ocean. The British government had no objections and announced its full support. Greenpeace decided to take action as part of its long-running campaign against ocean dumping. On 30 April 1995, activists occupied the Brent Spar and footage of Greenpeace activists being attacked by water cannons captured the attention of a sizeable audience throughout the world. Greenpeace International and a number of other environmental groups organized popular protests and consumer boycotts against Shell's decision, which further reduced Shell's sales to a great extent. Greenpeace took action against Shell as part of a campaign that it had been running since the 1970s, which aimed to push governments and the industry to have a more responsible attitude towards the ocean environment. They organized their campaign around the guiding principle of 'the ocean is not a dumping ground' and aimed to prevent Shell setting a new trend for further pollution through irresponsible dumping of a variety of obsolete installations like platforms, oil storage buoys, and oil rigs. Greenpeace also aimed to prevent cumulative negative environmental effects of these dumping operations. Upon these pressures, Shell decided to retreat from its decision, and the Brent Spar was dismantled (Greenpeace International 1995).

Later on, Greenpeace admitted their excesses in estimating the potential damage of sinking the Brent Spar. The controversial issue concerned the level of oil left in the Brent Spar, and Greenpeace apologized for their error in calculations as soon as they realized their mistake. As was reported in the *Independent*, 'Greenpeace claimed the Brent Spar could have more than 5,000 tons of oil still in its tanks. Shell said there was only 100 tons of an oily sludge inside, most of which consisted of inert silt' (*Independent* 1995).

However, Greenpeace insisted on its original claim 'the ocean is not a dumping ground' and Susan Meyer, Greenpeace UK's head of science, claimed that she feels rather comfortable about the stance Greenpeace took against dumping this structure at sea (*Independent* 1995). This is the departure point for Collins, Weinel, and Evans as they argued that the Brent Spar was primarily a symbol of a willingness to pollute, or mix the clean with the dirty, it would set a precedent that would license many more similar actions. Thus sinking one rig would justify sinking any number of rigs and, perhaps, other items of industrial waste and this would cause long term pollution damage whether or not the Brent Spar was a potential pollutant on its own.

They also referred to the predominance of 'quasi-religious/populist symbolic argument' stating that 'the North Sea should not be mixed with unnatural things like oil rigs' (Collins, Weinel and Evans 2010: 190).

Apart from miscalculations of the amount of waste on the Brent Spar, later on some other studies came out arguing in favour of sinking on this basis the role of quasi-religious/populist symbolic arguments were criticized by Collins, Weinel and Evans. They recommended scientists and technologists to insulate their work from the political and cultural environment. They also favoured those who 'know what they are talking about' and gave special weight to their views. The role of expertise under the third wave is different from the role of 'the scientist' under the first wave and the third wave's definition of a specialist 'expert' includes those who have experience-based expertise but no formal qualifications or training. Both the technical and political phases are necessary and neither can be reduced to the other and 'democracy cannot dominate every domain – that would destroy expertise – and expertise cannot dominate every domain – that would destroy democracy' (Collins, Weinel and Evans 2010: 188–89).

There are a number of guidelines and principles of the third wave such as:

- Recognize but do not endorse religious or populist reasons in the making of technological decisions in the public domain.
- Frame technological issues imaginatively so as to bring as many propositional questions and answers to the table as might bear on the technological decision.
- Never suppress or distort the opinions of experts even if they must always be treated as subservient to politics but, on the contrary, make sure that all relevant answers to all relevant propositional questions are as visible as possible.
- A good society will be informed by, among other things, scientific values for these are democratic values.
- A good society will facilitate maximum scope for discussion of political matters and maximum exposure of technical matters.

- Always aspire to keep the technical and the political phase separate even where they are combined in institutions or individuals expertise (Collins, Weinel and Evans 2010: 195).

Critiques of the Third Wave

These case studies and a number of other studies support the third wave arguments and clearly indicate that popular involvement of people in the policy process with some sort of unsubstantiated claims may entail some risks for the health and the well-being of societies. However, there are a number of other case studies that reflect the power of well-organized interests in manipulating research and setting the agenda for their own benefits. This section will summarize critiques of the third wave and analyse a number of other case studies in order to provide a more balanced view on the role of experts versus lay people in the policy process.

To start with critiques, there are a number of people who criticize the premises of third wave scientists. According to Tim Forsyth, expertise frequently forms parts of wider systems of governance and control, and individual agency frequently cannot change that. Moreover, 'science' does not simply generate knowledge in instantly trusted ways: it requires validation, recognition, and placements within paradigms of normality and recognized institutions. Simply asking experts to act cognitively to 'insulate their work from the political and cultural environment' cannot achieve neutrality (Forsyth 2011).

These arguments resemble second wave positions and refer to contextual factors at work. However, there are some other problems, for example in the Brent Spar case, that deserve attention. Although the British government was rather prompt in condemning Greenpeace's mistake, it also failed to consult scientists in its decision about the sinking of the platform. For instance, two government-funded marine scientists attacked assumptions put forward by Shell in justifying sea dumping. Dr John Gage and Dr John Gordon of the Dunstaffnage Marine Laboratory also asked why the government failed to consult them before approving the dumping. Their laboratory in Oban, Scotland, funded by the Natural Environment Research Council, is more knowledgeable than any other about conditions on the seabed of the dump site, the Rockall Trough. In a letter to Greenpeace, they criticize a Shell-commissioned report that justifies dumping by stating that relatively few species live at deep sea levels. They also say the analysis ignores the possibility undersea storms could bring pollution towards the surface (*Independent* 1995).

At the end of the day, the close ties the government has with industrial interests, their failure in consulting experts in the field, and the insistence on the views of certain experts attracts criticisms of other groups in society. This is why people approach governments cautiously, something that is also reflected in a number of other cases. It is not all about the ignorance, as in the case of MMR vaccines either. Other so-called emotional and irrational groups also resort to experts and on some occasions develop a larger understanding of rationality.

In this context, the Alar growth hormone case will be taken to critically analyse premises of the third wave concerning the role of experts versus people in the policy process. This case was cited in an earlier work by the author to illustrate the role of experts in informing parties of the policy process (Orhan 2006). In this case, the Natural Resources Defence Council (NRDC) in the US announced in 1989 that preschool children are at high risk for cancers and neurological disorders, because they ingest high levels of pesticides along with their fruits and vegetables. Their campaign focused on the Alar growth hormone used in apples and residues of Alar found in apple juice, apple sauce and raw apple itself, common in American children's diet. People refused to buy all those products and several cities took apples out of student cafeterias. After three months, the EPA issued a preliminary determination to cancel the use of Alar. Six months later, the company producing Alar voluntarily withdrew its registration (Tesh 2000: 89–90).

The Alar case generated an intense attack on the NRDC and it looked like a case in which citizens, acting through an interest group, pressed congress and the bureaucracy to make new policies, while experts criticized the logic underlying the citizens' position (Tesh 2000: 90). However, Tesh argued that the NRDC did not perceive the risks of pesticides by using a special form of reasoning and did not conclude that Alar is hazardous because it is unknown and dreaded; it did not publish an ethical treatise calling Alar dangerous, because exposure is involuntary, hidden, and uncontrollable; and it did not bring up values like fairness and equity. Instead, the NRDC used the same kind of scientific rationality by resorting to scientists sympathetic to environmental concerns. In that sense, the environmental movement resorted to scientists and experts to a large extent and based their arguments on expert opinions. The dichotomy between the 'lay knowledge' and 'scientific knowledge' or 'lay and expert risk perception' might be misleading since they both use a similar form of reasoning. Finally, the Alar case illustrates that when governments hear opposing judgments about the dangers of a technology, the two sides represent not solely lay people and experts but two groups of experts (Tesh 2000: 93).

There are some other examples on the dichotomy of lay people and experts. For instance, research in environment has indicated that 'received wisdom' about environmental problems such as deforestation and desertification have undergone changes according to how experts have changed their minds and widening participation has been a crucial part of these changes (Forsyth 2011).

Participation can also enhance how we understand environmental processes. But perhaps more importantly, it helps reframe empirical research to develop explanations and solutions to problems as they are experienced locally. In this context, the role of scientists has significantly changed regarding climate change. The initial predominance of meteorologists is somehow balanced by social scientists. Obviously, people cannot make predictions about climate modelling, however, for local climate adaptation, local people inform the policy process about the viability of alternative solutions (Forsyth 2011).

At the end of the day, difficulties in making generalizations characterized this section. Cases like MMR vaccines demonstrated that scientific misconduct and widespread media coverage resulted in serious health problems and the re-emergence of certain diseases even in developed regions of the world. However, other cases suggest that the dichotomy of experts versus laymen may not be valid, and groups of scientists/experts either in the form of discourse coalitions or advocacy coalitions compete with one other in informing the policy process. Furthermore, as it was demonstrated in the case of global climate change, having expertise is vital, but participation has the potential of enhancing the quality of policymaking and implementation as a whole.

Reflections on Turkey

There are some examples for both types of problems associated with the experts versus people dilemma in Turkey. In fact, Metin Münir's columns on attention deficit hyperactivity disorder (ADHD) sparked a discussion in Turkey similar to MMR vaccines debate. In his series published in *Milliyet Daily* in 2010, Münir questioned the irresponsible use of medicines on school children diagnosed with ADHD, without a thorough analysis of the situation. In fact, ADHD is a chronic condition that affects millions of children worldwide, and there are several thousands of children with similar symptoms in Turkey too. This problem often persists into adulthood and includes a combination of problems, such as difficulty sustaining attention, hyperactivity, and impulsive behaviour (Mayo Clinic).

Münir's reasoning is based on the distrust of experts (i.e. psychiatrists), large pharmaceutical companies who supply medication, and some educational professionals who would like to get rid of troubled students. Although, the diagnosis of ADHD requires elimination of all environmental and other sources of the problem, Münir points out potential problems likely to stem from the misconduct of certain practitioners and the risk children face of stigmatization without a serious diagnosis of their situation.

In the meantime, parents were confused over the allegations and some of them ceased using prescribed medications. Experts were furious over Münir's handling of the issue and accused him of misleading parents of children with ADHD. Münir could have possibly been right about the prescription of certain medication without a thorough examination, and the power of certain pharmaceutical groups in manipulating the process through a global campaign. However, there exists serious cases of ADHD and these children are very much in need of medication to pursue a healthy social life. A total rejection of these medical practices paved the way for rejecting medical treatment in some crucial cases. This style of journalism spread concern to families of a substantial number of children with ADHD and risk their education and wellbeing. According to Yankı Yazgan, such news about the excessive use of medication is not valid because a large percentage of children and adolescents with ADHD, roughly 85 per cent are not on medication. Such a problem is not about overmedication, but rather under treating those who are in need (Yazgan 2015).

This issue of experts versus the public has manifested itself in a number of other occasions in Turkey. It is especially the case when decisions are taken in a top-down manner without the involvement of stakeholders. Given the limited avenues for participation in Turkey, there are quite a few examples of confrontation, particularly regarding the environmental consequences of developmental projects such as dams, energy installations, large-scale mining projects, the conversion of urban green spaces, and new industrial zones. In those occasions, we cannot speak of experts and scientists playing the major role. Rather, centrally-planned development implemented in a top-down manner with political and economic concerns, and authorities resort to discourses on expertise, science, rationality, and economic development and progress in legitimizing their policy choices. Those groups who stood against the government's policies are easily labelled as 'irrational and emotional' if not a 'traitor and agents of foreign powers' or 'ideological, short-sided and biased'. We cannot speak of a rational speech situation where parties take their turn in voicing their concerns over the issues under consideration.

With such centralized processes of policymaking and implementation, genuine 'participation' of people and the involvement of experts and scientists can potentially make a serious contribution to quality of policies. One cannot risk missing voices of experts in the field. Even those so-called emotional and irrational environmental movements resort to experts in bringing their case to the forefront of public discussions. In the Bergama Gold Mine dispute, competing discourse coalitions formed on this issue and scientists informed both coalitions in different ways. In some occasions, representatives of certain NGOs were invited for consultation, yet again they were handpicked from pro-government or pro-industry groups. The failure of the government to be transparent and to consult the public, as well as relying solely on organized industrial interests, results in scepticism towards experts and authorities. This attitude, in turn, negatively affects the role of experts in our societies.

Conclusion

Nowadays we live in a world with a globalized policy process in which policy ideas, policy discourses as well as certain techniques and contents travel around the world. As it was outlined throughout the paper, the relationship between experts and public policies has been the subject of a number of periodical evaluations and paradigms. From the 1950s onwards, science, scientists, and experts enjoyed unquestioned authority in attending to social problems and policy problems as a whole. Yet again, there has been a critical approach to the role of science, scientists and experts in the policy process. This is partly related to the rise of interpretive approaches and their critical attitude to grand narratives and procedures of top-down policymaking and implementation. They have been particularly successful in bringing the social and political nature of policy problems and policies as such and especially the excessive role of certain powerful players into the policy process.

Democratization of the policy process was offered as a mechanism to solve policy problems stemming from excessive powers of experts as such. However, this reversal of power relations produced some unwanted consequences as in the case of MMR vaccination and in a number of other disputes like ADHD treatment. The third wave positions were offered the reinstalling of experts in the policy process.

'Can we take opinions of experts and layman as equals in the policy process?'

As critiques of the third wave approach have rightly put it expertise is necessary for the solution of the problems of modern societies. Yet again 'expertise needs transparency not blind trust' and 'blindly trusting expert facts is a dangerous game' (Forsyth 2011). Democratization of the policy process is vital, and experts should also be accountable to both the society in which they live and overall humanity as a whole.

'Do some groups of people develop an irrational and emotional attitude to problems or, do they have a more comprehensive and sound conception of rationality with the support of some other experts?'

There is a thin line between the expertise and engaged expertise as well as local knowledge on issues and sheer ignorance about the causes and consequences of policies. Yes, there are some occasions lay people act in total ignorance; yet again there are a number of other examples in which people develop a more comprehensive and sound conception of rationality with the support of some other experts. The vital issue will be democratization of the policy process in an accountable manner. The expertise should not be the legitimizing tool of centralized policy processes which then disregards other opinions through their top-down initiatives. Rather, it should be the guiding principle of the policy process that concerns of all stakeholders should be voiced in a rational speech situation.

References

Alazraki, M. 2011. 'The Autism Vaccine Fraud: Dr. Wakefield's Costly Lie to Society'. http://www.dailyfinance.com/2011/01/12/autism-vaccine-fraud-wakefield-cost-money-deaths/.

Collins, H., M. Weinel and R. Evans. 2010. 'The politics and policy of the Third Wave: new technologies and society.' *Critical Policy Studies* 4(2), 185–201.

Collins, H.M., and R.J. Evans. 2002. 'The third wave of science studies: studies of expertise and experience.' *Social Studies of Science*, 32(2), 235–96.

Forsyth, T. 2011. 'Expertise needs transparency not blind trust: a deliberative approach to integrating science and social participation.' *Critical Policy Studies* 5(3), October 2011, 317–22.

Greenpeace International. 1995. 'Shell reverses decision to dump the Brent Spar.' http://www.greenpeace.org/international/en/about/history/Victories-timeline/Brent-Spar/.

Head, B. 2009. 'Evidence-based policy: principles and requirements.' In *Strengthening Evidence-based Policy in the Australian Federation: Roundtable Proceedings.* http://www.pc.gov.au/__data/assets/pdf_file/0007/96208/03-chapter2.pdf pp. 13–26.

Independent. 1995. 'Greenpeace's Brent Spar apology.' http://www.independent.co.uk/news/greenpeaces-brent-spar-apology-1599647.html.

Irwin, A., and B. Wynne. (eds.). 1996. *Misunderstanding science? The public reconstruction of science and technology*. Cambridge: Cambridge University Press.

Lasswell, H.D. 1965. 'The Policy Orientation.' In D. Lerner & H.D. Lasswell (eds.). *The Policy Sciences*. Stanford: Stanford University Press. pp. 3–15.

Mayo Clinic. http://www.mayoclinic.org/diseases-conditions/adhd/basics/symptoms/con-20023647.

Miller, S. 2001. 'Public understanding of science at the crossroads.' *Public Understanding of Science*, 10(1), 115–20.

Orhan, G. 2006. 'The Politics of Risk Perception in Turkey: Discourse Coalitions in the Case of Bergama Gold Mine Dispute.' *Policy and Politics*, Vol. 34, No: 4, pp. 691–710.

———. 2014. 'Public Participation as a Depoliticisation Process: The Case of Environmental Policy.' In K. Göymen & O. Sazak (eds.). *Centralisation Decentralisation Debate Revisited*. Istanbul: Sabancı University IPC and Friedrich Neumann Stifting, 262–91.

Poland, G.A., and R.M. Jacobson. 2011. 'The Age-Old Struggle against the Antivaccinationists.' *New England Journal of Medicine* 364: 97–99.

Ring, R. (undated). 'Vaccines and Autism.' http://www.autismspeaks.org/science /policy-statements /information-about-vaccines-and-autism.

Sabatier, P.A. 1999. 'The Need for Better Theories.' In P. A. Sabatier (ed.). *Theories of the Policy Process*, Boulder: Westview. pp. 3–17.

Sugerman, D. E. et al. 2010. 'Measles Outbreak in a Highly Vaccinated Population, San Diego, 2008: Role of the Intentionally Undervaccinated.' *Pediatrics*, 25: 4, 747–55. http://pediatrics.aappublications.org/content/early/2010/03/22/peds.2009-1653.full.pdf+html.

Sunday Times. 2009. 'MMR doctor Andrew Wakefield fixed data on autism.' http://www.thesundaytimes.co.uk/sto/public/news/article148992.ece.

Tesh, S. N. 2000. *Uncertain Hazards: Environmental Activists and Scientific Proof*. Ithaca and London: Cornell University Press.

Wakefield, A.J., S.H. Murch, A. Anthony. et al. 1998. 'Ileal-lymphoid-nodular hyperplasia, non-specific colitis, and pervasive developmental disorder in children.' *Lancet*, 351: 637–41. [Retraction, *Lancet* 2010, 375: 445.]

Yazgan, Y. 2015. 'Kuyudaki Tas.' Birgün Pazar. 8 February. p. 6.

3 Participation of Civil Society Organizations in the United Nations in the Aid Effectiveness Discourse and Related Standard-setting Negotiations

Raymond Saner and Lichia Yiu

Abstract

This paper consists of two parts. The first part analyses the involvement of non-state actors in the United Nations (UN) and its agencies. The engagement of non-state actors, particularly of the international non-governmental organizations (I-NGOs) and the various national civil society organizations (CSOs) dates back to the founding of the United Nations in 1945 and the analyses show a growing participation of NGOs from developed and developing countries. The second part describes the role and participation of the I-NGOs in the deliberations and negotiations on global public policymaking and standard setting negotiations of aid effectiveness.

Introduction

International standards on aid effectiveness are negotiated in different International Organizations (IOs) by governments and non-state actor organizations such as CSOs. CSOs have been engaged over the past decade in the aid effectiveness discourse, which originated from the establishment of the Millennium Development Goals (MDGs). The MDGs delineated specific development goals and benchmarks to be achieved by 2015. Due to these ambitious goals and the monitoring processes put in place to track progress, it became apparent that aid was not producing the expected development results necessary to achieve the MDGs. The effectiveness of aid was plagued by the lack of coordination, overly ambitious targets, unrealistic timing, budget constraints, and political self-interest of states. Thus, the aid effectiveness discourse began as an attempt to improve aid in order to achieve the MDGs. In order to gain influence, CSOs have fought to be recognized as development actors at international level as well as within a domestic context (Göymen 2008). CSO's claim the right to contribute to the aid effectiveness negotiations at international and national levels. Additionally, CSOs have advocated for a paradigm shift away from focusing on technically-based aid effectiveness toward a focus on rights-based development effectiveness. This article describes how CSOs interact with other stakeholders to gain influence in international standard setting negotiations and how they participate in the aid effectiveness discourse.

Part I: Evolution of NGO Participation in the United Nations and Related Agencies

Technological advancements in the field of communication and information technology have dramatically accelerated global connectivity. Applications of these new technologies altered private and public relations and helped transform international relationships affecting the economic, social and political spheres of societies and their citizens. According to Saner and Michalun, this new wave of globalization 'is characterised by a complex set of interconnectivities and interdependencies with an increasing number of actors vying to influence the outcome of these relationships. They lay competing claims to resources, markets, and legitimacy, and are engaged in activities traditionally defined as belonging within the domain of diplomacy' (2009: 1).

This re-alignment of relationships has also affected the United Nations system. One can observe a much greater participation and influence of civil society organizations (CSOs) in the deliberation on global policies and relations within and outside the confines of the

UN system. Today, within the UN system, there is a liaison office which manages relations with the NGOs and other CSOs. The same holds for all major UN agencies and IOs. Most of these liaison offices were set up in the late 1990s or early 2000s.

Historical Background

The involvement of CSOs in the UN has evolved since the founding of the UN in 1945 and took the form of a consultative relationship with the Economic and Social Council (ECOSOC). As stated in the UN Charter, Article 71,

> The Economic and Social Council may make suitable arrangements for consultation with non-governmental organizations which are concerned with matters within its competence. Such arrangements may be made with international organizations and, where appropriate, with national organizations after consultation with the Member of the United Nations concerned (United Nations 1945)

Ever since, NGOs – mostly large international non-governmental bodies, have interacted with the UN Secretariat and agencies, participated in UN agencies' programmes, and have consulted with UN Member States. The 1970s and 1980s witnessed a significant increase in their participation in the activities of the UN organization. In this period, NGOs were recognized for their ability to shape the global agenda as well as for their important role as operational actors in delivery humanitarian and development assistance.

Turning Point

The relationship between the UN and NGOs changed dramatically in the 1990s. This change was triggered by both a UN resolution recognizing the importance of CSOs as part of the global community and also due to an angry outpouring of citizens across many countries expressing dissatisfaction with globalization, social hardships and increasing discrepancies between the wealthy and poor segments of society in many countries.

The fall of the Berlin Wall resulted in a sea change in Eastern European countries in 1989, which was preceded by the violent

Tiananmen Square Incident. The dramatic political changes created a global consensus that democratization of the public space and greater engagement of the public in affairs that affect the public were 'inevitable' and needed in order to ensure governmental legitimacy and to foster greater citizen satisfaction. In this climate, the UN decided to review the consultative status of NGOs with the Economic and Social Council (ECOSOC). Resolution 1296 of 1968 was replaced by Resolution 1996/31 adopted in 1996, which allows, among other things, sub-regional, regional, and national NGOs to be accredited by ECOSOC. Before that date, only international NGOs could apply for consultative status.

Today, the NGOs registered at the CSO Net under the auspices of UN-DESA (UN Department of Economic and Social Development) represent a vibrant community of civil society with diverse nationalities, different forms of organization, and wide range of interests. Even though not all registered NGOs enjoy a

Table 3.1: Organization Types of NGOs registered on the DESA CSO Net (2014)

Association	1364
Foundation	658
Institution	225
Inter-governmental Organization	200
Local Government	131
Non-Governmental Organization	22879
Media	94
Private Sector	474
Trade Union	58
Others	582
Academics	881
Indigenous Peoples Organizations	1788
Disability, Development and Rights Organizations	492
Open-ended Working Group on Ageing	93
Cooperative	82
Total	31365

Source: United Nations Department of Economic and Social Affairs 2014.

consultative status, they do engage in UN conferences and summits in different manner. Table 3.1 presents the types of organizations currently registered on the DESA CSO Net. It is interesting to note the wide range of organizations represented range from foundations to special interest groups, from inter-government bodies to NGOs, from private sector companies to cooperatives.

Today, there is also a fair representation of the regions across the world. Africa has the largest number of NGOs registered with DESA CSO Net (Table 3.2).

Table 3.2: Organizations by region as registered on the DESA CSO Net (2014)

Africa	7419	24%
Asia	5496	18%
Europe	4989	16%
North America	4490	14%
Oceania	748	2%
Latin America and Caribbean	3087	10%
Not Specified	4826	16%
Total	31'055	100%

Source: United Nations Department of Economic and Social Affairs 2014.

New Generations of NGO-UN Relations

The shift of the role and function of the CSOs within the UN environment were both quantitative and qualitative (Union of International Organizations 1995). This evolution took place gradually with the turning point at the end of the Cold War. Large numbers of non-governmental actors, in particular, national NGOs from developing countries, from the Western hemisphere and, albeit to a lesser extent, from East-Central European post-communist societies, appeared around the major UN Conferences on Environment and Development, Population and Development, Human Rights, Women's Rights, Social Development, Human Settlements and Food Security, and their preparatory and follow-up processes.

The success of the protests organized by the anti-globalization movement and the advocacy and lobbying by the debt relief campaigners were instrumental in ushering and consolidating greater openness of the UN and its related institutions. The former group bashed the World Trade Organization (WTO) Ministerial Meeting in Seattle in 1997 and disrupted a series of other important international meetings for instance the meetings of the WB/IMF (Washington DC 1998), G8 Summit (Genoa 1999) and WTO Ministerial Meeting (Geneva, 1999). The latter group was able to launch the debt forgiveness process for the most indebted poor countries and to replace the ineffectual structural adjustment programmes (SAP) at the IMF and the World Bank by the poverty reduction strategy plan (PRSP). Since then, eradication of poverty has become the *sine qua non* of CSO calls for change coupled with calls for redefinition of development results. NGOs with their own policy research capability and capacity have since been accepted as serious interlocutors in various policy forums and viewed as important partners in the democratic deliberations of global policy issues.

Since then NGOs have been allowed to be involved in the UN-organized world conferences, marking a turning point leading to the so-called 'Second Generation' of UN-NGO relations, a term coined by Hill (2004).

The necessity to strengthen relations between the UN and NGOs has been subsequently underlined in various documents, in particular in the United Nations Millennium Declaration of September 2000. The commitment of UN Member States to give greater opportunities to NGOs has been reaffirmed in the 2005 World Summit Outcome Document (para 172–74). This was again reaffirmed during the 2012 Rio+20 outcome document called 'The Future We Want'.

In 1946, only 41 I-NGOs were granted Consultative Status by ECOSOC. Relations were formal and lacked broad based representation. As a result of the Resolution 1996/31, the number of NGOs accredited at present with the Consultative Status reached 3,910 (United Nations Department of Economic and Social Affairs 2014) at the last count (Table 3), representing an exponential growth over the past 68 years.

This second generation of NGO engagement with the UN system has been marked by a much larger scale of the NGO presence across the UN system; a more diverse institutional character of the

Table 3.3: Organizations in Consultative Status with ECOSOC (2014)

General	146
Special	2,778
Roster	986
Total	3,910

Source: United Nations Department of Economic and Social Affairs 2014.

Table 3.4: Organizations by Fields of activity registered on the DESA CSO Net

Economic and Social	12,999
Financing for Development	2,368
Gender Issues and Advancement of Women	7,297
Population	2,475
Public Administration	2,555
Social Development	8,795
Statistics	1,731
Sustainable Development	9,196
Conflict Resolution in Africa	858
NEPAD	605

Source: United Nations Department of Economic and Social Affairs 2014.

organizations involved (Table 3.1); and a greater diversity of the issues that NGOs seek to address at the UN.

Today, in addition to the international NGOs, the second generation NGOs involved in the UN and UN agencies consist also of national and regional NGOs, networks and alliances. All said, there are more than 31,000 NGOs registered with the UNDESA (Table 3.2). 'Above all, the second generation of UN-NGOs relations are essentially political and reflect the motivation of NGOs to engage with the UN as part of the institutional architecture of global governance' (Hill 2004: 2).

Most of the registered NGOs are engaged in the economic and social areas, while NGOs focusing on sustainable development and social development hold the second and third spots (Table

3.4). NGOs are allowed to registered multiple interests and fields of activities.

The New Partnership for Africa's Development (NEPAD) is an African Union strategic framework for pan-African socio-economic development, spearheaded by African leaders in July 2001 in Lusaka, Zambia. The NEPAD group represents a pan-Africa alliance to address critical challenges facing the continent: poverty, development and Africa's marginalization internationally. It meant to support African countries to take full control of their development agenda, to work more closely together and to cooperate more effectively with international partners. NEPAD is also a new construction focusing on how the states could create hybrid coordination mechanisms to promote joint interest and move between the governmental and non-governmental space.

Facilitation Infrastructure for CSO Participation in the UN Process

Besides providing the legal framework, the Economic and Social Council (ECOSOC) within the UN General Assembly and the Department of Economic and Social Affairs (DESA) of the Secretariat are also required to ensure the participation of the NGOs. ECOSOC regulates the membership of NGOs in the UN process and meetings. DESA provides the secretariat support and transparency in terms of the NGO engagement.

The integrated Civil Society Organizations (iCSO) System, developed by the Department of Economic and Social Affairs (DESA), facilitates interactions between civil society organizations and DESA. 'The system provides online registration of general profiles for civil society organizations, including address, contacts, activities and meeting participation, facilitates the application procedure for consultative status with the Economic and Social Council (ECOSOC), and assists accredited NGOs in submitting quadrennial reports and in designating representatives to the United Nations' (United Nations Department of Economic and Social Affairs 2014).

DESA has also developed CSO Net – the Civil Society Network, a web portal devoted to non-governmental organizations in association with the United Nations, and to members of United Nations agencies, funds and programmes, to promote best practices in the field of economic and social development. The portal gives users the opportunity to publish news and to engage and moderate discussion forums. It facilitates online pre-registration to UN conferences open for civil society participation and allows for submission of NGO statements to the Economic and Social Council.

Part II: Non-State Actors' Engagements in the Deliberations on Aid Effectiveness

Civil society through NGOs has participated over the past decade in the aid effectiveness discourse that originated when the MDGs were negotiated. The MDGs delineate specific development goals and benchmarks to be achieved by 2015. The MDGs were ambitious and difficult to achieve. The monitoring processes put in place to track progress showed that aid was not producing the expected development results necessary to achieve the MDGs. The effectiveness of aid was plagued by the 'lack of coordination, overly ambitious targets, unrealistic timing, budget constraints, and political self-interest' of states (OECD 2014a). Thus, the aid effectiveness discourse began as an attempt to improve aid in order to achieve the MDGs.

International standards on aid effectiveness are negotiated at different international fora hosted by different IOs. Basic knowledge on how these IOs function and how decisions are taken were important sources of information which CSOs needed to meaningfully participate in and influence the international aid effectiveness debate.

A short case history is presented below to describe the NGOs engagement in the aid effectiveness discourse and negotiations from 2000–12. In order to gain influence, CSOs fought to be recognized as development actors with a right to contribute to the aid effectiveness deliberations and policy negotiations. Additionally, CSOs advocated for a paradigm shift away from focusing on technically-based aid effectiveness toward a focus on rights-based development effectiveness. While aid effectiveness aims at 'appropriate arrangement for the planning, management and deployment of aid that is efficient, reduces transaction costs and is targeted towards development outcomes' (OECD 2014b: vii); development effectiveness focuses on 'the achievement of sustainable development results related to MDGs that have country level impacts and discernible effects on the lives of the poor' (OECD: vii).

Context

Throughout the 1990s a series of international organizations hosted conferences, forums and meetings that brought poverty reduction and the importance of development to the forefront of the international aid agenda. Starting with the 'World Development Report 1990', published by the World Bank (1990), and the first 'Human Development Report', published by the United Nations Development Programme (UNDP 1990), international organizations highlighted poverty as a key issue. These initial reports set the tone for the international aid agenda in the 1990s and highlighted the importance of development policies that 'pursue ends (improved lives) and not just means (economic growth)' (Hulme 2009: 8). A series of international conferences throughout the 1990s, including the UN World Summit for Children, the United Nations Conference on Environment and the World Summit on Social Development, incorporated poverty reduction and development into their agendas. The World Conference on Human Rights in 1993 reaffirmed the UN's dedication to human rights. The principles of human rights informed and underpinned the international aid discourse of the 1990s that resulted in the MDGs (Hulme 2009).

Numerous conferences and summits resulted in a myriad of suggested benchmarks and goals. In order to consolidate and focus the global aid process, the Organisation for Economic Co-operation and Development (OECD), specifically the Development Assistance Committee (DAC), took the lead. The report 'Development Partnership in the New Global Context' (OECD 1995) was published by the OECD/DAC in 1995. The report reviewed the effectiveness of aid and asserted that 'development cooperation is an investment ... and that rich countries needed to increase aid, make it more effective and efficient and make their overall approach to development more coherent'. (Hulme 2009: 13)

Based on this assertion and resulting DAC meetings, the DAC published an outcome document 'Shaping the 21st Century: The Contribution of Development Co-operation' in 1996. This document synthesized the suggested goals from the preceding international conferences and produced a set of International Development Goals (IDGs). Although the document was endorsed at OECD ministerial meetings and by the G7 in 1996, it did not include a specific plan of action and therefore made little impact. The document had been produced by OECD member state representatives, with little to no input from developing countries or civil society organizations. As such, the document focused on the 'DAC frames of reference – aid transfers and resource constraints... projects, policies and programs (rather than rights and principles)' (Hulme 2009: 14). It was a technical document that needed to achieve OECD agreement and therefore did not include greater themes of inequality and right-based development that may have caused issues with some OECD members. CSO reactions to the IDG process varied depending on the extent to which the IDG fit with their own mandate and mission statements. There was a broad perception however that the IDGs were too narrow and technically focused. The stated goals had moved away from the rights-based approach that had been promoted at various conferences throughout the 1990s (Hulme 2009).

Leading up to the Millennium Assembly of the United Nations in 2000 various stakeholders, including states, CSOs and international agencies, lobbied to influence the aid agenda. The UN saw the Millennium Assembly as the opportunity to establish a more inclusive international development agenda. It recognized that the PECD and the IDGs, were tailored to a limited constituency of wealthy nations. Prior to the Assembly, the UN published a zero draft titled 'We the Peoples: The Role of the United Nations in the 21st Century' (Annan 2000) for review by the international community. The base document was much longer and inclusive than the DAC's IDG document but received mixed response (Hulme 2009).

In June 2000, the leaders of the four major international development organizations came together to produce a single document to guide international development: '2000. A Better World for All; Progress towards the International Development Goals'

(Annan, Johnston, Khöler and Wolfensolm 2000). The document was a gesture of solidarity among the four major institutions. Regardless, the parallel efforts OECD and UN continued with each supporting their own process, the IDGs and the expected Millennium Declaration. Negotiations and advocacy efforts continued leading up to the Millennium Conference. The final 'Millennium Declaration' (United Nations 2000) shows the changes made to the zero draft 'We the Peoples'.

Moving past the Millennium Summit, both the OECD and UN were trying to implement their own framework for development in the new millennium. At the World Bank meeting in 2001, it was acknowledged that having two separate sets of international development goals and processes would be ineffective and inefficient. Therefore, after a series of high-level negotiations, a task force was assembled to consolidate the two sets of goals. The four major international organizations, the World Bank, the DAC (representing the OECD), the UN and the IMF, were represented on the task force. Through this task force the Millennium Development Goals were determined and added to the Millennium Declaration as an annex. Although this final negotiation was officially recognized as purely a 'technical process', it carried great weight and set the agenda for development aid in the new millennium (Hulme 2009). The MDGs consisted of eight goals, seventeen targets, and sixty indicators (United Nations 2014).

Milestones of International Negotiations on Aid Effectiveness

Aid effectiveness policies and standards are determined through multilateral negotiations on an international level. International negotiations and diplomacy have become more complicated as the number of actors has proliferated. States are no longer the sole stakeholders in international policy debates. Now, non-state actors (NSAs), including international organizations (IOs), transnational corporations (TNCs), philanthropic foundations and Civil Society Organizations (CSOs), are trying to influence international standards. (Saner 2009: 7–8) States must engage with the other stakeholders in multilateral international negotiations. Each type of actor has a different approach or pathway to influence the negotiation as well as different strategies of engagement with the other stakeholders in the negotiation.

The Organisation for Economic Co-operation and Development (OECD) is the primary forum in which international aid effectiveness standards are negotiated. The Development Assistance Committee (DAC) is the OECD sub-forum for establishing norms and policies in regard to international aid. CSOs achieved representation over time within the OECD through participation in the WP-EFF, a sub-body of the DAC, and participation in the High Level Forums (HLFs). As established in the first section, the HLFs are the primary forums in which aid effectiveness policies are negotiated between an increasingly diverse group of stakeholders.

In order to implement the Millennium Development Goal (MDG) number 8, 'forming a global partnership for development' (OECD 2014e), the international community redoubled its effort in defining a more effective partnership arrangement so that MDGs 1 to 7 could be achieved within the time span of 15 years. Working Party on Aid Effectiveness (WP-EFF), a subsidiary body of the DAC, was formed in 2003 in order to facilitate the implementation of MDG 8 since it had become apparent that a partnership arrangement would be necessary to understand why development aid was not producing the expected results needed to achieve the MDGs (OECD 2014a).

The Working Party is an international collaborative forum that has evolved over time to incorporate 80 members from donor countries, recipient countries, CSOs, members of the private sector and multilateral organizations. Its purpose is to provide a space to discuss issues of aid effectiveness and development priorities such as (Organisation for Economic Co-operation and Development 2014e):

- Ownership and accountability
- Country systems
- Managing for development results
- Transparent and responsible aid

High Level Fora (HLF) brought together stakeholders in the aid effectiveness debate. Each HLF has produced a revised 'blueprint for maximizing the impact of aid' to be implemented

Figure 3.1: CSO Engagement in the DAC WP-EFF Process from 2002–12

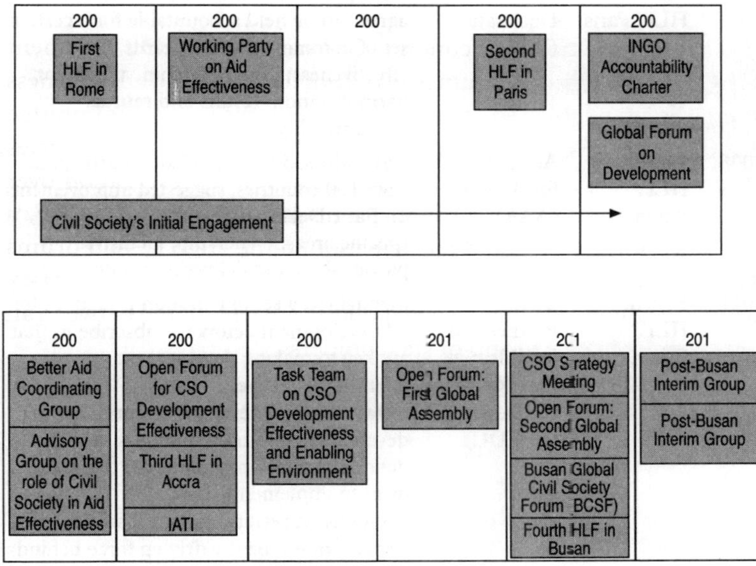

Source: Author.

on an international level (OECD 2014a). Figure 3.1 represents the milestones of the international negotiations under the auspice of DAC from 2002–12.

Outputs of these HLF meetings are a series of declarations, which serves as the blueprint and soft norms for observance by all actors within the context of aid implementation. Table 3.5 below summarized the various outcomes:

Table 3.5: Outcomes of HLF meetings

Year	Occasion	Name of the Declaration	Main Message
2002	First HLF, Rome	Rome Declaration (RD)	emphasized the important role of the recipient country and asserted specific priority actions

(Continued...)

(Table 3.5 continued...)

2005	Second HLF, Paris	Paris Declaration (PD)	for the first time donors and recipients agreed to be held accountable for a certain set of commitments in regards to aid effectiveness; i.e., ownership, alignment, harmonization, results and mutual accountability
2008	Third HLF, Accra	Accra Agenda for Action (AAA)	was endorsed by over 17,000 participants from 100 countries, suggested improvements on Paris Declaration strategies in three specific areas: ownership, inclusive partnership, and delivering results
2011	Fourth HLF, Busan	Busan Partnership for Effective Development Cooperation (BPEDC)	highlighted a set of common principles for all development actors to subscribe to that are key to making development co-operation effective. • Ownership of development priorities by developing counties: Countries should define the development model that they want to implement. • A focus on results: Having a sustainable impact should be the driving force behind investments and efforts in development policymaking • Partnerships for development: Development depends on the participation of all actors, and recognizes the diversity and complementariness of their functions. • Transparency and shared responsibility: Development co-operation must be transparent and accountable to all citizens.

Source: Author. (Based on Organisation for Economic Co-operation and Development 2014a and 2008.)

Milestones of CSOs Inching Forward in the Context of Aid Effectiveness Negotiations

While the formal DAC meeting convened every three years, a parallel process on the same issue also took place to coordinate and harmonize the NGO positions on the matter. The Working Party on Aid Effectiveness (WP-EFF) was created in 2003 to implement MDG 8 to 'form a global partnership for development' and to address the lack of aid effectiveness. At its conception, only donor countries were represented in the WP-EFF. In 2005 the WP-EFF developed into a partnership between donor and recipient countries as a result of the Paris Declaration and the recognition of the important role of recipient countries (OECD 2010).

Over time, the WP-EFF developed into a multilateral initiative in which CSOs gained recognition and credibility. Before its conclusion in 2012, five CSOs were among the 80 stakeholders represented in the development partnership. The CSOs that had representation status on the WP-EFF were:

- AWEPA (http://www.awepa.org/)
- BetterAid (http://www.betteraid.org/)
- Business and Industry Advisory Committee (BIAC) (http://www.biac.org/)
- Inter-Parliamentary Union (http://www.ipu.org/english/home.htm)
- Evaluation of the Paris Declaration (OECD 2010)

In June 2012, the WP-EFF gave way to the Global Partnership for Effective Development Co-operation, the current partnership 'to forge stronger and more inclusive partnerships for effective development' (Organisation for Economic Co-operation and Development 2014e).

Highlights of NGO Diplomacy and Building of Negotiation Momentum

Prior to the establishment of the Better Aid Coordinating Group (BACG) in 2007, CSOs' attempts to influence the aid effectiveness debate were relatively unsuccessful and disorganized. Reality of Aid (RoA) tried to influence the WP-EFF and OECD-DAC organizations for five years prior to the BACG. Through informal dialogue and the release of biennial global reports on the status of aid, RoA and other CSO networks gradually gained more recognition. CSOs also gained more popularity in other forums such as the Global Development Forum and in ENVIRONET and GENDERNET, two DAC subsidiary bodies. As mentioned above, CSOs tried to influence the second HLF in Paris but did not achieve access to the negotiation process itself (OECD 2014b).

A group of major International NGOs jointly signed the Accountability Charter marking a significant step toward multi-stakeholder commitment to 'better' aid. I-NGOs due to their maturity and access to resources have been instrumental in the aid debate. They tend to be active in all spheres of the policy arena (from policy initiation to evaluation) as well as taking operational roles in the field.

The Paris Declaration represented a major breakthrough in defining the aid relationship based on measurable targets. This normative guideline provided the NGO community with a yardstick to monitoring the funding, management approach and field operations of different donors and IOs. When gaps or relapse were identified, NGOs are quick in blowing the whistle and in demanding explanation and corrective measures. Governance of the aid architectural has since been slowly enhanced and democratized. In the meantime, since I-NGOs often serve as contractors in the field to deliver development assistance, they also need to ensure credibility by complying with the Paris Declaration and by taking one step further in developing their own code of conduct, i.e., the Accountability Charter, in regards to good governance, transparency and accountability (INGO Accountability Charter 2014). The Charter was established by leading I-NGOs based on discussions held at the 2005 International Advocacy Non-Government Organizations (IANGO) conference.

Founding members of the I-NGO charter included the following organizations (see Table 3.6): (INGO Accountability Charter 2014)

Table 3.6: Founding members of I-NGO charter

Organization	
Action Aid International	International Save the Children Alliance
Amnesty International	Survival International
CIVICUS World Alliance for Citizen Participation	International Federation Terre des Hommes
Consumers International	Transparency International
Greenpeace International	World YWCA
Oxfam International	

Source: Author. (Based on I-NGO website).

Full Members of the Charter are subject to audits and must submit annual accountability reports for review against standards of accountability and transparency. The reports must be written in the accepted Global Reporting Initiative's (GRI) NGO Sector Supplement format. (I-NGO 2014) GRI is a non-profit organization that provides a widely accepted sustainability reporting framework for a variety of sectors and organization types including the NGO Sector (Global Reporting Initiative 2011).

These CSO efforts were eventually recognized by the DAC. In November 2006, a small meeting was scheduled between the DAC Development Cooperation Directorate and a small group of CSOs. The meeting was attended by RoA members, i.e., ActionAid, BOND, CCIC, IBON and Coordination Sud as well as OXFAM, EURODAD, UKON and members of the European NGO Confederation for Relief and Development (CONCORD). This meeting was the foundation for a more formal relationship between the OECD-DAC and CSOs (Global Reporting Initiative 2011: 5–6).

Another access point for CSOs within OECD is the annual Global Forum on Development. Launched in 2006 as a platform for dialogue between non-member states, private sector actors and CSO, the forum helps define OECD's strategy for development. The first round, from 2006 to 2008, was focused on the effectiveness of international development finance (OECD 2014c). The forum is supported by the OECD Development Centre and by the Development Finance Network (DeFiNe). DeFiNe is a group of 'think tanks, research centres and academic institutions' that act as consultants to the Global Forum on Development in regards to issues of development finance. Originally consisting of only 12 institutions, DeFiNe now includes 39 organizations from all over the world (OECD 2014d). This was the first formal inclusion of CSOs within the OECD development dialogue.

In 2007, the Advisory Group on the Role of CSOs in Aid Effectiveness (AG-CS) was established by OECD's DAC to 'strengthen the dialogue between the Working Party on Aid Effectiveness and Civil Society'. (Advisory Group on Civil Society and Aid Effectiveness 2007) It was formed in response to the growing interest of CSOs to participate in the debate, expressed by CSOs' present at the HLF in Paris as well as by CIDA's conclusion about the importance of CSOs. AG-CS consisted of 'three representatives from each of the four stakeholder groups: donors, developing country governments, and CSOs from developed and developing countries' (Advisory Group on Civil Society and Aid Effectiveness 2007: 6).

The AG-CS provided CSOs with a voice through regional and international consultations. The AG-CS sought to establish a frame of reference for CSO involvement. Emerging from 2007, and leading up to the HFL in Accra, CSOs exerted influence through two different bodies. The AG-CS employed insider tactics, while the BACG employed outsider tactics, to influence the key donors and governments within the WP-EFF (Open Forum 2014).

Deliberations on the role of CSOs and its unique contribution to the development effort continued from 2008 and culminated in September 2010 when the first Global Assembly was held in Istanbul subsequent to which the process to identifying CSO principles of aid effectiveness was started. It was the first international meeting of stakeholders in the Open Forum process at which 'any interested civil society stakeholder who [was] familiar with the issues surrounding CSO development effectiveness' could register. The participant composition at the event included nine government representatives, 18 donor representatives, 31 international NGO representatives and 134 national CSO representatives totalling to 192 participants (Open Forum on CSO Development Effectiveness 2010).

At this meeting a 'draft holistic framework for CSO development effectiveness' was presented. The drafted framework synthesized information and perspectives gathered from hundreds of CSOs, as well as other development stakeholders, at over 70 national and thematic consultations. The initial draft then was adopted at the 2nd Global Assembly in 2011 prior to the fourth HLF in Busan (Open Forum on CSO Development Effectiveness 2010).

The 4th High Level Forum (HLF) in Busan brought together over 3,000 delegates to continue the process of analysing the successes and shortcomings of the implementation of PD and AAA standards. Eighteen Sherpas, including one CSO representative, were elected to represent a wide variety of stakeholders in the preliminary negotiations in Paris (Aid Effectiveness Portal 2014).

After the conclusion of the 4th HLF, a Post-Busan Interim Group was formed 'to propose a new structure for the follow up of the Busan commitments, laid down in the Busan Partnership document (BPd)' (Capacity and Institution Building Working Group 2012: 1). The final meeting of the WP-EFF occurred on 28–29 June 2012, and the Post-Busan Interim Group 'was mandated to propose a set of global indicators to assure the monitoring of the BPd and a Steering Committee to support the Global Partnership for Effective Development Cooperation (GPEDC) mechanism that [would] replace' the WP-EFF (Capacity and Institution Building Working Group 2012: 1). The final 'Guide to the Monitoring Framework of the Global Partnership' was released by the GPEDC in July 2013 and "explains the objectives, process and methodology for monitoring the implementation of the selected commitments made in the Busan Partnership agreement through the set of global indicators and targets agreed in June 2012"'. (Global Partnership for Effective Development Cooperation 2013: 2)

Inclusive Global Partnerships and Embeddedness of Private Sector

Over a decade of engagement, CSOs have gained influence within the aid effectiveness negotiation. The OECD and the DAC have influenced the aid effectiveness debate through the creation of the WP-EFF and by hosting the HLFs. These forums have produced the declarations, principles and standards that define international standards of aid effectiveness. Throughout this process, CSOs had the opportunity to voice their positions and influence the outcome by participating in developing the agenda, shaping the outcome documents alongside with the official representatives of countries.

The major achievement of CSO advocacy has been the shift from purely technical aid effectiveness to a holistic rights-based approach of development effectiveness. CSOs continue to play the role of Watchdog and Whistleblower in order to encourage governments to follow through on their commitments. The post-Busan process determined the future aid architecture that will hold governments accountable and implement a monitoring and evaluation system. CSOs have recognized the importance of this process and will remain engaged to ensure that the establishment of the Global Partnership for Effective Development Cooperation (GP) will hold stakeholders accountable and ensure rights-based development aid. In 2014 the first high-level meeting of the Global Partnership for Effective Development Cooperation (GPEDC) took place in Mexico.

Case Analysis and Lessons Learnt

International relations have long ceased to be the private domain of the states. Instead, multiple actors partake in this space and actively seek ways to influence the negotiated outcomes. This trend is particularly evident since the onset of the 21st century. Saner and Yiu (2003) call this enlargement of the operational sphere and changed nature of international relations the 'Post-Modern Variant' of diplomacy.

Although participation of non-state actors in foreign policy and international relations remains by and large a phenomenon that is more manifested in industrial countries; civil societies, however, all over the world are learning fast and are catching up due to the proliferation of ICT technology. Communication, information sharing and gathering, and mobilizing are no longer impossible or prohibitive. The costs of transportation have also been dropping steadily. The threshold for participating in the national or international affairs is no longer insurmountable and the resulting growing participation of NGOs from non-Western parts of the world has brought out diverse and dissenting voices to the status quo and contributed to the evolution of the role of NGOs within the UN proper and the global governance architecture. The next logical evolution is that people are self-organizing when their views and concerns are not included and/or considered in the national or international debates. This phenomenon can be seen all across the globally emerging citizen movements to various degrees of impact.

Therefore, it is more urgent than ever to understand the ways and means how all actors and stakeholders can participate in the global decision making process, especially in matters concerns us all, such as climate change, proliferation of nuclear weapons, right to information, sustainable development, water, migration etc.

The case presented in preceding section on the aid-effectiveness negotiations could serve as a 'roadmap' to see how national and southern NGOs through alliance building and coalitions could also participate and influence the process. It is interesting to note, today the boundary between state and non-state actors (including business organizations, philanthropic foundations and NGOs) are increasingly blurred. Therefore, such issue or principle based coalition or alliance might and have cut across the borderline of the government, NGOs, foundations and businesses.

Discussion below will reflect on the strategies deployed by the NGOs in order to ensure multi-stakeholder groups can be engaged in truly democratic form be they state, non-state or international actors. Analysis will also be made on how to re-conceptualize this multi-stakeholder engagement process in an inclusive and constructive manner. This goal of inclusive participation is of particular importance as the extent of interdependence brought on by the transportation revolution and ICT connectivity has changed fundamentally the scope and meaning of 'international affairs, international relations, and international security'. The current case of Ebola originating from three Western African countries is a good case in point.

Multi-Stakeholder Model in Policymaking Process

A multi-stakeholder model concerning global governance and public policymaking has been conceptualized in Figure 3.2 highlighting

Figure 3.2: Stakeholder Interaction in the Public Arena

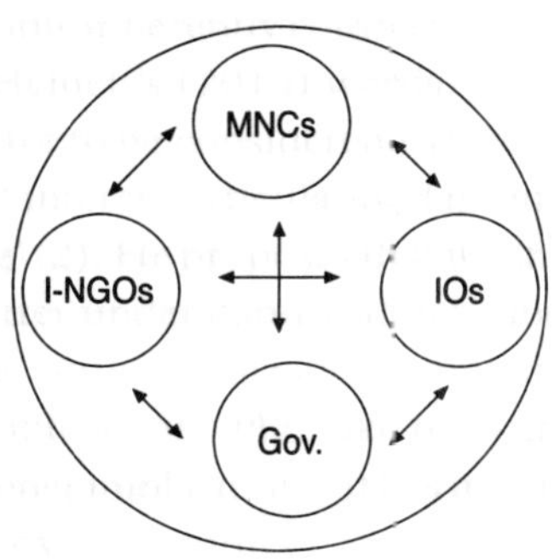

Source: Saner and Michalun 2009: 22.

the interactions and participation of varied actors in setting global agenda and standards consisting of governments, multinational companies, I-NGOs and IOs.

In this interaction model, political power of the state, resource power of business (especially the multinational corporations) and opinion power of the civil societies are brought to bear in making sure the policy choices made would be right, implementable and equitable. Development outcomes of these policy choices would also help the poor to move out of the poverty trap.

In the case of aid effectiveness debate, private sector actors have been accorded 'partner' status, recognizing their role in contributing to the infrastructure development and sustained economic growth.

Process Perspective in Public Policymaking and Policy Space

Reviewing the historical trajectory (Figure 3.1), a process of building up momentum which led to credibility and acceptance during the aid effectiveness negotiations could be discerned and correspond to the international policymaking cycle as depicted in Figure 3.3. Actions taken by the NGOs since 2002 when aid effectiveness rose

Figure 3.3: The International Policymaking Cycle and Space for Entry

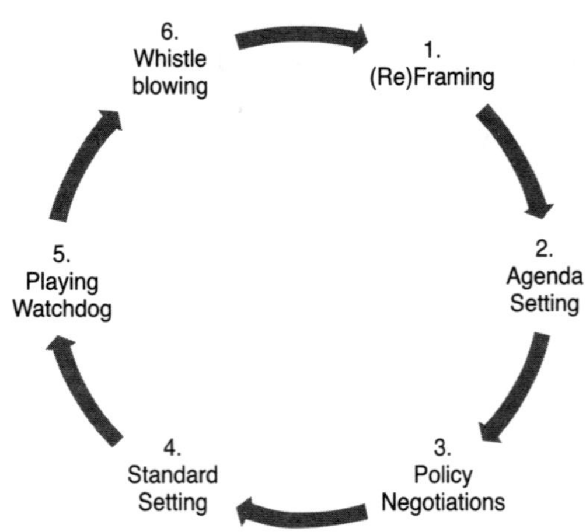

Source: Saner and Michalun 2009: 28.

up in the political agenda of the donor countries could be mapped along this cycle. Entry strategies exercised by the I-NGOs, national NGOs varied. The final impact by 2010 is the 'maturing' of the NGOs in its own governance structure and professionalism. This later development could lead to unspecified results in terms of global governance.

(Re) Framing

Each stakeholder frames the issue in order to establish a coherent position prior to entering into a negotiation and in a manner that will favour its ideal outcome (Saner and Michalun 2009: 29). CSOs can use the framing process to solidify and strengthen their position on an issue. Alliances based on common interests can arise among CSOs and social movements. A consolidation of power based on a common position can provide CSOs more influence in the agenda setting process. North-South CSOs coalitions have gained enough collective momentum to influence the agenda in IO forum such as the World Bank, the WTO (Green and Bloomer 2011) and the UN proper itself. CSOs can also use framing to mobilize citizens and gain support from the general public.

In the case of the aid effectiveness debate, the civil society alliance shifted the debate away from pure technical and efficiency based approach to rights based approach and redefine 'aid effectiveness' as 'development results' and 'development impact'.

Agenda Setting

Based on framing, actors choose certain issues to prioritize their agenda. Actors interact with one another to set a collective agenda through negotiations. CSOs can form alliances to increase their power of influence in the formation of the agenda. Some agenda setting processes are exclusive of non-state actors at the initial stage and then opened for review and minor negotiations at its final stages. Although the final agenda cannot be drastically altered at this point, it does create an opening for CSO involvement (Green and Bloomer 2011).

In the case of the aid effectiveness deliberation, CSOs were able to put the role of NGOs on the agenda and affirm its right to participate.

Policy Negotiations

Policy negotiations are normally based on consensual bargaining. In this process actors are more willing to compromise on some issues in order to gain traction in others. Concessions within policy negotiation are more technical and specific and are more acceptable to stakeholders than the ideological concessions inherent in the agenda setting process (Saner and Michalun 2009: 30).

However, the influencing of the CSOs tend to be informal and on the sideline of the formal negotiation process. In rare occasions, CSOs could gain entrance and get a seat at the table. The Aid Effectiveness negotiation is one of those rare occurrences. At this stage, CSOs tried to influence the outcome through policy studies, impact evaluation of past performance and identification of gaps, biases and oversights.

In the case of aid effectiveness, NGO representative eventually gained a seat as one of the 18 Sherpas during the preparatory process of the DAC setting leading up the 2011 Fourth High Level Forum on Aid Effectiveness in Busan, Korea.

Standard Setting

Standard setting institutions can operate unilaterally but their standards influence the outcome of the policy negotiations by influencing each actor's power in relation to the other actors. An example is the rating agency Standard and Poor's whose credit eligibility ratings of companies and countries impact the reputation of those actors and their respective power in business and politics (Saner and Michalun 2009).

IOs, although lacking enforcement power for many international standards, determine the international paradigm by facilitating the negotiation and consensus on international guidelines for global issues. Although implementation of such guidelines is dependent on the actions of member states, the IOs have become the repository and custodians of international standards. On the basis of these standards, other stakeholders, in particular CSOs, can hold states accountable for inaction through Watchdog and Whistleblowing activities.

Using standard setting to influencing the behaviour of private sectors and consumer has also gained currency in recent years. By vigorously promoting private and voluntary standards, environmental conservation groups have successfully promoted environmental standards in protecting forest, wildlife, water; fair pay standard in promoting 'fair' pay and making companies accountable in using child labour and in non-compliance with minimum labour standards and working conditions. These initiatives have been effective in generating consumer backlash against companies who disregard environmental sustainability and basic human rights.

In the case of aid effectiveness, the adoption of NGO accountability charter and a voluntary review process was the first step to move the NGO community further into the 'public trust' arena by leading the way in transparency and good governance. The potential impact of this move by the I-NGOs was not confined to shore up their reputation capital but to directly challenge the donor agencies on the same level of transparency and accountability. It will be critical to monitor whether the I-NGOs who have signed on to the Charter can stand the test of time.

Playing Watchdog

Monitoring and evaluating progress in the implementation and fulfilment of established international standards is an important step to ensure compliance. Engagement of CSOs, especially at the community level to review the actual practices and impact, is critical in achieving the desired goals and outcome.

CSOs have great influence at this point in the policymaking process by acting as external monitors. The goal of a Watchdog campaign is to pressure an actor to conform to the accepted international standards. Thus, campaigns gain support by building their message on the strong foundation of accepted international norms that appeal to a large audience. Within the context of international multilateral arrangements, CSOs can pressure both individual actors to implement norms while evaluating the international process and encouraging further negotiation to continue the development of norms (Doh and Yaziji 2009: 94–96). Once a CSO has identified a target for a Watchdog campaign, they engage through Whistleblowing tactics that bring attention to the stakeholders' failure to compile with international standards.

This watchdog function is critical in bringing the facts on ground to the global debate. It is also critical in identifying areas where more targeted and differentiated treatments are justified. Although there is a consensus that international community needs to avoid the bias of 'one size fits all', the practice remains by and large as such due to the lack of bottom up data and timely feedback. Therefore, CSOs can and should actively contribute to this Watchdog function and bring voices and data to the higher level of the international organizational hierarchy.

In the case of aid effectiveness campaign, civil society compiled their own data, published their own analysis to identify the uneven and unsustainable results of many development projects and programme. These information campaigns have helped to shift the focus of evaluation from outputs to development outcomes as well as the accepted political discourse.

Whistleblowing

The final step in policy negotiation is also the first step of a feedback loop that ensures a circular rather than a top down policymaking process. CSOs engage with stakeholders in the international community to highlight shortcomings in their commitments to the citizens of the world. As stated above, watchdog and whistleblowing campaigns identify and pressure individual stakeholders to fulfil their obligations while also encouraging the re-negotiation and improvement of international norms. This is a vital step of CSO participation in policy debates (Saner and Michalun 2009: 31–32).

In order to successfully represent their constituents, citizen groups, CSOs need to gain power of influence in the negotiation. Strategies of engagement include channelling or inciting public discontent. If public opinion expresses discontent that an issue is not being addressed on an agenda, CSOs can become the representative of the public in the negotiation. Media can be used as a tool to publicize citizens' discontent and force a CSO's entry into an agenda debate. The publication of CSO research and external monitoring results can be used to inform citizens, the stakeholder in questions and the international community about shortcomings in commitments. Ranking actors based on compliance with policies has also been an effective strategy employed by CSOs in the past (Saner and Michalun 2009: 31–32).

In the case of aid effectiveness, Southern NGOs have been actively making public their research findings which revealed the bias of neoliberal leaning of the international financial institutions (IFIs) and the continued SAP agenda and practices. This Whistleblowing action has exposed the inherent detrimental effect of many unchecked development projects and programmes. Agreeing on 'good' governance practices captured by 'good' principles and code of conduct became urgent and politically vital in the DAC context.

Advice for Aspiring NGOs

Information! Information! Depending on the resource availability, research capacity and organizational maturity, a CSO can determine their most effective sphere of operation and influence. There is no better or worse for each individual CSO's contribution to the betterment of this ONE world.

However, it can be said that 'watchdog' function could be an easy starting point for the start-up NGOs who would like to be engaged in the policy discourse. By monitoring the actual implementation of the policy commitments made public by the states, for example, the

Figure 3.4: The Boomerang Effect

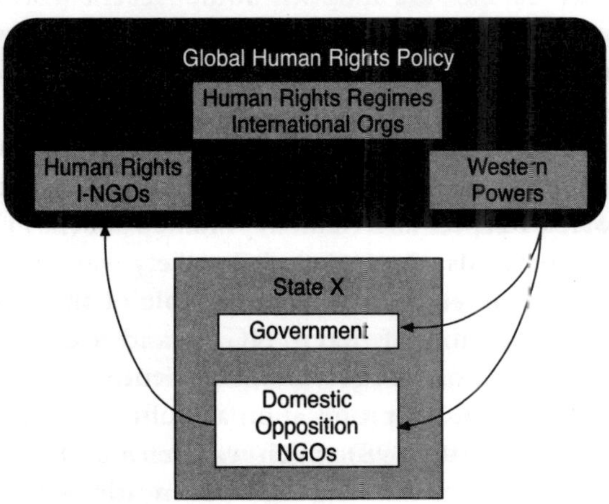

Source: Risse and Sikkink 1999: 19.

start-ups can accumulate the necessary information and knowledge on specific issues resulting in becoming a serious dialogue partners for other more established NGOs. Coupled with the Whistleblowing publicity, NGOs can create the 'boomerang effect' in the international public policy context (see Figure 3.4).

Issue Identification for Policy Advocacy by the Non-State Actors

Throughout the process of the Aid Effectiveness deliberation, there are three different types of advocacy in terms of *what* to advocate:

- *Positional advocacy:* The advocate influences the 'public' and stakeholders to choose particular policies or to accept particular values. In this case, a rights based approach to development was advocated.
- *Methodological advocacy:* The advocate influences the 'public' to become active as problem solvers and to use certain methods of problem solving, but is careful not to become an advocate for any particular position.
- *Standards-based advocacy*: The advocate influences the 'actors' to adhere and demands certain standards or codes of conduct of the 'public'.

For example, in promoting better working conditions and fair pay, NGOs who advocate for the adoption of the Decent Work Agenda (DWA) as part of the core of a PRSP development strategy, might approach the campaign from the rights perspective (Positional) or the accepted international norm perspective, such as the OECD Guidelines for the Multinational Enterprises (2011), or the Guiding Principles on Business and Human Rights: Implementing the United Nations 'Protect, Respect and Remedy' Framework (2011).

From 2007 onwards, the global civil society was organized as a large campaign under the coordinating role of the BetterAid. BetterAid is a coalition of major NGOs and a coordination mechanism grown out of the successful experience in campaigning globally against the OECD proposal on a Multilateral Agreement on Investment (MAI 1995–98) which was defeated by the NGO coalition. The strategy of the campaign was mostly positional and standard-based. Less known is the gender-based analysis developed by the NGOs over the years, which is methodological.

One current example is the effort of MATI Action 2015 Alliance in advocating a bottom up and inclusive approach to monitoring of the implementation of SDGs in the post 2015 era (Husch, Saner, Yiu and Zeitz 2014).

Conclusion

A global governance architecture is emerging where roles and rules of engagement for non-state actors are triggered and affected by this emerging process. Civil society has become a vital driver of democratization of the global decision making process.

Yet, the attitude and intentions of the other two stakeholder groups, i.e., governments and businesses, in regard to the proposal for an inclusive UN is relative unclear and mixed. Should the UN be just a talking shop where politicians meet to discuss without necessarily being obliged to follow through their comments? Should the UN be just a pulpit where high sounding principles and guidelines are being pronounced by political leaders without obligation for compliance by either the states or the businesses?

'Civil society is drawn to the UN because it provides fora based on the ethics, moral principles and aspirations of the Charter, in which governments exercise their power at the international level and in which even the smallest state has formal equality with the most powerful' (Hill 2004: 4). It is from this perspective that the review of the NGOs engagement with the deliberation on aid effectiveness becomes interesting. The authors' analysis shows that without political or financial resources, NGOs can deploy their social and network capitals and their 'opinion' power to affect change. This transformation towards more inclusive decision making might not be immediate, nor visible at first.

The engagement of civil society with the UN system and the global governance processes has come a long way. The national NGOs and other grassroots organizations from the global south have contributed to a constructive development of the UN system and the global governance system, but they also triggered an evolution of the established I-NGOs in regard to their way of perceiving the world and understanding the development issues. Therefore, with the case analysis presented here, the authors hope that their analysis will lead to broader participation of citizens from the emerging countries in the global governance debate.

Acknowledgement

The authors thank Amanda Borow for her excellent research support.

References

Advisory Group on Civil Society and Aid Effectiveness. 2007. Concept Paper. http://siteresources.worldbank.org/ACCRAEXT/Resources/4700790-1208545462880/AG-CS-Concept-Paper.pdf.

Aid Effectiveness Portal. 2014. http://www.aideffectiveness.org/index.html.

Annan, Kofi. 2000. 'We the Peoples: The Role of the United Nations in the 21st Century.' http://unpan1.un.org/intradoc/groups/public/documents/un/unpan000923.pdf.

———, Donald Johnston, Horst Köhler and James Wolfensolm. 2000. 'A Better World for All; Progress towards the International Development Goals.' http://www.keepeek.com/Digital-Asset-Management/oecd/development/a-better-world-for-all_9789264182561-en.

Capacity and Institution Building Working Group. 2012. 'Report of the WP-EFF Meeting.' http://www.cib-uclg.org/files/pdf/News/2012/10-07/Report_WP_EFF_meeting_28_29_June_2012.pdf.

Doh, Jonathan and Michael Yaziji. 2009. *NGOs and Corporations*. Cambridge: Cambridge University Press. pp. 94–96

Global Partnership for Effective Development Co-operation. 2013. 'Guide to the Monitoring Framework of the Global Partnership.' http://effectivecooperation.org/wordpress/wp-content/uploads/2013/10/BusanMonitoringF2Eng.pdf.

Global Reporting Initiative. 2011. 'Sustainability Reporting Guidelines & NGO Sector Supplement.' https://www.globalreporting.org/resourcelibrary/NGOSS-Complete.pdf.

Göymen, Korel. 2008. 'The evolving state- third sector relations in Turkey.' In Stephen P. Osborne (ed.). *The Third Sector in Europe*. London: Routledge. pp. 221–30.

Green, Duncan and Phil Bloomer. 2011. 'NGOs in Economic Diplomacy.' In Nicholas Bayne and Stephen Woolcock (eds.). *The New Economic Diplomacy: Decision-Making and Negotiation in International Economic Relations*. Farnham: Ashgate Publishing.

Guiding Principles on Business and Human Rights. 2011. 'Implementing the United Nations Protect, Respect and Remedy'. http://www.ohchr.org/documents/issues/business/A.HRC.17.31.pdf.

Hill, Tony. 2004. 'Three Generations of UN-Civil Society Relations: A Quick Sketch.' http://graduateinstitute.ch/files/live/sites/iheid/files/shared/executive_education/INP%202011/Syllabi%20_%26_Course_Materials/Hill%20-%20Three%20Generations%20of%20UN-Civil%20Society%20Relations.pdf.

Hulme, David. 2009. 'The Millennium Development Goals (MDGs): A Short History of the World's Biggest Promise.' Brooks World Poverty Institute. http://www.bwpi.manchester.ac.uk/resources/Working-Papers/bwpi-wp-10009.pdf.

Husch, Jerri, Raymond Saner, Lichia Yiu and Paul Zeitz. 2014. 'Monitoring of SGD Implementation: Infrastructure and Methodology – Proposal for Action.' *CSEND Policy Brief* No. 14. http://www.csend.org/images/articles/files/Monitoring_SDG_Infrastructure__Methodology.pdf.

I-NGO Accountability Charter. 2014. 'About the Charter.' http://www.ingoaccountabilitycharter.org/home/what-is-the-charter/.

New Partnership for Africa's Development. 2014. http://www.nepad.org/about.

Open Forum. 2014. 'History and Process.' http://www.cso-effectiveness.org/-histoire-du-processus,017-.html.

Organisation for Economic Co-operation and Development. 2014a. 'High Level Fora on Aid Effectiveness: A history.' http://www.Organsation for Economic Co-operation and Development.org/document/63/0,3746,en_2649_3236398_46310975_1_1_1_1,00.html.

———. 2014b. 'The Paris Declaration, Aid Effectiveness and Development Effectiveness.'

http://www.Organsation for Economic Co-operation and Development.org/development/evaluation/dcdndep/41807824.pdf.

———. 2014c, 'Global Forum on Development.' http://www.oecd.org/document/59/0,3746,en_21571361_37824719_37824763_1_1_1_1,00.html.

———. 2014d. 'OECD Development Finance Network (DeFiNe).' http://www.oecd.org/document/53/0,3746,en_2649_33993_43599669_1_1_1_1,00.html.

———. 2014e. 'Improving Partnership for Effective Development: The Working Party on Aid Effectiveness.' http://www.oecd.org/document/35/0,3746,en_2649_3236398_43382307_1_1_1_1,00.html.

———. 2011. 'Guidelines for Multinational Enterprises.' http://mneguidelines.Organsation for Economic Co-operation and Development.org/text/.

———. 2010. 'Working Party on Aid Effectiveness.' http://www.Organsation for Economic Co-operation and Development.org/dataOrgansation for Economic Co-operation and Development/0/40/45498646.pdf.

———. 2008. 'The Accra Agenda for Action.' http://www.oecd.org/dataoecd/22/2/45827311.pdf.

———. 1996. 'Shaping the 21st Century: The Contribution of Development Co-operation.' http://www.Organsation for Economic Co-operation and Development.org/dataOrgansation for Economic Co-operation and Development/23/35/2508761.pdf.

———. 1995. 'Development Partnerships in the New Global Context.' http://www.oecd.org/dataoecd/31/61/2755357.pdf.

Risse, Thomas, C. Ropp, Stephen, Sikkink, Kathryn (eds.). 1999. *The Power of Human Rights: International Norms and Domestic Change*. Cambridge: Cambridge University Press.

Saner, Raymond and M. Varinia Michalun (eds.). 2009. *Negotiations Between State Actors And Non State Actors: Case Analyses From Different Parts Of The World*. Dordrecht: Republic of Letters, B.V.

———. and Lichia Yiu. 2003. 'International Economic Diplomacy: Mutations in Post Modern Times.' In Mowby, S. (ed.) *Discussion Papers in Diplomacy*. The Hague: The Netherlands Institute of International Relations (Clingendael).

Union of International Organizations. 1995. 'Changing relationships between International Non-Governmental Organizations and the United Nations.' http://www.uia.org/archive/ingos-un.

United Nations. 2014. 'Millennium Development Goal.' http://mdgs.un.org/unsd/mdg/host.aspx?Content=indicators/officiallist.htm.

———. 2013. 'The Millennium Development Goals Report.' http://www.un.org/millenniumgoals/pdf/report-2013/mdg-report-2013-english.pdf.

———. 2000. 'United Nations Millennium Declaration'. http://www.un.org/millennium/declaration/ares552e.pdf.

———. 1945. 'Charter of the United Nations.' http://www.un.org/en/documents/charter/chapter10.shtml.

United Nations CSO Net. 2014. http://esango.un.org/civilsociety/login.do.

United Nations Development Programme. 1990. 'Human Development Report.' http://hdr.undp.org/en/media/hdr_1990_en_overview.pdf.

United Nations Department of Economic and Social Affairs. 2014. 'UN CSO Net.' http://esango.un.org/civilsociety/login.do.

World Bank. 1990. 'World Development Report 1990: Poverty.' http://www-wds.worldbank.org/external/default/WDSContentServer/IW3P/IB/2000/12/13/000178830_98101903345649/Rendered/PDF/multi_page.pdf.

4 How Great Expectations of International Organizations are Dashed at the Local Level

The Case of EU Structural Funds

Hubert Heinelt

Abstract

This paper considers the limits as well as the opportunities for democratic policymaking in a globalized world by reflecting on the EU structural funds (i.e. cohesion policy). The EU structural funds have been taken as a point of reference because it is, on the one hand, not only directly related to global competition and should achieve regional competitiveness in a globalized world. However, on the other, the EU structural funds are characterized by a high degree of political autonomy and democratic discretion in policymaking in the member states and their subnational levels of government.

Introduction

The title of my paper rephrases the subtitle 'How Great Expectations in Washington are Dashed in Oakland. Or, Why It's Amazing that Federal Programs Work at All?' from Pressman's and Wildavsky's 1973 book on implementation.[1] This question is relevant for the debate of public policymaking in a globalized world, because it focuses our attention on a decisive aspect of this debate. Policymaking in a globalized world may be characterized by interrelated 'driving forces' such as the market or technological developments as well as

[1] This paper is based on Chapter 5 of Heinelt 2010.

the growing importance of international organizations (including the European Union) through which attempts are made to steer or even control such societal 'driving forces' politically. This may question democratic self-government as Robert Dahl (1994) pointed out in one of his latest publications, namely in his article on 'democratic dilemma'. In this article, he argued that governability – or 'system effectiveness' in his words – may be assured by a bargaining system within and beyond the nation state at the expense of 'citizen participation' or 'citizen effectiveness' in policymaking. However, Pressman's and Wildavsky's work (as well as similar implementation studies such as those of Mayntz 1980; 1983; 1987) emphasize that we must be aware of resistance at the local level against 'driving forces' as well as attempts of guiding and controlling societal interactions politically from 'above'.[2] At the same time, we also must consider Pressman's and Wildavsky's point that it is amazing that programmes attempting to guide and control societal interactions work at all. I will try to address these issues by looking at EU structural funds (or cohesion policy).

The paper starts with a reflection on what governability might mean in a globalized world and in the context of multi-level governance. The following section summarizes the characteristics of EU structural funds, which in turn might shed more light as to why this policy works at all. The paper then provides an introduction to the concept of 'loose coupling' and outlines why governability can be assured by this concept. In a brief conclusion some lessons will be drawn.

What Does Governability Mean?

From the perspective of reflections in political science, governability should not be restricted to the question of whether or not certain policy objectives – such as 'cohesion' (the decrease of regional and social disparities) or 'sustainability' (reduction in energy consumption, emissions, etc. ...) – laid down in programmes or

[2] For an early contribution to the governance debate see the book on 'guidance and control' edited by Kaufmann et al. 1986.

other policy documents are achieved (see Knill and Liefferink 2007: 145–55 for general reflections on the problems of implementing such goals). Understanding whether or not objectives have been achieved might be sufficient for policy studies or for an efficiency-oriented analysis of (financial) inputs and outputs.[3] Instead, governability should be considered as the ability to guide or steer and to control societal interactions.[4] Against a background of widely-discussed (and accepted) complexity and contingency in modern society, this ability to steer and control has to be conceptualized in such a way that the picture of an all-powerful guiding and controlling entity is not the outcome. Instead, emphasis should be placed on context-related choices faced by groups of actors so that they can purposefully influence and act interactively with their current and future situations. This perspective has already been pointed out in contributions to early debates on policy networks focused on governance aspects (especially those of German and continental European scholars; see Marsh 1998). This perspective further calls for an actor-related capability indicating on the one hand that actors are not in a position to govern their social environment completely, i.e. there are exogenous constraints, but on the other, emphasizing that actors can influence their social environment with (potentially) available policy instruments on the basis of given (or changeable) institutional settings (Scharpf 1986: 12). From this perspective, governability can be related to endogenously, i.e. politically-determined constraints and opportunities for policymaking to realize what is desired and known by actors and perceived as collectively achievable by them (Scharpf 1988b: 63–64; see also Mayntz 1997: 192).[5]

[3] See for the EU structural funds Beugelsdijk and Eijffinger 2005; Cappelen et al. 2003; Castells and Espasa Queralt, 2003.

[4] In this respect, the understanding of governability presented here refers to what is called *'Steuerungsfähigkeit'* in German. With reference to the EU, see Grande and Jachtenfuchs, 2000.

[5] I am using here and below the terms the 'desired', the 'known' and the 'achievable' as apparently peculiar translations of parts of the following statement by Scharpf (1988b: 63–64; italics by the author). 'Die Rede [ist bei Steuerungsfähigkeit; added by the author] nicht von exogen bestimmtem Nicht-Können, sondern von endogen – aber nicht unüberwindlichen – Schwierigkeiten der Politik, das *Gewünschte*, *Gewußte* und objektiv *Erreichbare* auch zu tun.'

In this respect, governing a modern (functionally-differentiated) society is not in principle impossible (see the Luhmann-Scharpf controversy; Luhmann 1989; Scharpf 1989). Instead, first, the ability to govern, i.e. to influence deliberately societal interactions, has to be clarified depending on the specific issue under consideration. Second, specific actor-related and (endogenously) politically-determined opportunities to develop certain strategies and to pursue them have to be identified. Such opportunities are clearly related to institutional and organizational conditions, which may or may not allow for collective political actions. In certain circumstances, political actors may not be able to govern their societal environment completely but may be able to change policy instruments or organizational rules with the aim of deliberately influencing their societal environment. In other words, and to define a kind of bottom line, actors can develop a capacity to reform their social environment in line with their agreed upon policy objectives. Whether or not actors are actually able to achieve what is intended by a particular reform is another question (see Mayntz 1997: 192). From an actor-centred understanding of governability, they need to demonstrate a capacity to react politically to reform failure by altering the definition of the problem, by questioning the reasons for the failure, and by changing policy instruments, i.e. a new reform.

However, such a view on endogenously defined governability is dependent on how the ability to govern a certain issue is perceived within the relevant 'policy arena'. This raises the issue that the societal surroundings, which are to be influenced or altered by particular policy instruments according to the desires of involved actors, cannot be intellectually filtered through something 'objectively achievable'. Instead, they can only be filtered through what is known within the 'policy arena' or what can be conceptualized as politically hegemonic knowledge or a particular knowledge order (see Heinelt and Lamping 2015 in respect to local climate policy). Although it is clear that political knowledge does not develop independently from discourses in society, it is obvious that what is perceived as governable is dependent on processes taking place within the political system. In the case of the EU cohesion policy, this becomes clear when taking into account the paradigm shift in the

1980s, the intrusion of the New Public Management (NPM) ideas in the late 1990s (see Heinelt and Malek 2002), the more recent debate on competitiveness, and the strengthening of (urban) growth poles (as referred to in the so-called Lisbon process). Against this background, a distinction between what is determined politically as possible (and necessary) and what is an exogenously fixed 'mission impossible' may be blurred. Nevertheless, we must ask the questions regarding the endogenous political but not irresolvable constraints on policymaking to achieve what is desired, known, and perceived as possible by the actors involved.

Providing an answer to this question is not easy in any circumstance, but is even harder in the context of fragmented and multi-level policymaking – such as in the EU – where not only exogenously feasible conditions in the individual member states and their regions differ, but what is desired, known, and perceived as achievable by the multitude of actors involved at different levels and stages of policymaking also varies a great deal.

Taking into account the debate on the development and the specificities of the EU polity stimulated by the multi-level governance approach, it is important to emphasize for the purposes of this paper that this approach highlights the implications of a polity characterized by penetrating into the centre of the state and distributing tasks and competences between different nested territorial levels.

What does this mean for the question of how to achieve governability (as defined above) in multi-level policymaking? Maybe penetration into the centre of the state and the distribution of tasks and competences over nested territorial levels can fit in with a constellation of differing feasible conditions in individual member states (and their regions) and varying desires, knowledge, and perceptions of the multitude of involved actors. Therefore, it is worth looking at what characterizes multi-level policymaking in order to identify features and mechanisms in such constellations that might provide conditions to achieve governability in the sense outlined above. These will be done with reference to EU structural funds as one of the politically most important (in respect to political cohesion) and costly (in respect to spending) EU policy.

Characteristics of EU Structural Funds

The history of the EU structural funds points toward a continuous capacity for reform and does not confirm the 'joint decision trap' hypothesis that has been often associated with policymaking in the EU multi-level system (Scharpf 1988a). How can this capacity for reform be explained, taking into account the specific conditions of redistributive policies (Scharpf 2001; Heinelt 1996: 18–19)? The formation of the structural funds as a redistributive policy has typically been explained by reference to package deals and side-payments in the context of major steps toward European integration. However, is this sufficient, and what is the explanation for the further development of the structural funds and their relatively high stability over time? Furthermore, the EU structural funds have demonstrated that they are on the one hand leaving a lot of room for national and regional adaptation and variation, but on the other are shaping domestic regional (and labour market) policies. How can this kind of 'Europeanizing' be explained?

In some of the previous literature (Marks 1993; Hooghe 1996; Heinelt and Smith 1996), the main hypothesis has been that specific policy networks (actor relations) in the EU multi-level system are important. According to this hypothesis, the structural funds and their development as well as their adaptation at the national and regional level can be characterized as follows (Heinelt 1996: 16–17):

- Key players are not only regularly present at particular points in time at the European level, when decisions have to be made on programme structures, and budgeting. Due to the specific requirements of the policy field that funding measures must be dealt with according to programme targets and the flow of EU subsidies must be coordinated with national funding programmes, permanent policy networks have had to be created at the implementation level. These implementation networks form a permanent structure. Also, the key people involved have formed a 'policy community' (Heclo and Wildasky 1974: 389) between the EU, the member states, and the sub-national level, which has been held together by common interpretations of issues over the years.

- The decision network consists of a structure made up of member states and the Commission. This network makes decisions about funding objectives and resources after the period for individual programmes has expired. However, this network structure does not exist in isolation from the implementation networks which formed while the programme was being implemented, because the latter involves both the Commission and the departments of national governments as well as the sub-national interests directly involved. This is most apparent in the case of the monitoring committees used for evaluation and ensuring regular contact between key local players, national programme agencies, and the Commission.
- The stability and continuity of policy networks in relation to the structural funds result in redistribution and funding objectives, funding resources, and the implementation strategies remaining constant themes for the actors involved, and thus allow for 'organized feedback loops' in a multi-level policy arena (Marks 1993: 403). Thus, policy reactions can be continually fed into political processes, which not only relate to problems of implementation but also to policy issues and may result in changes in policy goals and objectives.

This seems to be a theoretically convincing hypothesis. Empirical research (for instance by Malek 2002 and Heinelt et al. 2005) on the historical development of the structural funds from the 1950s to the end of the 1990s and their implementation in a number of member states does, however, throw some doubt on the validity of this hypothesis. According to these findings, there is little evidence for a highly-integrated policy network that creates 'organized feedback loops' between policy implementation and policy reform. On the contrary, there is considerable evidence of a high degree of fragmentation within the policy network in the policy field under scrutiny. Fragmentation can be observed along at least four different lines:

- Vertical fragmentation can be observed between implementation and policy reform networks in member states. European decision making on the revision of structural funds regulations as well as on funding objectives and the allocation of resources at the EU level is undertaken by top-level representatives of the member states (together with the Commission) who lack close contact with those involved in the implementation of structural funds. The key players in the reform processes create a decision arena of their own without close links to the implementation of the funds.

- Horizontal fragmentation of policy specific implementation networks can be found in member states. Within the member states (to varying degrees) administrative structures (as well as their surrounding societal networks) are fragmented between different funds and policy areas. Implementation networks in the field of regional policy (i.e. the European Regional Development Fund [ERDF]), for example, rarely interact with implementation networks in the field of labour market policy (i.e. the European Social Fund [ESF]). This fragmentation is made more likely by variation in implementation rules and routines between different policies.
- Horizontal fragmentation of fund specific actor structures can be identified within the European Commission. In much the same way as in the member states, administrative structures within the Commission are fragmented into different Directorates-General (DGs), each of which is responsible for a separate fund.
- Vertical fragmentation between implementation and policy reform networks can be noted in the Commission. Within each DG, the units that are responsible for implementation in the different member states are clearly separate from the units that are responsible for coordination and more general 'political' tasks, including policy reform.

These fragmentations are not only formal organizational characteristics. They shape formal and informal interactions and influence communication and, thus, the transfer of experience and knowledge. In the light of these fragmentations, policy reforms in the field of EU structural funds cannot be explained by the existence of a single closely knit policy network that encompasses both policy implementation and policy reform and by direct, sustained personal interactions between actors in a single policy community. How can the hypothesis on the crucial importance of policy networks for the development of the EU structural funds be modified in light of these findings?

Achieving Governability by Loose Coupling

Do these observations question the relevance of linkages between different actors and layers within multi-level governance, or is it the nature of these linkages that has to be reviewed? Contrary to earlier literature, particularly on the EU structural funds, linkages between the different actors and levels are not tightly horizontal and vertical but rather loosely coupled. Against this background, a hypothesis could be put forward that governability is a result of policy networks characterized by different aspects of loose coupling between relatively autonomous actors and that the autonomy of actors assure not only 'system effectiveness' but allow at the same time for 'citizen effectiveness' or democratic self-determination particularly at the sub-national level.

The expression 'loose coupling' has its origin in older approaches developed in connection with organization studies, which emphasizes that a 'coupled' unit in an organization as well as an organization coupled with others can secure 'its own identity and some evidence of its physical or logical separateness' (Weick 1976: 3), although they are dependent on and influence each other. Based on an increasing use of the expression of 'loose coupling', which has further blurred the meaning, Orton and Weick (1990) helpfully identified different applications of the concept. Orton and Weick (1990: 204ff.) draw a distinction between a 'unidimensional' and a 'dialectical interpretation' of loose coupling. The first considers tight and loose coupling as extremes. Therefore, it puts systems characterized by closeness and openness or by 'independent' and 'responsive components' in opposition to each other. In contrast, the 'dialectical interpretation' of loose coupling (which has been adopted here) emphasizes the coexistence of closeness and openness as well as of 'distinctiveness' and 'responsiveness'. This interpretation highlights the fact that units separated by processes of differentiation are able to secure autonomy and to develop specific logic and orientations for their actions even though they still depend on and interact with each other (cf. Orton and Weick 1990: 205). This increases the opportunity to act more effectively with respect to specific problems and situations, whilst being oriented to common objectives and linked by overriding rules. In other words, it is the coexistence of coordination and autonomy, the ambiguity of overarching objectives and rules as well as selectivity on the part of key players that creates the conditions under which developments can come about quite quickly, and adaptability can be secured (cf. Weick 1985: 164–65).

This means (see Heinelt et al. 2003) that it is necessary to take serious account of the phenomena of differentiation, i.e.

- The internal organizational fragmentation of collective actors,[6] particularly in respect of (i) the vertical fragmentation between implementation and policy reform networks in the member states and (ii) the horizontal fragmentation of the different levels of implementation networks in the member states as well as of the European Commission (in DGs and their units) in line with specific responsibilities for individual funds, policies, sub-policies and even programmes;
- The functional differentiation between a decision-making arena at the EU level and (task specific) implementation arenas in the member states or regions;
- The sequentialization of decisions at the different levels of vertically fragmented policy sub-systems and between these sub-systems in terms of a break-up of the entire reform and implementation processes into manageable chunks that are

[6] See, for such phenomena, the argument put forward by Renate Mayntz. According to her a 'strong internal differentiation of the political-administrative system' is related to the 'observed change of fulfilling political tasks which can be described by a tendency to govern partial tasks through and in bargaining systems' (Mayntz 1996: 157; translation by the author). The internal differentiation of the political-administrative system is almost a basic requirement for bargaining by which 'the societal problems of interdependencies can get on the agenda of governmental actions' (ibid.), and 'intra-governmental bargains' are crucial for avoiding the danger that 'the shift of political decisions into sectoral policy networks only leads to fragmentation' (ibid.).

repeatedly processed at various levels and between the vertically fragmented parts of the decision system.[7]

On the other hand, we have to consider coherence mechanisms that can bring about loose coupling of the phenomena of differentiation. Such mechanisms include:

- Accepted rules and norms for the exchange of information and for coordinating actions;
- Ideas or paradigms (like sustainability or partnership)[8] that suggest specific objectives for actions as well as definitions and measures through which problems can be solved in a way which is commonly perceived as appropriate;
- Coupling institutions (like the monitoring committees in the case of the structural funds) where interactions are bound within a specific organizational context, i.e. where actors are forced to meet, to interact, and to explain/justify their particular choices of action as well as the underlying assumptions about causality and normative images of appropriateness;
- The anticipation of an authoritative final decision by an indirectly involved authority, for example, the 'shadow of hierarchy' within an organization or the possibility of a political decision (i) at a higher level in the negotiation system (e.g. by the Council) or (ii) from a higher level within a network of organizations (e.g. by the Commission); and
- The existence of a public sphere – whether a sectoral or professional one – which can complement the 'shadow of hierarchy' in so far as the relevance of the aforementioned rules and norms as well as ideas or paradigms is emphasized and their violation can be criticized in a public setting.

While the phenomena of differentiation reflect the autonomy of the units or parts of a system, the coherence mechanisms provide opportunities for coupling. This addresses the core of the 'dialectical interpretation' of loose coupling, i.e. 'to combine the

[7] It should be noted that these are probably not the only phenomena of differentiation within the EU cohesion policy – and even not for EU policies in general. But they are the most relevant ones for this policy area.

[8] See for the partnership principle in the context of the EU structural funds for instance Bauer 2002.

contradictory concepts of connection and autonomy' (Orton and Weick 1990: 216).

Loose coupling can be a result of the coherence mechanisms, but there is no inevitability in the development and the effectiveness of these mechanisms. Without these mechanisms, functional differentiation and organizational fragmentation can result in governance failure. The effectiveness of the coherence mechanisms depends on an alignment of orientations and routines of the – individual as well as collective – actors. This applies to ideas or paradigms as well as for the different dimensions of rules and norms for the exchange of information and the coordination of actions. Also, the anticipation of a possible final authoritative decision of an indirectly involved authority – especially a hierarchical intervention – could shape the incentive structure of actors, but could also lead to evasive manoeuvres by the (formally) subordinated actors. This is reflected in the 'dialectical interpretation' of loose coupling 'with its recognition of numerous structural dimensions, its emphasis on simultaneous coupling and decoupling, and its portrayal of structures as malleable through managerial intervention' in that it forces researchers 'to move more deeply into the human workings which underlie organizational structure' (Orton and Weick 1990: 218).

The emphasis on 'simultaneous coupling and decoupling' is particularly relevant with respect to hierarchical, one-sided, and power-based options and competences for making and enforcing decisions. In a multi-level system of joint decision making, they can lead to vetoes and blockages as well as to a reduction in the openness and the feasible set of involved actors (or units). Nonetheless, even in loosely coupled systems, the binding nature of interactions has to be enforced in order to avoid individual units becoming (too) independent and a real decoupling of collective actors is taking place.

As highlighted above, the internal organizational differentiation of collective actors, the differentiation (sequentialization) of decisions at different levels, as well as the functional differentiation between a decision-making arena at the EU level and implementation arenas in the member states/regions represent specific intra- and inter-organizational capabilities in a system of EU multi-level governance, which has been shown to be conducive to the development of innovative policies, responsive to their environment. They provide the actors involved in a multi-level system with space for taking decisions and offer area-related opportunities for institutional evolution and organizational learning. However, the various forms of differentiation need to be loosely coupled by specific coherence mechanisms. Otherwise there would be the risk of fragmentation in organizations and isolation of single sub-units within certain policy areas, which, in turn, could lead to implementation deficits and to the collapse of newly-gained insights and new outlooks.

Possible coherence mechanisms include the acceptance of rules and norms for the exchange of information and the coordination of actions (e.g. informal and formal norms for procedures), 'ideas' or paradigms suggesting specific objectives for actions, as well as definitions of and solutions to problems. Furthermore, the option of a clear decision imposed on the actors by an indirectly involved authority within an organization or the possibility of a political decision at a higher level in a bargaining system, as well as the option of being 'named' and 'shamed' in public, are crucial to enforce the coherence mechanisms referred to above. In this respect, the 'shadow of hierarchy' can be complemented by the 'light of the public'.

If coherence is guaranteed by such forms of loose coupling, then inter- and intra-organizational differentiation may prove to be a precondition for adaptation and learning processes by the units involved. This could be especially true for those at the 'operational' level as well as for governability with regard to the achievement of general policy objectives according to differing contextual conditions, whilst specific coherence mechanisms ensure that the actors still relate to each other within the frame of a multi-level system.

The fragmented structure and coherence mechanisms have not been developed and linked in a systematic and consistent way. They have emerged incrementally from pragmatic decisions determined by the specific structures of the EU multi-level governance system, as well as through the various path dependencies of policymaking in the member states. In other words, the array of formal and informal options open to actors in EU decision-making to secure the role of 'veto players' as well as the divergence of organizational structures in member states, which shape the development and implementation of the structural funds and environment policy at the EU level, prevent a successful systematic and consistent design.

Nevertheless, successful political attempts at structuring the multi-level system of the EU have had important consequences. This is demonstrated in the case of cohesion policy by the introduction of the principles of programming, implementation, and partnership through the 1988 reforms as well as by the partial withdrawal of the geographical units of the Commission from the implementation arenas after the reform of 1999, or the move away from the command and control approach in the case of environment policy in the early 1990s. Although there is some evidence that these attempts had been influenced by scholarly debate (see Hooghe 1996a, Heinelt and Malek 2002), they are mainly based or derived from the 'intelligence of practice'. In brief, through their involvement in the EU decision making process, actors are able to use favourable (historical and/or organizational) conditions to place their specific definition of the 'right' problem and a corresponding 'adequate' perspective on the relevant action to take in a hegemonic position. This constitutes policy or organizational learning (see Heinelt 2010: 41ff).

Conclusion

These reflections on loose coupling may provide an answer to the question as to how governability can be achieved in multi-level policymaking. Differentiation, usually seen as the reason for governance failure, can be used to realize what is desired, known, and perceived as achievable by key actors, providing coherence mechanisms are developed and used. This is crucial because what is desired, known, and perceived as achievable by key actors differs over time and space, according to historical and territorial contexts. Such a perspective

- denies the desirability of assimilation and uniformity, linked to a vision of state-based or state-like policymaking, and
- emphasizes, on one hand, the important influence of diversity but, on the other, tries to secure integration through fundamental rules and norms.

In this respect, the EU structural funds represent more or less a success story of a European model of policymaking, because a high degree of diversity at the regional and national level can be observed when it comes to the implementation of a common funding scheme.[9] This diversity allows not only the adaptability of the scheme to specific spatial and institutional as well as social and economic conditions but also to what is desired, known, and perceived as commonly achievable by the actors involved in implementation. At the same time, the acceptance of overall policy objectives and particular rules for adapting the scheme have been secured, which leads to coherence of policymaking and in the political interventions in this policy area. Furthermore, the EU structural funds demonstrated the ability to change policy objectives and particular rules for adapting the scheme over time according to (i) changing conditions (particularly further steps toward European integration and enlargement) as well as (ii) political debates about the effectiveness and legitimacy of this (re) distributive policy. These changes have been achieved without losing core understanding of what the policy is or should be about. However, it may well be that these characteristics of the EU structural funds are fragile. It is, for example, an open question (which will be answered in practice in the near future) how the structural funds will develop in times of severe crisis, not only financial but also political ones, which may challenge stages of European integration.

References

Bauer, Michael W. 2002. 'The EU "partnership principle". Still a sustainable governance device across multiple administrative arenas?' *Public Administration*, Vol. 80, No. 4, pp. 769–89.

Beugelsdijk, Maaike and Sylvester C.W. Eijffinger. 2005. 'The Effectiveness of Structural Policy in the European Union: An Empirical Analysis for the EU-15 During the Period 1995–2001.' *Journal for Common Market Studies*, Vol. 43, No. 1, 37–51. See also: http://onlinelibrary.wiley.com/doi/10.1111/j.0021-9886.2005.00545.x/abstract

[9] This observation can be linked to the concept of 'democratic experimentalism' (within a 'directly-deliberative polyarchy') see Cohen and Sabel 1997; Dorf and Sabel 1998; Sabel and Zeitlin 2007.

Cappelen, Aadne, Fulvio Castellacci, Jan Fagerberg and Bart Verspagen. 2003. 'The Impact of EU Regional Support on Growth and Convergence in the European Union.' *Journal of Common Market Studies*, Vol. 41, No. 4, pp. 621–44.

Castells, Antoni and Marta Espasa Queralt. 2003. 'Do structural actions contribute to reduced regional disparities in the European Union?' In Bernard Funck (ed.). *European integration, regional policy, and growth*. Washington, DC: The World Bank. pp. 167–76.

Dahl, Robert A. 1994. 'A Democratic Dilemma. System Effectiveness versus Citizen Participation.' *Political Science Quarterly*, Vol. 10, No. 1, 23–34.

Dorf, Michael C., and Charles F. Sabel. 1998. 'A Constitution of Democratic Experimentalism.' *Columbia Law Review*, Vol. 98, No. 2, pp. 267–473.

Grande, Edgar and Markus Jachtenfuchs (eds.). 2000. *Wie problemlösungsfähig ist die EU?* Baden-Baden: Nomos.

Heinelt, Hubert. 1996. 'Multilevel Governance in the European Union and the structural Funds.' In Heinelt, Hubert and Randall Smith (eds.). *Policy Networks and European Structural Funds*. Aldershot, Bookfield, Hong Kong, Singapore, Sydney: Avebury. pp. 9–25.

———. 2010: *Governing Modern Societies: Towards Participatory Governance*. London and New York: Routledge.

———, and Wolfram Lamping. 2015. 'The development of local knowledge orders: A conceptional framework to explain differences in climate policy at the local level.' *Urban Research & Practice* (forthcoming).

———, and Tanja Malek. 2002. 'Neuere Steuerungsformen im europäischen Mehrebenen system.' In Thomas Conzelmann and Michèle Knodt (eds.). Regionales Europa – europäisierte Regionen, Frankfurt am Main: Campus, pp. 69–86.

———, and Randall Smith (eds.). 1996. *Policy Networks and European Structural Funds*. Aldershot, Bookfield, Hong Kong, Singapore, Sydney: Avebury.

———, Tanja Kopp-Malek, Jochen Lang and Bernd Reissert. 2003. 'Policymaking in Fragmented Systems. How to Explain Success.' In Beate Kohler-Koch (ed.). *Linking EU and National Governance*. Oxford: Oxford University Press. pp. 135–53.

———, 2005a. Die Entwicklung der EU-Strukturfonds als kumulativer Politikprozess. Baden-Baden: Nomos. *Die Entwicklung der EU-Strukturfonds als kumulativer Politikprozess*. Baden-Baden: Nomos.

Hooghe, Liesbeth (ed.). 1996. *Cohesion Policy and European Integration: Building Multi-level Governance*. Oxford: Oxford University Press.

Kaufmann, Franz-Xaver, Giandomenico Majone and Vincent Ostrom (eds.). 1986. *Guidance, Control, and Evaluation in the Public Sector.* Berlin: Walter de Gruyter.

Knill, Christoph and Duncan Liefferink. 2007. *Environmental Politics in the European Union*. Manchester: Manchester University Press.

Luhmann, Niklas. 1989. 'Politische Steuerung. Ein Diskussionsbeitrag.' In Hans Hermann Hartwich (ed.). *Macht und Ohnmacht politischer Institutionen*. Opladen: Westdeutscher Verlag. pp. 12–16.

Malek, Tanja. 2002. *Politikgestaltung auf europäischer Ebene*. Baden-Baden: Nomos.

Marks, Gary. 1993. 'Structural Policy and Multilevel Governance in the EC.' In Alan W. Cafruny and Glenda G. Rosenthal (eds.). *The State of the European Community*, Vol. 2: 'The Maastricht Debates and Beyond.' Boulder: Lynne Rienner Publishers. pp. 391–410.

Marsh, David. 1998. 'The Development of the Policy Network Approach.' In David Marsh (ed.). *Comparing Policy Networks*. Buckingham: Open University Press.

Mayntz, Renate. (ed.). 1980. 'Implementation politischer Programme.' Empirische Forschungsberichte, Königstein/Taunus: Athanaum.

———. (ed.). 1983. 'Implementation politischer Programme II.' Opladen: Westdeutscher Verlag.

———. 1987. 'Politische Steuerung und gesellschaftliche Steuerungsprobleme – Anmerkungen zu einem steuerungstheoretischen Paradigma.' In *Jahrbuch zur Staats- und Verwaltungswissenschaft 1*, Baden-Baden: Nomos. pp. 89–110.

———. 1996. 'Politische Steuerung: Aufstieg, Niedergang und Transformation Einer Theorie.' In Klaus von Beyme and Claus Offe (eds.). *Politische Theorien in der Ära Der Transformation*. Opladen: Westdeutscher Verlag. pp. 148–68.

———. 1997. *Soziale Dynamik und politische Steuerung. Theoretische und methodologische Überlegungen*. Frankfurt am Main and New York: Campus.

Orton, J. Douglas and Karl E. Weick. 1990. 'Loosely Coupled Systems. A Reconceptualization.' *Academy of Management Review*, Vol. 15, No. 2, pp. 203–23.

Pressman, Jeffrey L., and Aron Wildavsky. 1973. *Implementation. How Great Expectations in Washington are Dashed in Oakland. Or, Why its's Amazing that Federal Programs Work At All.* Berkeley: University California Press.

Sabel, Charles F., and Jonathan Zeitlin. 2007. 'Learning from Difference. The New Architecture of Experimentalist Governance in the European

Union.' *European Governance Papers* (EUROGOV) Nr. C-07-02. http:/ www.connexnetwork.org/eurogov/pdf/egp-connex-C-07 02.pdf.

Scharpf, Fritz W. 1986. 'War die Massenarbeitslosigkeit unabwendbar? Von der Schwierigkeitbeschäftigungspolitischer Optionen.' In Hans E. Maier and Thomas Schmid (eds.). *Der goldene Topf. Vorschläge zur Auflockerung des Arbeitsmarktes*. Berlin: Wagenbach. pp. 9–37.

———. 1988a. 'The Joint-Decision Trap: Lessons from German Federalism for European Integration.' *Public Administration*, Vol. 66, No. 3, pp. 239–78.

———. 1988b: 'Verhandlungssysteme, Verteilungskonflikte und Pathologiender politischen Steuerung.' In Manfred G. Schmidt (ed.). *Staatstätigkeit. International und historisch vergleichende Analysen*. Opladen: Westdeutscher Verlag. pp. 61–87.

———. 1989. 'Politische Steuerung und politische Institutionen.' In Hans-Hermann Hartwich (ed.). *Macht und Ohnmacht politischer Institutionen*. Opladen: Westdeut scher Verlag. pp. 17–29.

———. 2001. 'What Have We Learned? Problem-Solving Capacity of the Multilevel European Polity.' Cologne: MPIfG Working Paper 01/4.

Weick, Karl E. 1976. 'Educational Organizations as Loosely Coupled Systems.' *Administrative Science Quarterly*, Vol. 21, No. 1, pp. 1–19.

———. 1985. *Prozeß des Organisierens*. Frankfurt am Main: Suhrkamp.

PART II

REFLECTIONS ON POLICYMAKING AND POLICY ANALYSIS

5 Public Policy as a Practice[1]

Reflection Inspired by Alasdair MacIntyre's *After Virtue*[2]

Ramaswamy Sudarshan[3]

Abstract

This paper attempts to relate the pedagogy of public policy to the concept of practice articulated by Alasdair MacIntyre. It first discusses the challenges of establishing public policy as a discipline in India, where it has been long assumed that only those employed in government need to acquire skills and knowledge essential for policy formulation. It was also assumed that, by definition, all policies made by the government must be in the interest of the public. This assumption is being challenged in recent times, opening up the possibility of fashioning a pedagogy for public policy that could make the subject meaningful to a variety of practitioners besides those serving in the government. In the quest for a philosophy of public policy as a practice, this essay examines an understanding of external and internal goods, the role of virtues, and limitations of economics, a dominant discipline in public policy schools. This contribution further underlines the importance of public policy practitioners connecting with the public, whose interests and concerns provide the raison d'être for the practice of public policy. The paper concludes by raising a paradoxical possibility that while

[1] Paper prepared for the Istanbul Policy Center at Sabancı University workshop on Public Policymaking in a Globalized World, 28–29 November 2014, Istanbul.

[2] This paper draws extensively upon MacIntyre, A. C. (1984). After virtue: A study in moral theory (2nd ed.), Notre Dame, Indiana: University of Notre Dame Press. Cited hereafter as MacIntyre, 1984.

[3] Dean, Jindal School of Government and Public Policy (JSGP), O.P. Jindal Global University, Sonepat, India.

public policy can be a practice as defined by MacIntyre, teaching public policy may not be a practice.

Introduction

Teaching public policy in India has posed several challenges. In the first place, it is a new discipline in Indian universities.[4] Hitherto, public policy has been regarded as a discipline that is meant exclusively for government officials. Public policymaking has been assumed to be the exclusive concern of bureaucrats, not meant for those outside government. This attitude towards public policy as the sole preserve of officers serving the government is a legacy of the British Raj.

The Indian Civil Service (ICS) was established in 1858. Officers were recruited by a competitive examination initially held in London but later also in India. These officers held all the key posts ranging from policymaking in the Viceroy's office to managing the business of government in the 250 districts that comprised British India. Jawaharlal Nehru, later to be the first prime minister of India, declared in 1934 that he would have nothing to do with the ICS tradition. But when the constitution of India was drafted, a successor service, the Indian Administrative Service (IAS), was created, incorporating safeguards protecting the tenure of service of its members. The last ICS officer inducted into the IAS retired in 1980 as the Cabinet Secretary.

Based on the advice of Paul Appleby (Dean, Maxwell School of Citizenship and Public Affairs, Syracuse University, and Ford Foundation consultant), the Indian Institute of Public Administration was established in 1954 with the Prime Minister as its founding president. Many other training centres for government officials were subsequently established in all the states of India. The Centre for Public Policy (CPP) was established in 2000 in the Indian Institute of Management, Bangalore, through a partnership agreement between the Government of India and the United Nations Development Programme, collaborating with the Kennedy School, Harvard, and the Maxwell School, Syracuse.

[4] The first group in India with an M.A. in Public Policy graduated only in August 2012.

All these institutions focused on public administration, understood as involving an investigation of the different ways public services can be delivered, and to a lesser extent on public policy, which was understood as the study of principles of public decision-making and the formulation of programmes to solve policy problems. In practice, this may be a distinction without much difference.[5] All primarily cater to the training needs of government officials and, to a lesser extent, on executive education for managers from the corporate sector and civil society organizations. They generally award diplomas, not degrees recognized by India's University Grants Commission.[6]

Against this background, the MA in Public Policy offered at O.P. Jindal University is a pioneering venture. It faces the challenge of novelty. The degree in public policy equips students with skills and knowledge needed for a growing variety of employment, via lateral entry, into governments, in public-private partnership (PPP) ventures, in corporate social responsibility, in international development-focused institutions, and in civil society organisations. Nevertheless, potential students continue to assume that public policy education is a requirement only for those who have already joined the government. India's British Raj legacy is again responsible for the desire to be familiar with public policy education.

At the policymaking level in the United States, there is no permanent civil service, unlike countries that are members of the British Commonwealth. In the US, there has been a steady movement of professionals from academia and the corporate sector into and out of government. Many professionals, in anticipation of working within or with governments at the federal, state, and local level, value public policy education to a much greater extent than is the case in the Commonwealth till recently. One of the more recent consequences of globalisation, and the influence of international actors and institutions on national public policymaking, has been to create a greater awareness of the usefulness of public policy education.

[5] Y. Hur and M. Hackbart. 2009. 'MPA vs. MPP: A Distinction without a Difference?' *Journal of Public Affairs Education* (JPAE 15(4): 397–424).

[6] Master's courses in public administration (not public policy) in Indian universities began in the 1970s, mostly as electives in master's programmes in political science.

A second challenge for public policy education in India is the lack of fit between Indian realties and the availability of concepts and categories to grasp and adequately describe those realities. We live in a time when the dominant form of political institutions is liberal democracy. For liberal individualism, a community is simply an arena in which individuals each pursue their own self-chosen conception of the good life, and political institutions exist to provide that degree of order which makes such self-determined activity possible. Government and law are, or ought to be, neutral between rival conceptions of the good life for people, although it is the task of government to promote the rule of law. In the liberal view, the government cannot, in any part of its legitimate function, inculcate any one moral outlook in the people.

The dilemma posed by the lack of adequate concepts and categories to articulate and describe realities in non-western countries that do not share the same history and experience of liberal democracy has been articulated in a 'manifesto'. This 'manifesto' was drawn up after a series of 'global conversations on democracy', organized by the Centre for the Study of Developing Societies, New Delhi.[7]

The manifesto states:

> Current definitions of democracy threaten to reduce it to an institutional checklist derived from idealized notions of the experience of a small part of the globe. The ideal of democracy is seen to be synonymous with the historical form of liberal democracy in advanced capitalist societies of Western Europe and North America. Often this is further reduced down to a few key institutional features. Yet, the historical experience of democracy in most of the world provides overwhelming evidence against this approach. More often than not, imported institutions do not produce the same consequences that they did in their home context. Similarity of form is no guarantee of democratic substance. In fact, a search for familiar form is an invitation to cynical and superficial

[7] Bishnu N. Mohapatra. 2011. 'The Democracy Manifesto: Re-imagining Democracy'. *Open Democracy*. www.opendemocracy.net/bishnu-n-mohapatra/democracy-manifesto-re-imagining-democracy-in-our-time.

> copying for extraneous gains. On the one hand, experience of 'established democracies' shows that appearance of democratic form of government can be made compatible with rule of experts, dominance of corporates, control by private networks and decline of citizen participation. On the other hand, experience of democratic success outside the global North suggests that a departure from the mandated institutional form is often a pre-condition to the success. Mass democracies of post-colonial societies tend to acquire depth through practices that may not have a legitimate institutional expression in the received wisdom on democracy. Institutions are no doubt crucial to the formation and strengthening of democracies, but what institutions do depends on the context in which these are located.

We need to shift the focus from the form of an institution to its real life consequences in a given context. This is a challenge for public policy pedagogy because the West's intellectual hegemony determining terms of discourse used in different disciplines makes it difficult to find more appropriate formulations to better grasp Indian and other non-western realities.

A third challenge for public policy pedagogy is posed by the predominance of neoliberal prescriptions about what governments should do and not do. New Public Management (NPM), for instance, has inspired many government reforms all over the world. Market-oriented reform strategies have aimed to increase effectiveness, diminish bureaucracy, and reduce public spending. However, the goals of greater efficiency and accountability, leaner and stronger governments, have proved to be elusive.

Challenges for Public Policy to Evolve into a Practice

The hegemonic assumptions of public policy pedagogy are based on European Enlightenment ideas, especially positivism, developed and elaborated in the 18th and 19th centuries. 'The Enlightenment Project' as Alasdair Macintyre called it, attempted to justify morality by universally accessible reason. This project failed, according to

MacIntyre, because the Enlightenment started from the idea of 'man-as-he-happens-to-be' (MacIntyre, 1984, p. 54).

In the Aristotelian tradition, a good man is one who has developed his attitudes and abilities in the appropriate way, given his possibilities and capacities. A 'man living well' is like a harpist playing well, a functional conception of man. Moral judgments are related to 'man-as-he-could-be-if-he-realized-his-essential-nature'. In developing and actually 'living' his virtues, such a man is oriented toward the telos of human life: the good life and, ultimately, happiness (*eudaimonia*). Modern individuals can claim their individual rights or proclaim utilitarian rules, but they cannot justify them in terms of the individual and collective ends they are supposed to help in realizing. As modern politics is devoid of thinking about the good life and the good society, public policymaking, acting as the servant of democratic politics, can also be aimless, lacking a telos, focusing only in expediency of means to achieve ends that are chosen, not discovered or given.

MacIntyre uses the notion of characters to show that there is something fundamentally wrong with modern society and its culture. He does so by exposing flaws in the claims that are basic to these modern characters. The authority of managers' claims, in particular, rests on (a) 'the existence of a domain of morally neutral fact about which the manager is to be expert' and (b) the possibility of 'law-like generalizations and their application to particular cases derived from the study of this domain'. MacIntyre dismisses these two assumptions of moral neutrality and scientific expertise as false by stating:

> There are strong grounds for rejecting the claim that effectiveness is a morally neutral value. For the whole concept of effectiveness is...inseparable from a mode of human existence in which the contrivance of means is in central part the manipulation of human beings into compliant patterns of behaviour; and it is by appeal to his own effectiveness in this respect that the manager claims authority within the manipulative mode (MacIntyre 1984, p. 74).

Management, according to MacIntyre, is both an instrument and perpetrator of manipulation. Public managers contribute to the manipulative character of the modern state.

A practice, in his definition, is

> Any coherent and complex form of socially established cooperative human activity through which goods internal to that form of activity are realized in the course of trying to achieve those standards of excellence which are appropriate to, and partially definitive of, that form of activity, with the result that human powers to achieve excellence, and human conceptions of the ends and goods involved, are systematically extended (MacIntyre 1984, p. 187).

What this means is that throwing a ball with some skill is not a practice, but soccer as a game is a practice. Laying brick is not a practice, but architecture is a practice. Putting splashes of colour on canvas is not a practice, but painting as an art form is a practice. Being an argumentative Indian is not a practice, but being a lawyer able to put arguments to use for the sake of delivering justice is a practice.

With respect to this definition of 'practice', MacIntyre makes some important distinctions. The first is between internal and external goods, or between goods of excellence and goods of effectiveness (MacIntyre 1984, pp. 188–91). With chess playing, or any other practice, one can usually gain money, honour, and the like. But these goods could also be obtained in other ways. They are in principle unrelated to the particular practice of chess. MacIntyre calls them external goods. However, there are also goods that cannot be achieved in any other way than by the act of performing this particular practice, such as enjoyment and admiration of the brilliance and beauty of certain moves on the chess board (even when they are made by the opponent in the game). These goods cannot be obtained in any other way than in being involved in the game of chess (even if in the audience). Such goods are called internal goods of the practice.

MacIntyre points out that institutions are indispensable for practices to exist, but they also often pose a threat to them. He says:

> Institutions are characteristically and necessarily concerned with what I have called external goods. They are involved in acquiring money and other material goods; they are structured in terms of power and status, and they distribute money, power and status as

> rewards. Nor could they do otherwise if they are to sustain not only themselves, but also the practices of which they are the bearers. For no practice can survive for any length of time unsustained by institutions. Indeed so intimate is the relationship of practices to institutions – and consequently of the goods external to the goods internal to the practices in question – that institutions and practices characteristically form a single causal order in which the ideals and the creativity of the practice are always vulnerable to the acquisitiveness of the institution, in which the cooperative care for common goods of the practice is always vulnerable to the competitiveness of the institution (MacIntyre 1984, p. 194).

The point is that public policymaking and public managers have helped to build their institutions within the capitalistic-bureaucratic state, which could obstruct aspirations for the realization of the good life and the good society.

The Role of Virtues

To guarantee the well-functioning of practices and to prevent damage to them by institutions, virtues are of the utmost importance, 'Without them, without justice, courage, and truthfulness, practices could not resist the corrupting power of institutions' (MacIntyre 1984, p. 194).

In MacIntyre's analysis, virtues play a crucial role in practices and the achievement of internal goods: 'A virtue is an acquired human quality the possession and exercise of which tends to enable us to achieve those goods which are internal to practices and the lack of which effectively prevents us from achieving any such goods'.

Public policymaking and management cannot be readily regarded as a practice, because they are predominantly concerned with realizing given ends and achieving external goods. This is often at the cost of sacrificing internal goods of the kind that proper practices, like healing, teaching and playing games, all have. We teach public policy students an amalgam of the social sciences to equip them to be effective, expecting that they will have the capacity to make law-like generalizations that would enable them to predict and control the social environment.

The Challenge of Hermeneutics: People are Self-Interpreting Agents

The methods of the natural sciences are well suited to understanding the behaviour of Nature, the movements of the planets, or how a wheat plant will grow under certain conditions. However, those methods are not well-suited to understanding human behaviour. The essence of freedom in human beings consists in the inherent degree of unpredictability. We are self-interpreting agents. The moment a theory is advanced by a well-known economist about how people will behave, the chances are that people will read that account and either make it into a self-fulfilling prophecy or do exactly the opposite. The heavenly bodies, however, are always unmindful about theories scientists may advance about their movements.

One source of unpredictability in human behaviour is the possibility of external incidents that cannot be anticipated. Human unpredictability also flows from the ability to decide and makes choices. The outcome of decisions that are not made yet cannot be predicted. A third level of uncertainty can arise, because it is inherently impossible to predict the development of radical new concepts, as one would need those concepts in the first place to formulate the prediction. As MacIntyre puts it, to an extent, we can outsmart Fortuna, the 'bitch-Goddess' of unpredictability, but we cannot dethrone her (MacIntyre 1984, p. 93).

The study of economics attempts to imitate the methods of the natural sciences which are well-suited to understanding nature, but not so well suited to grasping human behaviour. Sir Peter Medawar once suggested that economics could be properly described as an 'unnatural science'.

We must not belittle the enormous understanding and advances in human knowledge that the discipline of economics has made possible. This is because a good deal (though not all) of human behaviour, with regularities, conditioned by habits, is predictable. Understanding these patterns of behaviour using analytical tools of economics, econometrics and statistics, which are all disciplines with their own internal standards of excellence, can equip its practitioners to be in the front ranks of public policymaking.

However, we also must appreciate what economists cannot do. They can explain market failure, but they not are able to explain our failure in upholding public values, or all of the ways in which public policy can be so corrupted until it is no longer a practice infused with ideals. The rise of professional policy analysis has in many ways contributed to the ascendance of the market failure model and the pervasiveness of microeconomics in public policy.

Policy analysis more easily speaks the language of economics than the language of the common good or, for that matter, politics. 'Policy-analysis-in-use' typically involves the translation of decision alternatives into benefits, costs, discount rates, and transitive economic values, none of which accommodates the common good. The colossal failure of economists to anticipate the recent global financial crisis has not diminished the influence of 'ecocrats'. Ironically, the same set of 'experts' is in greater demand now to carry out post-mortems as to why they failed. Economics masks certain kinds of conflicts over contestable concepts, imagining a world that is much more predictable and manageable than it really is. Bureaucracies legitimize their authority by using its methodology, and ironically, even the unsuccessful employment of such social scientific knowledge results in more support for the same kind of knowledge.

The Way Forward for Public Policy Pedagogy

Public policy pedagogy should aim at bringing out all possible corrupting instrumental tendencies in public institutions. It should help public policy practitioners in identifying important virtues, which they should cultivate to counter the corrosive influence of institutions on public policymaking conceived as a practice. As a practice, the primary duty of public policy ought to be sustaining the political community. The telos of politics and public policy as practices ought to be the common good, which differs from the public interest or general good as it is often understood in modern discourses.

The public interest is often understood to be an aggregation of individual preferences. But the common good is concerned with the desirable (virtuous) development of individuals and not just their current preferences. The realization of the common good entails public policies that enable and ensure the participation of the public because it is only by participating in the pursuit of the common good that one can develop the virtues and competencies required for that enterprise to be successful. The forms of public participation must not only give a voice to citizens to promote their particular interests but must also contribute to training people to cultivate the virtues for the purpose of realising the common good.

For public policy to evolve into a proper practice, the discipline must meet MacIntyre's criteria:

- Have coherence and complexity
- Adhere to socially established norms
- Require human cooperation
- Involve technical skills, which are exercised within evolving traditions of values and principles
- Be organized to achieve certain standards of excellence
- Produce 'internal goods' in pursuit of excellence
- Increase human capability to achieve internal standards of excellence
- Systematically extend our conceptions of goods internal to the practice

'Public' in Public Policy

The institution most vital for public policy to become a practice, so that it does not remain a collective noun for technological fixes unrelated to the common good, is democracy. Democracy has intrinsic, as well as instrumental, value. Although some values of democracy are means to non-political values, others grow out of democratic processes themselves.

Participation completes individuals, in part by enabling them to discover and develop their public dimensions, in part by providing the kinds of interactions that develop capacities for autonomous judgments. The 'public' must be brought back into public policymaking. This is easier said than done. Ordinary people are, for the most part, rationally ignorant and cannot be expected to take an interest in all public policy debates. They also know that their vote in a democratic election, one in millions, can make little difference.

But it does not mean they are unable to voice their views on matters related to public policy.

Public policy practitioners ought to uphold the right information. If there is an institutional design in which those practitioners can become seriously engaged in weighing competing arguments, they could make informed and thoughtful judgments. The best way to pursue long-term democratic reform is to provide a context where the deliberative democracy of the people flourishes and can give voice to key concerns. Policy choices have to be made consonant with the informed preferences of the population. The public should be consulted about issues of collective political will, about the trade-offs they are willing to accept for the basic direction of policy. They should be consulted about whether we should build nuclear power plants. They need not be consulted about the choice of nuclear reactors.

Public policy, if it is to evolve into a practice, with a teleological commitment to the common good, ought to draw the general public into dialogue and discussions. The purpose here need not be hammering out a consensus. The purpose is simply deliberation and public understanding of policy issues. Public policy as a practice ought to cultivate the channels of public deliberation in order to change a flawed representative democracy into a deliberative democracy.

Conclusion

If public policy is conceived to be a practice having its own internal goods, standards of excellence and proper purposes which it is meant to serve, can the teaching of public policy also be regarded a practice? MacIntyre believes that teaching by itself cannot be a practice, because it is an ingredient in all practices, it is a means to other ends, and will be different depending upon what is being taught. People teaching public policy have to first internalize and appreciate why it is important to conceive of public policy as a practice. Next, they need to cultivate the virtues necessary to impart the knowledge and skills that are essential for the practice of public policy. The virtues of justice, courage and honesty, which are essential for all proper practices with internal goods and standards of excellence, are also essential for those engaged in the pedagogy of public policy. Teaching how to use the tools and techniques of designing and implementing public policies is important. However, even more important is the challenge of helping public policy students become a particular kind of person who can appreciate the intrinsic worth of the calling and not be drawn to it by the lure of external goods and inducements. After all, education is what remains after much that was learnt in schools is forgotten.

References

Hur, Y., and M. Hackbart. 2009. 'MPA vs. MPP: A Distinction without a Difference?' *Journal of Public Affairs Education*, JPAE 15(4): 397–424.

MacIntyre, Alasdair. 1984. *After Virtue: A study in moral theory* (2nd Ed.). Notre Dame, Indiana: University of Notre Dame Press.

Mohapatra, Bishnu N. 2011. 'The Democracy Manifesto: Re-imagining Democracy'. *Open Democracy*. www.opendemocracy.net/bishnu-n-mohapatra/democracy-manifesto-re-imagining-democracy-in-our-time.

6 Policymaking as an Art and a Practice

Erhard Friedberg[1]

Abstract

This article argues that the overemphasis of policy design over the teaching of policy implementation characteristic of present day policy schools tends to bias policy education towards a technocratic understanding of policymaking, and is incapable of training its students in what is above all an art and a craft, not an exercise in technical expertise.

Introduction

The mushrooming and multiplication of graduate programmes in public policy and more recently of graduate policy schools have many observers saying that policy schools will be, or already are, the business schools of tomorrow, progressively replacing their older sisters in their role as the training ground for the future elites of their countries and as the agents of rationalization, modernization, and professionalization of the world of policymaking, just like their older sisters had done for the practice of management in the business world.

There are good reasons for this, as the world of policymaking promises indeed to be an exciting world for ambitious young professionals wanting to make a difference in the world. For now is a time of watersheds, where linear change processes come to a peak and produce major shifts, calling for new institutional arrangements.

[1] This paper has been published in a slightly different version in *Strategic Review*, No. 1, (January–March, 2014).

Many areas come to mind where such change is now taking place. Let us just point out three crucial ones.

The Changing Context and Scope of Policymaking

The first is the foreseeable end of unilateralism. In the emerging multi-polar world, the capacity of any superpower to take on an issue singlehandedly is more and more constrained. The world of today does not have a clear hegemony anymore, on which it could depend in the past to produce and maintain a stable architecture of international relations. Today, the world has to search for, and establish, new mechanisms of international crisis management, a new regime of international relations where multilateral initiatives have to be pieced together and maintained in new ways to assure long term peace-building and conflict resolution processes. Diplomats and policymakers know what they cannot count on any more, but they do not know with what to replace it.

The second area is what could be called the 'end of the new frontier'. The world of today has become a finite world with less and less unknown reserves as well as less and less possibilities to 'get out'. Policymakers the world over still want to ignore this fact. They continue to cling to the myth of the unlimited resources of the still-to-be-discovered El Dorado (the fracking craze is the latest example of this tendency). However, new frontiers become scarcer and scarcer. The Arctic is on the verge of becoming one, as Siberia might soon be freed from permafrost. Outer space could be considered in this role and propositions have already been heard to, among other things, put our nuclear waste out on the moon.

However, policymakers as well as the man on the street distinctly feel that it is not the true thing anymore. Whether we like it or not, we are entering a finite world, and this situation basically cannot be changed. In a finite world, our usual modes of collective action cannot be sustained. We cannot have extensive growth without worrying about its consequences on our resources and the sustainability of our productive capacities. We cannot pursue profit maximizing without computing the negative costs of such a course of action. Clearly, this means that we have to begin thinking about how to internalize the negative costs of our actions in order to control and manage them. This increases immensely the complexity of human affairs and places huge demands on our social fabric as well as on policymaking, as externalization has traditionally been our favourite way of managing conflict and articulating conflicting interests. Organizations traditionally rely on externalization; societies as well have externalized the costs of their development; treaties rely on the exclusion of relevant parties, i.e. are based on externalization. Make externalization more difficult if not impossible, and you have to integrate a larger number of contradictory interests in any collective action process. The multiplication of legitimate and recognized stakeholders in an ever-growing number of policy issues continuously increasing the complexity of the policy-process is an illustration of this difficulty.

Here again, the policy world is far from having found the solution. Policymakers, politicians as well as corporate leaders, are groping around in the dark, trying to measure up to the challenge. Notions or catchwords like Sustainable Development, Corporate Social Responsibility or Ethical Investment, as imperfect as they might be, as misused as they might be in public relations operations, try to address this issue, without really convincing the observer. It is obvious that we are only at the beginning of something the magnitude of which will become apparent with time.

The third area, the challenge of diversity, covers many different elements: the recognition of the legitimacy of differences of all sorts (cultural, sexual, gender); a new sensibility to, and critique of, hidden premises justifying different treatments in our societies; the development of different forms of 'positive discrimination' in the name of equality; the increased questioning of the 'occidental way of doing things'. What's behind all of this is the increasing difficulty of imposing one set of premises as superior to another one and as the basis for integration and/or exclusion. The lack of legitimacy of such overarching principles is patent and growing. The 'one best way' philosophy is behind us, and we do not yet know with what to replace it. The overload and the increase in complexity that this creates for the policy process is still another question for which policymakers have yet to invent viable solutions.

However, there is more than just the newness or the new acuteness of the context, i.e. the problems. What makes everything even more problematic is the growing awareness that the old solutions will not do any more. Overcome repertoires have all shown their weaknesses, meaning that the world of policymaking will have to become genuinely inventive and innovative.

Looking back on the last fifty years of public policymaking, one can say that the policy world has come full circle in terms of believing in a single set of solutions. After the disasters of the Great Depression and World War II, the Keynesian synthesis (you could also call it the Bretton Woods Consensus) was built on blind trust in the virtues of planning, regulation and state intervention: markets were prone to failure, and planning and state intervention were there to compensate. Public initiative was implicitly identified with the public good, and all the results of studies showing the contrary were considered to be deviations from what ought to be.

In the sixties and seventies, this simplistic conception was increasingly questioned, due in particular to the progress in public policy analysis. The neoliberal revolutions that were ushered in by the Reagan and Thatcher administrations brought this criticism to the policy process, and a new consensus replaced the old one. Now the emphasis was on policy failures, and blind trust in the market mechanism replaced the previous pro-state bias.

Today, there is growing disillusionment with both the market and the market mechanism. In some parts of the world, this produces tendencies to swing the pendulum back to statist conceptions, making more state intervention again the solution for everything. However, policymakers as well as civil society have learnt from experience that it is not enough to trust the simple solutions of yesterday. The solution is not to be found in systematically more or less state, more or less rules. It lies in a new kind of public intervention, in a new kind of socialization based on new alignments of private and public interests that need yet to be invented and implemented.

Other examples could have been chosen, but I think that the thrust is clear. Future policymakers will have to be active in a risky world, where unprecedented problems call for unprecedented solutions. However, this also means an exciting world, with unprecedented opportunities to innovate, to invent new solutions and to drive institutional change, a world, in other words, where the enthusiasm, the spirit of initiative and the capacity to think out of the box by young, well-trained professionals are badly needed and will find ample opportunity to be deployed.

The Rise of Policy Schools in Response to these Changes

With their growing attractiveness for young people with an entrepreneurial spirit and in response to their changing context, the policy schools themselves have changed. What helped them in this process of reinventing themselves was the basic rethinking of policymaking brought about by the intellectual revolutions of public choice theory as well as operations research and micro-economic modelling applied to the public domain, all of which seemed to open an era where rational decision-making and scientific policy design would complement, if not gradually replace the traditional ways of policymaking. Traditional schools of Public Administration have been increasingly subverted by this revolution and have progressively been replaced by graduate schools and programmes of Public Management, Public Policy and Public Affairs seeing themselves as the agents and promoters of the rationalization of policymaking through its infusion with science and scientific methods, much like the business schools had seen themselves as the bearers of the rationalization of the practice of management.

What this change of denomination documents is indeed a transformation and rethinking of the basic mission of policy schools. Policymaking is not seen as the exclusive product of the activity of public administrators and cannot therefore be confined solely to the public sector. It is understood as the outcome of the interaction between multiple stakeholders from different sectors of society having to come to a common understanding and having to coordinate their conflicting interests. And policymakers cannot be viewed any more as administrators of a fundamentally administrative process. They become the manager of a process where the traditional division between private and public, between public and civil society becomes blurred.

In other words, policy education has increasingly come to view policymaking as a management process involving many of the techniques and using many of the tools which were close if not identical to a good deal of what was taught in business schools. In fact, just as its older sisters the business schools did for management, policy education increasingly tended to identify the policy process as a technical management problem the solution of which lay in the development of policy sciences, and the use of scientific methods and models in and for policy design.

This evolution is not problematic per se. It has meant great progress not only in our understanding of policymaking, but also in our practical capacity to devise new policy solutions and new institutional arrangements to carry them out. In short, it has increased the relevance of policy education for the solution or at least the serious tackling of the policy problems of today's world. But like all good things, when pushed too far, it seems to have become counterproductive and to produce results that are far from desirable.

In his 2004 book *Managers, not MBAs*, Henry Mintzberg,[2] the well-known specialist of management, has written an abrasive and highly documented critique of what the business schools have become in the last twenty to thirty years. The thrust of his critique could be summarized as follows: when taught to young inexperienced students just out of their bachelor's degree, the curricula of even the best business schools do not properly train for the practice of management (do not develop managers), because they overemphasize and overdevelop the analytical, logical and scientific side of management, producing replicable 'best practices', and accordingly underemphasize, undervalue and underdevelop other dimensions which call more on imagination, creative insights and practical experience, all dimensions which bring management closer to an art or a craft. To sum up Mintzberg's perspective, present day curricula of business schools tend to reduce management to analytical problem-solving, which itself is understood narrowly as problem-solving thanks to and with the help of the analytical techniques and the scientific

[2] H. Mintzberg, *Managers, not MBAs*. San Francisco: Berret-Koehler Publishers Inc., 2004.

methods that have been taught[3]. It is no wonder, says Mintzberg, if the acronym of MBA has often mockingly been translated into 'Management by Analysis'. As a consequence, business schools do the corporate world no good service. At best, they produce whiz kids convinced that the superiority of their analytical training puts them ahead and therefore above experienced managers, whiz kids who think that designing clear, analytical solutions can replace the much murkier practice of management, which basically consists in assiduously attempting to devise contextual solutions and to bring them to bear on reality in a complex interactive and iterative process. At worst, they produce technicians and consultants distorting the practice of management because they are incapable of facing and mastering the complex combination of art, craft and science it needs.

Policymaking Cannot be Reduced to a Technical Management Problem

Reading Mintzberg's book, which is much richer and insightful than this very short summary, one cannot help but draw the parallel to what has been taking place in policy education. Even if the evolution is fortunately less pronounced, even if the homogenizing influence of ratings and accreditation authorities is fortunately and for the present less institutionalized than in the world of business schools, many of the elements criticized by Mintzberg can, *mutatis mutandis*, be found in the recent evolution of policy education. Here too, young, inexperienced bachelor's degree-holders are put through curricula heavily weighted in favour of analytical methods, quantitative measurement and model-building in the service of theory and policy design. Here too, the practice of policymaking is left to be discovered after graduation, if, instead of taking a job in a public policy consultancy or think tank in which (s)he can continue to theorize about benchmarks, best solutions and the latest fad of the policy world, the graduate is lucky enough to find a job where (s)he will actually encounter and have to learn the practice of policymaking.

It is understandable why policy schools tend to overemphasize policy design over the practice of policymaking, which is really all

[3] H. Mintzberg, ibid. p. 92–104

about the implementation of policy. Policy design fits the academic world and can be taught easily. Notwithstanding its rhetoric, it is basically a neat, linear world in which seemingly highly complex understandings of the social fabric end up in clean solutions that have all the appearance of sound and reasonable policy, as long as one does not bring into the open many of the implicit behavioural assumptions on which such a policy would be based. Policy design is also amenable to the disciplinary structure of academe. Its main disciplinary roots have come to lie in economics, which explains why so often it is reduced to applying economic reasoning and concepts to the analysis and design of policy. It is amenable to analytical and quantitative methods and can easily be linked to the teaching and the construction of complex econometrical models of the policy world, which can claim to be interdisciplinary because they integrate elements of other social sciences (history, sociology, organization theory). In short, policy design is popular in policy schools not only because it is deemed important, but also (mainly?) because it fits the format of classroom teaching, draws on predominantly quantitative data and is thus easy to organize and administer.[4]

Let me be quite clear. To reflect on, and learn about, policy design is of course important, and policy education cannot do without these. But policy programmes should never lose sight of the fact that policy design is nothing but a theory of policymaking. However sophisticated, however relevant and based on the latest social science knowledge and findings this policy design might be, it will remain theory until it has undergone the test of implementation which, if conducted successfully, will allow the designed policy to have the desired impact on the ground, by changing the behaviour of the relevant actors targeted by the policy.

The Overemphasis of Policy Design Contributes to a Distortion of the Practice of Policymaking

By developing curricula and programs too heavily weighted in favour of the study and teaching of policy design, policy education thus

[4] Not to speak of another 'advantage', which is to enlarge the labour market for learned economists and econometricians.

contributes to the distortion of the practice of policymaking and produces not the reflective practitioners policymaking needs and calls for, but policy consultants and technocrats with a push-button understanding of public policy who are convinced that applying the right analytical tools and techniques will guarantee the success of a policy.

It would be a pity if in its pursuit of the promise of the rationalization of policymaking through its infusion with science and scientific methods, policy education, notwithstanding what is written in the mission statements of its schools, lost sight of the fact that policymaking is a practice and an art that can certainly be improved by technical knowledge and scientific methods, but cannot be made into a science or taught as a scientific discipline. A policy cannot be subsumed in a decision or a law and policy design cannot be separated from the process of implementation which becomes the crucial issue for a policy school. Policy design is certainly important, but in itself it is no guarantee for implementation. Policy design is nothing but intentions, preferably good intentions. But as the saying goes: Hell is paved with good intentions. A policy is only as good and as efficient as its implementation process allows it to be, it is nothing more than what it becomes in its process of implementation, which is its test of reality. A policy is a process, it is the deliberate attempt to change the state of affairs in a given policy field. The crux of policymaking is thus in implementation, not in policy design: it is in initiating and monitoring a process of social change whose ultimate success can only be measured and appreciated by its success in reshaping the behaviour of the relevant actors in their respective policy fields through a sustainable restructuring of the policy system they are part of.

Teaching the Skills and Abilities which Successful Policymaking Draws on by Taking the Classroom to the Policy Field

If they want to train policymakers, not mindless technocrats, policy schools must focus on the study and the teaching of the complex, contradictory and often counterintuitive and dysfunctional dynamics that can be observed and must be monitored in the implementation of policies. And this is where the problem starts. Because how does one teach something that is a practice and an art, how does one fit into a curriculum a process that evolves over time, how does one teach the skills and abilities which successful policymaking draws on?

Devising a course in implementation which focuses on the dynamics observed in the implementation of programmes and policies is a necessary beginning. Like all teaching of this sort, however, it might well rapidly develop a tendency to design what 'good' implementation would have to be and look like. It would most likely become an academic exercise, an academic sub-discipline, which in no way can replace the experience in real time that the implementation of a policy brings with it.

Following the footsteps of business schools, policy schools have turned to case studies of successes and failures in policy implementation to help bridge the gap between theory and practice characteristic of the teaching in so many policy programmes. However, the critique already made of business cases can be extended to policy cases: their seeming concreteness in reality conceals many simplifications and/or normative premises that are inherent to the exercise of writing case studies. While they are certainly better than no cases at all, they cannot by themselves fill the implementation deficit of public policy programmes.

So the question becomes: how to capture in a curriculum the real complexities of policy fields, how to give students the opportunity to not only learn about it, but experience it directly by discovering it themselves. Only then will it be more than just an intellectual understanding, and will have a chance to impact on their future practice. It seems to me that this can only be accomplished through a basic rethinking of policy programmes which not only makes implementation the focus of teaching and learning, but takes the classroom to the policy fields in order to confront students directly with the problems of implementation by providing them with the opportunity to observe and study them.

What this amounts to is to give a central place in policy training to pedagogical sequences structured around experiences of empirical, quasi-anthropological field research accompanied and prepared for by the necessary training in qualitative, descriptive empirical research. The philosophy of such sequences could be seen as, and to some extent is, close to what in some policy schools is called a capstone project: like the capstones in some two-year programmes, the idea is to provide a space for integration of the different perspectives students have been taught during the year, and to give them the opportunity to confront these perspectives with what can be observed in the field. But unlike capstones, which are mostly done towards the end of programmes and resemble consultancy projects that often amount to first steps back to the job market, the sequences of field research would be in the centre of the curriculum and should be an integral part of the academic programme: there would be no direct client other than the programme and its academic requirements, and the assignment would only be observation, description and reflective analysis, never prescription or the study of solutions. The idea of these sequences is 'simply' to equip students with the necessary conceptual frameworks and methodological tools and skills enabling them to go to various policy fields with only the assignment to explore, describe and analyse what a given policy becomes in the hands of all the relevant stakeholders (the policy actors) participating in the implementation of that policy in a given territory.

Such sequences will only bear fruit and fulfil their function if (1) they have a central place in the curriculum (as indicated and signalled by the number of credits they command), and (2) they comprise a full sequence, starting from the substantive as well as methodological preparation, to doing the actual fieldwork, write-up and discussion of the results, as well as of their significance for the understanding of the practice of policymaking. If this is the case, then they can help driving home the central point that policy solutions cannot be found without a thorough understanding of a given policy field, of the configuration of its actor networks, of the nature of its power structure, of its 'culture' and 'rules of the game', all of which will in the end condition whether a policy will succeed to 'make a difference', whether it will have the desired results—or will remain theory.

Conclusion: Beware of the Technocrat Slumbering in Each Budding Policymaker

If policy education is about training young professionals in the practice of policymaking, it has to safeguard against the technocratic bias that comes with the mastery of analytical methods and techniques that policy schools teach their graduates. It has to find a way to demonstrate to its graduates the relativity and biases incorporated in the scientific methods they have learned when applied to the policy world, in order to experientially convince them that technical expertise and mastery of sophisticated techniques are never ends in themselves, nor a guaranty for the success of a policy. It has to familiarize its graduates with the reality of policy fields and encourage them never to lose contact with this reality in order to be able to develop the contextualized solutions which will fit the characteristics of these fields and be able to build on these characteristics to initiate a positive change process. It has to remind them and help them realize how frequently the undesired results of a policy can be traced not to the lack of cooperation of a dominant actor in the field (playing the role of the 'bad guy'), but to the incomplete, ideological and biased understanding the responsible policymakers had of their policy field, or even simpler, to their basic neglect of it. And it must produce graduates who are not afraid, but curious of the reality of their policy fields, who feel at ease with them and have learned to read and diagnose what is going on in them, instead of protecting themselves from this reality and neglecting the constraints it carries, in order to be able to freely dream their policies. And it must produce graduates who know that politics, i.e. the fight for a negotiated common ground, is the normal, inevitable ingredient of any policy process, an ingredient that has to be accepted and monitored instead of being looked down on or avoided.

References

Mintzberg, H. 2004. *Managers, not MBAs*. San Francisco: Berret-Koehler Publishers.

7 Public Policy in the Framework of the Happiness Index

Sergey Zuev

The text submitted below is a part of a large research study conducted since 2011 at the School of Public Policy of the Presidential Academy (Moscow, Russia). The research is focused on the understanding of basic current trends in the feelings of different social groups concerning socio-economic and cultural environment in Russia. Its organization (three surveys per year with coverage of about 6,000 respondents in different regions of the country) allows us to consider the trends, which are interesting to researchers, in the medium- and long-term dynamics.

One of the problem areas, as in many other similar studies around the world, is the apparent insufficiency of many so-called 'objective' development indicators. Formal economic or social indicators are far from being in coincidence with the quality of well-being and its internal assessment by individual respondents or entire groups. This fact has been repeatedly discussed in the professional community and is a source of new research methods and tools.

'The Happiness Index' is one of those tools, and its test use in the framework of extensive collection of sociological empiric data allowed us to propose a number of new and often unexpected interpretations and hypotheses with regard to the Russian material. There is no doubt that the experimental nature in the use of this particular focus of the interpretation of sociological data suggests its further verification and validation.

Since the beginning of its usage, 'objective' country, region, or city development indicators (indices) were closely related to the issues of macroeconomic policy. For example, the most common and widespread economic progress index, Gross domestic product (GDP), was introduced by Simon Kuznets in 1934 for empirical evaluation of macroeconomic growth rates.

However, strong doubts started to arise almost immediately about the adequacy of using of statistical aggregates as reflectors of development level. The very existence of links between aggregative macroeconomic indicators and relevant concepts of progress was criticized. In comparison with the linear (quantitative) nature of economic growth, 'progress' was seen as a more complex and systemic concept. Thus, in 1950–60s in particular, there were already doubts about directly relating macroeconomic indicators of growth to a population's well-being and quality of life.

This doubt is based on two mutually dependent contexts. The methodological context: a wide distribution of methods for quality-of-life research and research on the socio-economic well-being of the population, based on a subjective evaluation of happiness and life satisfaction. The political context: a shift in political priorities from problems of the purely economic growth exclusively to much wider areas – social, communicative, territorial development, etc.

Methodological Context

The evaluation of subjective perception of life quality (happiness) was approached more or less seriously approximately 40 years ago. For example, in academic circles in the 1970–80s, broad debates were held about the methods that could be used to evaluate the general life quality of people – living in a certain area (country, region, city). The debates were provoked by the confidence in the fact that GNP or GDP per capita reflected solely the economic welfare of a state, while a measurement of life quality involved a broader set of indicators. A number of attempts were made to create a unique integrative indicator that could adequately serve these purposes.[1]

[1] Liu, B.C. 1976. *Quality of Life Indicator in U.S. Metropolitan Areas: A Statistical Analysis*. New York: Praeger. Johnston, D.F. 1988. 'Toward a comprehensive quality-of-life index.' *Social Indicators Research*, Vol. 20, No. 4 (November 1988), pp. 473–96. Selen, J. 1985. 'Multidimensional Descriptions of Social Indicators.' *Social Indicators Research*, Vol. 17, No. 4 (November 1985), pp. 435–45.

That was how the specific ratings of happiness and life satisfaction were created. They were fundamentally different from other ratings, because they were built on the basis of data received from mass surveys about population's subjective perception of different aspects of life.[2]

A compromise position was suggested as a result of the evolution of this approach.[3] It was based on the premise that subjective evaluations were necessary, but insufficient for life quality estimation. According to this logic, the researches combined the usage of statistics with the subjective evaluation of life satisfaction, or happiness perception. The most common life satisfaction aggregate is the OECD 'better life index'. It is based on both aggregated statistics and the results of surveys carried out in populations of different countries.[4]

This index includes eleven indicators of various subjects: housing, income, employment, social situation, education, ecology, civil rights, healthcare, life satisfaction, safety, work/leisure. Whilst these indicators are mainly statistical, the criteria of satisfaction are based on data from a 'subjective' survey.

There are two main perspectives on how indices of the subjective evaluation on a person's quality of life and well-being should be built: a 'strong' one and a 'weak' one.

[2] For example, Happy Planet Index is based on the following question from Gallup World Poll: 'Please imagine stairs where each stair is numbered from 0 at the bottom till 10 at the top. Let us assume that the top stair represents the best possible version of your life and the lowest stair represents the worst. In your opinion, which stair are you standing on at the moment? (Assuming that the higher your position on the stairs is, the higher you evaluate your life)?'

[3] In general there are two methodical positions describing the ways we can create an index of subjective life quality and well-being evaluation: a 'strong' and a 'weak' one. 'Strong' logic is usually criticized since a person cannot always adequately evaluate the degree of his life satisfaction. Depending on the mood and the local situation of respondent at the moment of the question there may be shifts in subjective evaluations.

[4] The index includes eleven indicators of different aspects: housing conditions, income, work, social situations, education, ecology, civil rights, health care, safety, work/leisure. Despite the fact that most of this indicators are statistical, the 'satisfaction' criteria are based on survey data. 'Life satisfaction gives us an idea of how people evaluate their lives as a whole, rather than their feelings at a certain moment. It provides an evaluation of life circumstances and conditions that are important for subjective well-being'.

The 'strong' viewpoint can be formulated as follows: 'Since [subjective] evaluations can take into account the role and the importance that people assign to various sources of their welfare, someone's own personal evaluation is the only main standard of estimating their quality of life'.

At the same time, this logic is often criticized on the grounds that a person cannot always adequately evaluate their own level of satisfaction with their life. There might be a bias in subjective evaluations depending on the mood and the respondent's local situation in the survey. As a result of the criticism a more established ('weak') methodology of happiness and life quality estimation was offered to complement the 'strong' viewpoint. It is based on the statement that subjective evaluations are necessary, but insufficient for estimating a person's quality of life.

It is evident, from the literature on the methods of measuring social attitudes and the creation of aggregates, that there is an increasingly imperative need to combine descriptive and subjective evaluations. Currently the 'weak (subjective) viewpoint' is the most common in real research practices.

Political Context

The shift of methodological priorities towards subjective evaluations of happiness and life satisfaction did not take place in a vacuum. It went hand in hand with a change in political priorities and the realization of the importance of people's personal evaluation of their happiness and well-being. The criticism of a direct relation between economic progress indicators and population's well-being created a favorable ground for political discourse. This was aimed at shifting a state's political priorities from economic growth to the problems of people's social well-being.[5]

At the level of practical politics happiness and life satisfaction indicators have been widely used since 2000s. Initially, the focus of policies based on these indicators was on the issues of

[5] See, for example, Richard Layard. 2005. *Happiness: Lessons from a New Science*. London: Penguin.

community development, improvement of interpersonal trust and the development of the urban environment. This is substantial, because the concepts of cultural and social capital, social cohesion, and confidence level, i.e. concepts that cannot be easily quantified, are gaining further importance both in the academic and applied public policy fields.

Now the indices of well-being, happiness and life satisfaction are used for a wider range of purposes:

- The determination of 'risk groups' and purposeful work with them;
- The detection of key factors that increase the socio-economic well-being of a population;
- The search for compromise solutions or the determination of long-term public development priorities;
- The evaluation of the social costs of proposed policies, etc.

Perhaps the biggest victory of subjective indicators was seen in the statement made in 2010 by British Prime Minister David Cameron, when he said that the feeling of population's well-being should be the main target variable of the state's long-term development. Since then, several committees dealing with the analysis of subjective evaluation of population's well-being have been set up in Great Britain: the Measuring National Wellbeing Advisory Forum, the Legatum Institute Commission for Wellbeing Policy, etc.

Russian Context (Practical Case)

Using Russia as an example, we can emphasize two cases illustrating the importance of subjective evaluations of happiness and well-being for determining the efficiency of implemented policies.

The first case (Republic of Dagestan) resembles a paradox. It illustrates the clearly seen contradiction between the subjective evaluation of life satisfaction and 'objective' indicators of economic progress.

The statistics of economic progress show that Dagestan is one of the most unfavorable regions of Russia. For example, the GRP per capita in Dagestan is 2.5 times lower than GDP per capita in

Russia (98,000 rubles versus 250,000 rubles according to the Russian Federal State Statistics Service).

The average monthly income of a Dagestani citizen is about 15,000 rubles lower than the average income in Russia. However, Dagestan outruns all other regions of Russia in the subjective evaluation of life satisfaction and happiness. Ninety per cent of the people in Dagestani are happy and satisfied with their living conditions. The index of happiness rates in Dagestan are 30 per cent higher than the average rate in Russia.

We observe the most striking difference between the objective and subjective indicators of life quality in this particular example. Despite the low GRP per capita and the actual income of population, the Dagestanis are the 'happiest' people in Russia. It is impossible to explain this paradox using the logic of objectified indicators of regional development.

However, the second case perfectly explains the paradox of the first one. It turns out that a high level of income is not directly connected with the evaluation of happiness and life satisfaction. Thus, the results of an all-Russian poll showed that people with the highest income per capita (above 50,000 rubles per family member) feel 20–25 per cent less happy than those who have an average income (20,000–25,000 rubles per family member).

As more profound analysis shows, the happiness level indicator is connected with the number and intimacy of social contacts. At the same time, the most important of these contacts are the so-called 'strong relations' – the number of close contacts with people that one can rely on in difficult situations (a specific question in the questionnaire). Primarily, these are close friends and relatives. The happiest groups of respondents are those with more than 10 'strong relations'.

The Dagestani paradox can be explained by the density and branching of 'social networks' of people in the region. Dagestanis have three times more 'strong relations', than people in other regions of Russia.

Of course, this fact affects the formation of a special (regional) type of social and economic policy, taking into account the basic values of the territory.

Interpretation of Results

Using Russia as an example, we can emphasize a case that illustrates the importance of using subjective evaluations of happiness and well-being when determining the efficiency of the practices which are currently used.

This example illustrates the lack of a direct relationship between the 'objective' indicators of economic development and the subjective evaluation of life satisfaction.

According to the statistical indicators of economic development, Dagestan is one of the most underprivileged regions of Russia. For example, GRP per capita in Dagestan is 2.5 times lower than the GDP per capita in Russia (98,000 rubles compared to 250,000 rubles according to the Russian Federal State Statistics Service). Half the population of Dagestan has an average monthly income of 5,000 rubles per family member, which is 15,000 rubles less than the average income in Russia.

Moreover, according to indicators on political satisfaction, almost 40 per cent of Dagestan's population has negatively evaluated the

Diagram 7.1: Average monthly income per family member in Dagestan

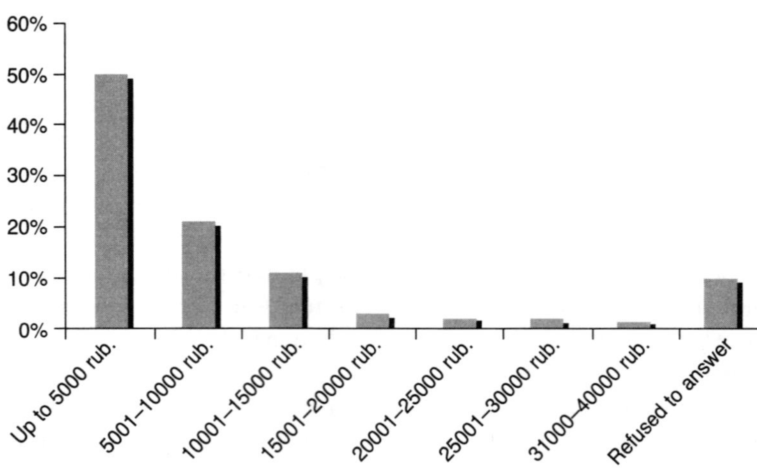

Source: Russian Barometer 2014.

Diagram 7.2: Comparison of political satisfaction of Dagestani residents and Russian population as a whole

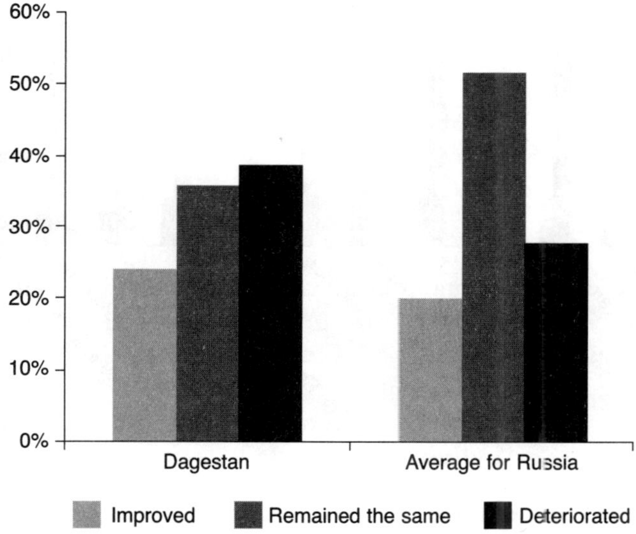

Source: Russian Barometer 2014.

political changes that have taken place over the last five years. Thirty-eight per cent of people in the region want to go abroad themselves or send their child abroad, and this percentage is higher than in almost all the other regions of Russia.

However, in terms of subjective evaluations of happiness and life satisfaction, Dagestan supersedes all other regions of the Russian Federation. Ninety per cent of Dagestanis are happy and satisfied with their living conditions. The indicators of happiness index in Dagestan are 30 per cent higher than in other regions of the Russian Federation.

Why does Dagestan remain a 'territory of happiness' in spite its unfavorable economic and political situation? It is not possible to explain this paradox using the logic of objectified indicators of regional development. In order to gain a better understanding of this matter, we will turn to the analysis of satisfaction with various aspects of life among the Russian population.

Diagram 7.3: Dagestan is the happiest region of Russia

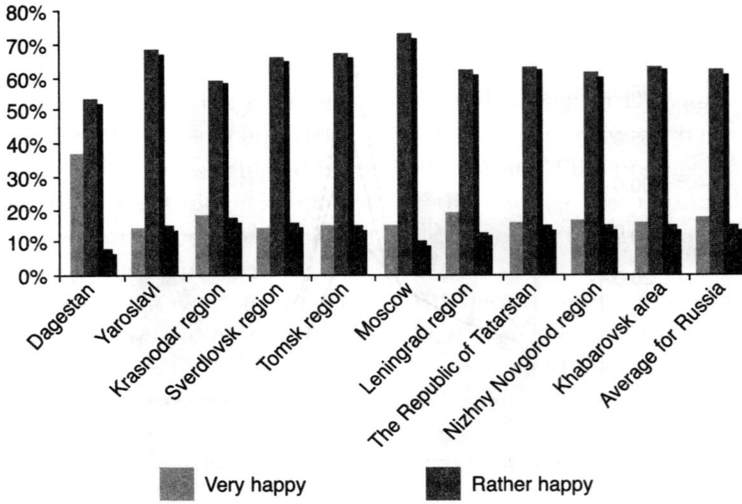

Source: Russian Barometer 2014.

The Happiness Index and Economic Well-being

The happiness index in Russia is relatively high. Approximately 70 per cent of the population is happy, which is 23–25 per cent higher than the indicators of happiness in Western Europe and the United States. At the same time, the average economic and political satisfaction is below 10–15 per cent.

Does this mean that the population's happiness does not depend on political and economic conditions of life? Not entirely. The correlation coefficients between these indicators are relatively high. Thus, the level of happiness has a correlation coefficient of 38 per cent for the level of economic satisfaction, while the correlation coefficient for the level of satisfaction with the political conditions is 20 per cent. In turn, the correlation coefficient for satisfaction with political and economic conditions is 28 per cent. Consequently, we can say that there is a statistically significant relationship between these indicators. But the level of happiness cannot be completely explained by the satisfaction with either political or economic conditions.

Diagram 7.4: Frequency distribution of life satisfaction indices

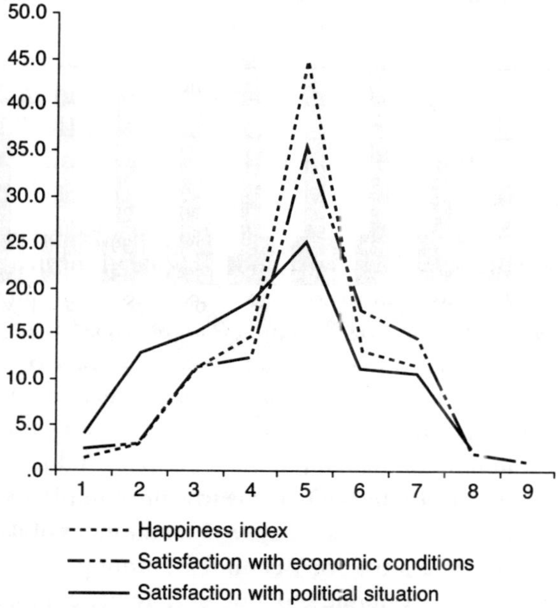

Source: Russian Barometer 2014.

This raises a question about the nature of the relationship between various aspects of satisfaction with the current situation in the country. As is evident from Diagram 2.1, satisfaction with economic conditions of life increases alongside the happiness index.

People who are not satisfied with their economic conditions – rarely consider themselves happy. However, when a certain degree of economic satisfaction is attained, the happiness index becomes independent of people's personal evaluation of their economic situation.

In other words, the less a person is satisfied with the economic conditions of life, the unhappier they are. However, those who are completely satisfied with the economic situation in the country are rather more complicated than the dissatisfied part of population. Economic well-being itself does not influence (or has a weak influence) on the self-esteem of people who can be ranked as being middle class in terms of their income.

Table 7.1: Correlation between happiness and satisfaction with economic conditions Happiness index/ Index of satisfaction with the economic situation

		Happiness						
		1	2	3	4	5	6	7
Index of satisfaction with the economic situation	1	16%	18%	23%	24%	14%	4%	2%
	2	8%	7%	26%	21%	26%	13%	1%
	3	3%	8%	22%	25%	28%	11%	4%
	4	3%	3%	16%	22%	39%	12%	5%
	5	%	2%	10%	15%	49%	13%	12%
	6	%	2%	7%	9%	53%	16%	13%
	7	%	1%	3%	6%	59%	14%	18%
	8	%	%	3%	4%	32%	31%	31%
	9	%	%	%	9%	33%	5%	53%

Source: Russian Barometer 2014.

As can be seen from the table, those who are completely satisfied with their economic conditions (values 8–9 for the index of satisfaction with their economic situation) cannot be unhappy. Therefore, satisfaction with the economic situation determines a 'basic' level of happiness, but does not guarantee high values of the index.

The analysis of the data showed that the respondent's social activity is the main factor of happiness. A social network of contacts is the least developed for people who do not have close friends and acquaintances. Conversely, the more friends and acquaintances a person has, the more likely he or she will be happy. At the same time the decisive role belongs to the so-called 'strong relations' – the number of close contacts that a person can rely on in difficult situations. These are primarily close friends and relatives. The happiest groups of respondents are those with more than 10 'strong relations'.

An analysis of the coefficients in the linear regression model 2 showed that, in comparison with the number of friends and acquaintances income has a two times weaker impact on the level of happiness. Often people with high levels of income per capita (more than 30,000 rubles per family member) are 10–15 per cent less happy than those who have an average income per capita (20,000–25,000 rubles per family member).

Diagram 7.5: Comparison of the number of 'strong relations' of Dagestani residents and Russian population

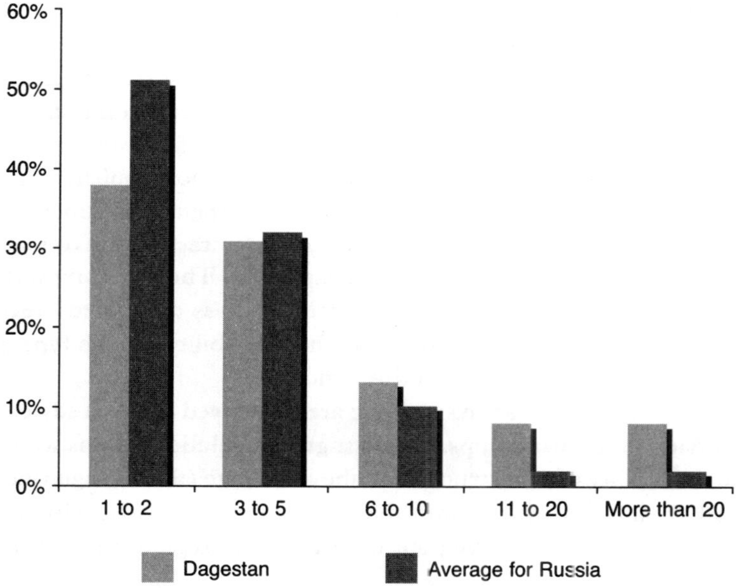

Source: Russian Barometer 2014.

The Dagestani paradox can be explained by the density and branching of people's 'social networks' in the region. Dagestanis have three times more 'strong relations', than people in other regions of Russia.

Why do strong relations play a decisive role in the feeling of happiness? What makes the Russians, who have more friends and acquaintances, feel more satisfied with their lives? In fact, it is the number of strong relations that determines social security and people's level of interpersonal trust.

Happiness Index and Political Satisfaction

The dependence of happiness level on political satisfaction is significantly lower if we compare this group of factors with their satisfaction with the economic situation. This is illustrated by the values of the correlation coefficients; the relationship between the evaluation of political conditions and happiness is almost two times weaker than the relationship between happiness and satisfaction with the economic situation.

Nevertheless, there is also a correlation here. These studies tend to suggest that political satisfaction depends mainly on the community's level of solidarity – the number of close relations a person has at a local level. According to the data, political satisfaction is substantially symmetric with the evaluation of the quality of urban environment, to the factor of availability of a social and cultural infrastructure (quality index of the urban environment) in particular. This is a composite index, meaning, that the index of each region is calculated based on the aggregate set of indicators on the availability of each type of urban environment objects in this region.

According to the analysis all the areas involved in the study can be divided into two groups. The first group includes regions where the availability of infrastructure is above average (the average value is 100 points): Moscow (with the exception of the wider Moscow region), the Sverdlovsk region, the Leningrad region, the Nizhny

Diagram 7.6: Rating of Russian regions depending on the availability of the elements of urban environment

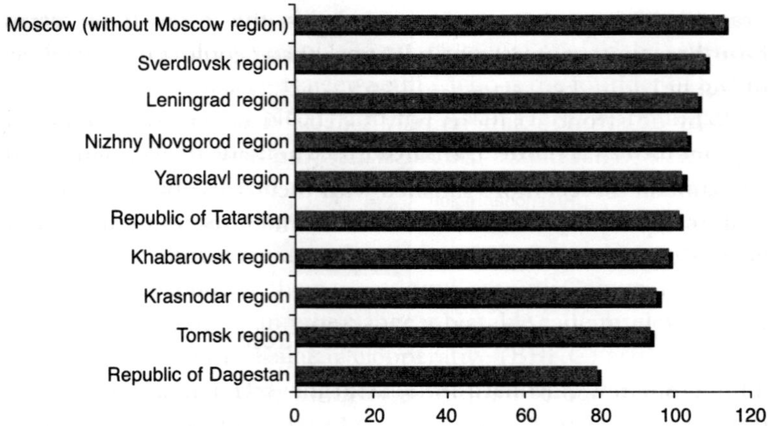

Source: Russian Barometer 2014.

Novgorod region, the Yaroslavl region, the Republic of Tatarstan. The second group consists of regions with a relatively low availability of urban environment objects: Khabarovsk, Krasnodar, Tomsk and the Republic of Dagestan.

When considering the indicators of individual infrastructures, it is evident that we are discussing the top three regions: Moscow, Sverdlovsk and Leningrad.

As the analysis shows, there is a direct relationship between the quality of urban environment in the region and an indicator of political satisfaction: they are correlated with a coefficient of 0.438. The relationship between these two indicators can be seen in Diagram 7.7.

However, the general pattern has two significant exceptions: the Moscow and Yaroslavl region. According to our data, the level of

Diagram 7.7: Dependence of satisfaction with the political situation on the quality of urban environment by region

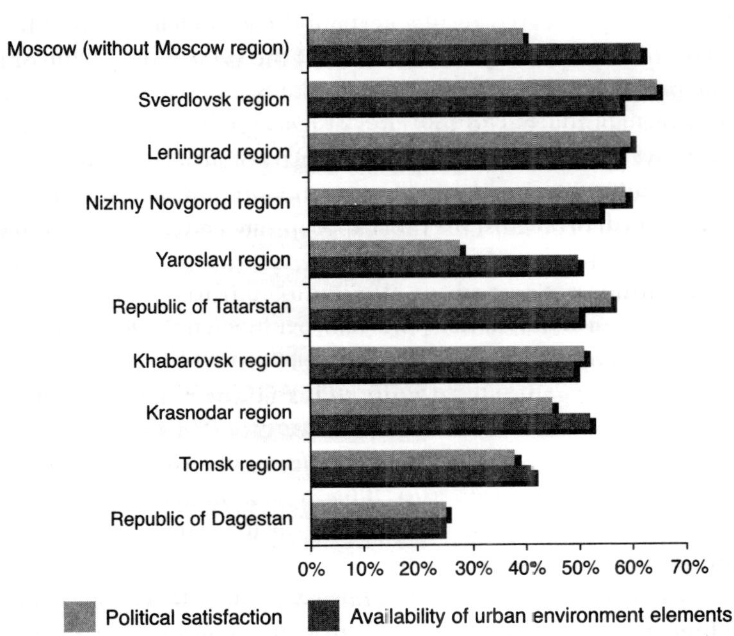

Source: Russian Barometer 2014.

political satisfaction in these regions is the lowest, with relatively high indicators of the development of urban environment (for Yaroslavl Region) and the highest (for Moscow).

These exceptions can be explained by two factors. Firstly, Moscow has the lowest solidarity rate of local communities, and Moscow's residents have the least developed strong contacts with people who live near them. However, the good quality of the urban environment does not compensate for the negative effect from the absence of local communities.

In the case of Yaroslavl a different factor comes into play – the level of the community's involvement in corruption transactions. Usually, personal experience of involvement in corruption reduces political satisfaction by 1.3–1.4 times. For Yaroslavl this indicator exceeds most of the other regions that were included in the research.

Happiness and Trust

Preliminary research results certainly have a clear trend. Almost all of the factors analyzed which affect the growth or decline of the 'happiness index' ultimately rest on the basis of social contacts. In previous approaches to this kind of research, this group of factors may have various designations: the density of social communication, social (cultural) capital, social coherence, etc. In this case, in terms of analytical problems, the most appropriate concept is the concept of 'trust'.

In social studies there are three types of trust:

Firstly, personal trust. This is a trust in a particular person or a group of people (usually familiar people);

Secondly, generalized trust. This is not trust in particular individuals, but a trust in a 'generalized other', a stranger that one could potentially meet in a certain place or in a social situation;

Thirdly, institutional trust. This is trust in institutions such as educational (schools or universities), health care systems, public authorities, churches or media.

Nowadays, the level of generalized trust in Russia is very low. Three quarters of the population treat strangers with suspicion and distrust. The level of generalized trust is the lowest in large cities (with over a million dwellers) and small economically challenged settlements. The lowest rates of generalized trust are in urban villages which were built during the soviet period around city-forming projects that were closed down in the 1990s. In these places, the level of distrust of strangers is approaching 100 per cent.

In general, according to the Public Opinion Foundation, few Russians believe that most people can be trusted (16 per cent).

The level of trust in the government, which is measured by the Public Opinion Foundation[4], shows that the population of Russia trusts key political figures much more than the institute of public authorities. For example, at the moment, the State Duma trust index is 36 points and the Government of Russia trust index is 47 points. This means that the majority of the Russian population is wary of the public authorities. At the same time specific individuals in governmental positions (such as the Prime Minister and the President) are trusted by a significantly larger number of respondents, with their trust indices scoring over 50 points.

Therefore, the level of institutional and generalized trust in Russia is very low, so who do the Russians trust?

According to our data, the majority of social relations in Russia are not based on a generalized or institutional trust – but instead on personal trust. People trust their friends and acquaintances the most. Personal connections (but not social institutions) in particular, which are based on a high level of personal trust, serve as the resources that are used by people in case of emergency.

For example, should someone urgently need to raise some money, 44 per cent of Russia's population would prefer to borrow it from relatives and friends, and not to take a loan from a bank (16 per cent). Within three days, an average citizen would be able to raise about 75,000 rubles from their family and friends. People are also willing to actively help their friends should they have any difficulties: 42 per cent of Russians regularly lend money to their friends and acquaintances. These relationships are based on personal trust – people are certain that the money they loaned will be returned to them. Institutional resources such as receipts are practically not involved.

Generally, the presence of a large number of friends and acquaintances who people can trust greatly increase people's level of happiness. Those who have more friends and acquaintances that they can rely on are happier by 15–20 per cent.

The diffusion index is calculated on the basis of responses to questions about trust. The index value of less than 50 indicates the predominance of negative evaluations.

As suggested in this article, 'paradoxes of the Russian consciousness' are, in the opinion of the author, no more than a starting point for theoretical reasoning. A number of contexts associated with the correct understanding of 'the Happiness Index' have not been discussed in the article. Thus, for example, a more careful consideration of social and cultural differences between people existing in a more traditional, even archaic way of life (e.g., Dagestan) and the groups that are organic to dynamics and system requirements of large cities (Moscow and St. Petersburg) is required. The value of cultural and social capital in such different conditions, as well as ways of their production and multiplication differ significantly. Likewise, the very system of values being the background for social and economic well-being, a set of samples to build professional and personal trajectories, the degree of social control are the most important 'indices' for more or less valid conclusions.

However, the fundamental heuristic use of 'subjective' indicators of 'the Happiness Index' to interpret large volumes of sociological empirical data should be noted, as well as a number of additional opportunities that appear while using these tools. Here we mean the attempts to reach a new understanding of the social stratification of contemporary Russian society, and curious contexts associated with the processes of regionalization of the country, and even more applied aspects oriented to the forecast of economic and social behavior of large groups of people in a rapidly changing situation in Russia.

References

Johnston, D.F. 1988. 'Toward a comprehensive quality-of-life index.' *Social Indicators Research*, Vol. 20, No. 4, pp. 473–96.

Layard, Richard. 2005. *Happiness: Lessons from a New Science*. London: Penguin.

Liu, B.C. 1976. *Quality of Life Indicator in U.S. Metropolitan Areas: A Statistical Analysis*. New York: Praeger.

Russian Barometer. 2012–2017. Moscow: Russian Presidential Academy of National Economy and Public Administration (RANEPA).

Selen, J. 1985. 'Multidimensional Descriptions of Social Indicators.' *Social Indicators Research*, Vol. 17, No. 4, pp. 435–45.

8 From Public Policy Analysis to Complex Governance Networks Studies[1]

Göktuğ Morçöl

Abstract

The main aim of this paper is to answer and discuss whether policy analysis is still relevant in the age of complex governance networks. This paper also proposes an ideal typical definition of policy analysis, which is that a government can solve society's problems based on the good advice provided by expert policy analysts and can measure the impacts of its policies. This paper argues that policy analysis and policymaking processes are more complex than the ideal type suggested by policy analysis and that governance is a better term, than policy, to capture this complexity and better reflect the realities of our times. To make the case for these arguments, this article first traces the history of policy analysis then cites the observations of governance: that in today's world governments are not unified actors that can make cohesive decisions, let alone their decisions being implemented as intended, and that governmental actors do not necessarily represent the 'public interest' or the collective will of the society. This paper further argues that the primary role of governmental actors should be to enhance the capacities of governmental and non-governmental actors to self-organize in order to generate desired outcomes.

Introduction

In the following sections, I will attempt to answer the question as to if public policy analysis is still relevant in the era of complex governance

[1] This is a revised version of the paper that was written for the Workshop on Public Policymaking in a Globalized World, Istanbul, Turkey, 28–29 November 2014.

networks. In order to explain why we even need to ask this question, I will trace the evolution of public policy analysis and make the case for the conceptualization of complex governance networks.

To understand the relevance of the question, one should consider the core concepts and history of public policy analysis. Although the location and time of the beginning of public policy analysis cannot be pinpointed, it would not be inaccurate to say that the concepts and methods of public policy analysis were formulated after the Great Depression and particularly post-World War II in the United States. The deeper sentiment they represent has universal resonance. The sentiment that governments should solve social problems, in the name of 'the public', resonates well with most, if not all, human societies. The relevance of public policymaking as a discipline and practice has increased worldwide in the last few decades, as is indicated by the increasing number of Master of Public Policy programmes in the United States and other countries.[2]

Then is it even meaningful to ask the above question if public policy is still relevant where there is a worldwide spread and increased interest in it? Yes, it is a meaningful question, and I will make the case in this paper that although not all the concepts and methods of public policy analysis have been outdated, many of them should be re-thought and re-configured to understand the increasingly complex workings of governance networks.

To make this case, I will make some simplifications about public policy analysis. I will define an 'ideal type' for it. Then I will compare this ideal type of public policy analysis with the concepts and implications of the complex governance networks (CGN) conceptualization.

[2] At the time of the writing of this paper, the information at the website of the Network of Schools of Public Policy, Affairs, and Administration (NASPAA) was that there were 37 NASPAA-affiliated Master of Public Policy Programmes in the United States and five others in China, South Korea, Egypt, the United Kingdom, and New Zealand (naspaa.org). The participation by the representatives of the public policy schools and programmes in China, Russia, South Africa, Germany, India, Brazil, Indonesia, and Egypt in the Workshop on 'Public Policymaking in a Globalized World' (November 2014) is another indication that public policy studies and analysis has spread around the world (http://ipc.sabanciuniv.edu/en/event/international-workshop-on-public-policymaking-in-a-globalized-world/).

The Ideal Type of Public Policy Analysis

An ideal type is a conceptual tool Max Weber (2011) used in his sociological theory. It is a composite image of the most common characteristics of a phenomenon. In his own words,

> An ideal type is formed by the one-sided accentuation of one or more points of view and by the synthesis of a great many diffuse, discrete, more or less present and occasionally absent concrete individual phenomena, which are arranged according to those one-sidedly emphasized viewpoints into a unified analytical construct... (90).

He used the ideal type of bureaucracy to help understand the organizational phenomena of his time. His ideal type of bureaucracy so astutely captured the common characteristics those organizations that even today, over a century after its original formulation, it helps us understand most of our organizational experiences.

This leads us to then ask about the ideal type of public policy analysis. The ideal typical construction of public policy analysis can be summed up as this vision: A government can solve society's problems based on the good (rational, objective, scientific) advice provided by expert policy analysts and measure the impacts of its policies. DeLeon (1997) finds the intellectual roots of this vision in the utilitarian philosophical tradition, positivism, and liberal rationalism (45–65). Simon (2007) cites classical liberalism as the intellectual roots of public policy analysis (7). This ideal typical vision for policy analysis includes a series of explicit and implicit assumptions/conceptualizations. Each assumption has some theoretical roots and has been critiqued by others, as I note briefly below.

1. The first of these assumptions is that *governments should and can solve social problems*, such as the problem of ensuring more equitable distribution of wealth in society (Simon 2007: 7). DeLeon (1997) traces the roots of this assumption to the 'benevolent government' notion of 'liberal rationalism' (57).
2. The second assumption is that a '*government' is a unified rational actor that can make cohesive decisions and take actions* (Simon 2007: 7). This assumption has been challenged by rational choice

theorists, who contend that actually governments are not unified rational actors, but they are composed of self-seeking individual actors (Mueller 1997).

3. It is also assumed that this *unified actor represents the 'public interest'* and/or the collective will of the society and defends it against private interests. This was one of the founding assumptions of 'public administration' as a distinct area of study in the beginning of the 20th century in the US; public administrators were conceived to be selfless and benevolent defenders of public interest, against private interests. This categorical definition of public interest has been critiqued by rational choice theorists (Mueller 1997) and postmodern theorists (Miller and Fox 2007).
4. Another assumption is that *neutral policy analysts who work on behalf of the 'government' and represent the public interest can generate 'good policy advice'* (Radin 2013). In other words, a 'good government' can solve these problems using 'good policy advice' (Simon 2007: 8).
5. It is also assumed that the *government's collective (unified) decisions can be implemented, as intended.* The implicit assumption is that there is a *linear and knowable causal link between governmental actions and their 'outcomes'*. Scholars like Pressman and Wildavsky (1984) demonstrated that actually there were major gaps between policy intentions and implementations and the causal links between the two were not linear.
6. If the link between policy intention and implementation is assumed to be linear, then it should be possible to determine objectively whether the government's actions reached their intended goals. *Once policies are implemented, neutral analysts can trace, identify, and measure their impacts.* This is a foundational assumption of policy/programme evaluation in its most classical form (Rossi, Lipsey and Freeman 2004). Alternatives to this classical form have been offered (for a comprehensive typology of alternative approaches, see Vedung 1997).

To sum up, in the ideal type definition of public policy analysis, policy analysts, on behalf of a benevolent government, identify the problems of a society, find objective solutions to them, implement the solutions, and then verify that policy goals have been reached.

This ideal typical definition has been critiqued by many scholars, from various theoretical perspectives, for over about half a century, some of which I noted above. In more general terms, critical theorists, postmodernists, implementation theorists, and public choice theorists all questioned one or a few of these assumptions. I will only briefly mention these critiques in this paper.

My main focus will be to make the case that the complex governance networks conceptualization better represents the actual workings of 'policy advice' today and that therefore the assumptions of the above ideal type should be reconsidered and re-conceptualized. This framework does not mean that all the elements of the ideal type should be abandoned; rather they should be adapted so that we can better understand complex governance processes. Later in this paper, I discuss a new set of concepts and methodological tools that should be used.

A Brief History of Public Policy Analysis

To better understand the above-stated assumptions of the ideal type, one should go back to the beginnings of public policy analysis. American political scientist Harold Laswell's conceptualization of the 'policy sciences of democracy' can be considered as the 'beginning' of what is known today as 'public policy analysis' (1951). Lasswell's conceptualization came after and built on centuries of developments in the use of what Dunn (2012) calls 'policy relevant knowledge' (5). In that sense, Lasswell's conceptualization was not a true beginning, but it was the first coherent articulations of the key concepts of the ideal typical policy analysis. Dunn points out that policy analysis is actually as old as human civilization, and it evolved to find its modern expression in the second half of the 20th century (32–42). Dunn specifically points to Lasswell's works as the sources of the early articulation of this modern expression.

According to Dunn (2012), even the earliest agricultural human societies, he notes, had 'symbol specialists', who acquired 'valid' and 'relevant' knowledge and gave advice for action to the rulers of their times about what would be the appropriate planting season and when and whether declaring war against the next tribe would be beneficial.

In many of these early practices, policy-relevant knowledge was based on mysticism and occult, which by today's standards would not be considered valid. Nevertheless, the advice by these symbols specialists was policy relevant and actionable by the rulers. The policy-relevant knowledge of symbol specialists was codified in the more advanced societies. Dunn cites the Code of Hammurabi in the 18th century BC and works by Aristotle, Confucius, and Kautilya in the 4th and 5th centuries BC as primary examples of this codified knowledge.

More systematic and more scientific policy-relevant knowledge was generated beginning in the 19th century (Dunn 2012: 35–36). The population censuses in the US and England and the surveys conducted on the social problems in various countries in Europe in this century were the first examples of empirically based (hence observationally valid) examples of policy-relevant knowledge production. During the first half of the 20th century, particularly after the First World War and during the Great Depression, the US federal government employed social scientists to generate policy-relevant knowledge. Lasswell's formulation of 'policy sciences of democracy' (Lasswell 1971) emerged from this background of systematic applications of scientific/empirical knowledge in solving society's problems. He wrote: 'policy sciences of democracy... is directed toward knowledge needed to improve the practice of democracy' (15).

What are the most valid and relevant methods that can be applied in policy sciences? To answer this question, Lasswell (1971) proposed a dual framework: information *about* policy processes and information *in* policy processes. There should be a group of studies *about* how actually policies are made. Typically political scientists who study policy processes produce this kind of knowledge. They study, for example, institutional structures in which policies are made. Later, this group of studies was called 'public policy studies', which is conducted by scholars whose primary professional organization is Policy Studies Organization (http://www.ipsonet.org/).

The studies *in* policymaking (also known as, analysis for policymaking, or analysis for policy advice) are conducted by policy analysts who produce knowledge to give advice to policymakers (elected politicians, presidents, parliamentarians, etc.), based on their applications of available methods of inquiry (e.g., quasi-experimental designs, regression models). Studies in policymaking involve two kinds of activities: *policy analysis and planning* (prospective analysis) and *policy and programme evaluation* (retrospective analysis) (Dunn 2012). Policy analysis and planning is prospective in the sense that a policy analyst conducts his/her analyses for the future. The analyst tries to predict what will happen in the future and recommends policy options and proposes plans for future policy actions to policymakers. Policy and programme evaluation is retrospective in the sense that a programme evaluator conducts analyses on past policies and programmes. The evaluator aims to determine whether the programmes were implemented properly and whether they have reached their goals and sometimes makes generalizations about multiple programmes and general policies as well. The purpose of the evaluator is to draw lessons from the past to inform the policymaking in the future.

Lasswell's original formulation of the policy sciences of democracy has been criticized by many for its incompatibility with real-life policy processes. However, its elements, which I summarized in the ideal typical reconstruction above, are still alive and they are being used at least as the reference point in the academic debates on public policy analysis. For example, the 'process model' (Dye 2013; Wheelan 2007: 10–13), or the 'stages heuristic' (Sabatier 2007), and 'rationalism' (Dye 30–33), which is an extension of Laswell's vision, is deeply ingrained in the public policy analysis thinking. It involves a 'rational' and linear process of decision making and giving policy advice. So much so that even Dunn (2012), who is keenly aware of the history of thinking in public policy and the intellectual debates, still uses it with some modifications (e.g., he uses a circular version of the policy process model instead of a linear model).

The assumption that 'government' is a unified and benevolent actor is reflected in the textbook definitions of public policy. For example, Dye (2013) defines public policy as 'whatever governments choose to do or not to do' (3). Simon (2007) offers a slight variation on the same theme by saying, 'public policy is...what government ought or ought not do, and does or does not do' (1). In both definitions, there is an actor (government) and action. It is implied that this action is or should be goal-oriented.

The conceptualizations of public policy and policy analysis have changed over time. The ideal typical model has been subjected to many critiques and alternative approaches have been offered. Many of these alternative approaches were based on the disappointments with and series of grievances the 'policy sciences of democracy'. The critics argued that policy sciences had not delivered what it had promised, which was solving society's problems through rational means.

Critical theorists like Fischer (1990, 1995, 2003, 2009) contend that the ideal type policy analysis actually masks the power relations in societies. So constructed, policy analysis helps reproduce the existing hierarchies and inequitable distribution of resources. Fischer particularly critiqued the distorting role of 'technocracy' in policy analysis processes and called for more participatory forms of policy analysis, planning, and policymaking. Interpretivists, such as Yanow (1996), and discourse theorists, such as Hajer (1995), contributed to the critical theory perspective by demonstrating that policies are interpretive tools and that their discursive contexts should be understood.

Rational choice theorists critique the ideal type from a different angle. These critiques took on different forms, such as the public choice school, policycentism, and the institutional rational choice (as examples, see Friedman 1995; McGinnis 1999; Mueller 1997; and Ostrom 1990). Even though all these theoretical perspectives have unique propositions, they share common assumptions. Rational choice theorists do not view 'government' as a unified actor that can make cohesive decisions and take actions. Instead, a government is composed of multiple 'self-seeking' actors (public choice). Thus the ideal typical assumption that 'the government' represents the 'public interest' and/or the collective will of the society becomes questionable and the distinction between the 'public' and 'private' realms is blurred.[3] This blurring of the realms is a key observation that is made by governance scholars as well (e.g. Kettl 2002; Salamon 2002). Rational choice theorists problematize the nature of collective

[3] Wheelan (2007) makes a subtle distinction between the public and private decisions in terms of the binding nature of the former and public decision are carried out by institutions (pp. 6–7).

actions and underscore the complexity of governance processes (Feiock 2013; Ostrom 1990).

Radin's (2013) history of the policy analysis theory and practice helps us better understand the criticisms of the ideal typical policy analysis and the evolution of policy analysis as a field of study. She summarizes its evolution in three stages: the 1960s, 1990s, and 2000s. In the 1960s, the US federal government established policy analysis units first in a select group of agencies (the Department of Defense and Education) and then a few others. Over time, the federal government's model of policy analysis units was replicated in the state governments in the US.

The practice of policy analysis spread to other countries in the following decades. According to Radin this globalization of policy analysis has been part of the globalization of the world economy. The globalization affected the 'boundaries' of the systems policy analysts considered as their frameworks. Initially the 'targets' of policies and programmes could be defined clearly; the boundaries of the geographic areas and social groups policies are intended to affect could be delineated within national borders. Radin notes that over time, the boundaries between 'domestic' and 'international' issues and those between the 'private' and 'public' realms became blurred.

These blurring trends became quite clear in the 1990s, as the policy 'think tanks' proliferated,[4] and as such the centres that produced policy relevant information and policy advice became diverse. More and more interest groups formed their policy think tanks to influence policymaking processes. Thus the notion that policy advice should be 'objective' gave way to the understanding that policy advice could and should be ideological, interest-driven, and even partisan.

Radin (2013) points out that the world of policy analysis and public decision making has become more complex in the early 21st century. She notes that in this century public decision making involves networks and collaborations, intergovernmental relations, relations with nongovernmental actors, and horizontal and vertical

[4] There were more than 1600 think tanks in the US in the early 1990s (Hellebust 1996).

relationships among all policy actors. She observes that we live in a 'pluralistic and fragmented policy world that operates in a society characterized by diversity' (x). Radin also notes that it has become more difficult to differentiate between 'analysis' and 'politics'. As a result of these developments, there are stronger disagreements among scholars about the nature of the field of policy analysis/policy studies today than in the previous century.

Public Policy and Complex Governance Networks

Radin's (2013) observations on the developments in the field of public policy analysis have similarities with those of some other social theorists and scholars of public policy/administration processes. Social theorists Castells (2000) and Jessop (1990) observe that societies have become multi-centred and networked. Kooiman (1993) asserts that in today's world no governmental or private actor has the capacity to solve the increasingly complex and dynamic problems of societies. There are several public policy and administration researchers who commonly make the observation that the roles of governments in policy processes have diminished, or at least changed (Kettl 2002; Koliba, Meek and Zia 2011; Rhodes 1997; Torfing, Peters, Pierre and Sørensen 2012). In these authors' analyses, nation states are no longer capable of policymaking by themselves. As the political and policymaking processes have become multi-centred and fragmented, with the participation of public, private, and quasi-public organizations, dealing with collective action problems have become inherently complex (Feiock 2013; Feiock and Scholz 2010). In Heinelt's (2010) words, particularly 'democratic political systems have to be considered as a complex and broad web of various forms of interest articulation and intermediation as well as decision-making' (2). He proposes that we should use the concept 'governance' to better understand and describe these webs.

The governance conceptualization is not simply an observation that there are multiple actors who take parts in policy processes; it has broader and deeper implications. It has implications, for example, for what we mean by 'government', or 'the state'? Heinelt (2010) argues that in the governance conceptualization 'the concept of citizenship needs to be re-conceptualized' (2). As Rhodes (1997: 57) observes, in the 'new era of governance' what we call 'the state' is no longer a unified entity that is sovereign over a territory; it is actually composed of networks of what is traditionally considered 'governmental' actors and other societal actors.

A theoretical and practical problem is who or what controls and/or coordinates the multiple actors of collective action processes? Do, or can, governmental actors control, or coordinate, other actors? According to Kettl (2002: 161) and Agranoff (2007: 192), 'governmental actors' (not the 'government' as a unified entity) still play special roles in governance processes: They can guide, or 'steer', non-governmental actors. Lynn, Heinrich, and Hill (2000) view the roles of governmental actors as coordination and control of partially autonomous individuals or organizations (235).

All these observations and theoretical arguments underscore the multi-centred and complex nature of governance processes. Governance processes are complex, as many scholars observe (e.g., Koliba, Meek and Zia 2011; Peters 1993; Sharkansky 2002). A group of my colleagues and I have adapted the complexity theory to understanding these complex governance processes (e.g. Morçöl 2012). I called this approach 'complex governance networks', which brings together the insights, concepts, and methods of complexity theory, governance studies, and network studies and methods (e.g., social network analyses) (Morçöl 2014). A journal has been launched to publish theoretical and empirical works in these three areas and their syntheses called *Complexity, Governance & Networks* (cgnj.info).

What are the contributions of complexity theory to understanding governance networks? Complexity theorists and researchers define the concept of complexity and offer a set of conceptual and methodological tools to be used in identifying and describing the complex patterns and mechanisms of natural and social systems. Complexity researchers applied complexity concepts (such as, nonlinearity, self-organization, emergence, and coevolution) and methods (such as, agent-based simulations and system dynamic simulations) in their studies of policy systems/governance networks (e.g., Gerrits 2012; Geyer and Rihani 2010; Kiel 1994; Morçöl 2012; Rhodes, Murphy, Muir and Murray 2011; Teisman, van Buuren and Gerrits 2009). In doing so, they help us better understand the structures and dynamics of governance networks and the patterns and nature of the relationships among the actors (agents) of these networks.

A key implication of complexity theory is that natural and social phenomena should be understood as systems. The properties of these systems are emergent; they are not designed nor can they be controlled directly or centrally. Particularly in social systems, systemic properties emerge from the self-organizing actions of their actors, and more broadly the micro-macro relations and dynamics. Translated to the language of governance conceptualizations, the actions of multiple self-organizing actors together constitute governance processes; this is why no governmental or private actor alone has the capacity to solve the increasingly complex problems of societies (Kooiman 1993). In other words, 'the government' (or 'the state') cannot control or solve the problems of a society centrally.

Governmental actors can, and do make policy decisions and take 'policy actions', but the relations between these actions and 'policy outcomes' are nonlinear. There is no linear causal connection between policy actions and social outcomes. In broader terms, social processes and structures, such as 'policy outcomes' emerge from the nonlinear interactions of self-conscious and self-organizing actors. This is why policy outcomes are not easily predictable or controllable (Salzano 2008). Complexity theorists do not suggest that the social world in general, and governance processes in particular, are random or entirely unknowable, however. They identified a few mechanisms of emergence in social systems (e.g. Axelrod 1997; Holland 1995, 1998).

A key implication of the emergent nature of policy outcomes is that policy actions by governmental actors can be viewed as 'policy interventions' into governance systems/networks. These interventions can 'nudge' systems toward 'socially desirable states' (Zia et al. 2014). In Stewart and Ayres's (2001) view, public policies are interventions into self-organizing social systems; as such, the aim of a policy intervention should not be to reach a pre-determined goal, but to enable the 'target system to enhance…its capacity for self-steering' (87). This conceptualization has important implications for our understanding of public policies and policy/programme evaluations. It means first that the success of a policy intervention should be determined in terms of how much it enhances the self-organizing capability of a social system.

Complexity researchers further posit that governance networks do not self-organize in isolation; they coevolve with natural systems. Ehrlich and Raven (1964) coined the term coevolution and Kauffman (1993, 1995) refined the theory of the coevolution of biological systems. Kauffman's observation is that organisms, which are self-organizing systems, adapt to their environments to survive, their environments (other species) adapt to their adaptive behaviours (i.e., all these systems coevolve). Gerrits (2008) and Zia and his colleagues (Zia 2013; Zia et al. 2014) demonstrated that social (policy/governance) systems coevolve with natural systems and these co-evolutionary processes lead to unexpected outcomes. The applications reflect the 'socio-ecological systems' view of governance networks, and they are primarily concerned about system- (macro-) level interactions and processes.

Others investigated and conceptualized the interactions among the actors of governance networks (i.e., the micro level) and the macro structures and patterns that emerge from these interactions. The 'micro–macro problem' (the problem of how the actions of individual actors generate collective outcomes and how, in turn, the collective structures, such as social institutions, systems of rules, affect individual actions) has been well known, but some other names have also been used: the 'agency–structure problem' (Simmel's sociology), the 'transformation problem' (European sociology), or the 'collective action problem' (Coleman 1986). Complexity researchers such as Axelrod (1997) and Holland (1995, 1998) made significant contributions to our understanding of the micro-macro processes and dynamics, but many theoretical problems remain to be investigated.

There are methods of investigating complex governance processes: social network analyses (SNA) and agent-based simulations (ABS). Both can be used to study the micro–macro interactions and transformations in governance processes. SNA methods are used to investigate 'how large-scale systemic transformations emerge out of the combined preferences and purposive actions of individuals....

[They provide] conceptual and methodological tools for linking changes in microlevel choices to macrolevel structural alterations' (Knoke and Yang 2008: 6). Kapucu (2006) and Kapucu, Arslan, and Collins (2010) applied these methods have been applied at increasing rates in the studies on the complex governance networks that deal with natural disasters. Several scholars used the ABS to study the dynamics of micro–macro relationships and transformations in various kinds of complex systems (e.g., Nan and Johnston 2009; Zia, Norton, Noonan, Rodgers and DeHart-David 2006). For an overview and assessment of SNA and ABS, see Morçöl (2012: 210–43).

Conclusion

Let us return to the question I asked in the beginning of this paper: Is public policy analysis still relevant in the era of complex governance networks? In other words, is 'good policy advice' still relevant (Radin 2013)? My short answers are 'yes' and 'yes', but policy analysis and good policy advice should be re-conceptualized. Although not all the concepts and methods of public policy analysis have been outdated, many should be re-thought and re-configured to understand the increasingly complex workings of governance networks. And newer analytical tools, like social network analyses and agent-based simulations, should be used.

A few observations that I made earlier in the paper need to be repeated here. Governments are not unified actors that can make cohesive decisions, let alone their decisions being implemented as intended. They do not necessarily represent the 'public interest' or the collective will of the society. Policy analysis and policymaking processes are more complex than the ideal type of policy analysis suggests. Governance is a better term than policy in capturing this complexity and better reflects the realities of our times. Then the nature of complex (polycentric, fragmented) governance processes and the roles of governmental actors in them should be re-conceptualized.

In this polycentric governance processes, the primary role of governmental actors would be to enhance the capacities of governmental and non-governmental actors to self-organize to generate desired outcomes, to paraphrase Stewart and Ayres (2001).

The success (effectiveness) of a governance network is an important problem that scholars and practitioners have to deal with. This can be judged on the basis of how much this self-organizing capacity of the governance system has been enhanced. Also we cannot simply say that governance processes are complex and therefore the outcomes of policies (intentions of governmental actors) are unpredictable. Governmental actors are still expected to help improve social conditions (not necessarily 'solve social problems'). The effectiveness of a governance system can be measured in terms of the compatibility of 'outcomes' with socially desired states without attributing linear casual connections between policies and outcomes.

References

Agranoff, R. 2007. *Managing within Networks: Adding Value to Public Organizations*. Washington, DC: Georgetown University Press.

Axelrod, R. 1997. *The Complexity of Cooperation: Agent-based Models of Competition and Collaboration*. Princeton: Princeton University Press.

Castells, M. 2000. *The Rise of the Network Society*. Oxford: Blackwell.

Coleman, J.S. 1986. 'Social theory, social research, and a theory of action.' *The American Journal of Sociology*, 91(6), pp. 1309–335.

DeLeon, P. 1997. *Democracy and the Policy Sciences*. Albany: State University of New York Press.

Dunn, W.N. 2012. *Public Policy Analysis* (5th Ed.). Boston: Pearson.

Dye, T.R. 2013. *Understanding Public Policy* (14th Ed.). Boston: Pearson.

Ehrlich, P.R. and P.H. Raven. 1964. 'Butterflies and plants: A study in coevolution.' *Evolution*, 18, pp. 586–608.

Feiock, R.C. 2013. 'The institutional collective action framework.' *Policy Studies Journal*, 41(3), 397–425.

———., and J.T. Scholz. (eds.). 2010. *Self-organizing Federalism: Collaborative Mechanisms to Mitigate Institutional Collective Action*. Cambridge: Cambridge University Press.

Fischer, F. 1990. *Technocracy and the Politics of Expertise*. Newbury Park: Sage.

———. 1995. *Evaluating Public Policy*. Chicago: Nelson-Hall Publishers.

———. 2003. *Reframing Public Policy: Discursive Politics and Deliberative Practices*. Oxford: Oxford University Press.

———. 2009. *Democracy & Expertise: Reorienting Policy Inquiry*. Oxford: Oxford University Press.

Friedman, J. (ed.). 1996. *The Rational Choice Controversy: Economic Models Of Politics Reconsidered*. New Haven: Yale University Press.

Gerrits, L. 2008. *The Gentle Art of Coevolution: A Complexity Theory Perspective on Decision Making Over Estuaries in Germany, Belgium and The Netherlands* (PhD Dissertation, Erasmus University Rotterdam). Retrieved from http://publishing.eur.nl/ir/repub/asset/11152.

———. 2012. *Punching Clouds: An Introduction to the Complexity of Public Decision-Making*. Litchfield Park, AZ: Emergent Publications.

Geyer, R., and S. Rihani. 2010. *Complexity and Public Policy: A New Approach to 21st Century Politics, Policy and Society*. London: Routledge.

Hajer, M. 1995. *The Politics of Environmental Discourse: Ecological Modernization and the Policy Process*. New York: Clarendon Press.

Heinelt, H. 2010. *Governing Modern Societies: Towards Participatory Governance*. New York: Routledge.

Hellebust, L. (ed.). 1996. *Think Tank Directory: A Guide to Nonprofit Public Policy Research Organizations*. Topeka, KS: Government Research Service.

Holland, J.H. 1995. *Hidden Order: How Adaptation Builds Complexity*. New York: Basic Books.

———. 1998. *Emergence: From Chaos to Order*. New York: Basic Books.

Jessop, B. 1990. *State Theory: Putting the Capitalist State in its Place*. State College: Pennsylvania State University Press.

Kapucu, N. 2006. 'Interagency communication networks during emergencies: Boundary spanners in multiagency coordination.' *American Review of Public Administration*, 26(2), pp. 207–25.

———. T. Arslan and M.L. Collins. 2010. 'Examining intergovernmental and interorganizational response to catastrophic disasters: Toward a network-centered approach.' *Administration & Society*, 42(2), pp. 222–47.

Kauffman, S. 1993. *The Origins of Order: Self-Organization and Selection in Evolution*. New York: Oxford University Press.

———. 1995. *At Home in the Universe: The Search for Laws of Self-Organization and Complexity*. New York: Oxford University Press.

Kettl, D.F. 2002. *The Transformation of Governance: Public Administration for Twenty-First Century America*. Baltimore: Johns Hopkins University Press.

Kiel, L.D. 1994. *Managing Chaos and Complexity in Government: A New Paradigm for Managing Change, Innovation, and Organizational Renewal*. San Francisco: Jossey-Bass.

Koliba, C., J.W. Meek and A. Zia. 2011. *Governance Networks in Public Administration and Policy*. Boca Raton: CRC Press.

Kooiman, J. 1993. 'Social-political governance: Introduction.' In *Modern Governance: New Government–Society Interactions*. J. Kooiman (ed.). London: Sage. pp. 1–6.

Knoke, D., and S. Yang. 2008. *Social Network Analysis* (2nd Ed.). Los Angeles: Sage.

Lasswell, H.D. 1951. 'The policy orientation.' In *The Policy Sciences: Recent Development in Scope and Method.* D. Lerner & H. Lasswell (eds.). Stanford: Stanford University Press. pp. 1–17.

———. 1971. *A Preview of Policy Sciences*. New York: American Elsevier.

Lynn, L. E., C.J. Heinrich and C.J. Hill. 2000. 'Studying governance and public management: Challenges and prospects.' *Journal of Public Administration Research and Theory*, 10, pp. 233–61.

McGinnis, M.D. (ed.). 1999. *Polycentricity and Local Public Economies: Readings from the Workshop in Political Theory and Policy Analysis*. Ann Arbor: University of Michigan Press.

Miller, H., and C.J. Fox. 2007. *Postmodern Public Administration* (Rev. Ed.). Armonk: M.E. Sharpe.

Morçöl, G. 2012. *A Complexity Theory for Public Policy*. London: Routledge.

———. 2014. 'Complexity of governance networks: An assessment of the state of the literature and proposals for future research.' *Complexity, Governance & Networks*, 1(1), pp. 5–16.

Mueller, D.C. (ed.). 1997. *Perspectives on Public Choice: A Handbook*. Cambridge: Cambridge University Press.

Nan, N., and E.W. Johnson. 2009. 'Using multi-agent simulation to explore the contribution of facilitation to GSS transition.' *Journal of the Association for Information Systems*, 10, pp. 252–277.

Ostrom, E. 1990. *Governing the Commons: The Evolution of Institutions for Collective Action*. Cambridge: Cambridge University Press.

Pressman, J.L., and A.B. Wildavsky. 1984. *Implementation: How Great Expectations in Washington Are Dashed in Oakland; Or, Why It's Amazing That Federal Programs Work At All* (3rd Ed.). Berkeley: University of California Press.

Radin, B.A. 2013. *Beyond Machiavelli: Policy Analysis Reaches Midlife* (2nd Ed.). Washington, DC: Georgetown University Press.

Rhodes, M. L., J. Murphy, J. Muir and J.A. Murray. 2011. *Public Management and Complexity Theory: Richer Decision-Making in Public Services*. London: Routledge.

Rhodes, R.A.W. 1997. *Understanding Governance: Policy Networks, Governance, Reflexivity and Accountability*. Maidenhead: Open University Press.

Rossi, P.H., M.W. Lipsey and H.E. Freeman. 2004. *Evaluation: A Systematic Approach* (7th Ed.). Thousand Oaks: Sage.

Sabatier, P.A. 2007. 'The need for better theories.' In *Theories of the Policy Process*. P. Sabatier (ed.). Cambridge: Westview Press. pp. 3–17.

Salamon, L.M. 2002. 'The new governance and the tools of public action: An introduction.' In *The Tools of Government: A Guide to New Governance*. L.M. Salamon (ed.). Oxford: Oxford University Press. pp. 1–47.

Salzano, M. 2008. 'Economic policy hints from heterogeneous agent-based simulations.' In *Complexity and Policy Analysis: Tools and Methods for Designing Robust Policies in a Complex World*. K. Richardson, L. Dennard & G. Morçöl (eds.). Goodyear: ISCE Publishing. pp. 167–96.

Sharkansky, I. 2002. *Politics and Policymaking: In Search of Simplicity*. London: Lynne Rienner Publishers.

Simon, A.A. 2007. *Public Policy: Preferences and Outcomes*. New York: Pearson/Longman.

Stewart, J., and R. Ayres. 2001. 'Systems theory and policy practice: An exploration.' *Policy Sciences*, 34(1), 79–94.

Teisman, G.R., A. van Buuren and L. Gerrits. (eds.). 2009. *Managing Complex Governance Systems: Dynamics, Self-organization and Coevolution in Public Investments*. London: Routledge.

Torfing, J., G.B. Peters, J. Pierre and E. Sørensen. 2012. *Interactive Governance: Advancing the Paradigm*. Oxford: Oxford University Press.

Vedung, E. 1997. *Public Policy and Program Evaluation*. New Brunswick: Transaction Publishers.

Weber, M. 2011. *Methodology of the social sciences* (reprint of the 1949 original translation by Edward A. Shils & Henry A. Finch). New Brunswick: Transaction Publishers.

Wheelan, C. 2007. *Introduction to Public Policy*. New York: W.W. Norton.

Yanow, D. 1996. *How Does a Policy Mean?* Washington, DC: Georgetown University Press.

Zia, A. 2013. *Post-Kyoto Climate Governance: Confronting the Politics of Scale, Ideology and Knowledge*. London: Routledge.

———., S. Kauffman, C. Koliba, B. Beckage, G. Vattay and A. Bomblies. 2014. 'From the habit of control to institutional enablement: Re-envisioning the governance of social-ecological systems from the perspective of complexity sciences.' *Complexity, Governance & Networks*, 1(1), 79–88.

———., B.G. Norton, D.S. Noonan, M.O. Rodgers and David L. DeHart. 2006. 'A quasi-experimental evaluation of high-emitter non-compliance and its impact on vehicular tailpipe emissions in Atlanta, 1997–2001.' *Transportation Research Part D*, 11, 77–96.

9 International Mechanisms of Human Capital Development and Knowledge Creation
The Role of Educational Institutions

Alexey Verbetsky

Abstract

The paper looks at the existing and potential instruments of knowledge and innovation transfer, exchange and creation that could be effectively utilized by universities and schools in order to build up human capital. In the global knowledge-based economy, the quality of interaction between the producers, distributors and users of innovations are one of the keys to successful and sustainable development. However, there are significant communication gaps between educational institutions, advanced businesses and policymakers, which prevent the efficient transfer of innovations and impede the processes of collaborative knowledge creation.

One of the working mechanisms for efficient human capital development, which has already been successfully employed by advanced universities around the world, is long-term bilateral or multilateral international partnerships. However, they are often limited to the participating educational institutions – while leaving aside other important knowledge-creation actors such as think tanks, advanced businesses (including global consultancies), and international development organizations which possess unique policy experience and knowledge related to implementation of large-scale developmental projects. It could be argued that there is a significant and urgent need for a comprehensive, systemic approach towards designing and utilizing multi-actor, consortium-based international partnerships between policy institutions, universities and businesses; such knowledge networks will enhance sustainable, equitable and democratic development.

External Trends in Innovation Management

The context of the present paper can be outlined through the analysis of several key factors – all of them directly related to **innovation management**. Firstly, the current stage of the global economy has often been called 'knowledge-based', implying the increasing importance of the contribution of human capital and associated productivity gains to global gross domestic product (GDP). While in industrial economies innovations were associated with investments in research and development (R&D), in the knowledge-based economy, according to the Organisation for Economic Co-operation and Development's (OECD) 2010 Innovation Strategy, innovations are based on investment in knowledge-based capital (software, data and skills).

The second trend deals with the growing complexity of policy issues and the global nature of challenges that are faced by decision-makers. These challenges are associated, for instance, with increasing international integration (political, economic, social and technological) and international competition, strong demographic and migration trends. These factors should be taken into the account in strategic decision-making and the search for new sources of economic growth in times of excessive fiscal burdens – partly due to the governmental measures taken during the 2008–09 global economic crisis and turbulent financial markets. As a result, in order to make quality public policy decisions, it is now necessary to build up not only conventional sets of skills and competencies (such as those related to budgeting, finance, human resource management, or legislative norms) but also new ones (e.g., those related to cross-sector communications, resource-sharing and IT-management). Further, it is also essential to collect and process much larger amounts of unstructured data.

Another global trend is related to the gradual but irreversible digitalization of various aspects of organizational business processes – from information search and storage (including, for example, crowdsourcing of ideas through Internet platforms such as Kickstarter) to innovative means of communication with stakeholder groups – public institution portals with feedback collection, engagement of local community groups through social networks, electronic voting, etc. The continuously increasing availability and spread of Internet access reduces administrative/bureaucratic barriers and leads to greater involvement of various stakeholders in the public policymaking process. In the education sector, straightforward examples of digitalization trends include development of e-learning platforms for universities and certified online courses available globally, 24/7. In fact, there are many more fundamental changes ahead (see, for example, Taleb's [2015] discussion on the 'Uberization of Education') that are, however, outside of the scope of the present paper.

Yet another important factor has been the increasing interdependence across organizations, industries and economies, leading to the notion of 'coopetition' – which is highly relevant not only for business management but also for the public policy agenda. In various business sectors (for example, telecoms and transportation), resource-sharing mechanisms have been successfully utilized; supporting/secondary business processes are sub-contracted or outsourced – even to direct competitors (e.g., the case of Apple and Samsung); and public-private partnerships (PPPs) become widespread both in developed and developing economies. The reason is again related to the need to possess an increasingly vast amount of knowledge, skills and competences in order to achieve sustainable success – which is often impossible for a single organization or business entity.

It could be seen that all these trends are especially relevant for knowledge-intensive projects, firms and industries. It has been demonstrated by policy researchers that in the knowledge-based economies, participants search for linkages to promote cross-organizational interactive learning (OECD 2013). In other words, in the knowledge-based world it is essential to share not only tangible resources (e.g., infrastructure) but also intangible ones (e.g., experience).

These factors highlight the importance of the quality of interactions between the producers, distributors, and consumers of innovations and knowledge that feed the development of human capital across industries and economies. The implications for public policy education could best be summarized by a statement from the Harvard Kennedy School:

Today's problems require novel approaches and non-traditional alliances that bring together leaders from government, civil society and business.

This paper focuses on cross-sector and international interactions related to public policy and specifically looks at the role of educational institutions in initiating, facilitating and promoting the mechanisms of efficient knowledge sharing – with specific reference to the Russian experience.

The Role of Networks in Public Policy: Recent Literature

Cross-organization, cross-industry and cross-regional interactions among multiple and diverse agents (stakeholders) who are not parts of the same organization are performed through networks. Researchers in the area of public policy (e.g., Smith 2000) differentiate between *policy networks* (informal, exclusive, long-term, non-transparent) and *advocacy coalitions* (inclusive, issue-based). The Advocacy Coalition Framework (Sabatier and Jenkins-Smith 1993) has proven to be an extremely useful model to understand and explain policies that involve multiple actors – government, research institutions and the media (Johns 2003).

Main contemporary trends of network usage in governance and public policymaking are summarized in Gül (2015). He explains, for example, the key drivers for knowledge-oriented institutional collaboration and increased use of policy networks that include diverse groups of stakeholders. The focus of research work by Castells (2000) is on societies becoming multi-centred and networked; this is explained by the rise of increasingly complex and dynamic problems that cannot be solved by either governmental or private actors. Radin (2013) also points out that in the 21st century, public decision-making involves networks and collaboration.

The specifics of networks composed of autonomous but interdependent actors and their role in the governance process is also discussed in Cepiku (2013). However, he states that the list of important actors within governance networks usually includes representatives from business, civil society, government and international organizations – while leaving out universities and educational organizations. At the same time, a number of works (e.g., Orhan 2015) stress and explain the crucial role for knowledge and expertise in policy analysis that are accumulated in public policy schools.

Kotilainen (2007) proposes the circulation of an innovation policy framework to explain the roles of various stakeholders in implementing public-private partnerships (in which, for example, public organizations set the policy agenda).

Figure 9.1: An innovation policy framework

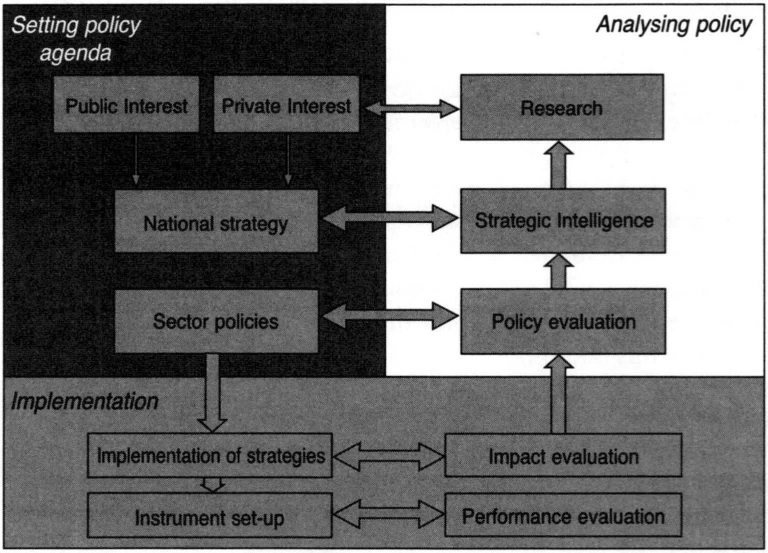

Source: Public-private partnership in innovation policy, Kotilainen 2007.

A European Research Area (2015) report describes how collaborative networks can contribute to the achievement of a broad range of objectives related to research and innovation. It analyses both vertical (cross-level) and horizontal (cross-area) types of policy coordination. In fact, *optimal transnational co-operation and competition* is one of five ERA (European Research Area) priorities (European Commission 2012). There are other examples of successful innovation networks with stakeholders from various sectors – in the UK, these are Knowledge Transfer Partnerships (KTP) funded by the Economic and Social Research Council and Knowledge Transfer Network (currently, there are over 1,000 partnerships). Each KTP is aimed at stimulating and enhancing business-relevant research and involves a company and a university/research organization; the UK government contributes over 50 per cent of the cost of each project.

It could be argued that effective networking is, in fact, one of the critical factors for success in public policy: to enrich the quality of decision-making, inputs (such as expert opinions, skills, frameworks, and techniques) from a number of expert areas are used, as policy analysts and policy advisers work in teams with economists, psychologists and lawyers. This has important implications for public policy education: in order to prepare successful leaders, public policy schools should engage both practitioners and techniques from areas such as information management, sociology, law and economics, and regional and environmental studies.

The Russian Education System as Potential Driver for Human Capital Development

In Russia, there has historically been a very serious institutional gap between research institutions (such as the Academy of Science, which was responsible for all types of research) and educational institutions (responsible for teaching). This gap was especially relevant for the public policy area – policy research activities were separated from the training and development programmes designed for public servants.

In recent years, the Russian government has implemented numerous polices aimed at reducing this gap: for example, financial support to the top universities is now contingent on the quality and practical applicability of their academic and policy research. Several long-term state-funded programmes were launched which stimulated cross-sector collaboration. In 2012, substantial resources were allocated for R&D projects implemented jointly by universities and large enterprises – 'producers' and 'consumers' of innovation. However, it could be argued that the Russian education sector could have a much more profound role as a source for innovation-driven growth by accumulating and re-directing knowledge and expertise within multiple stakeholder networks.

Despite the substantial progress that was driven by the changes in state policies, the lack of inter-sectoral cooperation is still a relevant issue. Among the top factors that prevent innovation development in Russia, businesses usually name the under-developed legal environment (and in particular protection of intellectual property rights), lack of infrastructure (both tangible and virtual), and serious communication gaps between science, education and industry.

The latter factor results in an *inadequately educated workforce* – this problem is often placed among the top factors in surveys which assess the climate for doing business in Russia. In other words, the sets of competencies acquired by most graduates in Russia are insufficient to be successful at work, either in business or in public organizations (see, for example, HeadHunter Group 2015). One of the global phenomena illustrating this gap is the spread of corporate universities – large businesses prefer to invest their own resources in human capital development. In the case of Russia there are, of course, a number of examples of successful cooperation between universities/colleges, public officials and business communities. However, the problem of inefficiency in communications among these stakeholders is of a systemic and chronic nature. In order to resolve this problem, detailed characteristics of 'demand' for human capital should be clearly formulated to the 'suppliers'; this communication should be continuous and involve active participation of the 'consumers' of human capital in the process of its 'production'.

The diagram from the Global Competitiveness Report (2015) below summarizes the strategic position of Russia compared to its neighbours. The overall stage of development at this point is considered as transitional from efficiency-driven to innovation-driven. It could be seen that one of the lowest scores has been assigned on the innovation scale; one of the innovation parameters used in this report that is especially relevant for the present paper is university-industry collaboration in R&D – which only got 3.6 out of 7.

The Russian education system has been seriously transforming itself over the past two decades, with recent trends focused on

Figure 9.2: Global Competitiveness Index: Stage of Development

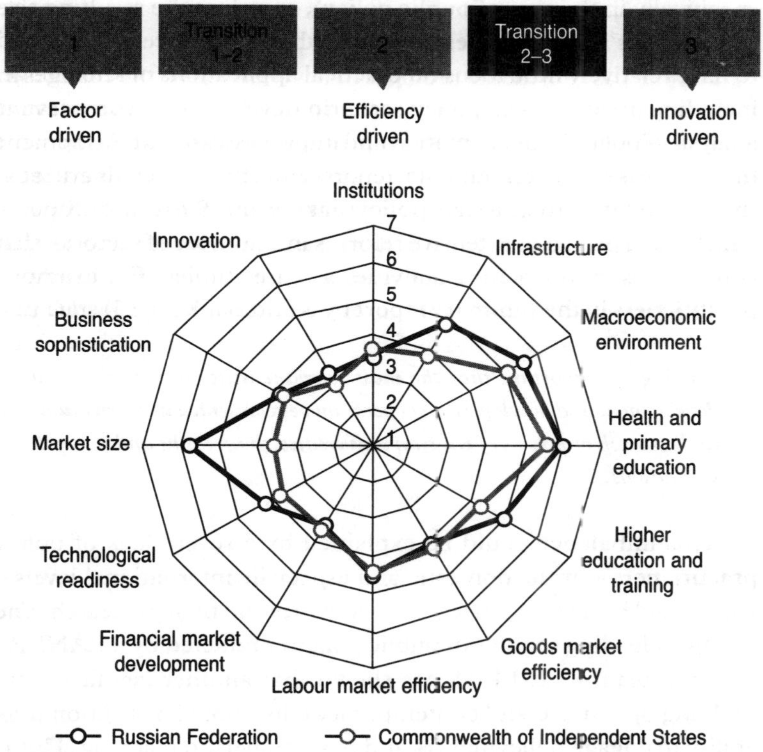

Source: Global Competitiveness Report (2015)
http://www3.weforum.org/docs/WEF_GlobalCompetitivenessReport_2014-15.pdf

increasing the transparency (e.g., funding for higher education is based on the results of unified state examinations) and the quality of education (measured across the set of internationally recognized, measurable and transparent indicators). A number of Russian high schools and universities are already successfully integrated into global academic life, and institutional partnerships and alliances with foreign schools and universities take various forms – from exchange visits to double-degree programmes – and enrich both teaching and research activities by bringing cross-regional and cross-cultural perspectives and sharing access to experienced and talented lecturers.

However, the teaching curricula of Russian schools (and specifically in the area of public policy), as well as the resulting sets of graduates' competencies, are still rather imbalanced. They tend to have relatively little focus on practical applications of knowledge, including areas such as policy scenario development, comparative analysis of policy implementation and impact assessment. At the same time, there is a lot of unique data, reports and other materials available that are related to Russian policymaking in 1990s and 2000s – which was a period of extensive reforms in a number of sectors – that could be used in teaching activities as case studies. For example, practitioners in the summary report by World Bank (2013) state that

> *it is highly important that the most relevant issues of international development and development cooperation be represented in curriculums and research programs of Russian universities, think tanks and research institutions.*

This imbalance could be explained by a severe lack of policy practitioners – at the domestic and especially international levels – who would be involved in teaching activities and policy research. The review of leading schools of public policy conducted by a RANEPA research team in 2014–15 has shown that another key factor for building up a successful contemporary educational institution is its ability to engage policymakers and practitioners in teaching. This is one of the major focal points within the public policy programmes at the School of International and Public Affairs (SIPA, Columbia University), the Maxwell School (Syracuse University), the Kennedy School (Harvard University), and the Lee Kuan Yew School (National University of Singapore). In Russia, the current practices in this area are limited to fragmented master-classes where policymakers are only involved in teaching and interacting with students on an occasional basis.

Another type of stakeholder whose input could increase the efficiency of such interactions are acting public officials (civil servants), who also need to be engaged in policy networking – e.g., explaining how decision-making works in practice, offering opportunities for student internships, clarifying government priorities, etc. At present, however, they are most often invited to universities, just to, formally address a panel at a conference. In other words, there is not yet a system where former policymakers could form their research teams at a university or a think tank, lead policy research projects and pass their expertise on to the next generation of policymakers.

Conclusion

The present paper aims at initiating a discussion of network effects that could lead to the increased efficiency of human capital development. One of the most effective – and already rather popular – types of such networks that stimulate the development of intellectual capital is cooperation among universities from various regions. The exchange of students, joint research activities by international teams, visits of teaching and administrative staff and double-degree programmes are examples of such networking. In fact, a high degree of internationalization and increasing student and faculty mobility are among the key success factors for schools around the globe.

However, networking should not be limited to cooperation and resource-sharing activities between educational institutions solely. To achieve maximum impact, it is essential to develop various systems of attracting other valuable sources of substantial knowledge and experience – such as acting public officials and civil servants, analysts from think tanks, representatives of the business community, and policy reform practitioners (including, for example, experts from the World Bank, IMF, USAID and other international development organizations). Universities could be viewed as the most convenient, independent and non-partisan venues for such cooperation among stakeholders with different priorities, but one clear common interest is the achievement of a higher quality of public policy decisions.

It could be argued that the resulting synergy between the academic, practical and public administration competencies – if concentrated within educational institutions – could serve as an effective source of high-quality human capital, able to adapt to complex geopolitical, socio-economic and environmental changes and stimulate innovative responses to global challenges. Universities could play a central role in such multiple-stakeholder networks.

References

Bartenev, Vladimir and Elena Glazunova (eds.). 2013. *International Development Cooperation. Set of Lectures.* Moscow: World Bank.

Castells, M. 2000. *The Rise of the Network Society.* Oxford, UK: Blackwell.

Cepiku, D. 2013. 'Unravelling the Concept of Public Governance: A Literature Review of Different Traditions.' In L. Gnan, A. Hinna and F. Monteduro (eds.). *Conceptualizing and Researching Governance in Public and Non-Profit Organizations*, Volume 1, 3–32, Emerald: Bingley, UK.

ERAWATCH. 2015. 'Platform on Research and Innovation Policies and Systems.' http://erawatch.jrc.ec.europa.eu/erawatch/opencms/information/reports/countries/eu/report_0031

Global Competitiveness Report. 2015. 'World Economic Forum', (full data edition). http://www3.weforum.org/docs/WEF_GlobalCompetitivenessReport_2014-15.pdf

Gül, Hüseyin. 2015. 'Global Governance and Public Policymaking: Trends and Values', presented at the conference Public Policymaking in a Globalized World, September 2014.

HeadHunter Group. 2015. expert forum, recruitment database and portal. www.hh.ru

Johns, P. 2003. 'Is there life after policy streams, advocacy coalitions, and punctuations: Using evolutionary theory to explain policy change?' *Policy Studies Journal*, 31(4), pp. 481–98.

Kotilainen, Heikki. 2007. *Public-Private Partnership in Innovation Policy.* S&T Balance, Finland.

OECD. 2013. 'New Sources of Growth: Knowledge-Based Capital, Key Analyses and Policy Conclusions.' *Synthesis Report.* Available at http://www.oecd.org/sti/inno/knowledge-based-capital-synthesis.pdf

Orhan, Gökhan. 2015. 'Dilemmas of Democratization in the Policy Process: The Role of Experts and People Revisited.' Presented at the conference 'Public Policymaking in a Globalized World', September 2014.

Radin, B.A. 2013. *Beyond Machiavelli: Policy Analysis Reaches Midlife* (Second Edition). Washington, DC: Georgetown University Press.

Sabatier, Paul A., and Hank C. Jenkins-Smith (eds.). 1993. *Policy Change and Learning. An Advocacy Coalition Approach.* Boulder: Westview Press.

Smith A. 2000. 'Policy Networks and Advocacy Coalitions: Explaining Policy Change and Stability in UK Industrial Pollution Policy.' *Environment and Planning C: Government and Policy* 18(1), pp. 95–114.

Taleb, Nassim. 2015. 'Uberization of Education.' *The Black Swan Report*, September 2015. http://www.blackswanreport.com/blog/2015/09/an-uberized-education-is-when/

PART III

GLOBAL CASE STUDIES: INDIA, CHINA, EGYPT, SOUTH AFRICA AND RWANDA

10 Public Policy and Corruption in a Globalized World

Case Studies from South Africa and Rwanda

Pregala Pillay and Firoz Khan

Abstract

The paper attempts to describe and elaborate on the relationship between policy analysis, planning and implementation and its relationship to development and state construction in a globalized world. In this attempt, the hurdles encountered in the complex and contradictory nature of planning and implementing public policy in the development of state construction are associated with the issues of global values, policy transfer, import of legislation, and restraining aspects of treaties and so forth. It is assumed that within this context, the attempts of individual states to carry through and successfully deliver socially inclusive and empowering developmental programmes and projects hinges on understanding and negotiating social change and transformation that 'works with the grain of societies' rather than brushing against it. This means exposing and refraining from imposing external public models that more often than not treat local political dynamics as dysfunctional. Acknowledging corruption and working within the public policy and political context in which it is rooted and functions, requires an in-depth understanding of the global dynamics and realities and their role as enabler and contributor to sustained/sustainable economic growth and development. To illustrate and ground this – to make it accessible to our students and development practitioners – we propose the utilization of case studies of Rwanda and South Africa which show that specific types of governance could be compatible with strong economic performance which can be considered broadly pro-growth, pro-rural and anchored in an institutional system that centralizes and distributes economic rents (with a view to the long term).

Introduction

State construction and sustainable development at all levels depend on a number of non-negotiable realities. These are rooted in historical development, developmental priorities, and the planning and implementation of public social policies shaped by the existing political, ideological, and economic circumstances of a particular country.

Given the dominance of the neoliberal paradigm in the context of globalization, successful delivery of socially-inclusive and empowering developmental programmes and projects hinges on understanding and negotiating social change and transformation processes that work according to the principle of 'going with the grain' of particular societies (as opposed to going against the grain; versus brushing against it). In this sense, 'indigenisation' of social development absorbs the lessons of history and learns from the successes and failures present in external public models, thus gaining invaluable understanding of global dynamics and realities.

Given existing international realities, and from Africa in particular, the acknowledgement of indigenization and its intersection with corruption is of paramount importance. The proliferation of international bodies, committees, commissions, and other new and fledgling research institutes and institutions, reveals the vast extent of the corruption scourge and hints at its dire consequences for communities, regions, countries and (even) continents.

This paper is framed within this policy framework and social context, utilizing the case studies of South Africa and Rwanda.

On Corruption, Policy and Development

Research related to the corruption of individuals, groups, syndicates, the private, and/or the public sector cannot be a purely academic exercise. Corruption is a currently existing phenomenon that will extend into the foreseeable future and that also has historical, sociological, psychological, economic, political, policy, and social roots. Its well-established foundations have resulted in manifest outcomes of a major magnitude with deeply-seated political associations and problems.

Due to the historical and current significance of corruption, a multiplicity of definitions has sprung from an assortment of academics, policy professionals, international consultants, auditor firms, and activists. These focus largely on the public sector and record volumes of the damaging economic and social consequences of this scourge.

All the valuable research, technical advice, and solutions advocating for action against corruption emanate from the Organisation for Economic Cooperation and Development (OECD), the World Bank (WB), international development agencies, as well as Transparency International (TI) (an international anti-corruption, non-governmental organization (NGO). These organizations and agencies have for many years been guiding governments and the private sector in successfully utilizing internationally-accepted methodologies. In the same way, as the well-equipped, anti-corruption agencies in the UK, Canada, New Zealand, and the Netherlands do, these guidelines provide a wide range of tangible and applicable solutions. Yet, as a result of the 2008 'financial collapse', there is now conclusive proof that corruption also occurs outside the developing world.

In her seminal work *Corruption and Government*, Rose-Ackerman relates how low rates of economic growth in under-developed countries lead to corruption associated with 'dysfunctional public and private institutions' (1999: 1–3). This, she asserts, is prevalent in 'non-Western countries', where rent-seeking activities divert resources from economically productive activities, thus limiting economic growth. This suggests that countries with high levels of public sector corruption will struggle to achieve sustainable economic growth and that the only way to reverse this negative trend is by adopting decisive structural and institutional reforms, as well as following the World Bank's and OECD's technical, but substantive, guidelines of 'good, anti-corruption-driven governance'.

The solution of maintaining a competitive market for sustainable development will turn rent-seeking on its head and lead instead to productive activities and economic and social growth that will be instrumental in breaking up rent-seeking tendencies. Such an approach, based on a selection of case studies of 'non-Western' countries, points to human and societal limitations that fundamentally ignore specific national, regional, and continental historical realities. This includes the dynamic and ever-changing nature of internal and external factors and their consequences in the building of a 'developmental state devoid of corruption'.

In this context, the realities of human relations (e.g. power, authority, greed, need or want) cannot be separated from policies, regulations, jurisdictions, and the conduct of public servants, politicians, senior business executives, and risk of procurement by middle managers. The degree of honesty or impartial performance through official or business functions is not dependent only on policies, regulations, or legislation, but also on ethics, integrity, and honesty.

Corruption distorts development and is nothing more than an infection leading to decay of politics, economics, and society at large – it is a 'foreign element' (Euben 1989: 221). Corruption thus, at any given level or sector, is a deviation from rules, policies and regulations, organizational and institutional imperatives. It is conduct that damages public interest by deviating from the formal duties of office by flouting legal norms and intending to abuse and design authority so as to maximize the income of an official, a politician or that of a business executive (Philp 1997).

In fact, Philp (1997: 29–30) is correct when he points out that the wide variety of disputes emanating from definitions of corruption have obscured the indisputable reality that the basic meaning of corruption is that the phenomenon 'is rooted in the sense of a thing being changed from its naturally sound condition, into something unsound, impure, debased, infected'.

The Developmental Journeys

South Africa and Rwanda do not share many similar characteristics in terms of geographical and physical dynamics, physical composition, social and political characteristics, and human resources. They share, perhaps, periods of tragic histories, divisions, heroism, and cowardice. In this instance, the case studies presented demonstrate examples of key differences in the political will of ruling political regimes. By showing how, in fighting corruption and expanding the horizons of even a preliminary state construction, a journey of a thousand miles can be started by taking the first step forward. As this article unfolds, it will become evident that basic planning of public social policies, shaped by existing political, ideological, and economic circumstance of a particular country, is not in itself enough to combat corruption. Only rigorous implementation of such policies can lead to social, sustainable, and people-centred social development that learns from the lessons of history, absorbs the successes and failures of external public models and gains invaluable understanding of global dynamics and realities.

Within this context, and in the light of past and present realities internationally and in Africa in particular, the acknowledgement of corruption as a dangerous infection is of importance for a number of reasons. This is articulated more extensively elsewhere in the article and is summarized in the following paragraph.

Corruption has a negative and debilitating effect on national development at all levels of society and existence – national, regional and continental. Economically, corruption raises the cost of living, especially for the poor and the working class. It also raises the cost of doing business, erodes trust in the private sector, creates social uncertainty, is instrumental in the misallocation and wastage of resources, discourages foreign investment and retards economic growth and development. At the political level, corruption undermines the confidence of the people in their government and public institutions. It erodes the capacity and legitimacy of the state, making a travesty of the concept of the rule of law (Mantzaris 2013).

Socially, corruption is detrimental to equitable and sustainable service delivery and results in the inefficient functioning of such social services as health, education, roads, water supply and telecommunications. It exacerbates social inequalities and increases social tensions in society (Woods and Mantzaris 2012).

Hence it is expected that individual governments will feel obligated to put in place mechanisms to mitigate and fight corruption, especially because of its negative linkage to development, growth and state construction. This is a truism that finds its empirical realization in the analysis of the developmental processes evident in the countries under scrutiny.

After 20 years of democracy, the continuing struggle of South Africa and its government in building a new, free society without racism or sexism is based on the premise of an intent aimed at remedying the negative legacies of centuries of colonization and oppression. Such a society will be built on a vision common to all sectors of society and will be driven by the acceptance, planning, design and implementation of a 'developmental state'.

This vision saw a number of policy initiatives such as ASGISA, JIPSA, the New Paths (Bond 2005; Alexander 2010) and the National Development Plan (NDP), all collectively described as the foundation for the latest attempts to make a 'developmental state' operational at all levels of society. The latter plan (NDP) is considered a fundamental instrument for sustainable growth and development.

Two key chapters in the voluminous NDP document are significant: chapter 13 sets the tone and steps to be taken for a 'capable state' and chapter 14 sets out the fundamental steps aimed at eliminating corruption, greed, avarice and fraud and explains how these steps would lead to 'good governance' (NDP 2013).

After 1994 the new South African government had limited policy choices. The political compromises made during the transition period left few possibilities for adopting radically new policies to replace the old. The new government's leaders were obliged to compromise and were forced to assess models, influences, policies and trends and consider the changing international balance of power. Under such circumstances, it cherry-picked the 'seeds' of a 'developmental state' inhering in the 1955 Freedom Charter, the Harare Declaration of 1990 and the Reconstruction and Development Programme (1994). The initial steps of the new regime intended to create 'stable state institutions' (Becker & Goldstone 2005: 194) are now derailed by (and include) patronage and gatekeeper politics. The 'developmental state' had to be built on the ashes of the old and the harsh realities of a society deeply divided in terms of class, race, gender and social inequalities that gradually led to decisions to replace the old bureaucratic elite with a new one, thus creating a new stratum of a layered middle class, mostly adhering to the principles basic to the ANC's National Democratic Revolution (NDR) (Mantzaris and Pillay 2013).

Unlike the empirically-verified realities that globally impact the evolution of state designs, their diffusion and implementation, in what has been a 'very slow process' (Becker & Goldstone 2005: 206), the new democratic regime introduced a series of equity-based transformations at most levels of society, hoping for an avalanche of effective action – especially with regard to the public sector. Such actions would, hopefully, lead to the development of an effective state and the expansion of its scope and action (Rueschemeyer 2005: 153).

Following the international 'apotheosis' of the transition, the transformation of the ANC from liberation movement to political party now having to guide, plan and implement the 'developmental state', has led to a relentless slide into corruption; authoritarianism; misguided, technocratic rule; centralization of power; unsavoury and corrupt relationships between public and private sectors; bad institutional design and poor service delivery – despite the coercive strands of 'good governance' and 'sound fundamentals' endlessly glorified in the business press and the conservative political elite.

The Broad-Based Black Economic Empowerment (BBBEE) laws and regulations led to a minimal restructuring of economic power dynamics, as the post-1994 state redirected slices/segments of the private/public sector in a conundrum of capital sharing into a few (Black) hands, thus creating a small group of new elites under the tutelage and hegemony of the old (white) monopolies and oligopolies. Such policies and their continued implementation were not un-instrumental in throwing into these groups a selected few political heavyweights that became the toast of the free-enterprise set and sparkled in the social and print media (see the multiple editions of the business-speak, the daily newspaper Business Day, for countless examples).

ANC past and present heavyweights that became multi-billionaires within a space of several years, including BBBEE tycoons such as Cyril Ramaphosa (presently the ANC and country's Deputy President), Saki Macozoma, Tokyo Sexwale and Mzi Khumalo.

In a continuous process of policy changes targeting 'sustainable development and growth' and failed 'quasi-neoliberal initiatives', driven by highly-centralized political power, contributed to widening of the gulf between super rich and downtrodden poor.

No one can deny the fact that, in absolute quantitative terms, poverty has decreased since 1994, but the same cannot be said about income inequality. Access to sanitation, electricity, gross education enrolment rates and immunization cover has also improved, but economic growth has been highly uneven in its distribution, perpetuating inequality and exclusion. With an income Gini coefficient of around 0.70 in 2008 and a consumption Gini coefficient of 0.63 in 2011 (World Bank 2012), South Africa stands recognized as one of the most unequal countries in the world. The social (racial) underpinnings of inequality in South Africa are evident at all levels of society, as Black Africans (almost 80 per cent of the population) garner only 44 per cent of income and contribute to 41 per cent of total expenditure, while Whites (who account for only 9 per cent of the population) secure 40.3 per cent of income and 40.9 per cent of total expenditure (Woolard, Leibbrandt and McEwen 2009).

The rising levels of inequality amongst the Black African population have been rooted primarily, but not exclusively, in the high rate of African unemployment (on the one hand) and increasing incomes at the very top of the distribution graph (on the other). In 2011, 59 per cent of overall income inequality was driven by differences within 'races', while the remaining 41 per cent resulted from income inequality between 'racial groups'. In the first quarter of 2012, unemployment in South Africa stood at 25.2 per cent (33.0 per cent when including 'discouraged' workers); among the world's highest (World Bank 2012).

The unemployment rate in South Africa averaged 25.27 per cent from 2000 until 2014, reaching an all-time high of 31.2 per cent in the first quarter of 2003 and a record low of 21.5 per cent in the fourth quarter of 2008. The unemployment rate in South Africa, as reported by Statistics South Africa, increased to 25.5 per cent in the second quarter of 2014 from 25.2 in the previous quarter (Trading Economics 2014).

The social grants positively impacted the lives of the most vulnerable members of society, specifically the disabled, the aged and children. But it has also created a vast client base for the ruling party. Not only has the share of social grant expenditure in terms of GDP increased significantly, but the number of social grant recipients has also increased meaningfully. By April 2009, 13.4 million people were benefiting from social grants. Of these, 2.3 million were receiving old-age pensions, 1.4 million were receiving disability grants and 9.1 million children were benefiting from child-support grants (Bhorat and Van der Westhuizen 2011). A crucial aspect of post-apartheid fiscal expenditure patterns has been a widening and deepening of South Africa's social security system (presently paid out to over 16.7 million). Spending on social grants will increase from R118bn in 2013–14 to R145bn in 2016–17.

The budget review mentions that social assistance is government's most direct means of combating poverty. Over the past five decades the number of social-grant beneficiaries has doubled from 7.9 million in 2003–04 to 15.8 million in 2013–14. This was largely due to the expansion of the child-support grant. About 11 million received the child-support grants in 2013–14, 2.9 million people old-age grants, 1.1 million disability grants and 519,000 received foster-care grants (Fin24 2014).

The Expanded Public Works Programme (EPWP) in 2004 and the EPWP Phase 2 in 2009 (of which more later) have also made a positive difference to the lives of millions, as most of the unemployed beneficiaries are unskilled and EPWP work opportunities are potentially beneficial if combined with training, education or skills development.

Rwanda, on the other hand, following the massacre of over 800,000 people, has been ruled by the Rwandan Patriotic Front (RPF), which took over in 2004 under the leadership of Paul Kagame. They had faced a civil war initially and in 1996 his forces were forced to invade Zaire [now the Democratic Republic of Congo (DRC)] to counter the threat posed by exiled troops. Eritrean troops were sent to assist the new regime in Rwanda, helping in the overthrow of Zaire's pro-Hutu President Mobutu and installing Laurent Kabila in his stead (Prunier 2009).

By 1998 Rwandan troops had re-invaded DRC, remaining there until 2002. Kagame meanwhile, for a number of reasons, earned serious African and international accolades, especially for maintaining stability in Rwanda, overseeing economic recovery, and implementing a truth and reconciliation process through traditional Gacaca courts. His (justified) disdain for the UN, because of its resolute decision not to intervene during the genocide and its act of allowing UN refugee camps in eastern DRC to be taken over by exiled soldiers and Hutu militias who had carried out the genocide, won the regime some new friends. Rwanda's armed forces have, since 1998, made half a dozen serious incursions into eastern DRC, accompanied by accusations of looting of Congolese natural resources (Pottier 2002).

The Rwandan government, from its inception, concentrated on a serious fight against corruption. Its developmental efforts revolved around vigorous programmes, carefully monitored by state institutions, and driven by a high concentration of power in the hands of the President and his close collaborators. While many would object to this political and programmatic frame, Rwanda has received over US$2billion of overseas development assistance in the 2005–09 period (notwithstanding Kagame's distaste for aid and an insistence on self-reliance). This is one of the reasons that the initial and continued developmental efforts concentrated initially on subsistence agriculture. In the process, this has been transformed into a mainstream, cooperative effort, tackling poverty and improving livelihoods, while being managed through the use of highly centralized machinery, controlled by members of the ruling party who dominate the private sector (Lemarchand 2009).

Kagame's unquestionable commitment to transforming Rwanda into a middle-income, 'knowledge-based economy', by exploiting competitive advantages in information and communications technology (ICT), horticulture, tourism and tea and coffee growing, are collectively underpinned by major strides in agricultural production, economic diversification efforts, and new sources of employment.

Against this backdrop, the realization of significant infrastructure projects has attracted international funding, including a rail link with Burundi and Tanzania and a new international airport at Bugesera.

Kagame skilfully took advantage of the international sympathy following the genocide and also garnered extremely high levels of domestic popularity. This was despite criticism of the Rwandan leader, intensified during 2010, following reports indicating possible infringements of humanitarian law in the DRC by Rwandan troops since 1993 (allAfrica 2003).

Within this context it can be argued, as previous research shows, (Golooba-Mutebi 2008a; Golooba-Mutebi 2008b; Gray and Mushtag 2010; Kelsall 2011; Kelsall and Booth 2010) that neo-patrimonialism is compatible with strong economic performance and that, in some cases, neo-patrimonialism could be harnessed for developmental ends. This does not mean that neo-patrimonialism is not problematic, especially in developing countries. Seemingly, Rwanda has to a large extent managed to avoid such problems by combining a multi-party democracy with the presence of an institutional vehicle that serves as 'mid-wife' between state and party.

Tristar, for example, is a party-controlled holding company that has over the years provided capital for joint ventures in previously-ignored areas, i.e. with untapped economic and developmental potential. It has also financed the Rwandan Patriotic Front in its electoral campaigns, assisted in mass mobilisation of its constituency, and funded general purpose campaigns. In addition, it directs profits into developmental and other socially-important infrastructure projects with a rural bias. The efforts by Tristar and the successful fight against corruption have provided opportunity for the ruling party not only to create a substantial hike and spurt in public goods creation and development, but also enlarged its public support base.

Tristar's basis and success are tributes to similar experiments in Asia of party-based and controlled holding companies that are directed and regulated by a politically-involved state whose developmental growth could increase and not unsustainably. Inevitably class and ethic contradictions and possible adverse shifts in the global economy lead to crisis and slow down economic performance. However, amongst existing and prospective developmental patrimonialists (Rwanda, Angola, South Africa, Malawi, and perhaps Eritrea and Ethiopia), Rwanda seems to have cast solid foundations of a dynamic economic and public policy, with a well-planned and properly-implemented rural public policy (Booth and Golooba-Mutebi 2011).

The Developmental Policy Antitheses: The Case Studies

As elucidated earlier, South Africa and Rwanda had in their first phase chosen different developmental policies to fight poverty and unemployment, which, in the long run, would supposedly deliver sustainable development.

South Africa chose the route of the Expanded Public Works Programme (EPWP) as a vehicle for job creation. A key priority for such massive projects is to develop, from the outset, some degree of suitable skills. Such a process empowers the beneficiaries with appropriate capacity to meet progressively the demands of the mainstream economy.

As mentioned elsewhere in the paper, after almost two decades of democratic rule, unemployment continues to be a serious problem. Despite some periodic signs of economic growth in the country, especially during the first decade after apartheid, new ways of tackling the lack of sustained development will have to be devised.

Expanded public works programmes have been introduced as instruments of job creation in a number of developing countries. Through massive financial injections by the government and/or donor agencies that fund such programmes, temporary employment is initially created for beneficiaries who may then, through upgrading of their skills, be transformed into workers suitable for permanent employment.

The fight against poverty and unemployment was the main reason for the introduction of the first EPWP in 2003 by the South African government, who considered it a key strategy to alleviate unemployment (Department of Public Works 2008). The programme was announced, with considerable fanfare, as an initiative aimed at providing unemployed people with temporary jobs in productive sectors. These jobs would combine to furnish the beneficiaries with a source of income and some measure of training that would be instrumental to their future absorption into the job market. Initially the EPWP, in its first phase from 2004 to 2009, was intended to create one million jobs. Moreover, it was aimed at providing skills, training and work experience (McCord 2005).

The second phase of the EPWP targeted the creation of 'at least 4.9 million jobs'; a highly ambitious target. The process would involve incorporating methods of labour-intensive production, through government-funded projects, so as to create more job opportunities of mostly a manual nature (Thwala 2011; Phillips 2004).

It can be understood that the key aim of such initiatives is to create short-term job opportunities that are pivotal to increasing the income levels of the poor and unemployed, while enhancing aspects of community-based service delivery through infrastructure development (Del Nino, Subbarao and Milazzo 2009).

It has been noted that the implementation of public works programmes does not really significantly advance their objectives. This holds even in those cases that are implemented as longer-running, anti-poverty programmes which provide income to poor households through wages (McCord 2012). On the other hand, some public works programmes have a strong training component that allows participants to gain new abilities and improve their necessary skills, thus entering the labour market better equipped (Del Nino, Subbarao and Milazzo 2009).

Inevitably, the initiators of such projects elsewhere have based their ideas of planning, design and implementation on the relatively successful experiences of such initiatives in developing countries such as India and Argentina, where similar programmes were considered a success, especially in terms of the combination of wages and/or skills training in groups (Del Nino, Subbarao and Milazzo 2009).

Judging from the official documents reflecting the public policy position of the South African government in respect of the programme, the 'strategy' can only be successful if it combines efforts to alleviate unemployment and improve skills development. Both objectives are treated as equal. In fact, the documents on the EPWP public policy framework are adamant that the skills development as part of the programme is of great significance, because it leads to sustainability (Thwala 2011).

As stated earlier, the EPWP filled a serious vacuum in the temporary job creation environment and, to a certain extent, in meeting the existing unemployment challenges. In this process, it became evident that all state departments played a role in utilizing their individual budgets and thus contributed towards the fulfilment of the target of one million job opportunities by 2009 (Del Nino, Subbarao and Milazzo 2009).

It can be assumed that such initiatives, by their very nature, cannot be equated with 'sustainable development'. One of the key reasons for such a reality is the short duration of the beneficiaries' involvement. The programme cannot make a significant contribution to the fight against unemployment, due to the non-sustainability of the jobs. This happens where there is either non-substantial training or, when provided, it is extremely short and not accredited. The consequences are that participants, who have left these programmes without acquiring skills that may lead to profitable employment, return to 'unemployed status'.

The existing financial and budget deficiencies also militate against such a programme, as the government puts more budgetary emphasis on social security and welfare projects. The lack of appropriate methodologies, planning, design and implementation of the programmes in these circumstances has also dented their capacity to deliver (Khanyile 2008; Nattrass 2002).

On the other hand, the success of cooperatives in Rwanda in terms of their positive contribution to society (the outcome of a carefully-planned and implemented public policy) shows political will and strategy that have paid dividends on the road to sustainable development.

Rwandan cooperative law, promulgated in 2007, defines cooperatives as 'associations of natural or legal persons, operating together in activities aimed at promoting their members in accordance with values of mutual responsibility and self-help, democracy, equity and equal rights to assets... subscribing to honesty, openness and securing the common interests of members' (Republic of Rwanda: Official Gazette 2007: 21).

Cooperatives have a long history in Rwanda and have over the years taken on a variety of formats with significant fluctuation in membership.[1] Already from inception, they have provided opportunities for their members to resist poverty and unemployment. The establishment of the Rwanda Cooperative Agency formalised the relationship between the cooperatives and the state.

Cooperatives have been instrumental in elevating the social and economic circumstances of its members and creating bonds of social solidarity at all levels. In this sense, their members take advantage of the public policy of the government as well as the agricultural potential of the country. Poverty has thus been reduced from a high of 60 per cent below the national poverty datum line to a current 45 per cent. The support by the government of the cooperatives' credit measures has raised their financial viability and sustainability (ICA 2011).

The successes of Rwandan cooperatives have been supported both by public policy initiatives and through the positive role of their government in its quest for sustainability. This reality is directly related to the RPF government's position that the cooperatives are and will remain major electoral machinery, guaranteeing future political support and its continued strength through the development of constituencies.

This political strategy, underlined by the endorsement of a legal framework and the subsequent establishment of the Rwanda Cooperative Agency, has helped strengthen the RPF. The laying down of regulations and strategies and the institution of an action plan – aimed at ensuring that cooperatives become an important instrument for bottom-up sustainable development – have won it admiration and political support at the polls.

The Countries' Anti-Corruption Policies and their Outcomes

In a comparative perspective, South Africa, when compared to Rwanda, has a more 'complete' and diversified set of anti-corruption policies in place.

[1] Formally there are at present over 4,000 such entities involved in various fields such as agriculture, consumption, production, marketing, credit and saving, housing, handicrafts and others. Credit and saving cooperatives are very common among farmers, civil servants and the military (Kantengwa n.d.).

This includes its participation in international anti-corruption agreements and treaties such as the United Nations Convention against Corruption (UNCAC), the Southern African Development Community (SADC) Protocol against Corruption, the African Union (AU) Convention on Preventing and Combating Corruption and the OECD Convention on Bribery of Foreign Public Officials in International Business Trade and Transactions. South Africa has also promulgated the following comprehensive pieces of legislation and accepted the tenets of policy regulations from these and other protocols dealing with various aspects of corruption:

- Prevention and Combating of Corrupt Activities Act (PRECCA) no. 12 of 2004
- Promotion of Administrative Justice Act (PAJA) no. 3 of 2000
- Protected Disclosure Act (PDA) no. 26 of 2000 otherwise known as 'The Whistle-blowing Act')
- Promotion of Access to Information Act (PAIA) no. 2 of 2000
- Financial Intelligence Centre Act (FICA) no. 38 of 2001
- Prevention of Organised Crime Act (POCA) no. 121 of 1998
- International laws and the laws of Revised Public Service Integrity Management Framework, the Public Service Anti-Corruption Strategy, the Public Service Charter, the Charter for the Public Service in Africa (5 February 2001)
- Public Services Act no. 103 of 1994
- Municipal Finance Management Act no. 56 of 2003
- Code of Conduct for the Public Service
- Code of Good Conduct for Supply Chain Management Practitioners
- Financial Disclosure Framework (FDF) and
- Asset Register for Accounting Officers

A number of statutory bodies exist to fight corruption. These include the:

- Financial Intelligence Centre
- South African Police Service (SAPS)
- Anti-Corruption Task Team
- Multi-Agency Working Group on Procurement
- Special Investigating Unit (SIU)
- National Prosecuting Authority (NPA)

- Specialized Commercial Crimes Courts and
- Asset Forfeiture Unit

  Other anti-corruption entities include the
- National Anti-Corruption Forum (NACF)
- Inter-Ministerial Committee on Auditor General
- Public Service Commission for Government Departments
- Public Protector
- National Public Service Anti-Corruption hotline system
- Anti-Corruption Coordinating Committee (ACCC) and
- Public Service Anti-Corruption Forum (Woods and Mantzaris 2012)

Despite the policy-legal-institutional infrastructure, South Africa has continued to slide down the international rankings of perceived corruption. According to Transparency International, a country's score indicates the perceived level of corruption in its public sector on a scale of zero to 100, where zero means the public sector is perceived as being totally corrupt. The ranking indicates a country's position relative to other countries surveyed for purposes of the index. The index ranks countries based on a variety of empirical studies related to the public's perception of public sector corruption and is the most widely-used indicator of official 'graft' globally. The survey also utilizes, in a number of ways, data from a variety of organisations, such as the African Development Bank and the World Bank, using altogether 13 surveys to compile the report (Woods and Mantzaris 2012: 121).

The latest Corruption Perceptions Index, compiled by Transparency International, reveals that South Africa fell to joint 72nd out of 177 countries surveyed this year (2014), from 69th last year. According to the report, South Africa scored 42 points in 2013, well below the minimum acceptable score of 50, and down from 43 the previous year. South Africa was on a par with countries such as Brazil and Serbia, but scored lower than other African countries such as Botswana and Rwanda (Transparency International 2013). It was also reported that 90 per cent of African states and two-thirds of all countries scored below 50, indicating a 'serious, worldwide corruption problem'.

The perceptions identified and recorded in the survey, indicated the expression of disapproval of and even anger at the high levels of corruption in the public service of South Africa. These have found their empirical realization in the hundreds of 'service-delivery protests' throughout the country (Alexander 2010).

Research on corruption at different levels and in various sectors has pinpointed the fact that, over the last few years, the levels of corruption have increased drastically. Trust in leaders, politically elected and administrative, has declined and concomitantly foreign and domestic investment has weakened too (Mantzaris and Pillay 2014a; Mantzaris and Pillay 2014b; Mantzaris and Pillay 2014c). The Transparency International Global Corruption Barometer has also revealed that 47 per cent of South Africans have paid bribes over the past year, against a global average of 27 per cent (Transparency International 2013).

Rwandan anti-corruption policy, on the other hand, is governed by the Constitution of the country, international treaties [such as the United Nations Convention against Corruption (UNCAC), the African Union Convention against Corruption (AUCAC) and the East African Community Treaty], organic law instituting the penal code, the leadership code of conduct and laws on prevention, suppression and punishment of corruption and related offences. Furthermore there are such measures as the prevention of and penalizing the crime of money laundering and financing of terrorism; ensuring proper public procurement policy; a law establishing the organization and functioning of the Office of the Ombudsman; and laws on appropriate state finance procedures.[2]

Research by the Rwandan Office of the Ombudsman has revealed that the main functional areas in Rwanda that constitute potential risks are found in the public finance management system, public

[2] See the Constitution of the Republic of Rwanda of 4 June 2003, as amended to date; organic law establishing internal rules of procedure for the Chamber of Deputies in Parliament; Law No. 23/2003 of 07/08/2003, relating to the prevention and suppression of corruption and related offences (O.G. Special of 3/09/2003); Law No. 65/2008 of 11/09/2008, regulating the Leadership Code of Conduct; and Law No. 22/2002 of 09/07/2002 on General Statutes for the Rwanda Public Service (O.G. No. 17 of 1/9/2002) and Republic of Rwanda: Office of the Ombudsman 2012a.

procurement processes, human resources management, traffic police, justice sector, land services offices, customs, licence issuing and construction permits. The most common forms of corruption in Rwanda include public funds embezzlement, fraudulent procurement practices, nepotism, abuse of office and power, corruption in enforcement and regulatory institutions and dealings within the private sector. This is also evidenced by the large number of corruption cases recorded annually: for instance, in the year 2009–10, 490 cases were lodged with the Rwanda National Police and the Office of the Ombudsman; of these, 292 cases led to prosecutions and 44 persons were convicted for corruption and related offences (Republic of Rwanda: Office of the Ombudsman 2012a).

As the institutional anti-corruption framework in Rwanda is categorized into two types (i.e. enforcement and oversight institutions), the government and anti-corruption strategists have admitted (unlike their South African counterparts) that they lack hard evidence on the extent and nature of corruption. This leads to the suggestion that fighting corruption by these institutions requires modern investigative tools, special investigative techniques and special investigative teams that are presently lacking (Republic of Rwanda: Office of the Ombudsman 2012b).

In addition, for proper decision-making, enforcement bodies in Rwanda lack statistical data on types, nature and causes of corruption. This inadequacy, they argue, may be avoided if there were constant surveys and research on all forms of corruption in Rwanda. With the aim of initiating reform, these surveys should entail analysis of the study and critiques of existing anti-corruption policies and laws, in tandem with appraisals of the efficacy of institutional and administrative structures operating within the public and private sectors (Republic of Rwanda: Office of the Ombudsman 2012a).

On the other hand, with the establishment of the Rwanda Public Procurement Authority – similar to the one lately established in South Africa, following the adoption of the National Development Plan (NDP) – and the enactment of the procurement law and regulations, public tender procedures are now properly respected, if compared to the times when there were no such regulatory frameworks. Failure to comply now leads to severe sanctions. The value of tenders awarded without the approval of the internal tender committees and the Rwanda Public Procurement Authority has plummeted dramatically, while the value of tenders awarded through open competition has inversely increased (Republic of Rwanda: Office of the Ombudsman 2012a).

It has been admitted that, despite the enactment of Rwandan procurement legislation and regulations, irregularities still exist in the allocation of public tenders and that the retrograde mind-set of key players in the financial management system remains a challenge. These may lead to corrupt practices affecting the whole financial management system. Through the use of such inappropriate public financial measures as unethical public procurement procedures and unscrupulous tax and revenue collection procedures, Rwandan authorities are forced to remain ever-vigilant (Republic of Rwanda: Office of the Ombudsman 2012b).

It has been openly admitted (unlike in the South African case) that oversight institutions also face a challenge of insufficiency of qualified personnel, both in numbers and expertise. Hence, for a better financial management system, the right people need to be recruited, their capacity needs to be developed and the effectiveness of internal audit functions need to be improved for the purpose of strengthening internal controls and active audit committees. This should help reduce the amount of expenditure, without supportive documents, which remains high as a result of failure to comply with the established procedures (Republic of Rwanda: Office of the Ombudsman 2012a:123).

Following concerted government efforts in the last five years to fight corruption, international reports have indicated that the battle has been won, at least in the surveys of Transparency International and its Corruption Barometer of 2013. As regards the corruption trend in Rwanda, the Global Corruption Barometer points out that 89 per cent of the respondents say corruption has decreased in Rwanda over the last two years.

The report indicates that the 2013 Transparency International Global Corruption Barometer generally ranks Rwanda as the only African country perceived to be 'least corrupt' (within the 10–14.9 per cent range). This means that, worldwide, the country is in the top three of nine categories of least corrupt nations. The third category, in which Rwanda falls, includes countries like Israel, Jamaica, Palestine, the Philippines, Argentina, Chile and Hungary. Rwanda is ranked the 13th least-corrupt country worldwide. The corruption trends in East Africa show that Rwanda is the least bribery-prone country in the region, with an average index of 2.5 per cent. The other EAC member states, i.e. Uganda, Tanzania and Kenya, fall within the 50–74.9 per cent category (Transparency International 2013). The report shows that there is strong political will to fight corruption, with the Rwandan government's effectiveness being rated the highest in Sub-Saharan Africa at 95 per cent.

In a nutshell, 'good governance' can be described as synonymous with transparency, accountability, integrity, the rule of law, stability and growth for the private sector and social compacts and synergy between the private and public sectors. The South African government, since 1994, has followed closely the guidelines and spirit of the 'new public management' school of thought, including the adoption of private sector management techniques such as performance management systems and the proliferation of 'public-private partnerships' (Mantzaris and Pillay 2014a).

However, the independence of the Reserve Bank, the (now defunct) Scorpions, the Competition Commission, state auditing watchdogs such as the Auditor General, public watchdogs such as the Public Service Commission, the Public Protector and over 15 well-structured laws, rules and regulations against corruption have created a sense of anti-corruption foundations militating for a high degree of autonomy. The reality on the ground and in the corridors of money and power, however, tell a different story.

Corruption and Sustainable Development: Some Observations

The preceding sections point out the differences between two African countries in terms of public policy towards sustainable development that have produced seemingly different results. In the sphere of public and social policy, the South African 'experiment' underlines the prevailing hegemony of the developmental orientation of 'liberal modes of governance' with sophisticated and expanded legislative frameworks against corruption and facilitating 'sustainable development'. Rwanda, by contrast, has embraced an emerging, possibly unorthodox, developmental agenda, anchored in the existing 'structures' of African society, resources and policies and enshrined it in their institutions.

Such a reality possibly points to empirically-verified writings that the 'the most successful developers in Africa all qualify as neo-patrimonial regimes'. These so-called developmental-patrimonial regimes have tended to centralize rent management within long-term horizons. Presiding over and administering the regime is a single ruling party (as in the case of the RPF), a leader with vision and a capable and competent economic technocracy. By contrast, the less developmental regimes demonstrate either a failure to centralise rents, or have a short-term perspective (Dawson and Kelsall 2012: 50).

On the other hand, the current demand for developing countries (as in the case of South Africa) to (immediately) adopt world-class institutions or face punishment, is at odds with the historical experience of the developed countries. Indeed, as Noman and Stiglitz (2012, 33) assert, 'no country has ever implemented the current "good governance" agenda before embarking on development – not the now developed countries, nor the rapidly "catching-up" countries of Asia'.

South African Section 9 institutions, such as the Public Protector, the Auditor General and the Public Service Commission, have shown high levels of independence in the struggle against corruption and it is accepted widely that the South African post-1994 state has acted on 'securing good governance', as the existing legislation and regulations show. However, the state has been unable or incapable of stopping rampant corruption at national, provincial and local government levels, as well as in the private and the public sectors, as has been shown elsewhere (Mantzaris and Pillay 2014a; Mantzaris and Pillay 2014c).

There are strong perceptions that in South Africa corrupt individuals and/or groups operate with relative impunity and that, because of the lack of decisive action, especially against prominent people in the political, public and private domains, the battle against corruption is being lost. In one of the most recent exposures of rampant corruption, the then-South African Minister of Justice announced that the government would publicly name and shame those convicted of fraud and corruption. He released the names of 42 people, mostly civil servants, who, after they had been directly implicated in 'priority cases involving huge amounts' of money, were found guilty of fraud and corruption. There was an undertaking that the names of others on a list of more than 3,000 individuals would be released later. Those names were never released.

The fact that the regional, specialized, commercial-crimes courts received 10,941 new, corruption-related cases to deal with in 2012–13 and that convictions were obtained against 3,968 people, 813 of whom were foreign nationals, in 3,763 cases, may to some (the uninformed) be an indication of reasonable success, but these convictions are basically only a drop in an ocean of corruption.

Due to the detrimental effect on service delivery, the fight against corruption was declared one of the South African government's top priorities. Thus, in 2012–13, a total of 242 people were criminally investigated in 89 priority cases, involving at least R5m per case and investigations were also under way against a further 193 accused. In addition, 152 employees in the government's departments of justice, crime prevention and security were convicted for corruption.

The investigations of 758 people by the specialized anti-corruption task team for corrupt activities, with its ability to secure orders for the total freezing of assets valued at R1.07bn, shows that, in the mind of the government at least, there is serious intensification in the fight against corruption via a dedicated anti-corruption bureau. The release of the names of culprits was to be regarded as a further strong message to criminals that their actions would not go without proper scrutiny in the public domain.

The security cluster's anti-corruption task team (ACTT), an interdepartmental body, has been involved in fast-tracking investigations into high-priority cases. According to ACTT's statistics, 758 people were under investigation for corrupt activities and orders for freezing R1.07bn had been obtained. The R1.07bn includes forfeiture orders for R14.7m brought against former Land Bank CEO Philemon Mohlahlane and Gauteng businessman Dan

Mofokeng. The two were accused of defrauding the Land Bank and transferring funds to a range of foreign entities for their own benefit. The Asset Forfeiture Unit recovered farms valued at R59m that had been lost through corruption in the government's land reform programme. Another five farms valued at R44m had been frozen and should be recovered soon. Other farms, with a total value of more than R52m, were under investigation for possible seizure in the next six months (Business Day 2013).

Within this context, and at least in the first few years of the South African 'miracle', very few within any sector of society could even dare question the impeccable democratic credentials of the ruling party as the epitome of representative democracy and 'good governance' (especially state-business relations) because of the imposing legacy of its first President, Nelson Mandela. As time passed and the increasing closeness to all sectors of capital became stronger, clientelism and co-option became the new state strategies as part of the cycle of 'embedded autonomy' (Evans 1995). This, through a relentless process, led to 'state capture', corruption and patronage (Mkandawire 1998).

Bearing in mind the material, legislative, social, institutional and political differences between South Africa and Rwanda, the key questions and answers arising within the ambit of social policy and its implementation are fundamental. For example, the much simpler and understandable policies of Rwanda have almost stopped an overriding preoccupation with looting resources, while in South Africa it seems the steady march to the bottom has continued with a relentless appetite for predatory materialistic accumulation, cutting across the elite, the middle class, and the working-class aristocracy associated with labour unions (Mantzaris and Pillay 2013).

In Rwanda, the penalties associated with corruption are not significantly different when compared to those in South Africa, but the key difference evidently lies in the implementation of anti-corruption policy. In the instance of Rwanda, there is persistent political will to uproot the scourge and dissipate a brutal and corrupt ethos, driven by those who seek personal enrichment. The fact that the South African government seems incapable of combating the corruption epidemic successfully, coupled to the false interpretation that 'Black Empowerment' should mean benefits mainly for small numbers and groups of politically-connected individuals, has led to a moral implosion in the populace (Mabandla 2013).

In the South African state's version of the developmental state, the private sector has been entrusted the role of maximising profits, serving to enhance development of a capitalist class and the concomitant relentless accumulation of wealth. By favouring this approach, the state inevitably ends up assisting corrupt practices through their perpetuation and enlargement.

Those in South Africa who lose out in the context of this peculiar type of 'developmental state' (in short, the poor and the workers) cannot in any way be happy and content. South Africa is ranked as high as 53rd on the international competitiveness list of the World Bank, to be placed second among the BRICS countries, even overtaking Brazil. It also does well in assessments of the quality of its institutions (41st), in terms of intellectual property protection (18th), property rights (20th), and in terms of the efficiency of the legal framework when challenging and settling disputes (13th and 12th respectively). According to the report, the high accountability of its private institutions (2nd) further supports the institutional framework. Its financial market development remains impressive in 3rd place, and it is ranked 35th in business sophistication and is 39th in innovation.

However, its performance in the macroeconomic environment has dropped sharply (from 69th to 95th); there are low scores for the diversion of public funds (99th), perceived wastefulness of government spending (79th) and a general lack of public trust in politicians (98th). The health of the workforce is ranked 133rd out of 148 economies; labour market efficiency is poor (116th); hiring-and-firing practices are extremely rigid (147th); companies cannot set wages flexibly (144th) and significant tensions in labour-employer relations exist (148th) (World Bank 2013:14).

Thus the World Economic Forum's Global Competitiveness Report, that for the second year in a row puts South Africa at the bottom of 147 countries in terms of labour-employer relations, not only scapegoats organized labour unions, but does not hesitate to buttonhole the government's failed economic policies for being squarely responsible. This is in spite of allowing for the international financial and social crises. While the developmental state is unfolding, workers are blamed for resisting the 'dictates of flexibility' and fighting for better wages.

On the other hand, Rwanda's 'developmental patrimonialism' (in which the ruling party has utilized its interest in a state-run company to transform the livelihoods, in a more or less transformational mode, of the rural poor) has enhanced the capacities and capabilities of local populations. This has been achieved through the imposition of a centrally-based, direct discipline, both with the political elite and the beneficiaries of such initiatives.

In this case, utilization of the state's apparatuses has had positive results, not only because substantial numbers of the rural and urban poor have benefited, but also since social cohesion has been strengthened in the process. This is an example of how accelerated development – relatively well-planned, appropriately-designed and properly-implemented – can lead to success. Public policymaking in Rwanda is driven by the belief that economic and social development is the optimal choice for the government. It is epitomized by the Rwanda Vision 2020 document that aspires to create an enlightened generation, suitably enabled to establish a 'new national identity' and erase the destructive divisions of the past.

The characteristics of the viable governing and governance regime in Rwanda indicate that external behavioural models have not been imposed and that the relationships of power, authority, clientelism and appropriate organizational modes, especially in the countryside, are understood. The support for cooperatives by the general populace has increased the 'political legitimacy' of the government at ground level. So too has the latter's continuous emphasis on the fight against corruption as a key enabler and contributor to sustained/sustainable economic growth and development, delivered belief in the value of its uninterrupted rule.

Within this context it is important to understand that Rwandan public policies essentially dictate that 'things need to be done' before development can proceed (Grindle 2011) and that the state apparatuses are therefore mobilized to implement policies based on good-enough governance and anti-corruption reforms. These have become instrumental through reward or punishment in the developmental process.

Conclusion

The present comparison between two 'developmental, patrimonial regimes', with different social, economic, political, geographical and historical trajectories, pinpoints their diverse path to development through public and social policy initiatives. The comparison poses the question of the role of state structure and construction, the difference between indigenous and external developmental models, issues complementing local centres of power, authority, and the part played by organizational modes in pursuit of development.

Instrumental in this comparison is public policy and its implementation in relation to corruption and governance. Although, in both cases, the acknowledgement of corruption is a common feature and anti-corruption policies have been introduced, the success of the Rwandan patrimonial regime and the political context in which it is rooted and functions, is substantially more successful, most likely because of the smaller and better-trained public bureaucracy. Despite the fact that both regimes are rooted in strong clientelism patterns, the Rwandan one has skilfully utilized a party-state private firm as enabler and contributor to sustained/sustainable economic growth and development, unlike the South African one. In Rwanda then, in essence, the regime of 'developmental patrimonialism' by the ruling regime has driven an agenda concentrating and driving financial, political and social interests through creating both capability and capacity within significant sections of the rural population in a centralized way, but one that operates in a developmental and transformative manner.

In South Africa, rampant corruption, greed and avarice underline a mainly imported social policy paradigm that started with experiments of Thatcherism and Reaganism, passed on as 'inevitable' policies to 'adjust' to new global realities and impersonal labour-market forces. These were continued as central principles of the government's macro-economic Growth Employment and Redistribution (GEAR) policy/strategy, all but disconnecting the poor from direct involvement in planning their economic survival.

The suffering of the poor, despite the important social grants to over 16 million recipients, is a direct result of the imitation of models imposed on South Africa by the globalized market and transnational imperatives; South Africa thus finds itself, through past and present social policies, exhibiting symptoms of gross inequalities.

As indicated in the paper, the EPWPs have been successful in a few countries, but their South African 'transplantation' fell short because of public policy weaknesses and lacking implementation procedures. Moreover, the lack of training opportunities, implementation weaknesses, the absence of a well-designed, equitable and comprehensive public-private partnership to bring together business, formal education and training institutions and the state together undermined success. Such a partnership would safeguard the training opportunities offered to the unemployed in every given sector and ensure that they are in line with the current labour demands of industry.

There is no doubt that the EPWPs have made a significant and positive difference to the lives of millions of poor and unemployed people throughout South Africa, but one of its key objectives, i.e. to provide sustainable skills to the unemployed, has not been met because of gaps in the letter, content and implementation of the public policy upon which it was founded.

On the other hand, the cooperatives in Rwanda have, through the creation of partnerships that have brought visible development, contributed significantly to the developmental path in their more backward agricultural societies. The strengthening and expansion of cooperatives have made a significantly positive contribution to millions of people, especially in the rural areas.

References

Alexander, P. 2010. 'Rebellion of the Poor'. *Review of African Political Economy 37*, no.123: 25–40.

Amsden, A.H. 1997. 'Bringing Production Back In: Understanding Government's Economic Role in Late Industrialisation.' *World Development 25*, no. 4: 480–96.

Becker, J., and J.A. Goldstone. 2005. 'How Fast Can You Build a State? State Building in Revolutions.' In *States and Development: Historical*

Antecedents of Stagnation and Advance. M. Lange and D. Rueschmeyer (eds.). Basingstoke: Palgrave Macmillan. pp. 183–210.

Bhorat, H., and C. van der Westhuizen. 2011. 'Pro-poor Growth and Social Protection in South Africa: Exploring the Interactions.' Input paper prepared for the National Planning Commission.

Bond, P. 2005. *Elite Transition*. Pietermaritzburg: University of KwaZulu-Natal Press.

Booth, D., and F. Golooba-Mutebi. 2011. 'Developmental Patrimonialism: The Case of Rwanda.' *Africa Power and Politics*. Working Paper 16.

Business Day. 2013. 'Corruption Watch head lauds state's antigraft initiatives.' http://www.bdlive.co.za/national/2013/06/10/corruption-watch-head-lauds-states-antigraft-initiatives.

Dawson, M., and T. Kelsall. 2012. 'Anti-developmental patrimonialism in Zimbabwe.' *Journal of Contemporary African Studies 30*, no. 1: 4966.

Del Nino, C., K. Subbarao and A. Milazzo. 2009. 'How to make public works work: A review of the experiences.' *Social Protection Discussion Paper No. 0905*.Washington DC: World Bank.

Department of Public Works, South Africa. 2008. 'Expanded Public Works Programme: Reaching the one million target.' http://www.epwp.gov.za/downloads/EPWP_Five_Year_Report.pdf.

Euben, J.P. 1989. 'Corruption.' In *Political innovation and conceptual change*. T. Ball, J. Farr & R.L. Hanson (eds.). Cambridge: Cambridge University Press.

Evans, P. 1995. *Embedded Autonomy: States and Industrial Transformation*. Princeton: Princeton University Press.

Leuvennink, J. 2014. 'Spending on social grants goes up.' *Fin24*. http://www.fin24.com/Budget/Spending-on-social-grants-goes-up-20140226.

Gray, H., and K. Mushtaq. 2010. 'Good Governance and Growth in Africa: What Can We Learn from Tanzania?' In *The Political Economy of Africa*. V. Padayachee (ed.). London: Routledge. 339–56.

Grindle, M.S. 2011. 'Good enough governance revisited.' *Development Policy Review 29*: s199–s221.

Golooba-Mutebi, F. 2008a. 'Collapse, War and Reconstruction in Rwanda: An Analytical Narrative on State-Making.' *Working Paper 2*. London: Crisis States Research Centre.

———. 2008b. 'Collapse, War and Reconstruction in Uganda: An Analytical Narrative on State-Making.' *Working Paper 2*. London: Crisis States Research Centre.

ICA. 2011. New opportunities for cooperatives. Abstracts. Helsinki.

International Labour Organization (ILO). 2001. Report V (1) Promotion of Cooperatives, International Labour Office, Geneva.

Kantengwa, A. 'Financial cooperatives in Rwanda.' Kigali: BNR, n. d.

Kelsall, T. 2011. 'Rethinking the Relationship between Neo-Patrimonialism and Economic Development in Africa.' *IDS Bulletin 42*, no. 2: 76–87.

———., and D. Booth. 2010. 'Developmental Patrimonialism Questioning: the Orthodoxy on Political Governance and Economic Progress in Africa.' *Working Paper 9*. London: Africa Power and Politics Programme.

Khanyile, B.K. 2008. *A Study of the Impact of the Expanded Public Works Programme on Job Creation in the Zululand District Municipality.* Pietermaritzburg: University of KwaZulu- Natal.

Lemarchand, R. 2009. 'The Dynamics of Violence in Central Africa.' Philadelphia: University of Pennsylvania Press.

Mabandla, 2012. 'The ANC is a vehicle for rapacious material accumulation.' CityPress. http://www.citypress.co.za/columnists/the-anc-is-a-vehicle-for-rapacious-material-accumulation-20121020/.

Mantzaris, E. A. 2013. 'Ethics and Public Sociology: A South African Case Study.' Keynote Address, Pan-African Conference of Government Officials. Livingstone: Zambia.

———. 2013. 'Towards a Marxist Conceptualisation of Corruption: The South African Case.' *African Journal of Public Affairs 6*, no. 3: 112–28.

———. 2014a. 'Corruption and Accountability: South African Case Studies.' Democracy Development Programme.

———. 2014b. 'Corruption in the Private Sector: The South African Construction Cartel.' Paper presented at ECMLG 2014, Croatia.

———. 2014c. 'Corruption in the bread industry: The South African Case.' Paper presented at ECMLG 2014, Croatia.

McCord, A. A. 2005. 'Critical evaluation of training within the South African National Public Works Programme.' *Journal of Vocational Education and Training 57*, no. 4: 565–88.

———. 2012. 'The politics of social protection: Why are public works programmes so popular with government and donors?' *Overseas Development Institute Background Note.* Maastricht: European Centre for Development Policy Management.

Mkandawire, T. 1998. 'Thinking about developmental states in Africa.' Paper presented at a United Nations University workshop on Institutions and Development in Africa. http://www.unu.edu/hq/academic/pg_area4/Mkandawire.html.

Mugisha, S. 2013. 'Rwanda least corrupt country in Africa.' *All Africa*. http://allafrica.com/stories/201307110440.html.

National Development Plan (NDP). 2013. *Vision for 2030*. Pretoria: Government Printers.

Nattrass, N. 2002. 'Should youth unemployment be targeted as part of a comprehensive welfare policy in South Africa?' *Social Dynamics: A Journal of African Studies 28*, no. 2: 207–36.

Noman, A., and J.E. Stiglitz. 2012. 'Strategies for African development.' In *Good Growth and Governance in Africa: Rethinking Development Strategies*. A. Noman, K. Botchway, H. Stein and J.E. Stiglitz (eds.). Oxford: Oxford University Press. pp. 3–49.

Phillips, S. 2004. 'The Expanded Public Works Programme.' Paper presented at Overcoming underdevelopment in South Africa's Second Economy, jointly hosted by the UNDP, HSRC and DBSA, Pretoria, 28–29 October.

Philp, M. 1997. 'Defining political corruption.' In *Political Corruption*. P. Heywood (ed.). Oxford: Blackwell, pp. 20–46.

Pottier, J. 2002. *Re-imagining Rwanda: Conflict, Survival and Disinformation in the Late Twentieth Century*. Cambridge: Cambridge University Press.

Prunier, G. 2009. *Africa's World War*. Oxford: Oxford University Press.

Republic of Rwanda. 2007. *Official Gazette, 21: Art. 2*.

———. 2012a. 'Office of the Ombudsman. Strengthening Good Governance in Rwanda.' Kigali: Government Printers.

———. 2012b. 'Office of the Ombudsman. Anti-Corruption Policy.' Kigali: Government Printers.

Rose-Ackerman, S. 1999. 'Corruption and government: causes, consequences and reform.' Cambridge and New York: Cambridge University Press.

Rueschemeyer, D. 2005. 'Building states – inherently a long-term process? An argument from theory.' In *States and Development: Historical Antecedents of Stagnation and Advance*. M. Lange and D. Rueschmeyer (eds.). New York: Palgrave Macmillan. 143–64.

Trading Economics. 2014. 'South Africa unemployment rate.' http://www.tradingeconomics.com/south-africa/unemployment-rate.

Transparency International. 2013. 'Global Corruption Barometer.' Bonn: Germany.

Thwala, W.D. 2011. 'Public works programmes as a tool to address unemployment and skills shortages among the youth in South Africa.' *African Journal of Business Management 5*, no. 15: 6011–20.

Woods, G., and E. Mantzaris, 2012. 'The Anti-Corruption Reader.' ACCERUS: University of Stellenbosch.

Woolard I., M. Leibbrandt and H. McEwen. 2009. 'Poverty and inequality.' In *Recession and Recovery*. J. Hofmyr (ed.). Cape Town: African Minds/ IJR. pp. 98–107.

World Bank. 2012. 'Focus on inequality of opportunities.' *South Africa Economic Update*. Washington, DC: World Bank.

———. 2013. 'The Global Competitiveness Report 2013–2014 Country Profile Highlights.' Washington, DC: World Bank.

11 Urban Poverty Policies and Politics in India

Public-Private Partnership in Slum Redevelopment

Bhuvaneswari Raman

Abstract

This paper analyses the politics of participatory development in a state-led urban poverty reduction programme. Rajiv Awas Yojana (RAY) was launched in 2009 by the Government of India with a vision to 'create slum-free cities and promote an inclusive and sustainable' growth agenda. Squatter citizens were to participate in RAY within the framework of Public-Private Partnership (PPP). The paper draws on findings from the Kathputli Colony slum redevelopment project, piloted in New Delhi under RAY that institutionalized citizens' participation, but led to a prolonged conflict among the various players. The paper argues that this conflict between squatter citizens and the state cannot be explained as a gap in implementation, for this line of thought misses the political-economic context of land and real estate in contemporary cities.

Introduction

This paper is an account of democracy in practice and explores the practices of citizens' participation in an Urban Poverty Alleviation Programme (UPAP) in India. The Government of India (GoI) introduced Rajiv Awas Yojana (RAY) in 2009, with the objective of creating slum-free cities and promoting inclusive and sustainable growth agenda. To this end, the programme proposed legalizing the tenure status of squatter settlements and providing legal titles to its occupants in the joint name of men and women (MHUPA 2013). The scheme proposed a three-pronged strategy – in-situ upgradation,[1] squatter re-development, and relocation – for legalization of land tenure. Unlike the earlier generation of poverty alleviation programmes funded by the GoI or those supported with bilateral assistance, RAY targeted all types of squatter settlements in a city, irrespective of their legal status.[2] Furthermore, the programme aimed to develop a comprehensive information infrastructure, comprising spatial and demographic information, on squatter citizens (MHUPA 2013).

Participation of squatter citizens is a key component of RAY. The paper design of RAY envisioned their participation in three domains of decision-making, viz., surveying the process for identifying eligible programme participants, mapping the physical layout of the settlement along with demarcating individual plots and designing the settlement layout and houses (GOI MHUPA 2009; Dupont 2014). Although the participation of squatter citizens had been emphasized in earlier generations of UPA projects, RAY expanded the scope of citizen's participation (CP) beyond self-help labour in housing construction to include other aspects of decision-making. This paper explores the experience of squatter citizens as partners in RAY.

This essay also argues for situating the analysis of citizens' participation in the wider context of the political economy of land and urban development. Squatter citizens participate in RAY scheme within a framework of (Public Private Partnership) PPP arrangements under which partnerships are forged between large real estate developers in land and housing, Non-Governmental Agencies (NGOs), the state agencies and squatter citizens. In addition, the instruments of PPP arrangements are designed to provide incentives to large developers and include the Transfer of Development Rights (TDR), land sharing, and the relaxation of Floor Space Index (FSI) (GOI MHUPA 2009, 2013). The TDR involves eviction of citizens from their territory and its transfer to developers for redevelopment.

[1] The in-situ upgradation process involves providing basic infrastructure with minimal realignment of existing houses, while in-situ redevelopment necessitate re-construction of houses often as multi-storeyed tenements.

[2] including both notified and non-notified ones in a city.

In theory, part of the land value gains was meant to be utilized for the construction of housing for low-income households.

The narrative of squatter citizens' participation in decision-making and their claims to legal title to land under RAY runs alongside the lucrative incentives to large developers in the form of land in prime locations and flexibility in development rules. It is also useful to note here that there is rapid restructuring of physical spaces in Indian cities as elsewhere in Asia to attract foreign direct investment. This urban transformation led by the state in Indian cities, as elsewhere in Asia, requires land and has been marked by eviction and displacement of low-income households from prime locations within the city boundaries (Shaktin 2011; Benjamin and Raman 2001; Roy 2009). In this light, several questions arise as to how the regime of participation was instituted and practised? How are decisions relating to sharing of land made? How is the information underpinning key decisions with respect to land sharing, allocation of land and housing shared? How far can citizens influence such decisions? How do citizens respond to state decisions?

As Roy (2009) notes, recent studies on urban transformation have documented extensively the contours of exclusion; however, the politics of inclusion in urban development projects has received less attention. I explore this politics drawing on the experience of citizens residing in a squatter colony, named the Kathputli Colony, in New Delhi, the capital city of India. The colony is one of the three locations where RAY was piloted. The struggle of Kathputli Colony inhabitants to secure their claims to land and housing at their present location(traced in section 2) spans over two and a half decades. The survey process for RAY is one of the series of state interventions in Kathputli Colony. It led to a prolonged conflict between residents, developers, and the state. Drawing on an ethnographic research undertaken in Kathputli Colony between November 2013 and July 2014, this paper examines the factors that led to the conflict. It draws on semi-structured interviews with NGOs, field bureaucrats of the concerned state agency, professionals involved in drafting the plan, activists, lawyers and the developer. The information thus gathered is supported by the author's role as participant observer and as a mediator between the community, the activists and the lawyers during the court proceeding between March 2014 and July 2014 over RAY.

Ever since RAY was instituted and the conflict broke out, Kathputli Colony has been swamped by researchers, media persons, party politicians, expat artists, lawyers, interested citizens, and university students, all seeking to represent the cause of colony citizens. The common explanation given for the conflict that erupted between the colony residents and the state agencies is failure of implementation. In other words, it is presumed that participation as a norm is intrinsically beneficial and its failure is linked to the unwillingness of the field bureaucrats to institute proper procedures (see for example, Dupont 2014). By contrast, this paper argues that the conflict masks the deeper conflict of interest between various agents over land and their differing interpretations of what constitutes access to legal title for squatter citizens.

In conceptualizing the politics of inclusion in RAY, I draw on Fergusson's (1994) thesis on anti-politics machine and Flyvberg's (2003) conceptualization of the relationship between rationality and power. Adopting Fergusson (1994), I argue that attributing the conflict between squatter citizens and the state to implementation gap misses out the political-economic context of land and real estate in contemporary cities in which RAY is being implemented. Conflicts witnessed in the Kathputli Colony context are an outcome of politics by intent, contrary to Dupont's analysis which attributes it to failure to implement procedures. The procedures and laws were shaped to limit the boundaries of participation and led to conflict between the state, the developer, and the community over issues of location, house design and importantly, the information about the community on which other decisions are premised. RAY is implemented in a political milieu where land and real estate are promoted as key strategies for driving growth. The politics of inclusion under RAY needs to be situated in a wider context, beyond the limited scheme framework. Often, the technical rationality of participation is mobilized to serve as a useful entry point for an intervention of a very different nature. I build on Flyvberg's conceptualization of the relationship between rationality and power to contest the Weberian understanding of rationality as a neutral norm, to demonstrate how power influences what is rational and rationalizes certain decisions over contested resources. The logic of technical rationality and crafting of rules of the game as law via the master plan, limited the boundaries of participation of citizens in key decisions pertaining to land sharing, which has a bearing on the design of housing and the location of projects.

The rest of the paper is divided into the following sections - a brief introduction to Kathputli Colony provided in the next section, followed by the history of colony citizens struggling to claim land and housing in the third section. The fourth section considers the key issues and lesson arising from this case study.

Introduction to Kathputli Colony

The case discussed in this paper draws on the experience of citizens residing in Kathputli Colony, a squatter settlement, in New Delhi. New Delhi has a population of 16.7 million and is one of the most rapidly growing metropolises in India. The city recorded a growth of 21 percent between 2001 and 2011 (Census of India, 2011). Around three million people reside in Delhi's slum, which is around 6 percent of total slum and squatter population in India (Solanki 2012). According to UN-HABITAT (2009), Delhi is the second largest megacity in terms of slum and squatter settlement population after Mumbai.

Kathputli Colony is located in Shadipur in the western part of Delhi metropolis. The term Kathputli is coined from two Rajasthani words, *Kat* meaning 'wood' and *putli* meaning 'puppet'. The colony is inhabited by migrant communities from different parts of India. The settlement derives its name from an artisan community from the western Indian state of Rajasthan, where string puppetry is practised. Besides puppeteers, other artisans from the same state, including musicians, magicians, jewellers, carpenters, metal workers, and snake charmers, reside in the colony. A majority of artisans are from the Bhatti community of Rajasthan. They were once seasonal migrants to Delhi, frequenting the city for three months in a year, but over time settled in the city. These migrants moved to Kathputli Colony in 1956, when their camps in Old Delhi localities were demolished. Overtime, they were joined by tribals from Andhra Pradesh who prepared and traded herbal medicines and migrant labour working in the nearby industrial estates. The latter group of migrants moved to the city from different Indian states such as Maharashtra, Kerala, and Bihar. Today, there are thirteen different communities in the colony. The artisans from Rajasthan are the dominant group constituting nearly 50 per cent of the colony's population. The 1,500–plus artisan households from Rajasthan trace their roots to 13 clans.

The colony is well-connected by the metro rail network and road transport to localities in central Delhi and other parts of the city. According to estimates, the number of households in the colony ranges from 3,200 to 3,400. The physical layout of the colony developed as dense enclaves of regional communities with low-rise structures. With the exception of houses along the main entry road of the settlement, access to settlement residences is difficult. The community lacks basic infrastructure. There is no piped water supply. The storm water drainage along the main entry road is used as sullage and sewage outlet. The main entry road to the settlement is paved, but the side roads are neither paved nor have they been provided with drainage. Consequently, the pathway is the place where sullage and sewage water is disposed. It gets inundated even with moderate rainfall and during the rainy seasons access to houses in the side-lanes is difficult.

Kathputli Colony was placed on the global map in the seventies by an influential artist – Rajeev Sethi – who is the founder of Sarthi (Friends of Artists in Need) and the Asian Heritage Foundation, with a mandate to preserve cultural heritage. Interviews with activists of Sarthi suggest Sethi mobilized the seasonal migrant artisans from Rajasthan camping at different locations in Delhi when their temporary camps were demolished in the early seventies, and the organization supported them to settle in Kathputli Colony. The Asian Heritage Foundation and the Sangeet Natak Academy elevated the status of Bhule Bisre Kalakar Cooperative (BBKC) artisans in the international arena. Drawing on his close friendship with the Gandhi family, Sethi enlisted the GoI's financial support to organize Festival of India shows outside the country to showcase arts and crafts of

Kathputli residents. By the 1980s, Kathputli puppeteers had gained recognition in the UK, France and the United States.

RAY was being implemented by three different local state institutions, namely, the Delhi Development Authority (DDA), Delhi Municipal Corporation and Delhi Urban Slum Improvement Board (DUSIB). With the exception of the DMC, the other two organizations are parastatal agencies headed by bureaucrats. Kathputli Colony is administered by one of the parastatal agencies, the DDA, which is also responsible for planning and regulating land development in the city. Kathputli was chosen as one of the three sites for piloting RAY, because the colony inhabitants had been lobbying to regularize land occupancy and house construction for over three decades (described in detail in the next section). Until the introduction of RAY, the struggle to claim land and housing was between the citizens of Kathputli Colony and the DDA. The PPP arrangement for the design and implementation of housing for the colony added a new dimension to land question, as shown in the third section.

History of Struggle to Claim Land and Housing

Kathputli Colony was demolished in 1976[3] along with a number of other settlements in the city, when emergency was proclaimed in the country (Tarlo 2003). The evictees were allotted plots in a resettlement site outside Delhi but many households returned to Kathputli Colony. With the help of Sarthi, they formed a cooperative called the Bhule Bisre Kalakar Cooperative (BBKC) in 1978. With the consolidation of the cooperative, the Asia Heritage Foundation and BBKC embarked on a dream project – an artisan village named – 'Anandgram' (1982), which was designed as a residential-cum-workspace for artisans. Subsequently in 1989, another plan was prepared called 'Nehru Kala Kunj'. The artisans argued that since they had been staying at Shadipur for more than fourteen years, the houses had to be constructed at the same location. These plans were drafted after extensive research on the artisans' ways of life

[3] 'Bhoole Bisre kalakaron ke sangharsh ki saalgirah.' *Hindustan*, 2 June 1978.

and work facilitated by some of the country's leading architects and a media organization. The dream of colony artisans still remains a plan in paper.

Both the plans – Anandgram and Nehru Kala Kunj – adopted a participatory approach, with citizens taking responsibility for design and implementation of their built environment. The model houses built by colony artisans were designed to preserve their rural lifestyle. There were several rounds of discussion between the colony citizens, the Delhi Development Authority, and Sarthi. The initial rounds were promising, as the then-DDA governor agreed to implement the plan and constituted an implementing committee in 1984. However, this remained a paper plan.

The DDA tried to demolish the settlement during the second round of demolition in the nineties, but the colony residents managed to ward it off. In the mid-nineties, under the Janata Dal regime, the then-prime minister regularized the occupancy status of all squatter citizens in the city and issued identification tokens. Protection was given against eviction, and an occupancy certificate, popularly known as the VP Singh Card, was issued to all squatter citizens in the city. However, the problem of demolition and evictions resurfaced after the turn of the millennium in all metro cities including Delhi, with GoI's policies for restructuring the image of cities to attract foreign direct investments.

The Anandgram plan was designed to accommodate 1,500 artisan households, with residential units organized around an open workshop. Each street was designed to showcase a particular craft and an open-air theatre was planned to educate visitors about the colony and the life of artisans. The plan was followed by lobbying for the transfer of land to the settlers. The DDA and the slum board instead, sought to plan a multi-storeyed structure, but failed twice. The Anandgram plan prepared by Rajeev Sethi did not move forward.

There were attempts to resettle Kathputli residents, first in 1986, and again in 1996, to the outskirts of South Delhi. Residents were identified and issued tokens, but they returned.[4] Subsequently, in

[4] Interviews with Puran, Puppeteer, Dilip – Pradhan, and Bhagawati Asia Heritage Foundation, February 2014.

2002, there was a proposal to relocate Kathputli residents to the outskirts of southwest Delhi, which also did not materialize. The idea of Anandgram continues to dominate the imagination of artisans till today, as an alternative to the DDA's multi-storeyed proposal.

Besides the BBKC, there are two other societies – Piyush Krotha (Leper) Society, and Mahila Cooperative Society (MCS). The MCS was formed to provide a platform to woman leaders to influence decisions relating to the community. It was constituted following a conflict between male leaders of BBKC and woman artisans. Another NGO, the Kalakar Trust, supported the formation of a women's thrift club with 400 active women, a youth club, an adolescent girls club, and a magicians club. Till date, such intra-community and intra-household conflicts and alliances play out time and again in the ongoing conflicts between the state and squatter citizens over issues of land and housing.

Technical Rationale, Conflict and Community Distrust

RAY comprised the following sequence of activities viz., generation of demographic and spatial information on squatter settlements; the design phase involving the preparation of a detailed development plan; and the construction phase. Squatter citizens were to be involved in all activities, namely the survey process, preparation of settlement plan, the design of houses and construction. External agencies such as NGOs and professional consultants would support the community to generate information at the settlement level and in detailed project report, which would constitute the legal document for implementation.

The Kathputli redevelopment plan under RAY was formally announced in 2009 by the then-Minister for Housing and Urban Poverty Alleviation, Mr Ajay Maken. The decision on in-situ redevelopment of Kathputli was made in 2006, when DDA invited tenders for empanelling consultants. The community was not involved in the initial design – the preparation of Development Plan Report (DPR) or the selection of agencies to undertake the survey – on the grounds that these require technical expertise, which was beyond the capacity of colony citizens. An architect and planning consultancy agency called the GPMA was chosen for preparing the DPR for Kathputli Colony. GPMA initiated a house-to-house survey in the colony for designing the development plan. The GPMA DPR proposed redevelopment in 40 per cent of land for Kathputli residents with 60 per cent land transferred to Raheja Developers Ltd. for sale in the open market. The 40:60 proportion of sharing the land was also stipulated in the Delhi Master Plan prepared by the DDA. The rationale for arriving at this decision was to provide an important incentive to private builders to participate in a low-income housing project.

The GPMA went ahead with the DPR despite contestations over the survey process, and the DDA decided to go ahead with the plan of construction by Raheja Developers under the PPP arrangement. According to the head of GPMA, their organization was employed only for consultancy, and it was known that the construction was to be awarded to another company. The GPMA decided to work on the Kathputli Colony DPR, since the DDA was one of their important clients and it was known at the time of DPR tender award that the PPP for construction would be awarded to a private developer named Raheja Developers Ltd.[5] Raheja Developers Ltd., chosen for the PPP in construction of housing for Kathputli, is one of the large developers in the country – known for their projects on shopping malls, IT parks, Special Economic Zones (SEZs) and high income luxury housing. The builders are based in Mumbai and largely rely on the state support to secure land for their projects under the PPP. Their dream plan for the location of Kathputli Colony envisioned high-rise towers predominantly for higher-end housing markets, evoking the image of Dubai in the middle of Delhi.

The land occupied by Kathputli Colony residents, measuring 5.22 acres, along with Rs 6.11 crore, was allocated to Raheja.[6] The first plan proposed by Raheja was along the same lines as the DPR prepared by GPMA which comprised 19 multi-storeyed buildings of a height of 190 metres with 54 floors. In 40 per cent

[5] Interview with chief architect GPMA and the team leader, GPMA November 2013.

[6] Internal Project Report DDA.

of land, earmarked for redevelopment, Kathputli residents would be accommodated in three multi-storeyed housing structures of 16 floors or 160 feet (50 metres). The houses for the colony residents were designed to have an area of 30 square feet, along with other common amenities. However, there were objections to the first plan from the Ministry of Environment, Forest and Climate Change and the Ministry of Civil Aviation, on the proposed height of the buildings. The Environment Ministry stalled the clearance of the project till October 2011, stating that the plan did not meet the environment clearance guidelines, and the Civil Aviation Ministry imposed height restrictions. Subsequently, in the revised plan, the housing structure would now have 13 floors instead of 16. Since the builder did not want to lose out land earmarked for commercial development, the new plan restricted the number of Kathputli households that could be accommodated in the 40 per cent of land area. This further reinforced the conflict. While the builder and the DDA worked to reduce the numbers further, colony residents fought for inclusion of all households in ownership tenure. This conflict over numbers set in process a web of surveys and alternative plans for housing.

Eventually, the DDA, the developer and the community entered into a tripartite agreement for implementation of the redevelopment project. The agreement guaranteed that the DDA would provide the builder with land that is free of encroachment and litigation[7] before the work commenced. The developer was made responsible for providing basic infrastructure (water supply, drainage and electricity), including securing permission from respective agencies. The project was to be completed in two years, i.e., 2011. As per the agreement, Raheja demanded vacant land before starting the work, meaning that all residents had to be shifted to a temporary camp, Anand Prabat, before the work could commence. The community refused to vacate the land, because the number of colony residents eligible for housing allocation remained unsettled. By this time, the community had lost trust in both the DDA and the builder. They feared that once they vacated the land, there was no guarantee that

[7] Interview with Sahil, ex-DDA planner, dated 23 June 2014.

they would be allocated housing in the same location and they would be forced to accept resettlement.

The location of Kathputli Colony is strategic from several aspects. It is well connected to the city centre, commanding a very high real estate price. Further, the colony abuts a main road, referred to as PR in this text, which connects the city centre to localities to the west of Delhi. The transport corridor planned along the PR road was proposed to be financed through a combination of rent and sale of shopping malls and luxury residential complex projects. As such, there was a bigger plan for land acquisition of other settlements in the locality. Not surprisingly, it ended in a conflict between the state, residents and the Raheja builders which played out in different domains – the state, the community, the courts and the media. It is not surprising that the developers involved in this case are still contesting the land occupied by Kathputli residents.

Institutionalized Participation and the Spiral Web of Surveys

Although RAY guidelines stipulate involvement of communities in enumeration and surveying, and a DDA circular also exists (F2(1)12001/LMClpt./296) to that effect, the DDA rarely provided information to the community about the date of survey or their visits to the site. Till the commencement of the first DDA survey, residents had almost no information about the project. Subsequently, GPMA associates claim, the DDA was supposed to publish the survey results but not the specifics of detailed development plan. On the other hand, residents claimed that the DDA did not share the survey result, stating that the analysis was not complete. In our interview with the survey team leader of GPMA associates, we were told that the DDA did not share the earlier survey with the community and that they were not aware of the reasons for DDA's action.

Subsequently, GPMA associates conducted a second survey in May 2008, which was approved by the Chief Architect on 23 September 2008 (http://www.pudr.org/?q=content/kathputli-colony-receiving-end). The GPMA survey counted 2,704 households and 13,250 residents. This data was used as the basis for preparing detailed development plans. The survey was verified in 2010 and 2011 and approved by the DDA. There were objections from residents to the list prepared by GPMA and they had filed complaints with the DDA.[8] In November 2013, when we first met GPMA, the survey team leader mentioned that they were busy in 'fixing the list' ... and visiting the area for a resurvey.

Residents argued that there was undercounting from the first survey and that many first floor households were not enumerated. The counting of households from different surveys and their outcomes told a contradictory story, with the numbers varying from 2,700 and 3,400. In March 2014, the DUSIB website listed 2,800 households as eligible for housing allotment in Kathputli Colony, and the conflict moved to the court. Despite its own count of 3,200 families in the colony in 2006, the DDA used 2,800 households as the basis for designing the detailed development project. The DDA did not share details of household listing from various other surveys, only informing the community of their count of the total number of households. Thus, who would be included in the housing programme of RAY remained unclear to the community.

Despite the disagreement over the numbers, the housing project for Kathputli Colony was inaugurated by the then- minister for urban development in January 2009. The residents had by then filed complaints with the DDA circle office about the undercounting in various surveys, but were told by a senior engineer that the office has no role to play in the survey process or in the allotment of houses, as these decisions are controlled by the DDA headquarters. The *pradhans* (community leaders) interviewed complained of the difficulty they faced in securing information about the survey results and said they had to resort to the Right to Information Act to elicit a response. Despite this, they were unable to secure any useful information from the DDA.

When the colony residents were asked to vacate the land and move to the transit camp, they refused to move. The DDA responded by organizing a third online survey in 2010, which accounted for 3,100

[8] Interview with Mr Dunu Roy, Hazards Centre, dated 12 April 2014; RTI documents shared by Ms Poornima, organizer of Friends of Kathputli Colony.

households. Apart from these four surveys, since the eighties, there have been community led surveys organized by NGOs and Friends of Kathputli.

The RAY guidelines also emphasized biometric mapping for the creation of a centralized data infrastructure. Banda, Vaidya, and Adler (2012) reported biometrics were recorded by DUSIB along with DDA. According to Banda et al. (2012), this survey was midway in 2012, but it was not clear whether it was completed. In our interview with the then DDA chairman in 2012, we were told that DUSIB did not proceed with the biometrics as they had, instead, decided to use the unique ID card issued under the AADHAR programme. Similarly, till date, the DDA has not revealed the GIS maps outlining the settlement boundary and houses as it exists now. The Kathputli conflict attracted the attention of the media, concerned citizens and activists as reiterated earlier. Until then not much was known about the settlement or the project. Citizens from different income groups formed a group called Friends of Kathputli to support the land and housing struggle of the colony citizens. The conflict between the DDA and the community had reached an impasse by the end of 2012, but there was not much action from the state until the end of 2013. When I was conducting fieldwork in November and December 2013, the colony residents mentioned the imminent redevelopment of the area but were not sure whether it would go ahead.

Entry of Political Parties

The announcement of Delhi state and Lok Sabha elections in October 2013 and subsequently in March 2014, brought new players into the Kathputli Colony discourse. Since October 2013, Aam Admi Party (AAP) representatives had been actively working with the community. They also supported the community against police harassment. In February 2014, AAP organized a public meeting with the concerned police inspector. Towards the end of April 2014, the Bharatiya Janata Party, widely predicted to take over the national government, was in discussion with the 13 *pradhan*s on the potential public interest litigation in the court. Post-elections, a BJP lawyer was to represent the community in future hearings. The lawyer, who had earlier fought the case for the community, was replaced. The second lawyer continues to work with the community.

Forced Eviction, Self-Enumeration for Contestation in Courts

The Kathputli redevelopment project picked up momentum at the beginning of 2014, with the DDA announcing a survey of its encroached land and digitization of land records. Until January 2014, the struggle for land and housing was led predominantly by the *pradhans*. The newspaper announcement of the DDA survey spurred a rumour in the colony about possible eviction within a few days. The *pradhans* feared that the DDA would evict them forcefully and decided to appeal against the demolition of their colony in the Delhi High Court. They began mobilizing support of NGOs and political parties to lobby for stalling of the survey. The NGO, Hazards Centre, which had been working with resettlement colonies, came forward to support them in their struggle against eviction.

In the midst of this frenzied lobbying, in February 2014, the Lieutenant Governor (LG), who heads the DDA, in the organization's Board meeting ordered the eviction of the citizens of the Kathputli Colony to start the construction of houses by Raheja Developers. Further, it was decided in this meeting that the DDA would allot housing to those households listed in the survey of 2010–11. When the DDA attempted to evict residents from the settlement in February 2014, women from the colony mobilized to block the entry of officials. The demolition was stalled. During that same month, the DDA attempted to demolish the settlement thrice, but could not succeed. Failing in the use of direct violence, the DDA resorted to other fear tactics like booking male members of households and the *pradhan*s under various petty criminal cases.

The fear of eviction and threats from the police influenced male heads of households to stay away from work. It is at this time that an NGO operating in the city entered the scene with an agenda to obtain legal rights to land for squatter dwellers in the city. The NGO mobilized residents to lobby the DDA and to protest actions around eviction of another squatter settlement. Following the questioning of the *pradhans*, the NGO organized a protest at the site, where the narrative moved from the list of households to design issues. Residents demanded that they be allotted plots instead of awarding the contract to Raheja.[9] (See also: http://www.gharabari.com/news-Delhi%20NCR-DDA%20goes%20ahead%20with%20Kathputli%20Colony%20plan-13339).

Self-Enumeration by Community

When the colony citizens along with the NGOs decided to appeal against the DDA plan in court, they organized their own 'participatory' survey to prove the case. The self-enumeration exercise was led by the colony *pradhans*. The Hazard Centre had mobilized university students to support the *pradhans* in this endeavour. The accuracy and details of record keeping differed between the *pradhans*. The *pradhans* from the artisan community of Rajasthan had conducted a survey of households dating back to the nineties and had collected photographs of each member, continuously updating this information over the years. They also maintained an informal record of property exchange within their community. Other migrant groups were not so organized and consequently, the community survey went on for nearly three months beginning in January 2014. The NGO also appointed itself as the mediator between the community and the DDA.

Towards the end of February 2014, the community registered a case at the Delhi High Court to stay the eviction. The first hearing was held on 24 February 2014. Following the refusal of the High Court to stay the DDA eviction, the NGO lobbied the LG, who agreed to stay the eviction till the end of March, and to consider the plan prepared by the community. From March 2014, the pressure from DDA increased. The artisan families were also struggling, as protest actions and regular visits to various offices affected their livelihoods. The preparation of community plan was controlled by the NGO. The first plan was developed with the assumption that the entire area of 5.22 acres would be transferred to the community.

[9] Interviews with Puran, Dilip, Bhule Biser Cooperative and members of Rajasthani community on 25 February 2014 and observation on 22 February 2014.

The NGO submitted the plan to the LG, but little was known to the residents about these meetings. The plan submission also resulted in a temporary fallout of the two NGOs connected with the community. With the planning exercise, a new narrative started to circulate among the *pradhans* – some of whom claimed that they were willing to move within 2 kilometres from their present location, provided all 3,200 households were allotted land. Others were ready to compromise on multi-storeyed apartments in the same location.

Towards mid-March, the community, encouraged by one of the NGOs, filed a case in the court for staying the redevelopment project. This was in response to the pressure from DDA to move the residents to a transit camp. While the community was in discussion with the NGOs and their lawyers, Raheja moved the court to issue an order to prevent any stay on the project. I went to the community on the day the community received this order. When the conflict had reached the court, there were three NGOs and one independent group working with the community – led by an NID graduate who came to learn puppetry, and wary of the NGOs' strategies, mobilized her group to work on this issue. There was competition between the NGOs in the appointment of the lawyer. At first, a lawyer (J), known to Friends of Kathputli, was appointed to represent the community. However, he was removed by Hazards Centre, and the NGO along with Rajeev Sethi, appointed a human rights lawyer (N) to represent the case.

The Role of the Court and Community Participation

The involvement of the court took the idea of community participation to a new level. There were three court hearings between February and July 2014. The first heard the plea seeking stay on any construction activity in the area. The DDA lawyer informed the court that the names of households entitled to a flat under the 'In-Situ Slum Rehabilitation Scheme' had been made public, and 2,641 residents had been identified who would be rehabilitated. The DDA along with Raheja Developers presented video evidence claiming that the survey was conducted in a transparent manner. The community objected to this. As the lawyer representing the community (N) arrived at the court late, the community was represented by J. By now, there was considerable confusion in the court. Eventually, the community's lawyer took over the process and disputed the evidence provided by the DDA and Raheja and sought an extension to disprove the DDA's claim. The first hearing dampened the community's spirit, as the court refused to stay eviction, but was willing to give an extension to the community to represent their case.

The second hearing was fixed for two weeks later, when the advocate appearing for the DDA told the court that under the proposed plan eight towers would be built with a capacity to house 2,800 economically weaker section (EWS) families. The DDA still would have a margin of about 160 flats, and would welcome genuine households who had been left out in the survey, the lawyer said. The community's lawyer pleaded that the authorities had wrongly assessed the residents of the colony at around 2,600, and the actual number was more than 3,200. He argued that many families were not covered by this list, and it had led to the court ordering the DDA to undertake a 'fresh' survey, and the community to prepare their plans.

The court, in the second hearing, asked the community to draft four plans for redevelopment. The NGO and Friends of Kathputli mobilized architects and planners in the city to prepare alternative plans (shown in annexure 1).One plan was drafted by a famous architect based in Mumbai who had worked on Slum Rehabilitation Authority (SRA) projects in Mumbai involving PPP. The other four plans were drafted by local architects/planners. The five plans were then presented to the community, out of which they were willing to consider three with much hesitation. Their first preference was for a plot which would allow them flexibility to develop vertically. The second preference was for G+3 and as a last option the plan with six-seven storeys. The process of drafting the community plan set in motion another narrative pertaining to the suitability of the DDA's design to meet their interests.

The third hearing held on 19 March 2014, ended in a verdict that in the court's view was a 'win-win' scenario. The Delhi High Court declined to stay the redevelopment project at Kathputli Colony and ordered the shifting of residents to a transit camp, 5 kilometres from the settlement. The court, however, provided relief to the residents in that the builder or the DDA could not force them to shift till all their demands were met. The court then directed a team of five representatives from the colony to survey the camp on 22 March 2014, taking note of the anxiety expressed by the residents over the facilities and basic amenities there. The community, the petitioner in this case, was told by the court that those residents of the slum colony whose names did not feature in the list of beneficiaries prepared by the Delhi Development Authority (DDA) should approach the land authority with their proof of identity for inclusion in the list.

Between these court hearings, there were continuous raids at the residences of *pradhans* and migrant households, for which the DDA had mobilized the police. Many were arrested and cases were slapped on them for petty crimes. On the day of the third court hearing, the DDA sought to prevent the *pradhans* from attending it by slotting another case hearing against them at the district court. Thus, while the case of the Kathputli residents vs. the DDA was heard at the High Court, many *pradhans* had to be present in the District Court for the hearing. Different lawyers were working for the residents at the District and High Courts.

Following the court judgment after the third hearing, the community visited the transit camp and held a meeting at the settlement to list the deficiencies in service provisioning at the transit camp. Hazard Centre, the NGO, prepared the list of demands to be fulfilled by Raheja Developers before the community would shift to the transit camp. The delay in the start of the project, in the words of Raheja's representative, affected the company. Raheja representatives held a meeting with the community to discuss the conflict over the number list. They argued that they had invested Rs 760 crore in the project, and that it was up to DDA to create the conditions for construction. The DDA response was that the agreement was between Raheja and the slum dwellers, and it was Raheja's obligation to fulfil the contract. At this meeting, the builders threatened to file a petition against the DDA in the court over the loss incurred by them since the start of the project. This remains a verbal threat till now.

In response to the court order issued on 20 April 2014, the community had identified the list, which was submitted to the DDA in May 2014. Around the first week of May 2014, nearly 400 of the more than 3,000 households moved to the transit camp but 100 of them returned. The remaining households, predominantly from the artisan community, are still adamant on the location. Even within their narrative, there is ambiguity in their interest with respect to location, heritage village and house. In the meantime, Raheja sent their representatives to the community to convince each household about the dream house they could own if they vacate the land and allow construction.

In the beginning of May 2014, an independent artist – P – who had moved to work with Kathputli puppeteers, decided to take a different approach. While the NGOs preferred to publicize the issue around land question, P decided to work to support their livelihoods, as by now the lobbying, meetings and court cases had affected the income of *pradhan* households. More than direct eviction, there was the everyday harassment from the police, fearing which men chose to remain in their houses. The DDA along with police officials frequently visited the site and forcibly handed over the *parchis* (tokens) for moving households to the transit site. Though the community would be shifting eventually, the artists were preparing a plan for a heritage village that would be designed to accommodate both their residential and work needs. The artist mobilized a new group, not linked to any of the three NGOs, to start a feasibility study to support the livelihoods of the artisans.

Progress Up to the Present

Till September 2014, the citizen squatters were staying at Kathputli Colony, with very few households moving to the transit site. While Raheja Developers had made it a condition that they would not commence work until all residents were moved to the transit camps; the residents, fearing that once the land is taken over it would be difficult to get it back, maintained that they would clear part of the land where Raheja could start construction. This was unacceptable to the DDA and the builder, who wanted the community to hand over the entire area.

In May 2014, mobilizing an intra-community conflict, the DDA managed to mobilize 400 households under the leadership of a mahila cooperative member. The remaining more than 2,800 families continued staying at Kathputli Colony. According to the *pradhans*, many among the 400 households are tenants who will not be eligible for house allocation under RAY guidelines.

Charulisa, an architect organization from the UK, offered to conduct participatory workshop between the developer, community and the DDA in August 2014. The jury is out, as the conflict over the list and the plan is far from over.

Conclusion

This paper aims to trace the politics of inclusion in the state-sponsored RAY programme for urban poverty alleviation. RAY, on paper, envisioned to enable low-income households secure legal access to housing. Citizens' participation was institutionalized in all aspects of the housing project, starting from the production of spatial and demographic information on squatter colonies, design of settlement layout and housing and its implementation. Low-income households participate in such projects under the PPP arrangements alongside professional consultants, developers and non-governmental agency. Further, the paper design of RAY is based on in-situ redevelopment, meaning that squatter citizens' occupancy at their existing location would be legalized and titles issued to each occupant. This promise of in-situ housing and legal titles is to be situated in an urban context marked by high land value gain. In addition, the locations occupied by squatter citizens within the city boundary are sought for high-end commercial or residential development. In this light, the paper contoured the experience of residents of a squatter colony, with institutionalized participation in a project for in-situ redevelopment.

Kathputli Colony is in a locality close to the city centre and marked by high land values. It is sought by large real estate developers. The paper analysed the manner in which participation was instituted and institutionalized by the state agency implementing the project and citizens responses. As Fergusson (1994) argued, the rhetoric of institutionalized participation served as an entry point for an intervention of a very different kind. Low income households are conflated with access to a physical structure at any location. This assumption in policy is at variance with the interest of low income households. Further, the land interest of developers was prioritized from the start of the project. The concerned agency – the DDA – deployed technical rationale to isolate key decisions with reference to land sharing, demographic and spatial information, and the design DPR. Kathputli Colony was not only the place of residence, but also the space of work. The place's identity is critical, particularly for artisans, to attract new clients and visitors who came to the site to purchase artisanal products. It led to conflicts between the DDA and Kathputli Colony residents, with the latter contesting the information generated by the state agency and decisions inscribed in the DPR. As illustrated in the paper, while institutionalized participation remained rhetorical, Kathputli residents contested the DDA generated information on which key decisions were premised. Their participation reshaped the decisions of the DDA in multiple domains of the state, courts and party channels, and forged flexible alliances with NGOs, concerned citizens, professionals and party politicians.

The Kathputli case discussed draws attention to the need to rethink the assumed relationship of low income residents with different agents in the city, specifically the given assumption that NGOs are natural allies of economically backward societies. Lobbying by both the NGOs and the developer happens at the level of national governments or international institutions – to which the poor have limited access. These attempts, though seemingly progressive, contribute to the erosion of political space at the local level. Another implication is the manner in which these new norms are enshrined via law. To counter this, there is a need to situate poverty strategies in relation to wider urban development strategies.

The Kathputli Colony case study is not an isolated incident. The PPP model with incentives for developers designed around tapping value gains is promoted dominantly as the model of housing provision for low-income households. This model of squatter upgradation was first experimented with in Mumbai – a milieu dominated by large real estate developers, even before real estate was officially declared as a policy for driving growth. The PPP strategy, which started as a way to attract private developers with an incentive to sell part of the product in the open market, morphed into the transfer of development rights from a locality with relatively low real estate value to localities commanding higher values. In addition, land in city centre localities was released often by forced eviction/buyout by the developers, and in some cases, shifted to locations that are less attractive to higher income residents. In many of these PPP projects, the state entered the partnership on the basis of providing land on a no-cost basis, and eliminating risks relating to acquisition. Paradoxically, the transfer as it happened in the Raheja case, benefits the developers in two ways – land on long lease at almost no cost and the floating of equity or mobilizing credit capital based on the land transferred for construction. The process of poverty in contemporary cities is as much a production of real estate-led urban development interventions, as illustrated by the case study. Poverty reduction policies and strategies need to be connected to urban planning and development. This calls for re-visioning the strategies of economic growth and the manner in which city spaces are produced and distributed between different sections of the population.

References

Banda, Subhadra, Yashas Vaidya and David Adler. 2013. 'The Case of Kathputli Colony: Mapping Delhi's First In-situ Slum Rehabilitation Project.' CPR Working Paper. New Delhi: Centre for Policy Research. http://www.cprindia.org/workingpapers/4638-case-kathputli-colonymapping-delhis-first-situ-slum-rehabilitation-project.

Benjamin, S., and B. Raman. 2001. 'Democracy, Inclusive Governance and Poverty in Bangalore.' In *Urban Governance, Partnership and Poverty Working Paper*. University of Birmingham.

Census of India. 2011. Government of India.

Dupont, V., S. Banda, Y. Vaidya, and M.M. Gowda 2014. 'Unpacking Participation in Kathputli Colony. Delhi's First Slum Redevelopment Project, Act I.' *Economic and Political Weekly*, Vol. XLIX, No. 24, 14 June 2014.

Ferguson, J. 1994. The Anti-politics Machine: Development, Depoliticization and Bureaucratic Power in Lesotho. Minneapolis: University of Minnesota Press.

Flyvberg, B. 2003. *Rationality and Power: Democracy in Practice*. Chicago: University of Chicago Press.

Ministry of Housing and Urban Poverty Alleviation (MHUPA). 2009. Rajiv Awas Yojana: Guidelines for Slum-Free City Planning, Government of India.

———. 2013. Rajiv Awas Yojana 2013–2022, Government of India. http://mhupa.gov.in/ray/ray_index.htm.

Roy, A. 2009. 'The 21st Century Metropolis: New Geographies of Theory.' *Regional Studies*, 43:6, 819–30.

Shatkin, Gavin. 2011. 'Privatapolis: Representation and Contestation in the Development of Urban Integrated Mega-Projects.' In *Worlding Cities. Asian Experiments and the Art of Being Global*. A. Roy and A. Ong (eds.). London: Routledge.

Solanki, V. 2012. 'Forward and Backward Linkages of Migrants: A Case Study of Delhi Slums.' Masters Dissertation, Department of Regional Planning. New Delhi: School of Planning & Architecture.

Tarlo, Emma. 2003. *Unsettling Memories*. New Delhi: Permanent Black.

UN-HABITAT. 2009. 'Global Report on Human Settlements: Planning Sustainable Cities.' London: Earthscan and UN-HABITAT.

12 The Hukou
China's Achilles' Heel?

Tian Fangmeng

Abstract

China's household registration system, or the hukou *system, has been established for over fifty years. Originally designed as a tool for controlling geographical mobility; in the reform era, it has evolved into one for welfare exclusion. The* hukou *system has divided China into multiple 'welfare states', particularly since the late 1990s, when municipal governments were entitled to make their own* hukou *admission policies. As the flow of migrant workers into cities swells unabatedly, the floating population – or urban residents without local* hukou *– has become a major policy issue in China. This paper analyses the origin and evolution of China's* hukou *system as well as its policy effects. It points out that the current* hukou *reform cannot fully solve the problem of the floating population without establishing proper fiscal and administrative institutions for transfer and allocation of resources across regions. It suggests that China should facilitate the transferability of migrants' social benefits and build up a nationally integrated social safety net for the entire population. The findings of this paper have strong policy implications for China's urbanization process.*

Introduction

Joseph Stiglitz, the Nobel Prize-winning economist, had once remarked that technological innovations in the United States and urbanization in China would become two key aspects of human development in the 21st century. The rapid pace of urbanization in

China has been fuelled by the swelling numbers of migrants each year. In 2030, China's cities will accommodate 1 billion people, or about 70 per cent of the population. In such a scenario, China must 'get its cities right'. China's *hukou* system, or the household registration institution, has been regulating its over 200 million migrants in its cities. The system has been criticized as the reason for several social problems. The ongoing reform by the central government aims to improve the management of *hukou* system and the services under it. The decentralization of fiscal and administrative powers in the late 1990s, further left little incentive for local governments to provide public services to migrants, and the majority of the floating population have not been covered under the urban welfare system. The problems brought on by the fragmented *hukou* system have become barriers for labour mobility and domestic consumption.

How did the *hukou* system originate and evolve into its current status? What consequences has it brought to Chinese society? Can the new reforms successfully address issues associated with the system? If not, what policies should China adopt for a better future? This paper tries to tentatively answer these questions. The first part reviews the origin of China's *hukou* system and its evolution by the late 1990s. The second part explains why and how the *hukou* policy at the local level has been 'internationalized'. The third section discusses the policy effects and consequences of the *hukou* system. The fourth part provides some policy suggestions after pointing out the inadequacy of the current reform. The final part concludes the paper.

Origin and Evolution of China's *Hukou* System

China adopted its household registration system, *hukou*, in 1958. *Hukou* combined the traditional imperial institution with a Soviet-style internal passport system in order to tightly control and restrict population flows within China, particularly those moving from rural areas to urban areas. Every citizen seeking a change in residence was required to apply for permission from the local authorities of both origin and destination locales (Wang 2004: 32–61).

The gradual development of a comprehensive *hukou* system was the demand of a planned economy (Chan 2009: 3). The *hukou* status of each Chinese citizen was determined by the economic type (agricultural/non-agricultural) and regional location (local/non-local) with respect to an administrative unit (such as city, town, or a village). Administrative control restricted migration flows not only between rural and urban areas, but also between towns and cities of different ranks, which formed a spatial hierarchy serving economic planning. The tight migration control prior to 1978, had ensured that almost all Chinese people lived in the place of their household registration, and only a small number of migrants stayed in places different from their de jure one (Chen 2009: 211).

Under such a restrictive internal migration regime, the *hukou* status remained the same wherever one moved, unless a citizen underwent *hukou* conversion. It was usually difficult to obtain approval for a conversion from 'agricultural' to 'non-agricultural' status or a relocation from a small town to a large city, as a limited quota of urban *hukou* was available for certain pathways. Non-local migrants could obtain an urban *hukou* status by getting married, attending college, being recruited in the military, or being formally employed in a state-owned enterprise (Wang 2005: 47–48).

The Chinese government provided basic social welfare and economic opportunities to those with a non-agricultural (urban) *hukou*, while those with an agricultural (rural) one were offered little public service. Urban residents could receive substantial benefits such as employment, housing, public education, and health care, but rural residents had limited benefits aside from the right to farm. Under the internal 'passport system', China literally became a sedentary world, divided into two different societies by the *hukou* institution (Wu and Treiman 2004).

However, Chinese people started becoming mobile after the state launched the 'reform and opening' meaning, reform of the economic system and opening of the economy to foreign trade, in 1978. From then on, daily commodities were gradually commercialized, and mobility control was also relaxed. From 1985, the central government formally permitted a temporary stay for migrants with a non-local *hukou* in urban areas. Medium-sized and large cities eliminated the quota of rural migrants applying for local permanent residence, and offered them temporary registration documents. During the same period, agricultural productivity rose substantially, which generated a large amount of surplus labour in the rural area, and the rural people were lured by industrial expansion and higher income in the urban sector. These 'peasant workers' were generally employed in cities, and took up informal jobs that urban residents did not want (Solinger 1999).

Though the geographical division turned permeable, the invisible divide has been persisting till now. Apart from a few migrants who had already acquired non-agricultural *hukou*, the majority of rural migrants were still excluded from the urban welfare system. In the official discourse, the former group is designated as the 'migrating population' and the latter as the 'floating population'. Here the de jure status is not necessarily consistent with the de facto status, as a 'floating' migrant might permanently settle in a Chinese city. The real distinction between them should be one of legal and identity status (Fan 2008).

The *hukou* system has continued to regulate the provision of social welfare and public service to Chinese citizens. Rural migrants are allowed to live in cities, but in most cases they do not have access to utility subsidies, housing benefits, health care, and public education for their children. The discriminatory system has generated 'cities with invisible walls' – cities where migrants with non-local *hukou* live but do not belong. In the reform era, the *hukou* system has evolved to function more as a tool for welfare exclusion than one for controlling geographical mobility. Such an institutional arrangement resembles the social protection system in contemporary Gulf countries (Abrar 2011).

The urban population of non-local *hukou* has expanded rapidly in the past three decades. About 245 million Chinese or one sixth of the national population now live in places other than where their *hukou* is registered (*Xinhua News* 2014a). They make up over one-third urban population in some large cities. Although China's urbanization rate has reached over 50 per cent now, the figure would be lowered to merely 36 per cent, if we calculate it on the basis of local *hukou* holders, instead of all residents (*The Economist* 2014).

'Internationalization' of the Hukou Reform

Roberts (1997) first pointed out that internal migration in China has several commonalities with international migration in both developing countries and developed ones. In this view, the migration of peasant workers in China shows five similarities with Mexican migration to the United States – circular migration, large income gap between source and destination, institutional restrictions, geographical proximity, and surplus labour in agriculture. Aside from these demographic and legal commonalities, the reform of the *hukou* system has generated some new features in recent years, which make it look more like immigration institutions of some developed countries.

Economic rationality has dominated *hukou* reform in the new wave of policy change. China's welfare system is largely fragmented, and the new policy reforms have led to local *hukou* policy evolving to resemble immigration policies in Western countries. For almost all major visa categories in the US, China's *hukou* policy has corresponding components similar to family-based, employment-based, or investment-based immigration programmes. The only missing category is probably one for admitting refugees and asylum seekers. The *hukou* policy has also evolved into a complex system in some large cities, and includes a variety of programmes targeting different groups of population. For example, Shanghai issued four types of residence cards for managing the floating population in early 2010: one for talent, one for overseas Chinese, one for general employment, and one for temporary residents (Li et al. 2010).

For the first four decades of the *hukou* system, the central government largely controlled household registration and population movements in China by setting the quota of *hukou* conversion and by subsidizing urban social welfare (Cheng and Selden 1994). From the early 1980s, China gradually devolved fiscal and administrative powers to local governments, which included policymaking for the local *hukou* system. As a result, local governments gained more power in the management of the floating population in their jurisdictions (Wu 2013). After national liberalization of the *hukou* restrictions in 1998, local governments largely obtained 'sovereignty' in determining the admission criteria of local urban *hukou* (Wang 2005: 93).

From the late 1990s, some municipal governments started eliminating the distinction between agricultural and non-agricultural *hukou* within the registered population of their jurisdiction by merging both economic types into a single version. The elimination of local agricultural *hukou* in a jurisdiction helped equalize the identity status of local permanent residents, thereby changing the nature of *hukou* management regime in China. As a result, the significance of *hukou* status in today's China is less about rural and urban than about local and non-local. Hence, the previous two-step *hukou* conversion has been simplified to a one-step procedure in many Chinese cities (Chan 2008: 594). However, such reform only applied to peasants with a local *hukou,* and not to migrant workers without local *hukou*.

Local governments have largely gained the power to decide the type and size of newly-admitted migrants to urban *hukou* in their jurisdictions. There powers over the *hukou* system have led to the formation of 'fiefdoms' at the local administrative level. For the purpose of economic development and fiscal revenue growth, local authorities usually have strong incentives to grant urban *hukou* to rich investors, highly-skilled workers, and their family members. By contrast, they only issue a temporary residence permit to most migrant workers who are less skilled and are not as wealthy.

For example, in 2004, Shanghai, Guangzhou, and other cities launched a new evaluation policy for the *hukou* application of non-local college graduates. These evaluation criteria for college graduates in Shanghai resemble Canada's point system, highlighting degree, score, foreign language, computer skills, and awards (Li et al. 2010). Some municipal governments also take the length of residence into consideration and adopt quota restrictions. In the case of Zhongshan in the Guangdong province, since 2007, migrants into the city can apply for urban *hukou* on the basis of points scored for the level of education, ownership of property, social-security contributions, and even volunteer work (such as blood donation). Since the admission scheme was launched, only about 30,000 out 1.6 million of migrants have gained local *hukou* (*The Economist* 2014).

Under China's current fiscal system, local governments must bear the financial burden of migrant workers' social benefits. Officials at the regional level worry that *hukou* relaxation would mean massive expenditure on public services to cover extra migrants under its umbrella. Therefore, few cities are keen to abandon *hukou* controls completely, as they fear that opening the floodgates will leave them bankrupt. Instead, local governments are inclined to set high admission criteria, so as to grant urban *hukou* only to a select group, such as rich businessmen who make a large amount of investment and those with an overseas degree or professional qualifications. Some family members of residents with local *hukou* are also eligible for admission.

In addition, the level of state-provided services and welfare are associated with the administrative rank of a city in China. The higher the rank of a city, the better is its social welfare to local residents, as large cities have more political influence when bargaining with the central government, and usually gain higher fiscal transfer in the redistribution of public benefits. Like the welfare state in North Europe, Chinese cities with better welfare system also set the bar higher for *hukou* admission. By contrast, obtaining a *hukou* status in many middle and small cities only requires stable employment and residence.

China's *hukou* policy is designed by local governments, but is directed by the central government. A national guidance issued by the State Council in July 2014 stated that '(local governments) should adopt differential *hukou* policies, and take local social and economic development, urban overall absorptive capacity, and supply ability of basic public service into consideration' (*Xinhua News* 2014b). To be specific, attaining a local *hukou* status is open to migrants with few requirements in small cities and towns (less 0.5 million population); is relatively liberal in middle-sized cities (0.5–1 million population), and certain criteria for settlement are relaxed in large cities (1–5 million population). However, the population of super large cities (over 5 million) is still under strict control. At the upper end, large metropolises like Beijing have superior education and health systems, and their admission criteria are also stringent. At the lower end, small cities and towns only require a stable residence to obtain a local *hukou*, but their level of welfare and quality of amenities are inferior to those in large cities.

(Although the new policy initiative is more liberal in admitting migrants in urban areas in general, it maintains the hierarchical management regime across different cities, as per their ranking. Hence, under the new *hukou* guidance, it can be even more difficult for the vast majority of migrants to settle in large cities permanently, especially super large ones, where numerous migrants congregate. For example, Beijing grants *hukou* to private business owners who pay tax of over three million yuan (close to 500,000 USD) in three years, and employ over 100 local residents (or more than 90 per cent of their employees should have local *hukou*). Some Chinese people complain that the *hukou* conversion criteria in Beijing are even more stringent than immigration admission requirements in some developed countries.

Using Wallerstein's concepts (Wallerstein 2011), it can thus be argued that the *hukou* system resembles the world system in terms of citizenship and social rights, as both the core and periphery regions are able to find their counterparts in China.

Policy Effects and Consequences

The 'internationalization' of China's *hukou* system has brought a series of negative consequences to the country. The primary one is that it hinders economic mobility. Although excluding migrant workers from the urban welfare system can substantially lower the labour price for attracting foreign investment and facilitating China's exports, it also generates institutional barriers to labour mobility across regions. As such, the system is not designed for workers who frequently change their jobs between locations.

Under the fragmented welfare regime, the government-subsidized social benefits are often not transferrable, or difficult to transfer, between provinces and even within one province. For instance, a migrant is required to contribute to a regional pension fund for fifteen years to qualify for the local benefit of retirement. When they move to another city, they may transfer their individual account to a new account, but lose their claim to their employer's contribution. Hence, it is impracticable for many mobile workers to join a regional welfare network, for they would rather bear more risks when seeking new jobs in another region.

The *hukou* system restricts the mobility of both less skilled and highly educated workers. It is not easy for even urban *hukou* holders to transfer their benefits geographically. Though they are more likely than those from rural areas to receive access to local social welfare, it takes considerable time to get through the administrative procedure. Some of them join job-related insurances in two or more cities, which can be both redundant and burdensome (Cheng 2013). In addition, Zhang (2010) finds that many professional jobs in state-owned enterprises are only open to local urban residents, so migrant workers are actually excluded from certain parts of the labour market. According to the author's calculation based on a national survey (NHFPC 2013), nearly 20 per cent of the floating population received a college education in China, and usually have a professional job. The lack of local *hukou* can discourage these skilled workers and professionals from seeking jobs away from their registered locations.

The disintegrated arrangement hinders the relocation of human resources significantly and makes labour market less responsive to the changing demands of production. The *hukou* restrictions and the lack of access to urban welfare have restrained migrant workers in moving from regions with lower productivity to those with higher-productivity, thus reducing scale economy and positive externalities associated with demographic agglomeration at different special levels. Au and Henderson (2006) find that insufficient urbanization has caused under agglomeration of individual cities.

Aside from deterring economic mobility, the fragmented *hukou* system leads to low coverage of social welfare and protection to migrant workers. This has resulted in many social problems. As fiscal transfer for social welfare from the central government is often based on population with a local *hukou*, social expenditure for migrant workers is not adequately taken into consideration when municipal governments estimate their annual public budget, indicating that over 200 million migrants in urban China are entitled to receive little or a fraction of public services.

According to a recent national survey (NHFPC 2013), around four out of five migrants do not participate in local pension, health, and injury insurance, though this indicator is higher in large cities and eastern China than in other regions. China's Labour Contract Law introduced in 2008 stipulates that migrant workers with formal employment contracts are entitled to certain social protections and entitlements. However, the law is poorly enforced at the local level. Most informal jobs simply do not provide a contract, and employers and sometimes migrants themselves are reluctant to contribute to the insurances for aforementioned reasons. As a consequence, migrant workers have to rely on their relatives and friends, or simply return to their hometown for help and assistance, if they encounter troubles such as illness, injury, or unemployment. For migrant workers, the lack of social protection might be an important reason for the high rate of saving among migrants, which reduces their consumption of domestic goods and services.

The *hukou* system has caused discrimination and exploitation of migrant workers, particularly those with a rural background. Many of them are employed with low wages and in harsh conditions. With weak bargaining power and lack of legal support, many workers are vulnerable, and often subjected to exploitation and labour abuses. Over two-thirds of these workers have experienced infringement of their civic rights, such as payment delay and excessive workload (Tian 2015). Without legal knowledge and institutional protection, many choose to remain quiet or turn to friends.

Geographical migration may have given migrant workers more bargaining power in negotiating with employers, since they are able to 'vote with their feet'; but this horizontal mobility does not necessarily imply vertical mobility in the sociological sense. One's *hukou* registration locale is inherited from his or her parents, and intergenerational social/economic mobility is institutionally restrained from birth. With no fair treatment from the start, and higher barriers of *hukou* conversion, many rural residents have little chance to obtain urban citizenship in their lifetime.

Such a trend of social stagnation and division is sharpest in super large cities, and it has been justified by official discourse on attracting highly-educated workers, which views less skilled migrants as unwelcomed sojourners. With migrants being treated as 'temporary residents' without equal status as urban dwellers, a hierarchical system of differential citizenship would persist in Chinese cities. This social division might lead to identity politics and political unrest, in the scenario where migrant workers are mobilized to request their 'right to the city' collectively.

China's New Policy Initiative and Orientation

According to a recent report, China's urban population will reach 1 billion in 2030, or about 70 per cent of the national population (World Bank 2013). Being aware of the problems associated with the *hukou* system, in 2013, Prime Minister Li Keqiang called for a 'human-centred new style of urbanization'. The new government raised two policy slogans related to urbanization – the first is 'citizenization', meaning turning a migrant into an urban citizen with local *hukou*; and the second is 'equalization', which refers to the endowment of equal rights and welfare to migrants as local citizens.

The national guidance issued in 2014, aims to grant 100 million of the floating population local *hukou* statuses in their destination cities by 2020 (*Xinhua News* 2014b). China's urbanization rate is estimated to reach 60 per cent by then, and 45 per cent of the national population will have urban *hukou*, indicating that the floating population will constitute 15 per cent of the nation. The share is lower than the level in 2013 (18 per cent), but remains substantial. Some commentators point out that the new guidance pushes little fundamental reform, and does not raise the prospect of admission for the majority of migrant workers (Chan 2014).

In addition, the issue of the floating population remains a structural problem for China. As mentioned above, the guidance requests small and mid-sized cities to ease their *hukou* restrictions, but attempts to further tighten migration flows to large ones. As most migrants live in or tend to move to the latter with more available jobs, the direction of the guidance can only favour a minority of migrant population. Considering the gap between economic driving forces and absorptive capacity of the *hukou* system, the floating population would continue to be phenomenal in the foreseeable future.

Recognizing that 'citizenization' or *hukou* conversion, cannot solve the problem of all migrants in urban China, the central government has stressed the responsibility of local government in the provision of public services, and issued directives from its functional ministries to address the inequality and injustice related to this group. For example, the central government has instructed local authorities to improve the health care coverage of migrants and to provide free services related to the family planning policy. However, in the absence of institutionalized coordination between the central and the local governments, the latter often spend a small amount of public funds in order to reduce financial pressure or avoid extra obligation.

The policy mismatch can be better illustrated in the area of public education. Over two-thirds of migrants bring their children to their host cities (NHFPC 2013), and the central government urged local governments to provide free compulsory education to children of migrants in both 2004 and 2008. However, it did not allocate adequate financial resources to accomplish the objective. Hence, many city governments continue to restrict access of children without a local *hukou* to primary and secondary schools in their jurisdictions.

However, some local governments, particularly those with more migrants, took innovative initiatives for better governance of the migrant population. For example, in 2007, Shanghai launched new policies to change social and economic conditions of the floating population. It introduced a comprehensive social security system specifically designed to cover migrant workers, and also spent a great deal of effort to absorb migrant children into public schools. Employers in Shanghai are also required to contribute to the social security fund and provide formal employment contract to all migrant workers.

Some cities in Zhejiang, Jiangsu, Guangdong, and other provinces, followed suit, and in 2009, introduced residence permit systems, entitling migrant workers to access local social services. Their residence permit systems operate independently of the *hukou* system and provide the floating population a limited number of services. As local governments are not actively responsive to the call for 'equalization' of welfare by the central government, and only achieved partial success, Lan (2014) depicts the policy practice as 'segmented incorporation', which replaces previous systematic exclusion with more subtle institutional segmentation.

Some people argue that the *hukou* system has actually facilitated China's economic growth, otherwise the country would not have abundant cheap labour, and its commodities would not become competitive in the international market. Even if this is the case, a fragmented policy cannot be justified on economic grounds alone, and policymakers should take its social price and human cost into consideration. Purely for the purpose of economic growth, Bao et al. (2011) shows that Chinese migrants are very responsive to the labour market when the *hukou* system is further liberalized. In their words, 'Even a modest reduction in restrictions can greatly strengthen the incentive to migrate. We find strong evidence that the sensitivity of migration to *hukou* has on balance risen over the last 30 years...' In order to facilitate economic mobility and spur domestic consumption, it is time the Chinese leadership overhauled the *hukou* system and led it toward a new direction.

The current *hukou* reform, as directed by the national guidance, has made limited progress in liberalizing the system. The central government can achieve more in the existing policy framework itself. China's urban welfare, such as pension, health care and injury insurance, is actually not bundled with local *hukou*, but connected with the nature of jobs. It is the informal jobs that make most migrant workers ineligible to enjoy such benefits. More migrants would join the social safety net if the regional authorities can enforce employment with labour contracts and offer more legal protection to migrant workers.

More importantly, China should have a long-term vision of *hukou* reform and aim to build a nationally integrated labour market, wherein every citizen can move freely, and easily realize his or her own social rights. The emerging system of residence permit has opened a pathway toward full urban citizenship for non-local residents, but the admission criteria are set too high in large cities and even a local *hukou* in Beijing is not transferrable across regions. As a result, mobile workers might be reluctant to take the pathway and contribute to local social insurances.

The Social Insurance Law enacted in 2011 entitles migrant workers to transfer their job-related insurances from one region to another. However, this does not work as easily in practice, partly because each province or city sets its own administrative requirements and contribution rates, and the level of welfare is much higher in larger cities than that in smaller ones. In addition, many social services, such as urban infrastructure and public education, are funded by local governments without taking the interests of the floating population into consideration. In the short term, China may learn from experiences and practices of the European Union, which has 28 member countries and also encounters the problem of welfare transfer for transnational migrant workers within the EU.

For reform in the middle term, it is important for China to address unbalanced regional development, which is driven by both market forces and political power. Large cities with high administrative rank have certain privileges in key aspects of social welfare, which greatly raise the value of *hukou* in these places. For example, it is much easier for students in Beijing to attend national leading colleges, simply because the higher education system allocates more quotas for admission to applicants in the capital city. As a national plan, China's 'equalization' policy should entail equal treatment for all its nationals within a city and also between cities.

In the long term, China should establish a nationwide social safety net, which will cover the entire population and provide them basic social services wherever they move. This kind of system resembles the national insurance networks in the US, which operate across states and offer migrant workers similar benefits following their relocation. For this purpose, the central government should reassume its responsibility for the provision of public services in the country, and rearrange the fiscal system and related institutions to transfer and allocate social funds according to the needs of total residents in each region. Commercial insurance or local welfare programmes can address regional variations, depending on their economic development and capacity.

Conclusion

A comprehensive *hukou* system, was developed by the planned economy in China in the late 1950s. The *hukou* status of a Chinese citizen was determined by his or her economic type and regional location. The tight control over population movement was gradually liberalized after the state launched the reform and opening policy in the late 1970s, and surplus labour in the rural area were attracted to find jobs with higher wages in the urban sector. With increasing numbers of migrant workers coming into cities, the floating population – or urban residents without local *hukou* – has become a major policy issue in China's urbanization process.

As the *hukou* system still regulates the provision of social welfare and public service to Chinese citizens, one's *hukou* status not only records demographic information, but also entails an entitlement of social rights. With the decentralization of fiscal and administrative power, local governments do not have much incentive to provide public services to migrant workers, and the majority of the floating population has not been covered under the urban welfare system. Instead of granting urban *hukou* to migrants, large cities in China selectively admit a small number of non-local residents who can bring economic benefits to them. This practice resembles the immigration policy practices in developed countries. The fragmented *hukou* system with special hierarchy has led to many social ills, which have become obstacles for labour mobility and domestic consumption.

This paper points out that the current *hukou* reform has not initiated fundamental changes into the existing policy framework. As such, it cannot achieve much success in solving the problems of the floating population, unless it establishes proper fiscal and administrative institutions for transferring and allocating resources across regions. After analysing the evolution of the *hukou* system, the paper suggests that China should learn from the European Union and facilitate the transferability of migrants' social benefits in the short term, and build up a nationally integrated social safety net for the entire population in the long term. It would probably take decades to transform and eliminate the *hukou* system, but the national leadership should have the determination to build a free, equal, and open society for all Chinese citizens.

References

Abrar, Chowdhury. 2011. 'Bangladeshi labour migrants in the Gulf: Coping with a large unmet need for social protection.' In *Migration and Social*

Protection-Claiming Social Rights Beyond Borders. Rachel Sabates-Wheeler and Rayah Feldman (eds.). Hampshire: Palgrave Macmillan. pp. 262–82.

Au, Chun-Chung and Vernon Henderson. 2006. '*How migration restrictions limit agglomeration and productivity in China.*' *Journal of Development Economics 80*, no. 2: 350–88.

Bao, Shuming, O¨ Rn B. Bodvarsson, Jack W. Hou, and Yaohui Zhao. 2011. 'The Regulation of migration in a transition economy: China's hukou system.' *Contemporary Economic Policy 29*, no. 4: 564–79.

Chan, Kam Wing and Will Buckingham. 2008. 'Is China abolishing the hukou system?' *The China Quarterly*, 195: 582–606.

Chan, Kam Wing. 2012: 'Crossing the 50 Percent Population Rubicon: Can China Urbanize to Prosperity?' *Eurasian Geography and Economics 53*: 63–86.

———. 2014. 'China's urbanization 2020: a new blueprint and direction.' *Eurasian Geography and Economics 55*, no. 1:1–9.

Cheng, Zhiming, Ingrid Nielsen and Russell Smyth. 2013. 'Access to social insurance in urban China.' Discussion paper 05/13. Department of Economics, Monash University, Australia.

Cheng, Tiejun and Mark Selden. 1994. 'The origins and social consequences of China's hukou system.' *The China Quarterly 139*: 644–68.

Fan, C. Cindy. 2008. 'Migration, hukou, and the Chinese city.' In *China Urbanizes: Consequences, Strategies, and Policies*. Shahid Yusuf and Anthony Saich (eds.). Washington DC: The World Bank. pp. 65–90.

Lan, Pei-chia. 2014. 'Segmented incorporation: the second generation of rural migrants in Shanghai.' *The China Quarterly 217*: 243–65.

Li, Limei, Si-ming Li and Yingfang Chen. 2010. 'Better city, better life, but for whom? The hukou and resident card system and the consequential citizenship stratification in Shanghai.' *City, Culture and Society 1*:145–54.

National Health and Family Planning Commission. 2013. 'Surveillance survey data on the dynamics of floating population.'

Roberts, Kenneth D. 1997. 'China's "tidal wave" of migrant labor: what can we learn from Mexican undocumented migration to the United States?' *International Migration Review 31*, no. 2: 249–93.

Solinger, Dorothy. 1999. *Contesting Citizenship in Urban China*. Oakland: University of California Press.

The Economist. 2014. 'Building the dream.' *The Economist*. 19 April 2014.

Tian, Fangmeng. 2015. 'Can floating population affect political stability in China?' [in Chinese]. *Beijing Cultural Review*, February.

Wallerstein, Immanuel. 2011. *The Modern World-System I*. Oakland: University of California Press.

Wang, Fei-ling. 2005. *Organizing Through Division and Exclusion: China's Hukou System*. Stanford: Stanford University Press.

World Bank. 2013. *China 2030 – Building a Modern, Harmonious, and Creative Society.* Washington DC: The World Bank.

Wu, Ling. 2013. 'Decentralization and hukou reforms in China.' *Policy and Society* 32: 33–42.

Wu, Xiaogang and Donald J. Treiman. 2004. 'The Household Registration System and Social Stratification in China: 1955–1996.' *Demography 41*, no. 2: 363–84.

Xinhua News. 2014a. 'Floating population in China has reached 245 million.' *Xinhua News Agency* [in Chinese]. http://politics.people.com.cn/n/2014/1119/c1001-26049933.html.

———. 2014b. 'A national guidance on further reform of the hukou system by the State Council.' *Xinhua News Agency* [in Chinese]. http://news.xinhuanet.com/2014-07/30/c_1111871925.htm.

Zhang, Huafeng. 2010. 'The hukou system's constraints on migrant workers' job mobility in Chinese cities.' *China Economic Review 21*, no. 1: 51–64.

13 The Evolving Role of Public Policy Education and Training in Egypt

Dina Wafa

Abstract

Globalization, economic, social and political changes are transforming approaches of teaching and training. Other nations have witnessed such an impact as with the 2007 economic crises in Europe and North America (Diamond and Liddle 2012). Education institutes are expected to play a key role to respond to society's changing needs. Initially, their role may be only responsive and reactive 'to external pressures rather than initiating or driving transformation' (Brennan et al. 2004); or it may be otherwise.

In Egypt, more than five years into the transition period, citizens' dissatisfaction with governmental services seems to be increasing and there is an urgent need for public service reform and for a new and at least different way of public policymaking. Furthermore, there is an urgent need for capacity building of imminent leaders who are anticipated to lead the transition period to meet the people's expectations.

Education institutes have an important role to play during periods of political transition and especially those offering programmes in public policy and public administration education and training. In Egypt, although there is an urgent need for highly capable public leaders, there are only four higher education institutions that offer master's programmes on public policy and public management: The American University in Cairo, Cairo University, Sadat Academy of Management Sciences, and the Arab Academy for Science and Technology (Bremer and El Baradei 2008). Additionally Cairo University offers a PhD programme in public administration, and Future University offers an undergraduate degree.

The aim of this research paper is to examine to what extent the teaching and training of public policy and public administration was impacted after the 25 January [2011] Revolution in Egypt.

Introduction

Globalization, political, economic and social changes have a critical role to play in affecting education in general. The implications for public policy and public management education and training are inevitable in Egypt's transitional period. These implications will naturally also bear significance on other specializations, as is the norm in interdisciplinary education, to include changes in media and journalism education, law and human rights, sociology, political science, economics and history.

Egypt's history of school curricula in general reflected a centralized government policy. The politicization of curriculum was utilized as a tool 'to inculcate students with specific cultural values and understandings' (Loveluck 2012a). The changes in leadership from Nasser's socialist era to Sadat's open market economy and to Mubarak's globalized capitalist outlook were clearly reflected in public schools' curricula (Baraka 2008; Graham 2004). Furthermore, prior to the 25 January uprising, the Ministry of Education removed all text referring to or praising Mubarak and the previous ruling National Democratic Party achievements, which comprised approximately 20 per cent of the curricula (Loveluck 2012a), an act which was again repeated after the removal of Morsi.

Nasser not only introduced a free for all, centralized, public education system, but he also offered guaranteed public sector employment, resulting in a rapid increase in university graduates and eventually to a strain on public resources and productivity. Egypt boasts more than 2.5 million students in higher education institutes and the majority are enrolled in public universities or public vocational colleges. Yet eighteen state-run universities have a limited ability to generate and disseminate knowledge, given their meagre resources (Lindsey 2012; Loveluck 2012b). Currently a few significant improvements may be seen at the university level. Students are encouraged to engage in discussions and debates.

Furthermore, student union free elections and a significant decrease in the appearance of police and intelligence services (Lindsey 2012) seem to indicate more freedom.

The impact of economic changes on politics and naturally on education, as we witnessed in the 2007 economic crises in Europe and North America, is inevitable (Diamond and Liddle 2012). To consider alternatives and assess suggestions by the political forces are urgent to the course of economic development in Egypt.

Education

Given the numerous challenges faced in Egypt, there is an urgent need for highly capable public leaders. Governments around the world base their public policies on theories developed through educational institutions, yet currently there are only four higher education institutions that offer master's programmes on public policy and public management: The American University in Cairo, Cairo University, Sadat Academy of Management Sciences, and the Arab Academy for Science and Technology (Bremer and El Baradei 2008). Additionally, Cairo University offers a PhD programme in public administration, and Future University offers an undergraduate degree. Nevertheless, these institutions have exerted numerous efforts.

Resuming operations after eighteen days of uncertainty and returning to school after weeks, where the streets witnessed million-man marches demanding change and empowerment, demanded a change in the teaching methods as well. The American University in Cairo (AUC) introduced several new courses and changes in the methodology of some existing courses. Among the new courses was an elective undergraduate history course to meet the high demand for learning more on current events. Three sections were opened for the course 'Al Shaab Youreed Iskat El Nizam', or 'the people want to overthrow the regime' – a popular cry during the revolution. According to the associate dean of the School of Global Affairs and Public Policy (GAPP), public administration faculty introduced debates and discussions on the implications of revolution in their existing classes.

GAPP was one of the leaders in offering public dialogues in response to the recent events and to assist in overcoming the challenges faced. The dialogues were designed to engage members of the media, civil society, academia, and political parties with the public. The dialogues focused on the fundamental issues facing the Egyptian people through a moderated panel debate of different viewpoints of renowned Egyptian analysts and leading public figures (Building a Better Egypt 2011; Haroun, M. Provost, AUC, 2011, personal communication to the American University in Cairo community).

Other schools were also quick to respond to the evident enthusiasm for knowledge, by introducing new initiatives. Cairo University introduced new courses, such as the 'Transformation of the Euro-Arab World Relations Post the Arab Spring' (El Khawaga O, Director, EuroMed Center, Faculty of Economics and Political Science, Cairo University, 2013, personal communication). Additionally, public university students were encouraged to engage in discussions and debates. Maintaining an education environment to enhance skills through debate and active participation in a classroom is an essential ingredient in the capacity building of leaders. Furthermore, student union free elections, a significant decrease in the appearance of police and intelligence services, and introducing elections for senior administrative positions as opposed to previous appointments (Lindsey 2012) seem to indicate more freedom.

There were also drawbacks, as the number of international students dropped significantly during the past three years (AUC Factbook 2014), thus affecting the potential benefit of mutual sharing of experience and cultural exposure. Additionally, research grants dropped by more than 50 per cent from USD 4,801,951 in 2010 to USD 1,826,353 in 2013 at the AUC. Nevertheless, according to the associate dean, the School of Global Affairs and Public Policy was able to secure a grant for three hundred fully-funded Master's fellowships in 2011 for the next twelve years through the Youssef Jameel Fund in addition to twelve others through the Ford Foundation, both based on their commitment to development and capacity building of the future generation of leaders.

According to a World Economic Forum report in 2013, higher education and training constitutes the fifth pillar of the Global

Competitiveness Index. This fifth pillar of higher education and training is considered the driving force for competitiveness and a mark of progressing to the efficiency-driven stage. Countries at this stage tend to 'nurture pools of well-educated workers who are able to perform complex tasks and adapt rapidly to their changing environment and evolving needs of the economy' (Schwab and Xavier 2013). According to the same report, Egypt has dropped 13 positions to reach number 107 out of 144, and will drop to 108 in 2014, according to the Egyptian Center for Economic Studies, and so continues to be placed in the transition phase to the efficiency stage (ECES 2014; Schwab and Xavier 2013).

Training

Egypt has a workforce of more than 27,690,000 ranked as the 21st largest workforce in 2013 (Indexmundi 2013). Egypt currently has an overinflated bureaucracy of over 5.7 million employees, which has been growing dramatically since Nasser's policy of guaranteed employment for university graduates, with a ratio of employees to citizens of approximately 1:17 (Abdel Hamid and El Baradei 2010; and CAPMAS). The total budget allocated to wages and salaries amounts to approximately 172.2 billion Egyptian pounds according to the Ministry of Finance Budget statement 2013/2014, reflecting an increase of 8.8 billion to offset the popular demand for increasing minimum wages, and 13.2 billion to rectify incentives and conditions of certain categories (Ministry of Finance 2013).

Egypt's civil service is currently faced with several challenges ranging from an over-inflated bureaucracy resulting from the guaranteed employment since Nasser's era, to the declining quality of the available pool of workers and to regulations that hinder its development.

Egypt currently has an overinflated governing structure that consumes a tremendous portion of public expenditure, coupled with a declining quality of the available pool of workers and to regulations that hinder its development. Yet the mere existence of institutions is insufficient for service delivery; according to several studies, it does not seem to be responsive to citizens' needs (BTI 2012; Gallup 2012; Radwan 2012; Reske 2011; Transparency International 2013).

One of the least strenuous areas of potential reform in public resources is that of training (World Bank 2013). Exploiting and mobilizing this abundance of resource effectively is necessary for advancement. According to several studies, the unrest continues, and Egyptians continue to be dissatisfied with government services (BTI 2012; Gallup 2012; Radwan 2012; Reske 2011; Transparency International 2013). There is an urgent need for reform and one of the least costly methods is through capacity building and training. Since training and executive education offer more flexibility and responsiveness to current trends (Wafa 2013), they would offer a swift response to help build the capacity of employees and create a cadre more capable of delivering to the public's high expectations. Public management literature implies that political will and government-endorsed reforms tend to have a higher rate of success (Meyer-Sahling 2011; Nakrosis 2014).

The fundamental purpose of training is the effective transfer of relevant knowledge and skills to the workplace, which may vary according to the enabling organizational characteristics (Lim D. and Morris M. 2006; Newcomer, Allen and El Baradei 2010). A government-endorsed organizational commitment that matches training needs with strategic goals and allows the proper transfer of acquired knowledge and skills would ultimately increase the opportunity for the success of capacity building programmes (Adetunji 2012; D.H. Lim and M. Morris 2006; Meyer-Sahling 2011; Majeed 2010; Nakrosis 2014; Newcomer, Allen and El Baradei 2010; OECD 1997; Rondineli 2004).

Capacity building and training programmes are crucial for organizational development, whether in the private or public sector (Goleman 1995; OECD 1997). Research indicates that leadership training can be taught through instilling implementation skills such as trust building, mentoring, updated trends and techniques, and situational analysis for assessing effective leadership behaviour (Robins et al. 2011). This is particularly viable in volatile situations, such as Egypt's current transition. Training leadership and instilling organizational citizenship is necessary for effective outcome and responsiveness. Effective governance requires the development of several government roles, of which evolving institutional capacity is the most critical since it sets the foundation for the development of all others (Rondineli 2004).

Since the 1960s most countries have established training institutions for public sector employees, each with various differing structural factors. Training took even greater importance as countries embarked on public service reform programmes in the 1970s and 1980s, including: reinventing government in the United States; Public Service 2000 in Canada's democratization; in Europe, reforming public management culture through democratization in Spain, de-bureaucratization in Germany, decentralization in France, and introducing private sector values in the UK (OECD 1997). In recognition of the importance of training and capacity building, some countries such as Spain, Italy and France have gone so far as to regulate in-service training, providing legal provisions to oblige governments to recognize civil servants' rights to in-house training (OECD 1997). Though each experience has its own challenges, which have been analysed in various literatures, yet the overall general commitment to the endorsement of capacity building as a tool for development and reform was evidently essential. Following are a few examples from Europe, North and South America, and Asia:

- France obligates civil servants according to the accord-cadre to take 5 to 6 training days annually. It enforces pre-entry exams, and preparatory training programmes by the National School for Public Administration (ENA), which, though not legally obligatory, is highly recommended, as it is almost impossible to pass the entry exam without having attended these programmes (OECD 1997).
- In an effort to increase efficiency and innovation, civil servants in Italy are allowed 150 hours of study leave annually (OECD 1997 and Rondinelli 2004).
- Training programmes for pre-entry exams are offered through the Federal Academy of Public Administration in Germany. Furthermore, a two-year training cycle after recruitment is obligatory (OECD 1997).
- Working toward the Singapore national goal of becoming a high-tech industrial centre, public servants are entitled up to 100 hours of training annually and they are required to develop a training

roadmap to upgrade their skills. Organization capabilities are identified by the Civil Service College in Singapore (Developing a First Class Civil Service and Rondinelli 2004).

- In the USA 80 per cent of government jobs are filled through competitive exams (Federal Jobs Network). Training is the main focus of the Civil Service Learning Institute, which is the central organization mandated with civil service training, and their mission is to 'Create a community of leaders more responsive to the demands of civil service reform' through the Professional Skills for Government framework (Adetunji 2012).
- The Escola Nacional de Administracao Publica is Brazil's national school responsible for training civil servants working toward the recruitment of qualified candidates and of revitalizing the public career system. Regular entry exams are held for public service recruitment (Majeed 2010).

In Egypt several programmes for training public servants have been offered, either through the government or through other sources; these programmes are designed to fill the gap of what the general education system had not provided to equip participants with necessary skills for the job market. These programmes are mainly for the entry-level positions. Additionally, other programmes aim to improve performance in the public sector, targeting mid- to senior-level officials. Training is becoming more globally recognized as a tool for effective leadership through technical, conceptual and human skills development (Goleman 1995; OECD 1997).

The Ministry of State for Administrative Development (MSAD) was established in 1976 with a mandate, as per the official website, 'to develop the state's administrative body so that it functions effectively and efficiently, enable it adapt to the fast pace of change, improve the management of state resources, and provide quality services to citizens'. However, as a ministry of state, the MSAD has limited authority despite the urgent need for reform in Egypt, which may reflect a modest political will for government-endorsed reforms. In 2008, the MSAD founded the National Management Institute, whose primary objective is to raise the capacity of public sector leaders. The MSAD had continued a revolving annexation to different ministries reporting to cabinet ministries. This was more pronounced in the past few years, as the MSAD was at times affiliated to the Ministry of Local Development, Ministry of International Cooperation, and in a few cabinet announcements was not mentioned altogether (Egypt Government Portal). However, there is currently perhaps more opportunity for an evolving role, as the MSAD offices have been combined with the Ministry of Strategic Planning, Evaluation and Administrative Reform.

Other programmes work to help raise the capacity of mid- to senior-level officials to reinforce and reinvigorate leadership capacities within government agencies and public institutions such as the School of Global Affairs and Public Policy (GAPP) Executive Education unit at the American University in Cairo, which was established in 2010 (GAPP Executive Education). While in Egypt and other countries in the region the time is ripe for change, yet the impact of the transition is presenting several challenges to education and training programmes, and will continue to do so for at least the near future. With turbulent changes came unexpected interruptions of operation in schools, cuts in funding, curriculum changes, and changes in perspectives.

Several challenges continue to hamper the delivery of training to public sector, particularly during Egypt's period of transition. One challenge is that of funding with Egypt's deteriorating economy. Budget cuts led to a decline in investment in training and development, as usually, 'training to support the individual career development of employees is more often embraced when budgets are flush' (El Baradei and Newcomer 2008). Furthermore, with the instability of the cabinet and changing the cabinet many times during the past few years, there was a noticeable decline in the discretion of utilizing funds, as senior officials became reluctant to take financial decisions.

Conclusion

Education and training institutions have the potential to play a vital role in partnering in Egypt's transition to democracy. The initial response to the impact of the economic, social and political changes on training in Egypt is naturally a reactionary one. Yet a more proactive, driving force toward transformation is needed in the coming phase of transition. Education institutes are expected to play a key role in economic, social, and political change, and in development.

One faster and more significant change can be seen more clearly in training and executive education, which offer more flexibility and responsiveness. As for public policy education, the bases of development curricula are already in place; the debate is on when, and if, policy issue changes do occur and how they will bear significance on education. A committed political will is necessary for effective reform.

References

Adetunji, J. 2012. 'Civil service training strategy cuts "massive duplication"'. *The Guardian.* http://www.theguardian.com/public-leaders-network/blog/2012/jun/29/central-government-civil-service.

AUC. 2011. 'Building a Better Egypt.' http://www.aucegypt.edu/GAPP/Pages/BuildingaBetterEgypt.aspx.

Baraka, P.E. 2008. 'Citizenship education in Egyptian public schools: What values to teach and in which administrative and political contexts?' *Journal of Education for International Development* 3(3): 1–18. http://www.equip123.net/jeid/articles/7/Baraka-CitizenshipEducation.pdf.

Bremer, J., and L. El Baradei. 2008. 'Developing Public Administration and Public Policy Master's Programs in Egypt.' *Journal of Public Affairs Education*, 14 (3):439–62.

Brennan, J. et al. 2004. 'The role of universities in the transformation of societies: An international research project.' London: Centre for Higher Education Research & Information and Association of Commonwealth Universities. http://www.open.ac.uk/cheri/documents/transf-final-report.pdf.

BTI. 2012. 'Egypt Country Report. Transformation Index.' Berlin: Bertelsmann Stiftung. http://www.bti-project.org/reports/country-reports/mena/egy/2012/index.nc.

CAOA (Central Agency for Organization and Administration). 2006. 'Laws and Regulations Governing Public Personnel' (in Arabic). http://www.caoa.gov.eg/laws.

CAPMAS (Central Agency for Public Mobilization and Statistics). http://www.capmas.gov.eg/.

Diamond, John and Joyce Liddle. 2012. 'Reflections and Speculations on Teaching and Learning in Public Administration.' *Public Policy and Administration* 27 (3)265–77.

Egypt Government Portal. https://www.egypt.gov.eg/english/guide/directory.aspx.

Egyptian Centre for Economic Studies (ECES). 2014. '2014–2015 Global Competitiveness Report.' Paper presentation on 3 September 2014.

El Baradei, L., and K. Newcomer. 2008. 'A human capital management assessment tool for identifying training and development needs: Application to Egyptian public organisations.' *International Journal Public Sector Performance Management* 1(2): 119–49.

Gallup. 2012. 'MENA residents put onus on government to help the poor.' http://www.gallup.com/poll/158906/mena-residents-put-onus-government-help-poor.aspx.

GAPP Executive Education official website. http://www.aucegypt.edu/gapp/execed/Pages/default.aspx.

Goleman, D. 1995. *Emotional Intelligence*. New York: Bantam Books.

Graham, E. 2004. 'Islamic extremism & modern Egypt.' http://www.mideastinfo.com/archive/paper4.htm.

Indexmundi. 2013. Available at: http://www.indexmundi.com/g/g.aspx?c=eg&v=72.

Lim, D., and M. Morris. 2006. 'Influence of trainee characteristics, instructional satisfaction, and organizational climate on perceived learning and training transfer.' *Human Resource Development Quarterly* 17(1): 85–115.

Lindsey, U. 2012. 'Freedom and reform at Egypt's universities.' Carnegie Endowment for International Peace. http://carnegieendowment.org/2012/09/04/freedom-and-reform-at-egypt-s-universities/drak.

Loveluck, L. 2012a. 'The contradictory aims of USAID in Egypt.' Available at: http://www.opendemocracy.net/louisa-loveluck/contradictory-aims-of-usaid-in-egypt.

——. 2012b 'Education in Egypt: Key challenges.' Chatham House. Available at: http://www.chathamhouse.org/publications/papers/view/182603.

Majeed, Rushda. 2010. 'Strengthening Public Administration: Brazil, 1995–1998. Policy Note. Innovations for Successful Societies. Princeton: Princeton University.

McMurray, D., and A. Ufheil-Somers. 2013. *The Arab Revolts: Dispatches on Militant Democracy in the Middle East*. Indiana: Indiana University Press.

Metz, H. (ed.). 1990. 'Egypt: A Country Study.' Washington: GPO for the Library of Congress. http://countrystudies.us/egypt/112.htm.

Meyer-Sahling, J. 2011. 'The durability of EU civil service policy in Central and Eastern Europe after accession.' *Governance: An International Journal of Policy, Administration, and Institutions* 24(2): 231–60.

Ministry of Finance. 2013. 'Financial Statement of State's General Budget for Fiscal Year 2013/ 2014.' http://www.mof.gov.eg/MOFGallerySource/English/PDF/Financial%20Statement2013-2014.pdf.

Ministry of State for Administrative Development (MSAD) official website. http://www.ad.gov.eg/About%20MSAD.

Nacrosis, V. 2014. 'Theory-based evaluation of capacity-building interventions.' *Evaluation* 20(1): 134–50.

Newcomer, K., H. Allen and L. El Baradei. 2010. 'Improving public service educational programs through assessing the performance of MPA alumni.' *International Journal of Public Administration* 33(6): 311–24.

OECD. 1997. 'Public service training in OECD countries.' SIGMA Papers, (16): OECD Publishing. http://dx.doi.org/10.1787/5kml619ljzzn-en.

Radwan, S. 2012. 'The Egyptian economy: waiting for a miracle?' http://carnegie-mec.org/publications/?fa=49929.

Reske, H. 2011. 'Egypt's Poverty, Unemployment Push Youths to Breaking Point.' *News Max*. http://www.newsmax.com/Newsfront/Egypt-poverty-unemployment-unrest/2011/01/31/id/384555.

Rondinelli, D. 2004. 'Reinventing government: The imperatives of innovation and quality.' US Small Business Administration. http://unpan1.un.org/intradoc/groups/public/documents/un/unpan010867.pdf.

Schwab, K., and S. Xavier (ed.). 'The Global Competitiveness Report 2012–2013.' World Economic Forum. www.weforum.org/gcr.

Singapore Public Service Division. 2008. 'Developing a First Class Civil Service.' http://app.psd.gov.sg/data/Corporatebook/developfirstclass.html.

Transparency International. 2013. 'Global corruption barometer.' http://www.transparency.org/gcb2013.

Wafa, D. 2013. 'The State of Higher Education and Training in Egypt Post the Arab Spring.' In *Critical Perspectives on International Public Sector Management Volume 2 - Looking for Consensus: Civil Society, Social Movements and Crises for Public Management*. John Diamond and Joyce Liddle (eds.). Bingley: Emerald Group Publishing Limited. pp. 89–104.

———. 2013. 'Egypt in Transition: Responding to social and political changes in executive education.' *Teaching Public Administration*, 31(2), 174–85.

———. 2015. 'Capacity-building for the transformation of public service: A case of managerial-level public servants in Egypt.' *Teaching Public Administration*, 33(1).

———. 2015. 'Arab Spring Impact on Executive Education in Egypt.' *International Journal of Educational Management*, 29 (6).

World Bank. 2013. 'Administrative and Civil Reform.' http://go.worldbank.org/G4FVQ9MI30.

14 The Case of Housing Policy in the 'New' South Africa (circa 1992–2003)

Firoz Khan

Abstract

Why and how is it that a left-of-centre government not hobbled by heavy external leverage, with (previous) developmental state precedents, potentially positive macroeconomic fundamentals, and well-developed alternative policies for housing and urban reconstruction, came to settle on a conservative housing policy founded on 'precepts of the pre-democratic period'? Arguably, this policy is even more conservative than World Bank strictures and paradigms, whose advice the incoming democratic government 'normally ignored' and 'tacitly rejected'. The paper proposes an answer residing in the mechanics and modalities of knowledge production in the shelter sector; the filtering of this knowledge through the workings and logics of post-apartheid state construction; and the (associated) state technologies of societal penetration and regime legitimization. The absence of a map and compass to guide, direct and assist post-Cold War statecraft; the weight of history and legacy; strategic blundering, and the blunt (government-engineered) techniques of consulting and advising, collectively contribute to the inherited and present defects and deformities of our two decade-old developmentalism, writ large in our dysfunctional human settlements. Alternatives to the technocratic market developmentalism of current housing praxis spotlights empowering shelter outcomes which strategically wrestle with the dynamics and dislocations of land, property and financial markets; urbanization and the wider spatial economy; and, a reconstruction and transformation project that affirms and strengthens citizenship and basic human rights. The role and contribution of planners, the rhetorical and argumentative framing of development/policy discourse, and the rewiring of the relationship between the elite and poor, are central and pivotal to democratically empowering and socially responsive housing praxis. Public policy teaching, in this context, must be alert and awake to the limitations and machinations of autopoiesis, rhetoric and agnotology.

Introduction

The African National Congress (ANC) government's delivery of housing to the poor is an unparalleled achievement in the history of humanity. Indeed, it is acknowledged by the United Nations Centre for Human Settlements as 'one of the most significant contributions of the process of settling people in secure tenure in the history of humanity' (Ahmedi Vawda, ex-Deputy Director-General of the Department of Housing 2003). When comparing South Africa to the very best success stories over the last 30 years – particularly in the first five years of the new administration (1994–99) – South Africans built 750,000 houses in five years, compared to Singapore, which built 585,000 in 26 years and 55,430 in the first five years; Cuba constructed 500,000 in 25 years (85,000 in five years); and Sweden delivered 1,000,000 in 10 years (250,000 in five years). Set alongside these examples[1], South Africa's delivery rate is a stunning achievement (Smit 1999), especially given our level of development and size of the budget. Sweden, for example, devoted between 6 per cent and 7.5 per cent of its gross national product (GNP) per annum to the housing sector over a ten-year period. At peak, the housing expenditure was nearly 20 per cent of government's annual budget. By contrast, South Africa's 1998/1999 housing allocation was only 1.9 per cent of the total government budget. Eighty per cent of the R3.6 billion housing budget at the time was allocated to subsidies (R2.8 billion or 1.6 per cent of national budget). This compares unfavourably with other countries. Housing subsidies, at the time, averaged 3.7 per cent of government budgets in a 19-country

[1] However, the quality and dimensions of housing stock provided in each case cannot be directly compared to South Africa's core houses.

World Bank study, with a range between 1 per cent and 14 per cent. At 16 per cent of budget, South Africa was is in the lowest quintile of the World Bank distribution (Smit 1999)

Almost a decade later, Minister Sisulu (2008) reproduced a similar result:

'When I took over as Minister of Housing in 2004, the government had produced one comma six million [1.6 m] houses. An achievement we were all rightly proud of, despite negative comments. Today, four years later, we have produced two comma six million [2.6m] houses. This means that in four years we have provided one million houses. The target that had seemed so elusive, we have finally achieved, not in five years, but in four years. In plain language, this would mean that we have provided houses for people in excess of five million in four years!'

No country in the world provides free housing for its people. No other country in the world has provided 2.6 million houses to its people, translating again to providing shelter for 13 million people, free of charge.

To put this into perspective [five million in four years], we have housed almost the entire population of Scotland [5.1m] in the past four years or if we want to bring it closer to South Africa, we have housed the combined population of Swaziland [1 million], Namibia [1.8 million] and Lesotho [2.2 million] in the last four years.

In 2010, the South African Banking Association pointed out that 'Government's most dramatic intervention in the welfare housing sector has been its national housing subsidy programme'. It is noteworthy that since 1994, the scale of delivery is 'second only to China' (Minister of Human Settlements, Tokyo Sexwale, cited in *politicsweb,* 21 April 2010).[2]

Set against the global and local recognition and celebration of this achievement and, more importantly, the millions of people to whom the housing intervention has delivered and/or restored some modicum of human dignity, senior politicians have however (since 1994) raised concerns about the poor standard, poor quality,

[2] http://www.politicsweb.co.za/politicsweb/view/politicsweb/en/page71656?oid=172539&sn=Detail.

poor location, poor socio-spatial integration, poor socio-economic integration, urban inefficiencies and spatial dysfunctionalities. The poor outcomes and results are, it is averred, related to a policy that is unable to engage with the (inherited) spatial structure and exclusionary market processes, which is now further fuelled by new and emerging forces, factors and processes, coupled with the inability of government to integrate planning, transport and housing functions in pro-growth and pro-poor formats. Repeated attempts to engage and wrestle with these multiple and interlinked challenges are frustrated and thwarted by an elite, who – over the two decades of democracy – appear unwilling to articulate and advance a transformation programme to address 'structural contradictions' (explained shortly) that were not externally imposed. These structural contradictions were by and large designed and engineered by the public sector elite. At the base of poor outcomes then is a series of decisions that one commentator has un-generously dubbed 'reformist reformism', i.e. elite decisions which strengthen the internal logic of the system (Bond 2014). Another critical commentator observes that the yawning gap between progressive 'intent' (expressed in 'policy' and rhetoric) is a consequence of post-1994 South Africa being 'stalled in a passive revolution', i.e. 'conserving and defending the status quo while simultaneously attempting to cure 'incurable structural contradictions' (Cronin 2014: 54).

The 'reformist reform' and 'cure-defend' decisions are attributed to the influence and power of a development discourse and orientation which not only obscures, but is indifferent to class divisions, inequality and poverty. The subsequent structural exclusions and violence inscribed in the development policies and programmes, its coercive and violent imposition on the poor, their subsequent rejection of it, and the deadly suppression of this rejection – evidenced in South Africa being dubbed the 'protest capital of the world' – compels rethinking and reformulation of the shelter question/problematic in radical and revolutionary schemas (Khan 2013).

This paper rebuts the conventional belief that policy transfer is a top-down process and/or foreign imposition. It also steers clear of conventional teleological explanations which suggest that (conservative) policy is a function of private-sector dominance in the policy process, not least because the incoming ANC government imposed on society a structural adjustment programme (explained shortly). Instead, while evidence points to the flow/diffusion of policies and ideas between powerful social groups in periphery and metropole as mutually constitutive, underscored here is the 'selective uptake' (Cutting 2006: 4) of policy informants and prescriptions within bureaucracies and policymaking circles and 'complex interaction and dialogue' among 'actors and institutions with "different world views"' (ibid.). The adoption and institutionalization of a conservative post-apartheid housing policy based on the 'precepts of the pre-democratic period' – and even more conservative than the strictures and paradigms of the World Bank, whose advice the incoming democratic government 'normally ignored' (Gilbert 2002a: 1926) and 'tacitly rejected' (Mackay 1999: 388) – alerts us to the central import of not imposing/imputing a master-slave (global-local, society/government-private sector) binary on local policy development. However, in relatively 'closed' and 'unexposed' policy communities like South Africa[3] rather than 'introducing new ideas', policy transfer through 'lesson'/'good practice' drawing – and its filtration through structurally uneven institutional terrains, perceived socio-economic and political imperatives and realities, and strategic (mis)/calculations of politicians and bureaucrats – tends to reinforce and strengthen the existing status quo (Dolowitz and Marsh 1996).

This process of policy diffusion – complemented by conservative economic policy/strategy – served (at most times, but not always) to 'manage' the adjustment of social boundaries in ways permitting the existing 'distribution of privilege to be modified rather than overthrown' (Lester et al. 2000: 135–36). Tracing the history of this dynamic from the early nineteenth century to the present, (Lester et al. 2000) posit that the previous radical reconstruction discourse of social groupings opposed to the apartheid state came to be managed/moderated by (amongst other things) the workings of the 1992–94 negotiation process; the accommodationist stance of moderate

[3] According to Mackay (1999: 388), the international development debates of the 1980s largely by-passed South African intellectuals/academics at a time when their efforts were concentrated on 'the struggle' and battling repression.

factions of the incoming opposing elite; the delegitimization of radical solutions[4]; and the influence wielded by a triumphalist (post-Cold War) West and other international organizations (also see Leftwich 1994; Swilling 1999). This atop the weight of history and legacy, strategic blundering, and the blunt (state-prescribed) techniques of consulting and advising, collectively contribute to why South Africa's much vaunted 'transformation' is characterized as more of 'transition' to a 'new, internationally and internally acceptable social and economic order than a radical break with the past' (Lester et al. 2000: 145).

This working paper is structured as follows. The first section sets the macro-context, surfacing the internally engineered and directed rightward shift of ANC economic policy and the long shadow this cast on the housing policy negotiations (1992–94) and 1994 Housing White Paper (WP) (RSA 1994). The second section delves into the modalities and mechanics of 'policy production' in the shelter sector, the filtering of this knowledge through the mechanics and logics of post-apartheid state construction and statecraft, and the (associated) techniques and technologies of societal legitimization and regime legitimation. The final section draws attention to the role and contribution of 'planners' and 'consultants' – who as legitimators of the status quo and handmaidens of repression organized in 'hegemonic discourse coalitions' – frustrated transformative policy (or any potential of its emergence). This does not however close the book on South Africa transiting towards (more) socially and democratically empowering shelter/housing praxis; instead, the 'turbulent, shifting forces taking shape in the arenas of everyday life' (Hart 2013) – here and elsewhere – prise open new vistas for re-thinking and

[4] The delegitimization of radical solutions is connected to the disillusionment flowing from the collapse of Soviet socialism, which over the decades came to occupy a prominent place in the liberation movement's imaginary. The collapse left the 'aspirant liberation movement ideologically rudderless'. In the absence of a critical stance toward Soviet socialism, having never partaken in the debates about the meaning of socialism – real and imaginary – the [South African] liberation movement in power found itself without a cognitive map to navigate the problems of national reconstruction. An 'exodus without a map', as Adler and Webster call it, became vulnerable to neoliberal redemption, especially when the entire globe is spellbound by the magic of the market (Buroway 1997: 1).

re-formulating praxis in radical and revolutionary schemas. This would only be possible via re-embedding and re-calibrating the shelter and housing intervention in ways that meaningfully alter the structural power relationship between the homeless poor, public authorities, and the private sector. Recent experiments in Latin America provide important clues in formulating and practically operationalizing radical re-embedding and recalibrating. Spotlighted in the section – with an eye on teaching public policy in a globalized world – is *poiesis:* making our world or 'our world' as product of social construction and human agency (Calhoun et al. 2013).

Snatching Defeat from the Jaws of Victory

The Macro-Context[5]

A very broad-brush narrative of the dynamics and forces undergirding the macro-transition explains why and how South Africa, spellbound by the 'magic of the market', came to install the 1996 'self-imposed structural adjustment programme' (Joel Netshitenze 2003 cited in Khan 2004: 28) dubbed the 'Growth, Economic and Redistribution Strategy (GEAR)' (RSA 1996).

A year before the election of the first non-racial government (1993), the ANC spent a great deal of time signing on as a party to a series of status-quo entrenching and preserving decisions, including an 'extraordinarily market-friendly Letter of Intent in order to guarantee a balance-of-payments loan [regarded by Fine (2001: 12) as 'unnecessary']... and joining the General Agreement on Tariffs and Trade (GATT)' (Saul 2005: 14). The 'Letter of Intent' pointed to the dangers of increases in real wages in both the public and private sectors; highlighted the importance of controlling inflation; promised monetary targeting, trade and industrial liberalization; and repeatedly espoused the virtues of 'market forces' over 'regulatory interventions' (ibid.).

The 'secret' Letter (Peet 2002: 73) committed the new government to the following policies: reduction of the budget deficit to 6 per cent

[5] This section is short and meant merely to provide a context – we will return to it again below in a more nuanced and textured way.

of GDP within a few years; 'expenditure containment rather than tax increases'; curbing the civil service wage bill; continuation of the tight monetary policies of the previous four to five years, and monetary targeting; policies coupling wage restraint with promoting training and fostering investment; maintenance of the financial rand mechanism without the introduction of new exchange controls (the ANC did however speedily and unceremoniously dispense with the finrand shortly after assuming power); and a simplification and rationalization of the tariff system and the phasing out of import licensing and non-tariff barriers (Padayachee 1997: 32). While Saul (2005) posits that the Transitional Executive Council (ANC and apartheid National Party administration) drafted the Letter, Habib and Padayachee (2000) state that the 'standard, neoliberal, draft Letter of Intent drawn up by the IMF [International Monetary Fund] was accepted by the ANC'. The important point made by (Habib et al. 2000) is that in spite of the many amendments/revisions to the Letter suggested by progressive economists allied to COSATU and the ANC and which the domestic elite had the necessary capabilities and power to effect, it 'was accepted without any changes' (250).

The rightward shift of the ANC not only 'cast the die for future policies' (Saul 2005: 14), it also negatively impacted housing policies under negotiation (1992–94) and later policies (the revised 2004 housing policy[6]) by way of preserving and propping up an urban development regime that was and continues to be out of synch with reconstruction and transformation imperatives and priorities of the post-apartheid period.

Spotlighting the 1992–94 period, the early 90s rightward shift in the economic policy orientation of the ANC played no small role in (the late) Joe Slovo – a member of the ANC's National Executive Committee, a long-time leader of the South African Communist Party, a key actor in the housing policy negotiation and first Minister of Housing – accepting an extremely conservative (the old apartheid 'toilets-in-the-veld': site and pit latrine in the bush) capital subsidy, which ostensibly offered poor families very little by way of housing quality, location and access to basic amenities.

[6] Beyond the remit and timeframe of this paper.

Given grassroots pressure around housing demands and with the other eye on the elections – while at the same time staying true to deficit targets – the ANC had to 'pretend that the subsidy would pay for finished houses' (Gilbert 2002: 1924). South Africa's basic premise, then, as in Colombia and Chile, for the introduction of the capital subsidy scheme was to 'reduce government spending'. 'While every minister of housing [SA, Colombia and Chile] was anxious to increase both total expenditure and the subsidy level, every finance minister tended to say no' (Gilbert 2004b: 33).

With little to no modification to the previous class and racial character of South Africa and the ANC's abandonment of efforts to discipline and direct capital, 'progressive' ideas on 'spatial engineering' – which the ANC had since 1994 being trying to drive (Oranje 2012: 173) – were trumped by a private sector that was (is) at 'once anxious to take advantage of profitable opportunities in the South African city, reluctant about long term investment in general, and recalcitrant about well-meaning schemes that [were and] are not on the face of them profitable' (Freund 2012: 10).

Indistinguishable from the past, this urban development regime – dominated by banks and investment companies – 'determines the direction of development rather than the state, and do this in ways that reinforce the [inevitably intertwined] class patterns of the past' (ibid.). It is for this reason that urban investment and development continues to:

i) favour the interests of the private sector, which seeks insulation for preferred activities and preferred actors through forms of exclusion;
ii) support the kinds of investments that are familiar and characteristically profitable, such as high-value housing and consumption projects, shopping malls linked to road transport and greenfield development;
iii) and that consequently social development aimed at upgrading the lives of the poor will depend heavily on the initiatives of the state, which in turn feels obliged to sustain private sector initiatives whenever possible (Freund 2012: 12).

The scaffolding of this set of structurally (interlocking) inequality-generating processes and outcomes is cemented by this regime's institutional capture of the state and/or its 'informalisation' of the state institutions and/or it resorting to informality and/or placing 'itself outside the law', especially when officialdom's regulatory power is compromised, weakened, or unenforceable (UN-Habitat 2010: 204). Termed 'deregulated governance', it is the process via which power is mobilized and leveraged not only between the state and society but also within state institutions and within and among civil society institutions' (ibid.). This system 'creates a different logic of resource allocation, accumulation and authority' (ibid.) and the 'interactions' between regulated and deregulated formal structures at 'different moments give rise to urban wealth enclaves [and] slums' (ibid.). This form of '"urbanisme de rocade" (bypass urbanism)' (Herve 2009: 58) benefits 'only rarely' low-income people and/or the 'settlements built by the government for the low-income population' (ibid.: 110). If the reasons for this development regime's durability and continuity are anchored in the 'negotiated terms of the transition' that 'precluded radical interventions in either private property or the accumulated wealth of the minority' (Pieterse 2009: 1) – it is exacerbated (underscored above) by the government not having in place any real policy to address the needs and integrate the poor into cities (Herve 2009: 114). In the absence of any 'real overhaul of the land ownership system' (ibid.: 93); 'the maintenance of existing property rights' and relations (ibid.: 93); 'expansion constraints and property taxes' that 'are only very little dissuasive for [socially exclusionary] private development' (ibid.: 111); municipalities that 'do not and cannot' revise 'zoning and assorted regulations' because of the perceived 'weight of the private sector' (ibid.: 94)[7]; 'limited involvement of the state to control development' (ibid.: 141); the financial dependence of municipalities on the private sector; and the 'weakness of the participatory mechanisms' for programmes and projects that benefit and/or aimed at the poor (ibid.), the poor are in effect structurally locked out from access to resources and institutions.

[7] Being unwilling to overhaul urban planning documents amounts to depriving oneself of a tool and allowing the past to continue to operate. This maintains a grey zone conducive to urban development that the government has a hard time managing and creates a considerable hindrance to the application of the desired spatial strategy (Herve 2010: 84).

Apartheid is Dead – Long Live Apartheid![8]

Negotiating Housing Policy: The Dynamics of Policy Production – Change and (Dis)/Continuity

The National Housing Forum was officially launched on 31 August 1992 with a mandate to negotiate a future housing policy and framework. The nineteen members of the Forum comprised major political groups; parastatal agencies (Development Bank of Southern Africa, Independent Development Trust [IDT], South African Housing Trust); representatives of the financial services, construction and insurance sectors; and, two 'non-governmental' organizations (Urban Foundation and Kagiso Trust). Both the IDT and the Urban Foundation (UF) had very close links with business and their credibility was seriously questioned. Created in 1991 by the (apartheid) de Klerk administration, the IDT was set up to finance large numbers of urban upgrading projects on terms 'defined by the logic of economic liberalism, legitimated by a politically correct board and justified by a conservative 'basic needs' approach to development' (Swilling 1998: 289). The Chairperson of the IDT was Jan Steyn, who incidentally was also the Chair of the Urban Foundation.

From its establishment in the aftermath of the 1976 uprising to its disbandment in 1995, the UF – while presenting itself as 'avowedly non-political' (Wilkinson 1998: 222) – was 'untiring first in its search for minor palliatives for apartheid'[9]; 'always' fell short of endorsing universal suffrage; and was the lead 'storm trooper for conservative "neoliberal" social policy' (Bond 2000a: 125–26). Its main aim was to 'promote improvement of the quality of life in urban (and primarily African urban) communities' (Urban Foundation n.d. cited in Wilkinson 1998: 222) through a re-definition of the (Apartheid) 'established parameters of housing policy'. The objective was to create a property-owning (mortgage-bonded) stable society, targeting African households in particular.[10] Pursuant to this end,

[8] Graffiti on a shack wall in Mandelaville in Soweto – post 1994 in *Sunday Independent – Reconstruct*, 12 November 2001.

[9] The Foundation drafted the Black Local Authorities Act of 1983.

[10] As liberal-capitalist political strategist Zach de Beer, [a few years later], (1998) put it, 'When people are housed – more especially when they are home owners – they

the Foundation came to aggressively promote 'self-help' based on individual freehold tenure, which, in their mind, was most suited to addressing the large and growing backlog of housing and creating the conditions for social stability.

A number of the leading 'radical' intellectuals of the 1980s – who 'did not challenge [apartheid] white hegemony' (Mabin 2000:13) and who sought to 'mobilise "free market" forces in an arena from which they [had] been excluded for some thirty years' (Wilkinson 1998: 222) – played a crucial role in the lobbying activities of the Foundation via generating pro-market policy documents and championing these positions in various forums.[11] These 'intellectuals' also piloted and implemented the approaches they developed while consulting for the Foundation, most notably the supply-side, once-off small capital subsidy that created the legendary apartheid-perpetuating 'toilet towns' (mentioned above) – through arms-length apartheid-funded institutions like the IDT (Bond 2000a: 125–26)

The balance of power within the Forum 'favoured the business interests which generally acted in concert with the state and parastatal institutions'. Nine of the sixteen founding members of the NHF were businesses representatives or were pro-business; i.e. 'business interests were over-represented' (Lalloo 1999: 38–39). Business interests were also 'favoured insofar as the deputy chair [of the NHF[12]], Matthew Nell, was a former employee of the Urban

---

are not only less likely to be troublesome, they are also likely to feel they have a stake in society and an interest in its stability' (cited in Bond 2006: 08).

[11] The names of Dan Smit and Jeff McCarthy stand out prominently here. As part of an 'ageing clique of white radical men', these intellectuals, during the late 1980s, 'sold out their earlier radical beliefs' and 'also showed a radical disdain for the emerging societal demand for transparency'. Where before Smit and McCarthy 'criticised capital's agenda with undisguised venom', they 'changed their stripes' even faster than 'apartheid bureaucrats..., transmogrified into the UF's [Urban Foundation's] leading guides to the Left and its most insipid apologists' (Bond 2000a: 129–30). During the 1990s, the work of these scholars, and those associated with them, centred around the promotion of 'informal settlement intervention simply as a form of housing delivery, dismissing a role for community organizations, supporting the imposition of individual freehold titles and promoting increased stakes for the private sector' (Huchzermeyer 2001a: 72).

[12] Rust (1997) lists Nell as the Chairperson of the NHF's Co-ordinating Committee.

Foundation' (Gilbert 2002: 1923) and "member" of the last apartheid task team to reform housing; namely, the De Loor Task Team (Rust 1997: 90). Nell's position in the negotiations was crucial – for not only being 'regularly pulled to the right by the NHF's banking, business and parastatal groupings' (Bond 2000: 134) – he 'appointed the majority of technical experts' (Gilbert 2002: 1923), drawn from the ranks of the Urban Foundation. These conservative technical experts 'guided the negotiations' (Jenkins 1999: 191) and 'controlled' (Bond 2000a: 133) and/or 'dominated most of the proceedings' (Bond 2000: 247).

Tilting the balance further in favour of business was its high level of organization and ability/capacity to generate positions very rapidly for consideration by the Forum. Civil society organizations, for example, battled to participate not only because of 'the lack of expertise, but also because of the lack of resources' (Sandi Mgidlana, leader of the South African National Civics Organisation (SANCO) cited in Nell et al. 1996: 64). This imbalance also tended to narrowly focus negotiations on 'credit' and expedient implementation (the 'possible' versus the 'appropriate').

> Because the financial institutions could develop their own positions for consideration by the NHF and because organizations like SANCO lacked similar capacity, the focus shifted to that which was possible rather than that which might have been more appropriate. The two are not always the same thing (Nell et al. 1996: 64–65).

What is striking here is that by both omission and commission, the 'social construction of knowledge' was configured – not a process – to 'depoliticise' (Nell et al. 1996: 65) housing to ensure its disconnection from political and structural realities. Recalling here the tract on deregulated governance, bypass urbanism and the conservative development regime, the hegemonic project of the powerful, their storm troopers and their institutions effectively excluded and/or chose not to engage oppositional views. Justifying this exclusion and non-engagement, the hegemonic coalition asserted that removing housing 'out of the political debates' was 'logical' and 'necessary' to reduce the 'risk that political interests seeking to gain favour with their constituencies could hijack the housing issue as a centre around which to mobilise' (Rust 1997: 93). Is it any small wonder then why 'housing' provision then became defined as 'a technical problem which could be solved on the basis of a subsidy formula and minimum standards'? (Rust 1997: 93) The technicist solution proposed (formula plus standards), by definition, decoupled/delinked housing problems as deriving from 'historical inequalities and injustices in the educational and political structure' (Mackay 1999: 389) and the workings of the land, financial sector, property and labour markets.

If this sounds a tad conspiratorial – sweeping the needs and priorities of the poor under the carpet – then how else to explain why the new government made short shrift of the planned second and third phases of the NHF agenda?[13] Worded differently, 'appropriate housing strategy' became confined to resource allocation matters only, and the third phase was 'abandoned altogether' (Lalloo 1999: 40). The new state, Jenkins and Smith (2001a) assert, 'did not continue the negotiation process on housing policy, reverting to the use of appointed Task Forces...and the review within parliamentary committees' (493) (which itself was co-opted and manipulated by the executive: see IDASA's magazine, *WHIP*, 18 October 1996; IDASA 1999). It is perhaps for this reason that the policy produced (and subsequent modifications) remains confined to the 'possible'/'implementable'; and 'reinforce[s] rather than reduce the spatial inequalities of the apartheid system' (Lalloo 1999: 45–46). The policy overlooks the special needs of rural women trapped in exploitative patriarchal and African customary relations and – in the absence of an urbanization strategy – is unresponsive to needs of migrant workers and long-distance commuters wherein mobility and maintaining multiple residential bases is pivotal to their livelihoods (see Lalloo 1999). In fact, mobility as part of a livelihood strategy is perceived as a '*problem*' (Huchzermeyer 2001a: 80 – original emphasis), given that the main aim of a capital subsidy scheme – with its emphasis on individual freehold tenure – is to 'permanently fix' people in hostile spaces and tie them into a full cost-recovery

[13] The second phase entailed the development of appropriate housing strategies and the third was about engaging the public in 'interactive policy discourse' (Lalloo 1999: 40).

system of (ill-affordable) payment of rates, taxes and service charges. Abandonment of RDP houses is not an unrelated outcome of 'fixing' poor people in space, whose survival depends on mobility, i.e. a 'transient and placeless existence' impelled by survival-based mobility is at odds with subsidy-'burdensome restrictions on movement' (Lalloo 1999: 37).

And again, if this sounds conspiratorial, then why did the UF and networked consultants – in three (housing finance) of the total eight NHF technical committees[14] – pay scant attention to the background of current financial difficulties within townships or squatter settlements? There was little discussion of political conditions; no appraisal of informal finance methods; no detailed discussions of how the poor housed themselves over the previous two decades; how they saved or the costs of informal credit. Moreover, the reports were largely uncritical of past experiences with supply-side housing subsidies in South Africa (like the IDT-type intervention) and abroad; and did not adequately engage with alternatives proposed by non-establishment sectors, most notably the trade unions, Urban Sector Network, and the South African Homeless People's Federation (Jones and Datta 2000: 399–400).

Although progressive and radical non-governmental organizations participated in the Forum discussions, their views carried less weight than establishment forces. More importantly though, the reasons for the Forum's non-engagement with these views – over and above the power differentials and the strategic selectivity of the discursive terrain of the Forum – is more appropriately located in their effective exclusion from the discussions. This is because direct inclusion of low-income groups was restricted to SANCO (umbrella body of civics), who at the time came under increasing pressure from the ANC to endorse and underwrite their conservative conception of 'society' and 'social transformation' that they were slowly coming to settle on, i.e. less political, consensus-seeking, technical and managerial (discussed in greater detail below). The absorption and co-option of key civic leaders into ANC structures and the emphasis placed

[14] Only one committee looked at land and there was no dedicated committee on infrastructure.

on a 'united front' in the 1994 elections played a not insignificant role in blunting the contribution of the civic sector in housing policy formulation.

Thus, the way that knowledge came to be produced in the NHF – discursive and programmatic frame-narrowing; depoliticization; elevation of the 'possible' over the 'appropriate'; exclusion of the voices of the most vulnerable segments of society versus the over-representation of experts from banking institutions; and non-recognition of the poor's lived reality – drastically hampered policy responsiveness to the livelihood and shelter needs and priorities of the poor.

On balance, though, it would be amiss to accord too much prominence and importance to external importation and (coercive) foreign imposition. While the extent of South Africa's conformity to the dominant market-enablement approach of the time is widely debated, at a very general level, it can plausibly be argued that post-apartheid policy does 'appear to be similar' to that of the Bank's (Goodlad 1996: 1642). However, it draws very selectively, based on narrow 'technical arguments' and with little consideration of beneficiaries' needs (Jones and Datta 2000: 397–98). Of the seven strategies outlined in the White Paper (RSA 1994), two concerned the development of housing finance (subsidy provision and the mobilization of savings and credit at scale), and the other centred on the 'stabilisation of housing environment', which had a finance component. The remaining strategies were cobbled together without reference to alternatives, to critiques of and learning from past policy, and most importantly, to the needs and priorities of the politically enfranchised but socio-economically disenfranchised poverty-struck majority.

(Quasi-)/Structural Predispositions

Whilst the rules dictating the composition and profile of the Forum, the relegation of housing policy to a technical fix, and the power imbalances arguably played not insignificant roles in narrowing policy and development horizons, it is problematic to argue that expansion of Forum membership and better power re-balancing between the members would have produced more developmental outcomes.[15] This is to underplay and misread the shared identity between liberal and radical political parties related to notions of how social change is to be organized, orchestrated and led. Both liberal and revolutionary parties – despite their rhetoric – share between them an understanding of social change underpinned by hierarchical relationships between rulers and ruled and the primacy of leadership over mass action in effecting processes of change. Both agendas, 'anchored in the tradition of the nation-state, conceive of change in narrowly statist terms despite their anti-statist rhetoric' (Johnson 2003: 02).

Consequently, despite the ANC's ideology and rhetoric of popular democracy and people-driven transformation – significantly watered down in the run-up to and during negotiations – the non-establishment and apartheid-establishment forces of the Housing Forum shared a similar understanding of the role of leadership, representation and participation. The leadership role surrendered by the civil society formations to the ANC, particularly the exile wing, with its (secretive) top-down bureaucratic organizational structure and leadership style, structurally predisposed the NHF negotiation process to be dominated by experts and consultants who were willing at all costs to ingratiate themselves with a leadership that since the beginning of the 1990s was coming under increasing pressure (from domestic and international elites) to 'moderate its aspirations for socio-economic transformation... as a precondition for achieving a smooth transition' (Saul 1999 cited in Johnson 2003: 214). In the housing sector, this moderation came to be effected via the various organs of civil society being disciplined by the ANC (largely, the exiles) to endorse their view of *society* and *social transformation*, and their decapitation of the leadership of civil society (via absorption and co-option). Complementing this was the elevation of the (old and new, public and private, liberal and Leninist) elite of the socially alienating expert knowledge – technocratic rationality allied to policy analytic/policy rhetoric produced in 'poor-free' quarantined environments – over knowledge emanating from the

[15] This is what 'planning' theories/approaches propose and underwrite, especially the mainstream school that is premised on Habermas and communicative action (see Watson 2006).

community halls and gatherings of the poor in their townships and squatter settlements.

Coherently, judiciously, and rigorously accounting for the ANC's 'moderation' is however a dangerous undertaking, given the dearth of literature recording the mechanisms and mechanics of the orchestration, especially the key forces and individuals involved, party-political and elite machinations, and so on. The dilemmas generated by democratic transition and consolidation add further levels of complexity. A useful way to commence thinking of change in transitional societies must of necessity combine (amongst others) political science, political economy and sociology. And here the work of Habib et al. (1998) is useful in their deployment of the 'transplacement' phenomenon.

'Transplacement', (Habib et al. 1998) opine, is guided by discursive adaptations that reformulate social boundaries of inclusion and exclusion in ways that do not threaten dominant established interests – a necessary precondition for elite pacting. 'Transplacement' is a common feature of transition wherein the dominant groups in both the (apartheid) government and the opposition (mass democratic movement) realize that they are incapable of unilaterally determining the nature of the future political and economic system, particularly in the context of global economic restructuring, the dominance of conservative elites (here and abroad) and development ideoscapes, and the demise of alternative visions and formats for organizing and governing society. Purging themselves of any remaining radical rhetoric and progressive ideas – an exorcism conducted by intellectuals (progressive economists)-turned-apologists [16] – reigning in and disciplining errant social movement forces under the banner

[16] Previously progressive academic economists played no a small part in the ANC's 'moderation'. With the ANC's 'leadership slide into neoliberalism' (most noticeable from early 1993), the impact on the decisions and choices of the progressive economics community was most dramatic. The main reason for this, argues Padayachee (1998), 'lies in the attraction to power, and loyalty to political patrons, that academics have displayed for most of this century'. Padayachee (1998), citing Said (1994), points to how willing intellectuals have been to respond to governments who recognized the importance of having

...as their servants those intellectuals who could be called upon not to lead, but to consolidate the government's policy, to spew out the propaganda against official enemies,

of 'unity' – in the hope of establishing the appropriate credentials with international financiers and domestic capital, comprised the essential rafters of the ANC's transplacement. But this is only one part of the complex tale.

During this period that it became an almost *universal* article of faith in development thinking that the optimal organizational route to secure consensus around 'acceptable' socio-economic policies – especially in societies undergoing transition that needed to bring disruptive social elements to heel – was through corporatist/ neocorporatist[17] institutional arrangements, strongly anchored, and very much so in our case, around notions of 'national unity', 'rainbow nation', and 'reconciliation' (discussed below). Corporatist institutional arrangements – usually a response to systemic crises in governance – are state creations that serve to defuse conflict and stabilize a new regime of state-society relations, i.e. re-embedding (Habib 1998; Jenkins 1999). Corporatist institutional arrangements appeal to elites as they serve to re-establish their authority, pre-empting a more thoroughgoing, participatory and self-empowering democratic alternative (Ginsburg 1996).

Transformation and Social Change Narratives

It is against this backdrop that the ANC came to embrace a 'liberal ecclesiastical discourse of forgiveness' (Hart 2011: 07) that further frustrated the realization of an empowering and people-centred housing policy. Loosely dubbed the 'let's-join-hands [LJH] paradigm

---

euphemisms and, on a larger scale whole systems of Orwellian Newspeak, which could disguise the truth of what was occurring in the name of institutional 'expediency' or 'national honour' (445, original emphasis).

Citing Johnson (1988), the right-wing commentator, intellectuals '*far from being highly individualist and non-conformist people, follow certain regular patterns…they are often ultra-conformist within circles formed by those whose approval they seek and value*' (Padayachee 1998: 445, original emphasis).

[17] Corporatism is defined as a system of interest representation welded by an ideology of national unity wherein organs of civil society, and in particular labour unions and employer associations, are given access to, and the possibility of informing policies decided in, state institutions, in exchange for restricting their demands, operating within the parameters laid down by and observing the ideology of national unity (Khan 1997).

of transition'[18], the thrust was to socialize a non-conflictual view of society. Thus, within the *Reconstruction and Development Programme* (ANC 1994)[19], for instance, 'there are no essentialist identities, no oppositional identities' (Leroke 1996: 244). Potential tensions, conflicts and disagreements around the notions of 'fundamental transformation', 'democratisation', 'restructuring', etc. are eliminated by *ideological fiat,* i.e. tensions around societal transformation 'are immediately offset by dissolving the differences into the goals' (Wolpe 1995: 97). The effect of adopting this consensual model of society as one's point of departure is that it permits contradictory goals to be accommodated within policy frameworks, thereby obscuring or eliminating the need to examine or meaningfully engage with conflict and power. In the housing and urban development sector, for instance, the interests of the white suburbanites, bankers, developers, construction material suppliers, industrial corporate polluters, estate agents, and slum landlords are presumed to be consistent with those remaking towns and cities in a productively inclusive, socially just and democratic manner (see Bond et al. 1996 for a full discussion).

Summarily, the nature of the NHF agreements struck was 'predicated' on perceptions of the balance of socio-political forces, institutional processes, and conservative development ideoscapes. The process of securing consensus 'essentially entailed groups with major differences reaching the "lowest common denominator" [LCD] in their agreements, i.e. that beyond which they would not concede' (Jenkins 1999a: 433). What is perhaps most disturbing about the policy outcome is that LCD-type agreements came to be forged around an uncritical understanding of the housing process prior to 1994 (Jones and Datta 2000), resting on 'unexamined assumptions about the needs of the population' (Wilkinson 1998: 224); and a largely apolitical/technical perspective centred around the production of dwellings rather than the development of viable

[18] See *Mail & Guardian: Quarterly Reconstruct Supplement,* 12–18 July 1996.

[19] The RDP was drawn up by the ANC-led alliance in consultation with other key mass organizations and assisted by a wide range of nongovernmental organisations (NGOs) and research organizations. This inclusive approach to developing and implementing policy – involving as many organizations as possible – is unique in South Africa's political history. See http://www.anc.org.za/show.php?id=234.

living environments. Institutional and technical capacity constraints drove the conservative nail further, with policy coming to settle on 'previously tested mechanisms' about which Urban Foundation staff working in the Forum were 'adamant that no other kind of subsidy programme was possible' (Gilbert 2002: 1920).

The 'new' policy – its silences, omissions and prejudices – is testimony to the genius of the planning and plotting, the schemes and scheming, and the strategies and stratagems of deregulated governance that successfully installed a housing programme that is little or no different from that of apartheid praxis. The complicity of the public sector elite either via 'reformist reformism' (at best) and emasculating 'cure-defend' (at worst) interventions is unlikely to stem the tide of daily protests centred on the diminishing progressivity of the social wage (Khan 2013), and the intensifying inequality 'alongside "wageless life"' (University of Georgia Press 2013: 1). With the declining effectiveness of official 'containment ranging from liberal interventions targeting specific populations to increasingly common police brutality' (ibid.), the limits and limitations of deregulated governance are starting to show.[20]

Section Three: Transformation, Consultants/Planners and Discourse Coalitions

Historical record reveals that 'nations in the developing world have been more than passive recipients of [foreign/external] ideas and programmes' (Harris 2003: 165). Their governments, in the area of housing praxis, have often 'resisted the pressures of colonial rulers and the blandishments of the technical experts deployed by international agencies'. This demonstrates, asserts Gilbert (2002a; 2004a; 2004b), that countries have considerable autonomy in negotiating their own shelter programme through (amongst others) clever officials playing off powerful institutions against one another and/or exercising their market power through sheer size and/or through mobilizing expert knowledge to counteract unwelcome intrusions into domestic policy.

[20] http://www.ugapress.org/index.php/books/rethinking_the_south_african_crisis.

In turn, the institutionalization and sustainability of an alternative housing policy depends on the configuration of structural power relationships between the homeless poor, public authorities and the private sector. Put baldly, and here drawing from the Latin American examples, this translates into re-establishing the command of the social and collective over the private and individual – or societal/social (re)-embedding of the economy and state in social democratic and developmental formats and schemas. Observed in numerous Latin American countries are state-led economic and industrial strategies centred on redistributing assets and incomes, stimulating demand, and significantly boosting development and structural transformation. Underpinning this reasonably successful strategy is a rapid and substantial expansion of the state's role in the economy, with strategic ownership of key sectors; active promotion of social ownership, particularly through a huge increase in co-operatives; pursuit of expansionary macroeconomic approaches; and progressive interventions to transform the labour market via formalizing employment, combating atypical work, raising wage levels and promoting collective bargaining (Khan and Mohamed 2014).

The active promotion of popular participation and improving the political and institutional clout of civil society and the poor is central to this battery of interventions. This promotion and empowerment of the poor assumes different formats ranging from Brazil's hybrid form of 'liberal new developmentalism', to Bolivia's reform and change from below (underpinned by social movements and the priorities of the poor) to Venezuela's inclusive state activism without statism. This 'effective defense of the weakest that no capitalist state can match' is testimony to the 'respect of minorities, differences and the weak' (Vattimo and Zabala 2011: 06).

What is notable in these experiments and experiences is the inclusion of the poor, their discourse, their needs and priorities via the simultaneous re-reorientation of the vertical (state-economy) and horizontal axes of governance that places the poor at the intersection of the axes. Put differently, in Latin American developmentalism, the state extends and deepens civil society or supersizes civil society as a 'supercivil society' (borrowing from Rodrik 1999: 20–1), characterized by a diversity and multiplicity of civil society organizations. These organizations, initiated, supported and empowered by the state, then utilize the formal democratic spaces and opportunities to push for deeper institutional reforms, to which the state responds by further strengthening the mechanisms for power-sharing, decentralization and democratization, and so virtuous circles of synergistic relations are catalysed with reforms permeating upwards, thereby dramatically altering the relationship between polity and economy.

With the socio-economic and institutional balance of forces tipped in favour of the poor via legislative reform, regulatory rightsizing, and the accompanying changes in the distribution of assets and capabilities, these government can more easily instantiate redistributive, poverty-ameliorating, inequality-reducing, employment-generating growth strategies through top-down axes re-orientation.

This is at great distance from the South African situation, where the policy and policy negotiation processes were designed and engineered to exclude the most vulnerable segments of society, their voices, and their champions – their experts. While some argue that the ANC strategically blundered by keeping the service organizations [21] of the poor out of the process – because they wanted the emphasis to fall on the direct representation by political and civic leaders 'rather than on "experts" from the service organisations' – ...this contrasted markedly with the strategy of organized business – in particular the banking institutions – which seconded large numbers of experts, and in so doing directly influenced policy... The democratic movement's overcommitted political and civic leaders were not equipped to deal with this army of technical experts entrusted with broad negotiating mandates (Swilling 1998: 295).

Even where civic and political leaders – who were denied access to independent sources of information and analysis via the policy formulation process of the NHF – drew on the advice of their own 'experts' (from service organizations), their 'alternatives' were slated as impractical/unworkable/unfeasible. The 'new, generalised, consensus' – 'policy analysis'/policy rhetoric discourse – wrapped

[21] Urban service organizations that traditionally supported CBOs, both technically and politically.

up in the 'abstract, positivist methodological validation rooted in traditional epistemology, including the "objectivity" of the analyst' – 'required, by definition, the suppression of [radical] discourses that reflected unmet demands and needs' (Swilling 1998: 293). Whereas in the past, these very same 'experts' put their services to empowering the poor by espousing strategies and solutions that supported their collective actions, grounded in their needs and demands, this uncoupling[22] generated a mindset of pragmatism.

This 'generalised consensus' and pragmatism – not disconnected (amongst others) from self-imposed structural adjustment programme, the depoliticization of the housing, and the delinking of housing from historical inequalities and injustices, the dominant conceptions of society and social transformation that the ANC came to generalize and impose – effectively obliterated any policy autonomy in formulating and designing an alternative to our technocratic market-driven housing praxis. At issue here is the matter of how policy is framed, the 'experts' framing it and the coalitions assembled to institutionalize them.

It is worth mentioning that official policies

> ...do not so much objectively represent the interests located in or beyond the state or objectively reflect 'real' problems in the

[22] A product of the transition process – or the shift from oppositional politics to 'preparing to govern' – which included the delegitimization of mass action by the ANC, the relegation of local struggles to a secondary status in the pursuit of the 'seizure of state power', and the domestication of the civic movement via the formation of a unitary SANCO. It is interesting to note here that a similar dynamic was at play in the sphere of economic policy. Padayachee (1998: 444) remarks that the:

> ...defeat, emasculation and disappearance of many civil society organisations in the 1990s, and the decision by many others, including COSATU, the SACP and SANCO, to accept the leadership of the ANC in the anti-apartheid struggle of the 1990s, effectively excluded civil society organizations from the policy world, as independent constituencies. As a result many progressive economists lost direct touch with the dynamic and more radical traditions of these mass-based labour and social movements. Progressive academic economists found themselves relating more and more to the ANC's elite leadership, whose concerns and agendas were increasingly being set by conservative forces and institutions. They followed the current into... the 'corporatist statism' of the 1990s. Many already conform to Mahmood Mamdani's characterisation of African intellectuals as 'state fetishists'.

> internal or external environments of the political system as they are discursively-mediated, if not discursively constituted, products of struggle to define and narrate 'problems' which can be dealt with in and through state action [that is, the 'possible'/'implementable' versus the 'appropriate']. In this sense the effectivity of policymaking is closely tied to its rhetorical and argumentative framing – especially as effectivity, like beauty, often exists in the eyes (or ears) of the beholder (Jessop 2001: 11; emphasis added).

'Framing' is not a neutral process. They are problem-setting stories/narratives linking casual accounts of policy problems to implicit/explicit proposals for action and 'facilitate the normative leap from "is" to "ought"' (Rein and Schon 1993: 148). Stories/narratives are the 'medium through which actors try to impose their view of reality on others, suggest certain social positions and practices, and criticize alternative social arrangements' (Hajer 1993: 46).

It is this rhetorical and argumentative framing contained in housing praxis scholarship/discourse that compromises our attempts to reform policy. This is because discourses are, following Foucault (Sheridan 1980: 129), instruments and objects of power. In the case of the National Housing Forum, selected (elite) experts 'framed' the problem and were drawn into working relationships with traditional economic and political elites, creating a 'discourse coalition' (Hajer 1993: 47), or more appropriately, an 'elite discourse coalition' (Fischer and Forester 1993: 8), i.e. a grouping of actors (elites) sharing an ensemble of ideas, concepts and categories via which a phenomenon is 'politically framed and given social meaning'. The 'elite discourse coalition', comprising experts from liberal and conservative 'think tanks' (the Urban Foundation) (Gilbert 2004a: 202), were pivotal to 'national policy agenda setting' and aligning the 'articulated advice of leading experts with the interests of economic and political elites' (Fischer and Forester 1993: 8–9). A discourse coalition comes to rule when 'it dominates the discursive space; that is, its central actors are persuaded by, or forced to accept, the rhetorical power of a new discourse (condition of discourse structuration)' (consultants framing the problem); reflected in the 'institutional practices of that political domain; that is, the actual policy process is conducted according to the ideas of a given discourse (condition of discourse institutionalisation)' (Hajer 1993: 48). This coalition was institutionally embedded in a forum driven by consensual modes of decision-making, 'fudging vital differences' (Tomlinson 1998: 4) and promoting LCD-type agreements.

It is this 'pragmatism', depoliticization and suppression of alternatives (not unrelated to and deepened by deregulated governance) that has bequeathed a lock in/path dependency – 'where we are stuck on a path and...cannot get off that path' (Vawda 2012). This path dependence – and cure/defend response – is manifested in the tension between 'government's long term visionary approach to sustainable urban development and its demand for visible short-term delivery' (Treasury 2003: 4); a state that strives to increase the rate of delivery whilst simultaneously seeking to enhance the product and settlement pattern (Richards 2001); and government acknowledgement of the need for bottom-up development processes (implying the devolution of power and authority to communities) but at the same time seeking to determine the nature of the process usually configured around an already defined output (ibid.). Greater responsiveness to household's needs and priorities is advocated but the subsidy instrument is still deemed inflexible and the necessary socio-institutional capability required to render it flexible is sorely lacking. Integrated human settlements are sought not through 'structural intervention' (ibid.: 4) and deep democracy, but through reliance on urban governance regimes[23] that are unable (not geared) to address the socially and spatially marginalizing outcomes of land markets, escalating construction costs, and the political economy of urban construction, more generally. Lastly, market-embedding/ market restoring/market-construction interventions of the state (social housing, for example) excludes the poor from housing in areas they deem more suitable (in the inner-city, for instance).

Re-thinking and re-formulating housing praxis in radical and revolutionary schemas requires not only a 'reconsideration of the imperatives of housing delivery and how this structurally links with

[23] Which are based on consensus and co-operation and the more (recent) top-down rightsizing of local development plans.

land availability, infrastructure, transport, economic opportunity, health care, social facilities, etc.' (ibid.: 10). More critical is the re-embedding and re-calibration of the shelter and housing intervention via the re-orientation and dynamic re-connection of the horizontal and vertical axes of governance which must of necessity directly confront informalization from above, state capture, and deregulated governance.

At the nub of this re-orientation and re-connection is a fundamental break from the 'reformist reform' and 'cure-defend' praxis horizon to one that establishes and secures the command of the social and collective over the private and elite, i.e. enhancing the leverage and power of the poor, diffusing power in their favour, and promoting the accountability of the elites to the vast majority of citizens (Habib 2013: 205–06). Fortunately, lessons from the financial crisis and new developmentalism put our governors and decision-makers on terra firma to regenerate and rethink housing praxis in progressive modes/modalities. Indeed, it could arguably serve as a useful springboard to bring back the re-emerging 'sound fundamentals' – as espoused by *civil society* and *their consultants* and *experts* – enshrined in Macroeconomic Research Group (MERG 1993), the Reconstruction and Development Programme (RDP) (ANC 1994), many criticisms of the 1994 White Paper; the ANC's Polokwane (2009) resolutions, and more recently, the ANC's 2012 Manguang Conference.[24,25]

[24] For the Polokwane and Manguang resolutions – See http://www.anc.org.za

[25] Proposals and recommendations lifted from these documents include:

- Tackling land speculation and addressing the highly cartelized building supplies industry;
- Upgrading state capacity to deliver separate but related components of the housing production (from land acquisition and assembly through to final finishing);
- Lending support to collective forms of tenure (example, housing associations) and public rental accommodation (which should not be precluded at the outset through an ideological commitment to owner-occupation). Rather than soliciting a housing programme through private sector finance (formal and/or informal and/or intermediaries), far more reliance should be placed on state finance to fund a public housing subsidized rental programme.

The degree of state intervention can vary over the range of functions involved – it can be a builder itself, or subcontract to an audited private sector; it can provide or guarantee loans; it can subsidize rents or charge at market value. Nor does extensive

Whether our governors can marshal and command this terrain in ways that make hope and history rhyme is highly debatable for three reasons, which together fundamentally impacts the teaching of public policy.

---

state intervention now preclude a more market-oriented stance in the future (MERG 1993: 84).

- Following World Bank (1993) advice – extending significant and substantial resources to the poor which would 'not necessarily be appropriate for medium- and long-term vertical and horizontal fiscal balance'.
- State intervention to address market failure via regulating the housing market and sector; breaking the white monopoly of contractors over local authority work through promoting black businesses that are more efficient and independent of white-controlled large-scale contractors; redressing the high degree of concentration in the cement industry.
- Compulsory purchase of privately-owned land and ensuring an equitable distribution of development gains.
- Effective functioning of housing supply; and urban and regional planning.
- Implementation hinged on institutional reform and capacity building, with the report proposing a 'unitary national housing authority with corresponding institutions at lower tiers of government'. The responsibilities of the authority would include: urban and regional planning; infrastructural provision; restructuring of the apartheid city; co-ordination of all aspects of housing delivery; formulation and monitoring of planning regulations and ensuring their effective functioning; and facilitating the release of land for housing (ibid.).

On balance, the nature of proposed state intervention (influenced in significant dimensions by readings and interpretations of the developmental state experience) was rooted in the belief that sustainable growth necessitated a radical redistributive programme to address the chief obstacles to growth rooted in structural inequality. The restructuring of the economy, it was said, could not be left to the autonomous actions of capital, but required decisive state leadership, in which capital would have to accept a subordinate role in returned for increased profitability. Restructuring the distribution of political and organizational power with a view to encouraging the construction of productive coalitions to support the reforms of the state was to be effected through a novel combination of consensual and inclusive embeddedness, distinct from East Asian state corporatism. Important in this growth path was the view that poverty eradication/reduction was not an 'add on'/'appendage' /'after-thought' affixed/appended to the growth strategy – as it presently is – but an integral part of it (see Makgetla 2004). Government would thus use large scale anti-poverty programmes while expanding domestic demand, skills, services and infrastructure – a strategy used to great effect in 1950s in the high-performing Asian economies (Makgetla 2004: 280). This was echoed in the RDP (ANC 1994), which emphasized land reform and support for co-operatives and micro enterprises, as well as massive expansion in basic infrastructure, housing, education, welfare, and health care for poor communities (Makgetla 2004: 270).

Firstly, teachers of public policy should be alert and aware to the 'absurdity of what is accepted as everyday reality', especially in a world where 'theory' now predates and determines policy (Ocampa 2006). These theories are replete with 'blind spots'

> ... areas where questions are not admitted of do not make sense within a specific conceptual framework. This affects, in turn, the nature of empirical research, and more generally, the way reality is read. The existence of these 'blind spots' is perhaps the most important channel through which ideology affects knowledge about social conditions in democratic societies, that is, by affecting the questions that are asked and the filters through which reality is read (Ocampo 2006: viii).

Secondly, with reference to 'blind spots', what frequently 'passes as knowledge is little more than opinions, which are susceptible to other influences and can spread like wildfire'. The scope and prospect of 'contagion' is rampant in institutional settings where 'deviation from mainstream and world views restricts 'access to power and influence' (Utting 2006: 07). Indeed, the main achievement of conservatives has 'been to make the ticket of entry into reputable discussion, a rite of passage for anyone who wants to be taken seriously on the public stage' (Galbraith 2009 cited in Berry 2014: 15–16).

Thirdly, and here bringing together the heady issues of 'blind spots', contagion and being 'taken seriously', teachers of public policy need to understand and appreciate the 'ideological underpinnings' of the many ideas that dominate the 'discourse of contemporary politics' (Vale 2014: 03). Of acute relevance here is 'governance' –

> ...the effective reduction of conflicting interests to idea of policymaking, a controlling process that paradoxically excludes deep voices in affairs that touch the lives of the citizenry. So governance, and the words that buttress it, aim to create a 'realm where the status quo cannot be questioned...' (Vale 2014: 03).

In conclusion, progressive ideas related to development emerge in settings where individuals and *institutions* (not organizations) challenge and break from the 'mainstream', and free themselves from the clutches of 'conditionality and dogmatism' (Utting 2006: 07). What animates and activates the challenge, resistance, rebellion and revolt is the realization and limitations of autopoiesis, rhetoric and agnotology. Underscored here is the concept/notion of *poiesis* – making our world and ourselves. The 'world', it is written,

> ...is created by people in history, both consciously and through cumulative unintended effects...From this foundation, scholars have argued that the fundamental features of our world that we often take to be natural, from race and gender to politics and economy, are actually products of human making. This is the basis for the twined concepts of social construction and human agency...While the terms *social construction* and *human agency* both point towards the study of creative activity, they tend to operate at a level of abstraction that seldom contains analysis of how things are actually created, including the conditions of creation as well as the products that come out of it (Calhoun et al. 2013: 195).

A rebellious and revolutionary pedagogy for public policy in the classroom and beyond demands that we as teachers should be mindful of *social construction* and *human agency*, and this means being alive and alert to the dynamics of agnotology, the questions that are omitted, and autopoiesis. On a practical level, teachers of public policy should pay close attention to analysing and deconstructing policymaking on four interlocking levels. The first relates to policy documents presented by governments or ruling parties. Next, these are underpinned by particular 'scholarly' or 'ideological' paradigms – which in many instances are a 'confused amalgam of what are often inconsistent approaches'. Third, the actual intent, or unintended consequences, of the policies is often 'shrouded in rhetoric' and routinely adjusted for different audiences to render them 'desirable, palatable or even unquestionable common sense (in the Gramscian frame). Finally, policies in practice 'often (but not always) differ markedly from those on paper, the underlying scholarship, and the rhetoric'. The relationships between [1] policy on paper, [2] scholarship, [3] rhetoric/ideology, and [4] policy in practice are not necessarily stable or consistent and can shift with context and across place, topic and over time (see Isaacs 2014). Analysing the shifts and movements across temporal, spatial and institutional planes and relaying these to our students (and wider) is the quintessential challenge in these troubled, complex and confusing times.

In *Heart of Darkness,* Conrad says: 'It is written that I should be loyal to the nightmare of my choice.' The task ahead of us is to make hope and history rhyme in democratic and empowering schemes and schema, frames and frameworks, in the classroom and beyond.

References

Adler, T., and M. Oelofse. 1996. 'The housing subsidy scheme.' In *A Mandate to Build: Developing Consensus around a National Housing Policy in South Africa.* K. Rust and S. Rubenstein (eds.). Johannesburg: National Housing Forum. pp. 109–37.

African National Congress (ANC). 1994. *The Reconstruction and Development Programme: A Policy Framework.* Johannesburg: Umanyano Publications.

Anonymous (a). nd. Housing and the Urban Poor.
http://www.dialogue.org.za/Documents/Outside%20Docs/.

Appadurai, A. 2002. 'Deep democracy: urban governmentality and the horizon of politics.' *Public Culture*, 14:1, pp. 21–47.

Baumann, T., and J. Bolnick. 2001. 'Out of the Frying Pan into the Fire: The Limits of Loan Finance in a Capital Subsidy Context.' *Environment & Urbanisation*, 13:2, pp. 103–15.

Bay Research and Consultancy Services (BRCS). 2001a. Review of Department of Housing Policy Document. Prepared by BCRS for *People's Dialogue* (e-mailed to writer by Ted Baumann on 1 June 2001).

———. 2001b. 'The South Alliance.' A Report Prepared for the Homeless International. Cape Town.

———. 2002. 'Delivering the Housing Subsidy in a People's Housing Process Context: Challenges, Experiences and Options.' Cape Town.

———. 2003. 'The People's Housing Process in South Africa.' Review for the People's Housing Partnership Trust. Cape Town.

Berry, M. 2014. 'Neoliberalism and the City: Or the Failure of Market Fundamentalism.' *Housing, Theory and Society*, 31:3, pp.1–18

Bond, P. 2000. *Cities of Gold, Townships of Coal: Essays on South Africa's New Urban Crisis*. Trenton: Africa World Press.

———. 2000a. *Elite Transition: From Apartheid to Neoliberalism in South Africa.* South Africa: Pluto Press & University of Natal Press.

———. 2006. 'Neoliberal Urban Policy: Are Those Planact Fingerprints.' Paper presented at the Conference on NGOs as Innovators and Agents of Change: A history interpreted by development practitioners. University of Witwatersrand, Johannesburg. 5 August.

———. 2014. '"Talk Left, Walk Right" in South African Social Policy. Tokenistic Extension of State Welfare versus Bottom-up Commoning of Services.' (Personal copy).

———, M. Mayekiso, D. Miller and M. Swilling. 1996. 'Response to Government's Draft Urban Strategy Document II.' *Urban Forum,* 7:1, pp. 101–20.

Buroway, M. 1997. 'Neoliberal Pitfalls – South Africa Through a Russian Lens.' Paper presented at the Harold Wolpe Memorial Trust Inaugural Conference, 1–2 April.

Calhoun, C., R. Sennett and H. Shapira. 2013. '*Poiesis* Means Making.' *Public Culture,* 25:2, pp. 195–200.

Council for Scientific and Industrial Research (CSIR). 1999. 'The State of Human Settlements South Africa 1994–1998.' Draft report for comment, prepared by the CSIR for the Department of Housing.

Cronin, J. 2014. 'Rethinking the South African Crisis: Nationalism, Populism, Hegemony – Review of Gillian Hart.' *New Agenda,* 54, Second Quarter, pp. 54–56. (Book review).

d'Cruz, C., and D. Satterthwaite. 2005. 'Building homes, changing official approaches: The work of urban poor organizations and their federations and their contributions to meeting the Millennium Development Goals in urban areas.' Human Settlements Programme. IIED Poverty Reduction in Urban Areas Series Working Paper 16, London.

De Loor, J.H. 1992. 'Housing in South Africa: Proposals on a Policy and Strategy.' The Task Group on National Housing Policy and Strategy of the South African Housing Advisory Council. Pretoria.

Dean, M. 2002. 'Liberal government and authoritarianism.' *Economy and Society,* 31:1, pp. 37–61.

Development Works. 2002. 'Cities Alliance Project on a pro-poor slum upgrading framework for South Africa for submission to the Cities Alliance/United Nations Centre for Human Settlements.' Report prepared by Development Works for People's Dialogue. Johannesburg.

Dolowitz, D., and D. Marsh. 1996. 'Who learns what from whom: a review of the policy transfer literature?' *Political Studies*, XLIV, pp. 343–57.

Fine, B., and Z. Rustomjee. 1996. *The Political Economy of South Africa: From Minerals-energy Complex to Industrialisation*. Johannesburg: Witwatersrand University Press.

———. 1999. 'Transition and the political economy of South Africa.' Revised version of paper presented to African Studies Association of Australasia & the Pacific, Perth, Australia, November.

Fischer, F., and J. Forester. 1993. Editor's Introduction. In *The Argumentative Turn in Policy Analysis and Planning*. F. Fischer and J. Forester (eds.). Durham & London: Duke University Press. pp. 1–17.

Foucault, M. 1983. Social security [Interview]. In *Michael Foucault: Politics Philosophy Culture: Interviews and Other Writings 1977–1984*. L.D. Kritzman (ed.). [1988]. London: Routledge. pp. 159–77.

Freund, B. 2010. 'Is there such a thing as a post-apartheid city?' *Urban Forum*, 21, pp. 283–98.

Isaacs, G. 2014. 'The Myth of "Neutrality" and the Rhetoric of "Stability": Macroeconomic Policy in Democratic South Africa.' Working Paper 1 for the Political Economy of Restructuring in South Africa. (Personal copy).

Gilbert, A. 2002. '"Scan Globally; Reinvent Locally": Reflecting on the Origins of South Africa's Capital Housing Subsidy Policy." *Urban Studies*, 39:10, pp. 1911–33.

———. 2002a. 'Power, Ideology and the Washington Consensus: The Development and Spread of the Chilean Housing Policy.' *Housing Studies*, 17, pp. 305–24.

———. 2004a. 'Learning from Others: The Spread of Capital Housing Subsidies.' *International Planning Studies*, 9:2/3, pp. 197–216.

———. 2004b. 'Helping the Poor through Housing Subsidies: Lessons from Chile, Colombia and South Africa.' *Habitat International*, 28, pp. 13–40.

Goodlad, R. 1996. 'The Housing Challenge in South Africa.' *Urban Studies*, 33:9, pp. 1629–45.

Habib, A. and V. Padayachee. 2000. 'Economic Policy and Power Relations in South Africa's Transition to Democracy.' *World Development*, 28:2, pp. 245–63.

Habib, A. 1998. *Structural Constraints, Resources and Decision-making: A Study of South Africa's Transition to Democracy*. Department of Politics, City University of New York (unpublished PhD).

———, D. Pillay and A. Desai. 1998. 'South Africa and the Global Order: The Structural Conditioning of a Transition to Democracy.' *Journal of Contemporary African Studies*, 16:1, pp. 95–115.

Habib, A. 2013. *South Africa's Suspended Revolution: Hopes and Prospects.* Johannesburg: Wits University Press

Hajer, M.A. 1993. 'Discourse Coalitions and the Institutionalization of Practice: The Case of Acid Rain in Britain.' In *The Argumentative Turn in Policy Analysis and Planning.* F. Fischer and J. Forester (eds.). Durham & London: Duke University Press. pp. 43–76.

Harris, R. 2003. 'Learning from the Past: International Housing Policy Since 1945 – An Introduction.' *Habitat International,* 27, pp. 163–66.

Hart, G. 2013. *Rethinking the South African Crisis: Nationalism, Populism, Hegemony.* Scottsville: University of KwaZulu-Natal Press.

Hervé, F. 2009. Integrating Poor Populations in South African Cities: A Challenge for Government Authorities. *Study produced under the supervision of Thierry Conzalez.* Agence Francaise de Dévelopment Research Department (France).

Huchzermeyer, M. 2001. 'Housing for the Poor? Negotiated Housing Policy in South Africa.' *Habitat International,* 25, 3, pp. 303–31.

———. 2001a. 'Consent and Contradiction: Scholarly Responses to the Capital Subsidy Model for Informal Settlement Intervention in South Africa.' *Urban Forum,* 12, 1, pp. 71–106.

Institute for Democratic Alternatives in South Africa (IDASA). 1999. 'Executive Policymaking in the New South Africa: Policymaking in the Department of Housing.' (Unpublished, available from IDASA Resource Centre in Cape Town).

Jenkins, P. 1999. 'The Role of Civil Society in the Development of Housing Policy: Some Lessons from Southern Africa.' *Third World Planning Review,* 21:2, pp. 177–99.

———. 1999a. 'Difficulties Encountered in Community Involvement in Delivery Under the New South African Housing Policy.' *Habitat International,* 23:4, pp. 431–46.

———, and H. Smith. 2001a. 'An Institutional Approach to Analysis of State Capacity in Housing Systems in the Developing World: Case Studies in South Africa and Costa Rica.' *Housing Studies,* 16:4, pp. 485–507.

Jessop, B. 2001. 'Institutional (Re)turns and the Strategic-relational Approach.' *Environment and Planning A,* 33, pp. 1213–35.

Johnson, K. 2003. 'Liberal or Liberation Framework? The Contradictions of ANC Rule in South Africa.' In *Limits to liberation in Southern Africa: The Unfinished Business of Democratic Consolidation.* H. Melber (ed.). Cape Town: HSRC Press. pp. 200–23.

Jones, G.A., and K. Datta. 2000. 'Enabling Markets to Work? Housing Policy in the "New" South Africa.' *International Planning Studies,* 5:3, pp. 393–416.

Kanbur, R. 2011. 'Structural Inequalities and the New Growth Path: A Response to Jeremy Cronin.' Deputy Minister of Transport, Republic of South Africa, 24 March. http://www.kanbur.dyson.cornell.edu.

Khan, F. 1997. 'Democracy, Forums, Social Compacts and the Fuzzy Relationship between Conflict and Development: A Reflection on the Cato Manor Experience.' In *Best Practices of Developmental Local Government.* Urban Sector Network (ed.). Johannesburg: USN (Unpublished).

———. 2004. 'The City and its Future? The Eternal Question.' *Development Update: Special Edition – The City and its Future,* 5:1, pp. 5–52.

———. 2013. 'Poverty, Grants, Revolution and "Real Utopias": Society Must be Defended By Any and All Means Necessary!' *Review of African Political Economy,* 40, 138, pp. 572–88.

———, and S. Mohamed. 2014. 'From the MEC to the Green Economy Conglomerate: Wiring a Green Economy-Green Society-Developmental State Circuit.' *New Agenda: South African Journal of Social and Economic Policy,* no. 56: 47–53.

Lalloo, K. 1999. 'Areas of Contested Citizenship: Housing Policy in South Africa.' *Habitat International,* 23:1, pp. 35–47.

Leftwich, A. 1994. 'Governance, the State and the Politics of Development.' *Development and Change,* 25:2, pp. 363–86.

Leroke, W. 1996. 'Development as a Post-modern Condition: Towards a Post-modern Development.' In *Reconstruction, Development and People.* J.K. Coetzee and J. Graff (eds.). South Africa: International Thomson Publishing Southern Africa (Pty) Ltd. pp. 222–45.

Lester, A., E. Nel and T. Binns. 2000. 'South Africa's Current Transition in Temporal and Spatial Context.' *Antipode,* 32:2, pp. 135–51.

Lupton, M. and S. Murphy. 1995. 'Housing and Urban Reconstruction in South Africa.' In A. Lemon (ed.). *The Geography of Change in South Africa.* New York: John Wiley & Sons. pp. 143–68.

Mabin, A. 2000. Urban development, urban policy and state action (mimeo)

Mackay, C.J. 1999. 'Housing Policy in South Africa: The Challenge of Delivery.' *Housing Studies,* 14: 3, pp. 387–99.

Macroeconomic Research Group (MERG). 1993. *Making Democracy Work: A Framework for Macroeconomic Policy in South Africa.* Bellville (Cape Town): Centre for Development Studies.

Makgetla, N.S. 2004. 'The Post-Apartheid Economy.' *Review of African Political Economy,* 100, pp. 263–81.

Napier, M. 2003. 'Supporting the People's Housing Process.' In *Housing Policy and Practice in Post-Apartheid South Africa.* F. Khan and P. Thring (eds.). Sandown: Heinemann. pp. 321–62.

Ocampo, J.S. 2006. 'Foreword: Some Reflections on the Links Between Social Knowledge and Policy.' In *Reclaiming Development Agendas: Knowledge, Power and International Policymaking.* P. Utting (ed.). New York: Palgrave, pp. viii-xiv.

Pieterse, E. 2009. 'Post-Apartheid Geographies in South Africa: Why are Urban Divides so Persistent?' Paper presented at Interdisciplinary Debates on Development and Cultures: Cities in Development – Spaces, Conflicts and Agency, Leuven University, 15 December.

Rodrik, D. 2000. 'Institutions for high-quality growth: what they are and how to acquire them.' Draft paper prepared for the International Monetary Fund Conference on Second-Generation Reforms, No. w7540. National Bureau of Economic Research (NBER).

Rolnik, R. 2009. 'Report of the Special Rapporteur on Adequate Housing as a Component of the Right to an Adequate Standard of Living, and on the Right to Non-discrimination in this Context.' United Nations General Assembly. http://daccess-dds-ny.un.org/doc/UNDOC/GEN/G09/106/32/PDF/G0910632.pdf?OpenElement.

Rust, K. 2002. 'No Short-cuts: Implementing the South African Housing Policy.' Paper prepared for the Institute for Housing of South Africa.

Saul, J.S. 2005. 'South Africa: Debating the Transition.' *South Africa: The Post-Apartheid Denouement.*

Sheridan, A. 1980. *The Will to Truth.* London and New York: Tavistock Publications.

Simon, D. 2001. 'Trading Spaces: Imagining and Positioning the "New" South Africa within the Regional and Global Economies.' *International Affairs,* 77:2, pp. 377–405.

Sisulu, L. 2008. Speech by L.N. Sisulu Minister of Housing at the Occasion of the Budget Vote of 2008/09 for the Department of Housing (RSA). http://www.pmg.org.za/briefing/20080528-housing-ministers-budget-speech.

Smit, D. 1999. 'Housing in South Africa: Significant Government Achievement based on Public-Private Partnership.' *CDE Focus,* November.

Swilling, M. 1998. 'Rival Futures.' In *Blank: Architecture, Apartheid and After.* H. Judin and I. Vladislavic. (eds.). Rotterdam: NAI Publishers. pp. 285–99.

———. 1999. 'Changing Conceptions of Governance.' *Africanus: Journal of Development Administration – Special Issue on Administrative Culture,* 29:2, pp. 20–40.

———. 2005. 'Thoughts and Notes' (Unpublished).

Tomlinson, M. 1998. 'South Africa's Housing Policy: An Assessment of the First Two Years, 1994–1996.' *International Journal of Urban and Regional Research,* 22, pp. 137–46

———. 1999. 'South Africa's Housing Policy: Lessons from Four Years of the New Housing Subsidy Scheme.' *Third World Planning Review,* 21, pp. 283–95.

———. 2002. 'Efforts and Errors: South Africa's Search to Extend Housing Finance to Low-Income Households.' *Housing Finance International,* XVII, pp. 8–14.

———. 2002. 'International Best Practice, Enabling Frameworks and the Policy Process: A South African Case Study.' *International Journal of Urban and Regional Research,* 26:2, pp. 377–88.

Treasury. 2003. Briefing Notes on Housing and Urban Development. Prepared by Sharon Lewis for the Director-General and Minister of Finance, July.

UN-Habitat. 2010. *The State of African Cities 2010: Governance, Inequality and Urban Land Markets.* London: Earthscan.

Utting, P. 2006. 'Introduction: Reclaiming Development Agendas.' In *Reclaiming Development Agendas: Knowledge, Power and International Policymaking.* P. Utting (ed.). New York: Palgrave. pp. 1–24.

Vale, P. 2014. 'Introduction – The New South Africa at Twenty: Some Brechtian Whispers.' In *The New South Africa at Twenty*. P. Vale and E.H. Prinsloo (eds.). Pietermaritzburg: University of KwaZulu-Natal Press. pp. 1–18.

Vawda, A. 2003. Address to the National Housing Policy and Strategy Workshop. Department of Housing. (Available from author).

———. 2012. 'Altering Path Dependencies: Sketching Contours of the Built Environment: A Sector's Response to Climate Change.' http://www.gsdpp.uct.ac.za/course-materials/viewcategory/42-wednesday-7-march-2012.html.

Vattimo, G., and S. Zabala. 2011. *Hermeneutic Communism: From Heidegger to Marx.* New York: Colombia University Press.

Watson, V. 2006. 'Deep Difference: Diversity, Planning and Ethics.' *Planning Theory,* 5:1, pp. 31–50.

———, and B. Agbola. 2013. 'Who will Plan Africa's Cities?' *Counterpoints,* September. London: African Research Institute.

Wilkinson, P. 1998. 'Housing Policy in South Africa.' *Habitat International,* 22:3, pp. 215–29.

Wilson, P.A., and C. Lowery. 2003. 'Building Deep Democracy: The Story of a Grassroots Learning Organization in South Africa.' *Planning Forum*, 9, pp. 47–64.

Wolpe, H. 1995. 'The Uneven Transition from Apartheid in South Africa.' *Transformation*, 27, pp. 88–102.

World Bank. 1993. 'Housing: Enabling Markets to Work.' World Bank Policy Paper. Washington, DC: World Bank.

PART IV

PUBLIC POLICY IN TURKEY: SECTORAL PERSPECTIVES

15 The Evolution of Institutions of Economic Policy in Turkey

İzak Atiyas

Abstract

The economic development regime in Turkey went through a fundamental change from one of inward-oriented import substitution industrialization to one where the market mechanism played a more significant role in the allocation of resources. The purpose of this chapter is to provide an account of the evolution of institutions of economic policy that accompanied the changes in the development regime.

The paper argues that economic liberalization notwithstanding, economic policy institutions in the 1980s and 1990s were overall characterized by increased centralization and a high degree of discretionary authority retained by the government. By contrast, during the 2000s more rule-based and relatively non-discriminatory institutions emerged, and substantial degree authority was delegated to relatively independent administrative agencies. The chapter discusses the roles of the economic crisis of 2000–01, global trends and the European Union accession process in this development. It also reviews policy areas where centralization and discretionary forms of intervention persisted or increased during this period, namely public procurement and construction where the government retained significant instruments that could be used to create and allocate rents to favoured companies. The chapter then discusses the reversal towards more discretionary forms of intervention in the last few years and the political underpinnings of this trend.

Introduction

The policy framework for economic development in Turkey underwent a fundamental change starting in 1980. Until 1980

Turkey had been following what has been called the Import Substitution Industrialization (ISI) model of development, a model that was characterized by high levels of protection from imports through both tariff and non-tariff barriers, extensive presence of public enterprises (especially in 'strategic' industries such as steel, refineries and chemicals), a repressed and underdeveloped financial system, strict controls over foreign exchange, typically overvalued exchange rates, and extensive controls of domestic prices, especially of the intermediate inputs produced by public enterprises. In addition, public banks played a crucial role in the distribution of credit.

A programme of reform that changed fundamentally the development model was launched in 1980. The programme entailed trade liberalization, reduction and/or removal of tariff and non-tariff barriers to trade, liberalization of international capital flows and foreign exchange, major adjustments in domestic prices or their liberalization, and the liberalization of domestic financial markets. The latter involved removal of controls on interest rates as well as major reductions in barriers to entry. The programme also entailed privatization and various means were devised to encourage private participation into infrastructure investments, which used to be carried out almost exclusively by the government. In summary, from a development regime where the state played a major role in the allocation of resources, Turkey moved into a regime where the market mechanism started to play a major role.

The purpose of this paper is to provide an account of the evolution of institutions of economic policy that accompanied the changes in the development regime. Section 2 lays out a simple analytical framework. Sections 3 and 4 discuss the evolution of economic policymaking institutions in the 1980s-90s and 2000s, respectively, and document a tendency in the last decade towards developing more rule-based institutions of economic policy resulting in a reduction of the discretionary powers of the executive. Section 5 examines the last few years of the Justice and Development Party (AKP) period and discusses the reversal away from rule-based economic policymaking. Section 6 concludes.

Institutions, Credible Commitment and Discretion

It is now generally accepted that even when the market mechanism plays the dominant role in the allocation of resources, interventions by the public authority are required to address various forms of market failures. Proper functioning of the market mechanism requires the existence of a legal and regulatory framework that ensures effective competition, prevents abuse by dominant enterprises, and above all ensures that public authority is used in the public's interest rather than the interests of the political authority or interest groups connected to it.

Government intervention creates opportunities for rent seeking, cronyism and favouritism towards politically connected firms. In the last two or three decades, the general solution found to this problem is to reduce the discretion of the political authority over these matters and establish relatively independent administrative bodies and delegate to them the authority to intervene. This solution entails leaving the authority to design policy to the executive, but delegating the authority to implement policy and to issue the necessary secondary legislation and enforce it to the administrative bodies. The idea was that the decision-making process of an administrative body would be guided by clearly defined rules designed to focus on market failures and thereby reduce the scope for discretionary interventions that may create opportunities for rent seeking and favouritism. This solution gained special importance especially after liberalization and privatization of network industries. The stated purpose of liberalization and privatization is to allow new entry, enhance competition and thereby encourage increases in productivity. However, these objectives can only be attained if anti-competitive behaviour by incumbents can be curtailed. This, in turn, requires close monitoring and regulation of the behaviour of incumbent companies. It was thought that delegation of these functions to independent regulatory authorities (IRAs) and insulating their decision process from political influence was a way to credibly commit to potential investors that decision-making in the sector would be guided by clear and fair rules rather than political discretion. While IRAs have often been discussed in the context of network industries, they exist in other industries where market failures necessitate frequent intervention and close monitoring by the public authority, such as the financial sector, environment or health and monetary policy. One could also add that in some policy areas, such as fiscal policy or the budget process, the solution often entailed not the creation of a separate administrative body (though some countries did exactly that in the area of tax policy) but setting rules and procedures that would limit discretionary behaviour of the government.

It can be argued that reducing the discretionary powers of the state and creating more rule-based institutions of economic policy are especially relevant for developing countries with histories of populism and clientelism. Turkey has been one such country. Turkey has a long history of populism and clientelism, where the use of public resources in exchange for votes and other forms of political support has been part of the normal process of political competition. During the import substitution era, trade protection and provision of investment incentives created state-business relations that were plagued by clientelism.[1] The fundamental change in the development model initiated in 1980 meant not only that a new legal and regulatory framework necessary for market-based development had to be created but also that the new framework would need to contain necessary institutional ingredients to address the legacy of populism and clientelism.

The 1980s and 1990s

The 1980s and 1990s were characterized by three dynamics that were reinforcing each other. One was an under-appreciation of possible welfare losses that market failures may inflict and the need for a regulatory framework to address these failures. There was a widespread if simplistic belief in the virtues of the market system and that any problems that would emerge as a result of liberalization would somehow correct themselves. The second characteristic was

[1] See the detailed discussion in Buğra (1994).

that even though the reform process initiated in 1980 did result in the 'withdrawal' of the state from many areas of economic activity, it also entailed significant increase in the discretionary powers of the state and significant centralization of bureaucratic control. Third, especially in the 1990s there was a significant amount of political fragmentation and the emergence of short-lived coalition governments. Perhaps one should add a fourth dimension, namely the continuation of the legacy of populism and clientelism.

The interaction of these characteristics determined to a large extent the evolutionary path of the institutions of economic policy in these two decades. The 1980s, especially until 1987, was a period when political competition was relatively restricted due to a ban on political parties that had existed before the coup of 1980 and their leaders. This was a period when Turgut Özal, first a technocrat, then a minister of the economy and eventually the leader of the party that reigned during those years, initiated a serious of reforms, and in the name of expediency simultaneously centralized policymaking authority in agencies that he could directly control. Admittedly, his reforms did meet with resistance from parts of the bureaucracy, a fact that may partly explain the centralization that occurred during that period. But this was not all. He also tried to make sure that his pet projects would be implemented without delay and, when necessary, acquire the necessary financing by bypassing possible veto players.

This tendency for centralization was most apparent in budgetary policy. In a very controversial move, the Treasury was separated from the Ministry of Finance and attached to the Prime Ministry. The Treasury became responsible for public debt and cash management, and the Ministry of Finance was left with the tasks of revenue collection and procedural control of the budget process. Another well-known example was the emergence of extra-budgetary funds (EBFs), which allowed the executive to circumvent parliamentary supervision and allocate public funds to pet projects.

While the emergence of EBFs started an unhealthy dynamic of moving public expenditures outside the purview of traditional budgetary institutions, during most of the 1980s fiscal policy was under control and the extent of budget deficits was relatively limited. The ban on political leaders was abolished in 1987. With the re-emergence of political competition, pressures on the budget emerged again, with serious consequences. Large budget deficits, increases in public debt and macroeconomic instability ensued throughout the 1990s. A good part of public debt was held by the banking system. In addition, however, by the end of the 1990s, 'budget unity' was broken down, that is, there were significant amounts of off-budget expenditures, especially through state owned banks. Such expenditures led to high quasi-fiscal deficits, but the exact size of these deficits was not known. Public banks were given certain non-banking functions such as lending to certain politically favoured borrowers through preferential lending rates and financing agricultural support programmes. The losses created by these activities were accumulated over time and created an additional amount of public debt that was not recognized in official statistics.

Another policy area that suffered from institutional shortcomings was the regulation and supervision of the banking system. The banking system experienced a high level of new entry after the liberalization in the 1980s. The supervision of the banking system was undertaken by the Treasury and the central bank, and ultimate decisions were taken by the political authority. Even though the banking law of 1985 did give the Treasury and the central bank significant powers to intervene in the banking system, there were two factors that led to inaction. The first was the fact that governments relied on the banking system to refinance the public debt and banks were the main holders of government instruments used to finance budget deficits. The second was lack of independence of the regulators. In fact, the regulators were directly responsible for managing the public debt. During the 1990s, macroeconomic instability in an environment of liberalized capital flows encouraged banks to borrow in foreign currency and lend, especially to the government by holding government securities, in domestic currency at very high real interest rates. This increased their foreign exchange exposure and made them vulnerable to devaluations. After the crisis in 2000–01, it turned out that some banks also engaged in excessive exposure to affiliated companies as well as tunnelling.

The area of privatization policy was a clear example of the main tendencies in this period. Privatization has been high on the agenda of most governments in the post-1980 period. Depending on the period and government priorities, privatization was seen as a means of curtailing state intervention, raising revenues for the budget, expanding popular capitalism by spreading share ownership, encouraging the private sector to participate in infrastructure investments and a vehicle for transferring rents to politically connected firms.

Nevertheless, privatization did not really take off in the 1980s and 1990s. There were numerous efforts by various governments to enact privatization laws but they were mostly shot down by the Constitutional Court, which found them unconstitutional. One of the main reasons for the Constitutional Court's objections was that the laws transferred legislative authority to the executive. What this meant was that the laws attempted to give too much discretion about privatization policy to the government. Indeed, in most cases these laws attempted to vest the authority to take a wide variety of decisions pertaining to privatization to a ministry or an agency directly controlled by the government. Rather than elucidating rules about, for example, the procedures to be followed in privatizations, valuation methods and what type of tender schemes would be followed, and the laws empowered a government body to make these decisions, with no precautions taken to ensure transparency or accountability. It was only in 1994 that a more comprehensive law was finally passed, and with further amendments until the end of the 1990s, the legal framework became acceptable according to the standards set by the constitutional court.

One characteristic of the privatization efforts during the 1980s and 1990s was that governments did not attempt to establish a legal and regulatory framework when they tried to privatize public monopolies in network industries; that meant that incumbent public monopolies would be transferred to private ownership with no measures to contain anti-competitive practices. In the telecommunications industry, for example, there was an attempt to privatize part of Türk Telekom without any measures to eliminate its monopoly rights, liberalize the industry or establish mechanisms that would prevent the company from abusing its dominant position.

There were also numerous efforts, especially in energy, that stopped short of full privatization, but which tried to encourage the private sector to participate in electricity generation and distribution activities through contracts (so-called 'build-operate-transfer', 'build-operate' and 'transfer of operating rights' contracts) that provided widespread exclusivity and monopoly rights, as well as various forms of government price and purchase guarantees. Some of these investment contracts in generation were approved without any competitive tender mechanism. Some of these contracts came under heavy criticism for very high prices paid by the state and some were investigated by the High Court of Accounts (Sayıştay). In electricity distribution, the government attempted to transfer operating rights to private companies, granting them monopoly rights over consumers in their regions; most were cancelled by the Council of State (Danıştay), which is the high appeals court in administrative law. Irrespective of the details of specific projects, it was clear that the government's approach to engaging private capital allowed for significant discretion and mechanisms whereby rents could be transferred to favoured firms.

One should emphasize that this process of de-institutionalization did not take place in a vacuum but within an overall global shift that undervalued the state's role in the economy, was suspicious of governments and the public sector in general, and overestimated the corrective capacities of the market mechanism. Especially during the 1980s international financial institutions such as the World Bank and the IMF were deeply engaged in 'structural adjustment', which basically meant macroeconomic stabilization through austerity on the one hand, and liberalization on the other. Government interventions were solely seen as a source of rents and other inefficiencies, and the best a country could do was to remove them. In this general framework there was no place for legal frameworks or institutions that were necessary for the workings of a modern capitalist economy. Reform and good policy were largely seen as matters of sufficient 'political will', and while the absence of good policy was seen as the direct result of politics messing up the policy process, there were no recommendations how the policy process could be insulated, if at all. It was not until the fall of the Berlin Wall that the Washington institutions suddenly became aware the need to study the institutional underpinnings of the market mechanism, and this realization plus the overall failure of structural adjustment programs in most developing countries pushed the World Bank and the IMF to recognize the importance of governance. Indeed, it was probably this new realization that eventually prompted the World Bank to devote a whole World Development Report to the issue of 'The State in a Changing World' in 1997.

Coming back to Turkey, there were a number of policy areas that presented counterexamples to the overall trend of increased discretion and centralization mentioned above. The most important one was competition policy. Turkey signed a Customs Union (CU) with the European Union in 1996, and as part of the requirements of the CU, enacted a Law for the Protection of Competition in 1994. The Competition Authority, which was an independent administrative authority entrusted the implementation of the law, was established in 1997. The establishment of the Competition Authority turned out to be a very significant step in the evolution of economic institutions. Its influence went beyond the straightforward implementation of competition law, which it did quite successfully, but had an impact on privatization and liberalization of network industries as well. These interventions had a very significant impact on the degree of competition in many markets, as discussed below.

Another important development actually predates the enactment of the competition law and has to do with the regulation of capital markets. A crisis in non-bank financial institutions in the early days of financial liberalization prompted the government back then to establish the first independent regulatory authority, the Capital Markets Board.

One should also mention industrial policy. During the 1980s, in line with the new development regime, the government used many instruments to support exports. These various forms of export subsidies were used in a non-transparent and discretionary manner with a high degree of variability across sectors and across years. The degree of discretion as well as the extent of financial support were both reduced in the 1990s, both because of membership in the World Trade Organization and the establishment of the Customs Union (both of which required restrictions on the scope and type of subsidies) and because of increasing lack of public funds.

The 2000–01 Crisis, the Golden Years and the Role of the EU

The excesses of the 1990s resulted in a major macroeconomic and financial crisis in 2000 and 2001. The crisis wiped out almost half of the banking system and created a major recession in 2001. The government called on Kemal Derviş, a vice president at the World Bank, to take responsibility as minister of economy and a major reform programme was announced with the support of the World Bank and the IMF. The reform programme was rich in institutional restructuring.

It should be pointed out that many elements of the reform programme were not foreign to the economic bureaucracy. They were areas where various preparations were already undertaken in various parts of government agencies, especially the State Planning Organization and the Treasury. Hence there were studies in the State Planning Organization, as early as 1994, underlining the need for regulation and the establishment of independent regulatory authorities in network industries such as telecommunications and electricity. Both the Treasury and the Ministry of Finance, as well as the State Planning Organization, were well aware of the disruptive effects of deterioration of budgetary institutions, the breakdown of budget unity and proliferation of off-budget expenditures and borrowing. In fact, many members of the economic team designing and implementing the reform programme were recruited from within existing managers of the agencies, though there were a few outside recruitments as well.

As extensively emphasized in the literature, the economic crisis played an important role in creating an environment conducive to reform. First of all, the crisis put international institutions in a much stronger bargaining position. Second, the reform also strengthened the position of bureaucrats who were well cognizant of reform, but could not pursue reform before the crisis because of the adverse political environment. Third, as the degree of incompetence, and worse, of corruption became public knowledge, the incumbent political class lost their public appeal. It was in this kind of a political environment when the Justice and Development Party (AKP) won the general elections by a landslide in 2002 and formed the first majority government in more than a decade. Interestingly, the AKP adopted the reform programme almost in its entirety.

Another important factor that facilitated the reform process was the EU. Turkey became a candidate country in 1999 and membership negotiations started in 2005, after the AKP implemented significant political reforms. The transformation of the institutions of economic policy actually has been an excellent area to gauge the importance of the EU. Being a candidate country, Turkey was set on the task of transposing EU regulations in many areas of economic policy. These were also areas that needed reform. The EU provided a template on the rules and regulations that needed to be adopted. The existence of a template meant that many delays that could occur because of costly bargaining among stakeholders could be avoided. It could be the case that a certain set of EU regulations for a particular policy area is not the first best. Nevertheless, it seems the benefit of the existence of a template that had legitimacy and on which parties could readily agree, dominated potentially higher but highly uncertain benefits that could be achieved as a result of costly bargaining.

The role of the EU goes beyond providing a legitimate template, however. It also provided a model of rules that would govern the policymaking process. Public consultations became much more widespread relative to earlier periods. Not only the IRAs but also the ministries started to publish annual reports of their activities and even strategic plans (though both have been of highly variable quality). For the IRAs, closer interaction with peers and colleagues in EU member-states and the possibility of twinning programmes created opportunities for learning, updated information and exchange of ideas. Finally, in many areas the EU also provided a benchmark against which both the performance of public agencies and the outcomes of rules and regulations could be evaluated. For example, in telecommunications and electricity, the publication by the European Commission of benchmark statistics on issues such as interconnection rates, development of competition, markets shares of new entrants and consumer switching rates provided metrics to evaluate developments in Turkey.

In fact, the role of the EU can also be seen as part of the global norms and standards about institutional preconditions of good public policy. By the end of the 1990s, the importance of good governance, delegation, independence of regulatory authorities, transparency, accountability and public consultations had become part of what have been called 'second generation reforms' in the phraseology of international financial institutions, especially the World Bank and the IMF. Although the details might differ, there was a high degree of congruence between the institutional and policy prescriptions in Brussels and Washington DC. So for anyone looking for credible models of what was considered as basic institutional principles of good public policy, there was a well agreed-upon model globally available.

The new economic programme first addressed the financial sector, which was in a deep crisis. A new banking law was enacted in 1999, forming the Banking Regulation and Supervision Agency (BRSA) as an independent authority with strong powers over the banking industry. Under the recovery programme, BRSA, together with the Savings Deposit Insurance Fund, undertook a massive restructuring of the banking sector and ensured its adequate capitalization. New rules governing capital requirements, accounting of risks and reporting requirements were introduced and properly implemented and monitored. The BRSA and the tight control of the banking system are widely credited for the resilience of the banking system in the face of the global financial crisis that hit the world in 2009.

The Central Bank became independent in 2001. Over time the Central Bank adopted several institutional measures to enhance its credibility and transparency. It followed a policy of inflation targeting, which successfully reduced inflation from high double digits to single digits towards the end of the first decade of the 2000s.

In the area of fiscal policy, several laws were adopted that eliminated possibilities of off-budget expenditures, increased the coverage of the budget, and improved transparency and reporting requirements on expenditures and public debt. Public banks were forbidden from engaging in quasi-fiscal activities unless there was an explicit appropriation in the budget.

IRAs were established in other sectors as well, such as energy, telecommunications (and in not-so-obvious industries such as tobacco and sugar). Both the institutional structure (i.e. establishment of

IRAs) and the laws and secondary legislation were largely inspired by the EU Directives, as well as decisions of the European Commission or national regulatory authorities of member-states.

The literature on regulation and independence of regulatory authorities makes a useful distinction between de jure and de facto independence. The concept of de jure independence focuses on formal/legal requirements or institutional measures that ensure the independence of IRAs from political pressure and from the industries that they regulate. Studies undertaken on Turkey have found that by and large Turkish IRAs meet the formal requirements of independence. Of course, formal independence does not always guarantee de facto independence. Governments may influence decision-making in IRAs by appointing people that may be easily influenced. The degree of de facto independence of IRAs in Turkey has been a source of concern, especially in the last few years. However, in order to show how the establishment of IRAs made an impact, it may be useful to look at individual sectors.

Take electronic communications, for example.[2] A new telecommunications act, adopted in 2000, established the Telecommunications Authority (later renamed as the Information and Communications Technologies Authority, ICTA), terminated the monopoly rights of the incumbent fixed line operator Türk Telekom, laid down rules for regulated access and interconnection rates, and prepared for the liberalization of the industry. Türk Telekom was privatized in 2005. The legal framework for the liberalization and regulation of the industry was very much influenced by that in the European Union. However, in practice, and especially in the early years of the liberalization process, the more competitive elements of the new framework were implemented slowly and half-heartedly, possibly reflecting both Türk Telekom's influence on the Ministry and the limited de facto independence of the regulatory authority, as well as a desire to fetch high revenues out of the privatization of Türk Telekom. Licensing of new entrants was delayed and interconnection rates (charges that operators pay to each other when they are given access to their rivals' network) were too high relative to those in the

[2] Atiyas and Doğan (2010).

European Union. As a result, the dominance of Türk Telekom in fixed-line telecommunications markets, especially in the market for internet services, is still too high when compared to many member-states of the EU.

However, the ICTA took a much more competitive stance in the mobile markets (Atiyas and Doğan 2010). This is possibly explained by the fact that Türk Telekom's subsidiary is a new entrant in the mobile telecommunications markets; hence ICTA tried to create a more competitive environment in the mobile industry so that new entrants could gain market share and the dominance of incumbent operators might be reduced. Here we see a case where the IRA is clearly not necessarily acting independently and its choices represent the preferences of the incumbent fixed line operator and/or the government. However, the interesting point is that even when the ICTA wanted to favour some operators, it had to carry this out within the established rules of the game. Rather than using more coarse instruments (such as outright harassment or predatory intervention using regulatory powers, see below), the ICTA chose to create a more competitive environment by reducing interconnection rates to levels that were among the lowest in the EU. Here we see the effect of the EU (or indeed of global norms) at several levels: First, the existence of a legal/regulatory framework limits and refines the extent of favouritism that the IRA can pursue. Second, the fact that the ICTA made publicly available at least some of its main regulatory decisions (such as interconnection rates) made it more accountable. Third, the availability of standardized measures of performance (such as published interconnection rates) in the EU (via the report of the European Commission) allows us to evaluate the actions and performance of the ICTA against their peers in the EU.

In energy as well, a new law was passed that established a regulatory authority with wide powers to regulate the industry (Atiyas et al. 2012). The law envisaged very low restrictions on new entry into generation, regulated third party access, and privatization. A wholesale market was eventually established, reducing significantly the influence of the government in the formation of wholesale prices. Government control of gas prices continues, and the degree of competition is still quite limited because of the presence of the incumbent government-owned electricity generation company. Despite that, the industry has been able to attract high levels of private investment into generation without any price guarantees.

It may be worthwhile to identify the important role of the Competition Authority (CA). Widely known for its high level of professionalism and competence (OECD 2005), the CA took an active role in the privatization process. It reviewed privatization transactions from the point of view of the effect of the transaction on the degree of competition in the respective markets. More specifically, in telecoms the CA required that the cable TV component be separated from the incumbent operator before privatization. In electricity, it required that retail arms of distribution companies (which are potentially competitive) be separated from the distribution business (which is a natural monopoly).[3]

However, there were also some policy areas where the overall trend has been in the opposite direction. One such area was public procurement. In 2002 a new Public Procurement Law was passed that established a regulatory authority, increased transparency of procurement, set rules for dissemination of information on public purchases, enhanced measures to ensure competition and covered a large part of the public sector. It was significantly revised as early as 2003 to exempt public utility companies in the oil and transportation sectors. Between 2003 and 2013 there have been 23 amendments covering more than a hundred changes that exempted state-owned enterprises and businesses established by municipalities, introduced various other exemptions and increased contract size below which less strict rules were applicable. Overall, the changes increased the scope of discretionary behaviour by public agencies engaged in procurement, especially by increasing opportunities for procurement other than the open tender method (restricted and negotiated tender methods as well as direct purchases).

The other area where institutions evolved in the direction of centralization and discretion has been construction, especially public housing. The Housing Development Administration of Turkey (TOKİ) was established in 1984. It was attached to the

[3] See Atiyas (2012) for a fuller discussion.

Prime Ministry in 2004. In time, the Directorate of Office of Land was abolished and TOKİ assumed control over almost all public land. Moreover, in 2005 TOKİ was exempted from the Public Finance and Control Law, which is the main law that ensures budget unity, transparency and efficiency of the budget process. TOKİ has been given the authority to use public land for joint projects with the private sector or transfer land to the private sector through land sales or designing income-sharing contracts for construction projects. It has tremendous power to develop projects and override the authority of local governments in developing urban plans, zoning arrangements etc. (e.g. urban renewal projects). There is a general perception in the public that these construction projects have become a major vehicle for the transfer of rents to politically connected companies. The mechanism seems to be rather simple. Consider an income sharing project. TOKİ has access to publicly owned land free of charge. The cost of the project may be inflated to ensure transfer of rents to the company. The total cost of the project may still be reasonable because the cost of land is zero. While in the 1980s and 1990s rents were created out of fiscal flows, with an adverse effect on the budget, in the above scheme rents are created out of stocks, with little immediate effect on budget expenditures or deficit. Furthermore, since there are no publicly available and transparent records of publicly owned land, and since TOKİ has almost no reporting requirements, these activities are undertaken without providing any information to the public.

It is widely accepted that the economic performance of Turkey after the crisis and during the early period of AKP rule has been exemplary. Especially the period until the great global recession of 2008–09 has been characterized by macroeconomic stability and high economic growth. There is also quite a bit of evidence that this high growth was 'shared' in the sense that new economic growth centres in Anatolia (dubbed the Anatolian Tigers) have participated in this growth (World Bank 2014). The traditional industrial provinces such as Istanbul, Izmir, Ankara, Kocaeli and Bursa still carry out a large portion of economic activity and still have higher levels of labour productivity compared to the Anatolian Tigers, but there is evidence of 'catch-up' in that the new centres are both increasing their shares in economic activity and exports, and also their productivity have been growing at rates which are higher than those of the traditional centres.

It is difficult to identify the particular role of institutional reform in these developments. It is generally believed that under a generally benign global economic environment, stability in the domestic macro-economy and lower public debt, and access to finance became easier, a factor that facilitated entry of new firms and expansion of existing small- and mid-size firms. However these developments are also consistent with the idea that with major reform in institutions of economic policy, a more competitive economic environment was created. With the benefit of a more level playing field, and a non-discriminatory environment, firms in these new centres of growth were able to grow, gain market share, and play a larger role in national economic activity.

There is one more qualification that needs to be underlined. Recent literature on political dynamics in Turkey has emphasized the emergence of a devout bourgeoisie as the main constituency of the AKP (for example, Gümüşçü and Sert 2009). One possible topic of discussion is whether the economic environment was actually not non-discriminatory, or whether it was actually discriminating in favour of the newly emergent constituency. There are many examples of instances where the AKP government has used discretion to favour particular politically connected business groups,[4] and whether what looks to be shared growth was actually positive discrimination in favour of these groups, is a legitimate question. A sufficiently convincing answer to this question will require more thorough empirical research. My tentative answer based on the narrative above and admittedly insufficient empirical evidence is that there was a two-pronged approach. In many sectors, especially manufacturing, the government's approach was non-discriminatory. Constraints on discretionary industrial activity imposed by the Customs Union and WTO membership mentioned above probably are partly responsible. In others, especially public procurement and construction, as well as in some instances media and energy, the government used its power

[4] See Buğra and Savaşkan (2014) for examples.

to favour particular businesses. There is also evidence of particular instances of explicitly exclusionary behaviour, especially in the case of business groups associated with media taking a critical position against the government. At the same time, in hindsight, evidence of such exclusionary behaviour during the early part of AKP rule is relatively scarce, especially as compared to the more recent years, or the so called post-Gezi period.

A Turn in the Wind

In the last few years, several developments in the political environment led to a stagnation or even reversal in the evolution of institutional economic policy. For various reasons the excitement over Turkey's EU candidacy weakened both in Europe and in Turkey, with the result that the institutional anchor provided by the EU started to weaken over time. A second development, which possibly is closely correlated with the first, is that the government increasingly became intolerant of dissent, a situation that reflected itself in the government's stance towards business. Specifically, businesses that voiced dissenting opinions on current political events increasingly risked a scolding by some member of government or worse, tax audits. This tendency became more evident after the Gezi incidents of May 2014, a wave of protests against the government's desires to turn an urban park into shopping malls and hotels in Taksim, Istanbul.[5]

An even more important development was that the coalition that characterized the early periods of AKP government broke down. During the first two AKP governments, the AKP and what is called the Gülen community, which is tightly organized both in business as well as in the police and the judiciary, cooperated, especially to curtail the political power of the military. In the last few years this coalition has unravelled: prosecutors and members of the police

[5] The term Gezi incidents refers to a wave of protests initially against government plans to turn Istanbul's Gezi Park into shopping malls and hotels. Subsequently, protests took place across many provinces of Turkey, covering a wide range of concerns, including the increasing authoritarianism of the government. The government took a non-conciliatory stance towards the protesters and blamed foreign powers and 'interest lobbies'.

administration widely associated with the Gülen movement initiated investigations against politicians, bureaucrats and business people known to be close to the AKP. This process culminated in a major investigation and a series of arrests or custodies with charges of major corruption in December 2013 and of course the recent purges in a variety of government-controlled sectors, whereby the government took major legal and administrative steps to rid the judiciary and the internal security apparatus of people suspected of being associated with the Gülen movement, with devastating implications for the independence of the judiciary.

It seems that these primarily political developments have started to take their toll on institutions of economic policy as well. Already in 2011 the government passed a decree-law which stated that regulatory agencies would be 'inspected' by ministries. This was widely seen as a serious restriction on the independence of regulatory agencies. Recent policy initiatives reflect a return to more traditional modes of policymaking, where rather than delegating authority, the government retains direct control. One example is in the area of macro-prudential regulation. Rather than following a solution that is similar to those found in the US and EU, where the task is delegated to independent agencies, the government opted for the establishment of a Financial Stability Committee chaired by the Minister responsible for Treasury (Ersel 2012).

Another policy area where the government's institutional choice reflects a preference for direct control rather than delegation is the area of nuclear energy. The government so far has launched two nuclear plant projects, one through an agreement with the Russian government, and the other with the Japanese government. Neither of these two projects was initiated through a consultative process. More importantly, in international comparison, and especially in comparison to EU directives or the legal frameworks of member states, the current legal and regulatory framework for nuclear energy in Turkey puts the regulatory process directly under the control of the prime ministry. The regulatory authority for nuclear energy does not comply with the formal norms of independence and there are no measures for transparency, or to the public's right to information or independent monitoring or appraisal (Atiyas and Sanin 2012).

More recent developments reflect a more serious desire to intervene in regulatory procedures. One telling story in this regard is the Bank Asya saga.[6] Bank Asya is widely known to be associated with the Gülen movement. The dispute between Bank Asya and the then-Prime Minister Erdoğan started after the police arrested a number of government officials in December 2013, on allegations of corruption and bribery, an operation during which the sons of two ministers were also implicated. State-owned and pro-government firms withdrew their deposits and by the second quarter of 2014, Bank Asya lost 25 per cent of its cash deposits. According to news reports, there were also rumours that Bank Asya was accused of acquiring information about the impending corruption investigations and purchasing large amounts of US dollars in expectation of a depreciation of the Turkish Lira.[7] This allegation was later dismissed, apparently when the Central Bank data showed that there was no abnormal purchase of foreign currency prior to the December investigations.[8] In any case, the government revoked Bank Asya's license to collect taxes on behalf of the state in August 2014. Pro-government newspapers have carried almost daily reports on Bank Asya, portraying it as a failing bank being propped up by members of Gülen's network. The *Financial Times* reported that Bank Asya's shares dropped by 55 per cent between December 2013 and September 2014.

In September, Erdoğan, by now the president, urged the Banking Regulation and Supervision Agency (BRSA) to 'make a decision' on the bank, otherwise 'it would be the BDDK that is responsible'.[9] Later rumours were reported that the President of the BRSA urged the Board, the decision making body of the agency, to undertake an

[6] See for example, Buttironi, 'The Dispute over Bank Asya'. *Business Network Magazine*. 14 October 2014. http://www.bnmagazine.co.uk/articles/2014/10/14/the-dispute-over-bank-asya-what-lies-ahead-in-erdogans-turkey; *Financial Times*. 'Turkey's Bank Asya dented by Erdoğan call.' 16 September 2014. http://www.ft.com/intl/cms/s/0/05361dd8-3d83-11e4-b782-00144feabdc0.html#axzz3HKkDJv00,

[7] http://t24.com.tr/haber/bddk-bank-asyanin-dolar-topladigi-iddiasini-inceliyor,247283. 31 December 2013.

[8] http://www.taraf.com.tr/haber-ankara-ekonomiye-kursun-sikiyor-144799/.

[9] *Financial Times*. 'Turkey's Bank Asya dented by Erdoğan call'. 16 September 2014. http://www.ft.com/intl/cms/s/0/05361dd8-3d83-11e4-b782-00144feabdc0.html#axzz3HKkDJv00

intervention that did not strictly follow procedures outlined in the law on steps that need to be carried out towards banks suspected of experiencing financial problems; the suggestion was apparently opposed by Board members, on the grounds that they would become legally liable if their interventions were not justified by regulations.[10]

Another interesting episode is the Competition Authority's investigation into Tüpraş' alleged abuse of its dominant position. Tüpraş is the largest petroleum refinery in Turkey. It was privatized in 2005 and was bought by a consortium of Koç Holding and Shell. After the Gezi incidents, Tüpraş has been subject to several audits, along with other companies owned by Koç Holding.[11] The Competition Authority investigation centred on Tüpraş' pricing practices over a period of three months and concluded that the company was guilty of excessive (or abusive) pricing. The company was fined a record 412 million TL. The decision was highly controversial. Excessive or abusive pricing is one area that competition authorities try to keep away from because it is hard to establish objective standards and also because investigating excessive pricing incidents is akin to price regulation. As commented by one observer, the Competition Authority had not issued a decision on excessive pricing for the last 13 years.[12] Proving the presence of excessive pricing requires that the excessiveness in the prices in question should be persistent and significant (against, say, costs). In the Tüpraş case, the duration was less than three months and the 'degree of excessiveness' (that is, the margin between the allegedly excessive prices and a benchmark cost or price) was a mere 15 per cent (and this relative not to costs but

[10] Sağlam 'BDDK'nın zor kararı'. 19 September 2014. http://sosyal.hurriyet.com.tr/yazar/erdal-saglam_8/bddk-nin-zor-karari_27218590. The same article also reported that pro-Gulen websites started to disseminate rumours about financial problems in other banks.

[11] During the Gezi incidents the Prime Minister had accused the Divan Hotel, owned by Koç Holding, of providing shelter to Gezi protesters fleeing the police. Shortly after the Prime Minister's reproach, finance ministry inspectors raided the offices of Tüpraş and Aygaz, while finance minister denied any connection between the protests and tax inspections. http://www.tmcnet.com/usubmit/2014/01/21/7640049.htm.

[12] http://www.academia.edu/7295475/The_Turkish_Competition_Authority_fines_an_ex-state-owned_oil_refinery_for_abusing_its_dominant_position_by_charging_excessive_prices_and_imposing_unfair_trading_conditions_TÜPRAŞ_.

to international benchmark prices. In the reasoned decision, one dissenting member also mentioned that much higher margins were found as not abusive in earlier Competition Board decisions. In addition Tüpraş was not making positive profits during this period but was making losses.

Admittedly, the treatment of a few cases does not provide sufficient evidence to decide whether there is a fundamental shift in the performance and independence of the IRAs, but the stories presented above do raise a concern about whether delegated powers to ensure that treatment of businesses is protected from political influence can be used in a predatory manner against businesses that fall out of favour with the government. This concern has been raised in the latest progress report issued by the European Commission, where, regarding the BRSA, it is stated: 'As part of the government's response to the December 2013 corruption allegations (see Political criteria — Government), an extensive reshuffling of the regulator's senior management took place. Perceptions of politically motivated decisions increased' (European Commission 2014: 32).

Conclusion: The Primacy of Politics

One of the main functions of the types of institutions reviewed in this paper is restraining the discretionary powers of the government. The aim is, through delegation of authority and additional measures, to ensure that this delegated authority will be used in a manner that is insulated from the government, and therefore from the short-run dynamics of political calculus. The interesting issue is that this very act of delegation and the creation of measures of independence are themselves outcomes of political acts.

Once created, formal measures of independence help maintain some degree of independence of the agencies. For example, the government cannot recall appointed directors, administrators, or board members unless there are major reasons such as health issues or improper use of power. However, ultimately when the terms of these administrators end, it is still the prerogative of the government to appoint new ones. Hence, ultimately the government has the ability to appoint friendly regulators if it wishes to do so. Ultimately, as emphasized by Acemoğlu and Robinson (2008), it is the nature of the political institutions that determine the nature of economic institutions.

In that sense, one should not be surprised that the evolution of institutions of economic policy in Turkey seems to reflect the evolution of political institutions. In the golden years of the 2000s, this evolution largely reflected a policy that apparently was interested in EU accession. Currently the evolution seems to be closely influenced by the survival instincts of the government.

The big dilemma that the government now faces is as follows: on the one hand, political imperatives seem to guide the government towards more discretionary rather than rule-based institutions in economic policy. At the same time, however, the AKP has been a political party that has always identified high economic growth as a most important political objective. Indeed, as discussed above, many observers believe that it was the dynamism of emergent middle classes that formed the main constituency of AKP in the first place. More discretionary institutions, discrimination among business groups, and using economic instruments to punish business groups that fall out of favour are most likely going to result in lower investment and lower economic growth. As this happens, one should not be surprised to witness the emergence of new instruments of economic policy that can be used in even more discretionary ways[13] to support investment, resulting in further deviations from rule-based institutions, resulting in still lower investment, etc. While these instruments will be highly effective in creating loyal politically connected firms, they will most likely further deteriorate the general investment environment.

References

Acemoğlu, D., and J.A. Robinson. 2008. 'The Role of Institutions in Growth and Development.' Working Paper No. 10. Commission on Growth and Development.

[13] This is already happening. The government recently issued a new regulation that allows the Treasury to issue guarantees for credits obtained for private-public joint investment projects such as Build Operate or Build Operate Transfer projects, reminiscent of the 1990s.

Atiyas, İ. 2012. 'Economic institutions and institutional change in Turkey during the neoliberal era.' *New Perspectives on Turkey*, No. 47, 57–81.

———., and P. Doğan. 2010. 'Glass Half Empty? Politics and Institutions in the Liberalization of the Fixed Line Telecommunications Industry in Turkey.' In *Understanding the Process of Economic Change in Turkey: An Institutional Approach*. Tamar Çetin and Feridun Yılmaz (eds.). New York: Nova Science Publishers. pp. 261–83.

———., and D. Sanin. 2012. 'A Regulatory Authority for Nuclear Energy: Country Experiences and Proposals for Turkey.' In *The Turkish Model for Transition to Nuclear Energy – II*. S. Ülgen (ed.). Centre for Economic and Foreign Policy Studies (EDAM) publication.

———. T. Çetin and G. Gülen. 2012. *Reforming Turkish Energy Markets*. New York: Springer.

Buğra, A. 1994. *State and Business in Modern Turkey: A Comparative Study*. Albany: State University of New York.

———., and O. Savaşkan. 2014. New Capitalism in Turkey: The Relationship between Politics, Religion and Business. Cheltenham, UK & Northampton, USA: Edward Elgar Publishing.

Ersel, H. 2012. 'Finansal İstikrarın Sağlanması İçin Nasıl Bir Mekanizma Tasarlanabilir?' *İktisat İşletme ve Finans*, 27(315), pp. 37–49.

Gümüşçü, Ş., and D. Sert. 2009. 'The Power of the Devout Bourgeoisie: The Case of the Justice and Development Party in Turkey.' *Middle Eastern Studies*, 45:6, pp. 953–68.

OECD. 2005. *Competition Law and Policy in Turkey*. Paris: OECD

World Bank. 2014. 'Turkey's Transitions: Integration, Inclusion, Institutions.' Washington, DC: World Bank.

16 Anti-corruption Policy in Turkey Instruments, Issues and Influences[1]

Muhittin Acar

Abstract

Corruption is an entrenched and enduring problem in Turkey. While political and popular discussions about fraudulent acts in politics and public administration have been intensified in recent months, 'anti-corruption as a public policy' has not yet attracted enough attention from the scholarly community. This current paper can thus be construed as one of the initial attempts toward framing anti-corruption as a complex public policy problem in Turkey dwelling on the interplay of instruments, issues, and influences to better capture the national context and constraints facing the present and future anti-corruption efforts.

After briefly describing the significance of studying anti-corruption as a complex public policy problem in a globalized world, the first section of this paper informs the reader about the research methodology utilized. The interview component of our field study involved 55 face-to-face interviews with a group of 60 highly-educated and well-experienced 'experts', including academicians, inspectors, journalists, activists, and politicians. The main thematic section further describes and discusses key policy instruments pertaining to anti-corruption policies, namely government programmes of AKP cabinets and the 'strategy for increasing transparency and strengthening the struggle against corruption'. This contribution then debates major issues related to identifying and getting corruption onto the agenda as a public problem by taking findings from

[1] The research activities leading to preparation of this paper were funded in part by the Seventh Framework Programme for Research and Technological Development of the European Union (ANTICORRP, Grant agreement no: 290529).

our field research in consideration. Finally, this essay takes into account the influences of the EU and other international actors in determining anti-corruption policies and practices in Turkey along with the relevant findings from the interview component of our field research. The paper then ends with a brief concluding section.

Introduction

There is growing global consensus regarding the pervasive and persistent nature of corruption encountered by many societies from around the world. As a deep-rooted problem and an overarching evil, corruption is considered as a serious threat to economic and democratic development, as it significantly endangers the effective functioning of political and administrative institutions as well as economic markets and financial mechanisms in a polity. Corruption also remains a significant obstacle to obtaining not only the rule of law, but also law and order in a given country since it impinges upon public security and safety. Last but not the least, corruption corrodes the ethical codes and moral foundations of communities and undermines the efforts toward achieving a just society (European Commission 2014a; Mungiu-Pippidi 2014; Persson, Rothstein and Tothstein 2012; Transparency International 2014).

Turkey is not immune to this reality. On the contrary, corruption has long been regarded as an entrenched and enduring problem in the country. Although political and popular discussions about fraudulent acts in politics and public administration have intensified in the months following the 17–23 December 2013 corruption scandals,[2] the widespread existence of this problem in Turkey has

[2] Due to time and otherwise constraints, a detailed description and critical analysis regarding the issues surrounding the 17 and 25 December 2013 will not be provided here. Instead, the following information taken verbatim from the European Commission's most recent Progress Report on Turkey (EU 2014b: 9) would be utilized to briefly inform the reader about those developments in the country:

'For most of the year attention was drawn to the 17 and 25 December 2013 corruption allegations targeting the Prime Minister, four ministers, their relatives, the head of the biggest public bank, public officials and businessmen. Ten out of twenty-five ministers were replaced in a Cabinet reshuffle on 25 December. There was a significant delay in submitting requests to parliament to lift the immunity of four

been recognized for quite some time by international organizations (e.g., Freedom House 2014; GCB 2010/11), official documents (e.g., Council of Ministers 2002; Tarhan et al. 2006) and individual studies (e.g., Özhabeş 2011; Sarlak and Bali 2007). To give an

Table 16.1: Turkey's Country Scores and Rankings in Corruption Perception Index (CPI)

Year	Country Score of Turkey	Country Rank of Turkey	Total Number of Countries Covered
2004	3.2	81	146
2005	3.5	69	159
2006	3.8	60	163
2007	4.1	64	179
2008	4.6	58	180
2009	4.4	61	180
2010	4.4	56	178
2011	4.2	61	183
2012	49	54	174
2013	50	53	177
2014	45	64	174

Source: Transparency International

former ministers implicated in corruption allegations. In response to the allegations of corruption, the government alleged that there had been an attempted judicial coup by a "parallel structure" within the state, controlled by the Gülen Movement. Prosecutors and police officers in charge of the original investigations of 17 and 25 December were removed from their posts. A significant number of reassignments and dismissals in the police, civil service and the judiciary followed, accompanied by legal measures in the judiciary. A significant number of police officers were detained. In September, the Istanbul Chief Prosecutor's Office decided not to prosecute 96 suspects allegedly involved in the December corruption case. As part of that response, key legislation, including on the High Council of Judges and Prosecutors and on the internet, was drafted and adopted in haste and without consultations.'

It must be added that the investigation commission established to examine the graft allegations within the Turkish Grand National Assembly (TGNA-Turkish Parliament) has decided not to commit for trial four former ministers accused in a corruption investigation on 5 January 2015. A floor vote on 20 January 2015 in the General Assembly of TGNA was in the same direction. Strictly speaking, both legislative-wise and in terms of judicial processing the case seemed to get closed.

example, the country's scores on the Corruption Perception Indexes (CPIs) prepared by Transparency International (TI) have remained at less-than-inspiring levels, despite some fluctuations and even improvements in the rankings of the country between the years 2004 and 2014 (see Table 16.1).

In a sense, corruption in Turkey has long been an 'open secret' for some segments of society, 'secrets in the sense that they are excluded from formal or official discourse; but they are open in the sense that they are familiar and referred to in idioms and language games, though these often require explanation for outsiders' (Ledeneva 2011: 725). For others, 'the politics of corruption' has always been at play; it has only intensified and become more visible in recent months, better reflecting the extensively politicized and extremely polarized nature of the debates related to corruption and anti-corruption in the country. As stated in the Turkey 2014 Progress Report prepared by the European Commission, 'the government response to corruption allegations, which amounted to interfering of the executive into the independence, impartiality and efficiency of the judiciary, raised serious concerns. This led to further polarization of political climate' (EC 2014: 10).

In any case, however, it is reasonable to argue that 'anti-corruption as a public policy' has not yet attracted adequate attention from the scholarly community in Turkey. Thus, this current paper can be regarded as one of the initial attempts toward treating anti-corruption as a major public policy problem in the country. It argues for a new analytical approach that takes into consideration the interplay of various instruments, issues, and influences in shaping and re-shaping the national agenda in the country vis-à-vis corruption and anti-corruption. It intends to illustrate that such an approach is better-equipped than single-issue frameworks to capture the national context and constraints facing the present and future anti-corruption efforts.

Nevertheless, to avoid repeating or duplicating previously published works of ours and others on relevant matters, a carefully-dosed selectivity here is deemed necessary. For instance, since we had described and discussed in detail the existing legal-institutional framework related to anti-corruption in Turkey elsewhere (e.g., Acar and Dede 2013), it has been necessary for us to skip them as much as possible and to focus instead on recent government programmes and strategy. Similarly, since the role and place of corruption in Turkey's relations with the EU have been examined extensively, if not exclusively, by different studies before us (e.g., Ömürgönülşen and Doig 2012), the potential contribution of this paper has instead been envisioned to utilize the findings from field research.

This said, the following section succinctly describes the research methodology utilized throughout this paper. The second major section of the paper deals with the key instruments, issues, and influences associated with corruption and anti-corruption in Turkey. The findings from the field research on issues and influences are also presented and discussed therein. Finally, the paper ends with a brief concluding section.

Research Methodology

The research strategy used in this study was largely determined by the purposes of the study and the nature of research questions posed, as well as by the extant resources and constraints. In addition to literature review and document (content) analysis, the current study has also benefitted from field research, including a survey of 'ordinary citizens' and interviews with 'experts'. The overarching purpose of the interview component of the field research has been to identify, describe, and evaluate the most critical issues and themes associated with corruption and anti-corruption in the country. Therefore, throughout the interviews, a more explicit and extensive inquiry into different dimensions of corruption and anti-corruption was attempted by posing a set of questions to the participants consisting of government officers, inspectors/auditors, politicians, entrepreneurs, anti-corruption activists, and so on.

The Interviews and the Informants

Once it was decided to conduct semi-structured interviews as part of the field research, the list of questions to be explored with the study participants became an important issue. After close consultation and collaboration with the coordinator of the ANTICORRP Work Package 4 and our colleagues, we were able to determine the key themes and issues to be covered during the interviews. In the process of drafting the list of questions to be asked, we greatly benefited from the content and style of sample questions provided by the WP4 Coordinator.[3] We translated some of them directly into Turkish, while adopting others with small revisions and further adding new questions. The questions asked were further grouped into nine key themes/issue areas.[4]

We utilized both elite sampling and purposive sampling in the process of selecting the interviewees. In other words, once the main themes and issues to be explored during the interview component of the field research was determined, we decided to approach a certain group of people consisting of inspectors/auditors, representatives of non-profit organizations, academicians, journalists, and so on, who were 'experiential experts' about a particular issue. That is to say, we sought after certain individuals for our study sample based on the premise of gaining as much information and insight as possible. The chief researcher's professional background and personal connections were also critical in contacting and recruiting the participants for the interviews.

Fifty-five face-to-face interviews were conducted during the interview component of the fieldwork between December 2012 and March 2013. All the interviews were conducted in the urban districts of metropolitan Ankara, except for the seven interviews that were conducted in Istanbul. The duration of the interviews ranged from 30 minutes to 2 hours, a typical one lasting around 60 minutes. Face-to-face interviews were generally conducted one-on-one with the ethnographer on one side and an interviewee on the other. However,

[3] Namely, Professor Davide Torsello of University of Bergamo, Italy.

[4] The nine thematic areas were: Institutional performance, satisfaction and trust; Definitions and perceptions of corruption; Forms of corruption; Causes of and local justifications for corruption; Targets and impacts of corrupt practices; Anti-corruption policies and practices; Social and cultural norms and corruption; National and local media; and Local politics and policies. It must be noted that only the findings gathered in response to three most relevant questions from the third thematic subsection will be presented here.

in three cases, more than one interviewee was involved in the process, thus bringing the total of people interviewed to 60. Fifty-three of the interviewees were males and seven were females. The age range for the interviewed people was around 35 to 55.

It should also be noted here that the people interviewed for the study were a highly-educated group of experts in that all were college graduates, and a significant portion of them also had or were at the time pursuing graduate degrees (masters and doctoral degrees). They were, in general, a professionally well-equipped and highly-experienced group. It is interesting to note here that some of the interviewees were wearing two hats, for example, being an auditor/inspector in a public organization *and* a representative of an association of auditors/inspectors at the same time.

As such, the following information about the interviewees reflects these dual roles, explaining why the total number of professional attributions below (70) is higher than the number of people interviewed (60).

- 24 Auditor Generals/Controllers/Inspectors
- 19 NGO-Association Representatives/Activists
- 9 Researchers/Academicians/Scholars
- 6 Businesspeople/Consultants
- 4 Journalists/Media Reporters
- 4 Politicians, including two MPs and two members of local municipal councils
- 2 Representatives from the judiciary (a Public Prosecutor and a Judge)
- 2 Public Managers

The existence of an interview guide enabled the ethnographer to have more control over data gathering than would have been possible with an informal conversational or a free-fall qualitative interview approach. While some questions were directed at the participants during the interviews as main venues of inquiry, others were used as tools of either warm-up or follow-up. It must also be noted here that not all questions were explored with every single participant, nor were these questions directed in the same order. A certain dose of flexibility was employed by the ethnographer during the interview processes, in terms of the number and order of the questions to be explored, depending largely on the institutional contexts as well as individual constraints surrounding the participants.

Framing Anti-corruption as a Complex Public Policy Problem: The Interplay of Instruments, Issues and Influences

As stated at the beginning of this paper, framing anti-corruption as a public policy issue requires paying more attention to the interplay of related policy instruments, issues, and influences in a connected manner. It thus calls for a much broader perspective in order to obtain a better-nuanced analysis of the contexts and constraints facing policymakers. In this section of the paper, we will attempt to contribute by advancing and exemplifying such an approach. Nevertheless, as was clearly pointed out earlier, the following information and discussion on anti-corruption as public policy in Turkey has no claim whatsoever over comprehensiveness or completeness. They should be treated as part of an initial attempt to test the value and practicality of such an approach as an analytical tool.

Instruments: Political Rhetoric about Corruption and Anti-corruption in the Government Programmes[5] of AKP Cabinets

From the beginning, the Justice and Development Party (Adalet ve Kalkınma Partisi – AKP hereafter) declared that it was going to fight three major problems facing society – poverty, corruption, and restrictions, the so-called three Ys in Turkish (*Yoksulluk*, *Yolsuzluk*, and *Yasaklar*, respectively). Thus, subsequent AKP governments formed between 2002 and 2014 have had in their programmes.

[5] Unless otherwise mentioned, the texts of government programs used in this paper were obtained from the official website of TBMM (the Turkish Grand National Assembly), which are available at:

http://www.tbmm.gov.tr/kutuphane/e_kaynaklar_kutuphane_hukumetler.html, http://www.tbmm.gov.tr/hukumetler/HP58.htm,

http://www.tbmm.gov.tr/hukumetler/HP59.htm, http://www.tbmm.gov.tr/hukumetler/HP60.htm,http://www.tbmm.gov.tr/hukumetler/HP61.htm.

Assessments about corruption and specific measures for fighting it, albeit with varying degrees of detail and depth.

The most detailed descriptions related to corruption and promises for eradicating it can be found in the first AKP government's programme. Headed by then-Prime Minister Abdullah Gül, the programme for the 58th government of the Republic of Turkey offers the following:

> Corruption, which is both a product and indication of social, economic, cultural, political, and most importantly before anything else of moral collapsing and decaying, undermines the people's sense of trust toward bureaucracy, politics, state in general and judiciary. Main priority in preventing corruption will be cleaning of the politics and public administration from corruption. In this struggle, the larger part of the society who remained clean and the civil society organizations will be brought in for solving of this problem and the fight will be owned by the society.

The programme further goes on to state that, 'in order to decrease corruption in the distribution mechanisms of public resources, transparency will be provided and favouritism will be prevented in taxes, procurements, state aids, loans, incentives, subsidies, customs transactions, recruitment, promotion, and assignment of public servants, and in the politics-business relations'.

This government programme lists the following as main measures to be taken in the context of anti-corruption:

- By taking into consideration the relevance of corruption to ethical decay, the standards in professional ethics and business ethics will be raised particularly, and honesty in public administration will be valued as much as technical competence.
- The Law on Political Parties will be changed so as to make political financing transparent and attached to objective criteria.
- Penalties for corruption and unlawfulness will be tightened, related legal processes will be accelerated, and no longer will the shadow of corruption fall on the justice system.
- There will be fight on 'culture of secrecy', which was expanded superfluously in public administration. In all works and

transactions of public sector, transparency will be the rule; secrecy will remain as an exemption. The 'Citizen's Right to Know Act' will be initiated and decision making processes and paper trails (document flows) systems of public organizations will be reoriented/reordered.

- The complex structure existing among auditing units in the public sector will be simplified, measures will be taken to obtain an efficient control practice focusing on performance auditing, and the areas remained out of auditing remits will be limited.
- The unwieldy and not-outcome-oriented public auditing system, which even prohibitively restraints decision makers from making decisions, will be transformed into an efficient and results-oriented auditing structure.
- It will be made sure that Turkey join the Group of States against Corruption (GRECO) existing within the framework of the Council of Europe, and that it sign and approve Crime Law Convention on Corruption and Private Law Convention on Corruption prepared by the Council of Europe. International cooperation in preventing corruption will be heeded.

Finally, this government programme includes a specific measure concerning public personnel policy, which was repeated almost verbatim in the subsequent AKP government's programme as well, 'in order to prevent favouritism and corruption, there are going to be objective criteria in (public) personnel recruitment whereas promotions will be based on merit and equal opportunity' (http://www.tbmm.gov.tr/hukumetler/HP58.htm).

Based largely on the aforementioned government programme, the Urgent Action Plan of the first AKP government contains, among others, the following measures within the section on 'public administration reform' under the subheading of 'anti-corruption':

- (The Council of Europe) Crime Law Convention on Corruption and Private Law Convention on Corruption will be approved;
- Penalties for corruption and unlawfulness will be made deterrent/dissuasive;
- The restrictions concerning the fields in which the public servants might work after leaving their posts will be expanded and the rules on this realm will be enforced more efficiently;

- Political financing will be made transparent;
- The concept of secrecy embodied in the existing legal statute will be redefined;
- The dialogue about corruption between government, public administration, judiciary, media and civil society will be improved;
- The benefits and costs of new legal initiatives will be featured in new laws (Başbakanlık 2003: 9).

The programme of the second AKP government, which was in power between 2003 and 2007 and was headed by Prime Minister Recep Tayyip Erdoğan, also points out the need for developing objective criteria in hiring of public personnel as well as competence and equal opportunity principles in promoting public bureaucrats. It briefly touches upon such concepts as transparency and accountability, ethical bureaucracy, a system of regulations, checks, and sanctions keeping up with universal standards along with initiatives for preventing corruption and tendency for committing crimes (http://www.tbmm.gov.tr/hukumetler/HP59.htm).

Reflecting the assertions and aspirations of Prime Minister Erdoğan and his second cabinet who were at the helm between 2007 and 2011, the 60th government's programme stipulated that 'Corruption is a major problem, which has made our country incur heavy costs and hurt the relationship of trust between the state and the citizenry…In the period of our rule, we have taken very serious measures in preventing corruption and holding to account (those who are involved in it). Our government will unwaveringly maintain its position against corruption' (http://www.tbmm.gov.tr/hukumetler/HP60.htm).

The fourth AKP government, the third and the last one headed by Erdoğan as its Prime Minister, ruled Turkey from July 2011 until August 2014. Its programme contains the following major assertions on corruption and anti-corruption:

> We have in the preceding period struggled against corruption with resolution. We have for the purpose of efficiently fighting against corruption taken part in seven important international conventions between 2003 and 2006 on this realm. Besides, we have become member of the Council of Europe Group States against Corruption

> (GRECO) in 2004. While Turkey was ranked 77th among 133 countries with a score of 3.1 in 2003 in Corruption Perception Index issues by the Transparency International, it has risen to 56th place among 178 countries with the score of 4.4 in 2010. Our efforts on this front will continue with determination and without disruption within the frame of an inclusive strategy. (http://www.tbmm.gov.tr/hukumetler/HP61.htm)

The AKP government led by Prime Minister Ahmet Davutoğlu was in power from the end of August 2014 to the middle of 2016. Its programme repeated in part some of the issues and policies alluded to earlier in the context of the preceding AKP government programme (e.g., the signing of international conventions in the realm of anti-corruption and the rise of the country's scores and rankings in CPI prepared by TI). The programme went on to say that,

> Turkey's great leap (jumping to another class) regarding economic development and welfare during the ruling of our four cabinets before us were only made possible by the determination and sagacity our governments have exhibited in the realms of transparency and anti-corruption.

It might be ironic to note in the midst of ongoing debates in the country regarding the fate of corruption probes emanating from the operations between 17 and 25 September 2013, the government under Ahmet Davutoğlu made, among others, the following contentions:

> Our government will continue its struggle with determination for reaching the goal of Turkey projected in 2023 as economically and politically predictable and transparent, democratically fortified, with zero-tolerance against corruption...We have displayed a very strong will power in the fight against corruption. We have put out an intensive effort for (making sure that) not a single corruption case is covered up, every kind of (corruption) claim is examined diligently, and the judicial processes about it proceed robust. (Başbakanlık, 2014).

Strategy for Increasing Transparency and Strengthening the Struggle against Corruption (2010–14)

Perhaps the most critical document in understanding anti-corruption policy in Turkey in the last decade or so may be the Council of Ministers decision number 2010/56, which was published in the Official Gazette on 22 February 2010. The 2010–14 'Strategy for Increasing Transparency and Strengthening the Struggle against Corruption' (hereafter the Strategy) is a 10-page policy decisional text, consisting of six short subsections laid out in six pages. There is also a four-page-long annex where a 'Table of Activities' lists in a more detailed manner the future actions to be taken to reach the targets listed throughout (Strateji 2010).

After a brief introduction defining corruption and explaining the rationale behind its initiation, the Strategy enumerates the 'main regulations that were so far realized in the country in the last couple of years in order to increase transparency and prevent corruption'. The list includes around twenty laws, ranging from most relevant regulations such as the Right to Know Act, the Penal Code, and the Law Concerning the Establishment of State Employees Board of Ethics, to vaguely-related ones such as the Special Provincial Administration Act, and the Social Security and General Health Insurance Law. In the same vein, the Strategy lists seven international conventions approved by Turkey in the most recent years and then cites the rise of Turkey's country score and ranking in CPI issued by TI (from 3.1-point score and 77th place among 133 countries in 2003, to a 4.4-point score with the 61st place among 180 countries in 2009).

The purpose of the Strategy has been explained as 'developing a more just, accountable, transparent and reliable administrative mentality by removing factors that inhibit transparency and feed on corruption ...' Three fundamental components of the Strategy have been explained in the fourth section as a) Prevention; b) Enforcement (of Sanctions); and c) (Increasing) Public Awareness and then the measures falling into each category have been enumerated therein.

The fifth section of the Strategy, entitled 'Realization of the Strategy', informs the public about the establishment of a

Commission for Increasing Transparency and Struggle against Corruption in Turkey (hereafter referred to as the Commission) and of an Execution Committee for Increasing Transparency and Struggle against Corruption (hereafter referred to as the Execution Committee) in Turkey, pursuant to Prime Ministry Circular 2009/19 which was published in the Official Gazette on 5 December 2009. Briefly told, the Commission is envisioned as a more politically-leaning, high-order mechanism consisting of ministers convening at least twice a year; while the Committee consists of high-level bureaucrats, preparing the groundwork for decisions to be made by the former, convening at least four times a year. The Prime Minister Inspection Board has been designated as the technical support and secretariat services unit for the both. The Strategy ends with a brief concluding section.

Following the Strategy, the Prime Minister Inspection Board, heeding the advice from the Commission and the Committee, has been influential in developing and following-up 'the Action Plan for the Strategy' in subsequent years. It is reasonable to assert that the involving members of the Board and the Committee have done a fairly good job given their remits and constraints. For instance, they were influential in shaping the anti-corruption agenda and pushing a number of measures through the bureaucratic ladders such as 'preventive regulations' (e.g., legislation related to the establishment of an Ombudsman and changing the organization and functions of the Court of Accounts) and anti-corruption-related activities and projects (e.g., national and international anti-corruption conferences and workshops; initiation and implementation of a large-scale EU-funded anti-corruption project, TYSAP – Strengthening the Coordination of Anti-corruption Policies and Practices in Turkey).

Nonetheless, measures that were put forward in the Strategy still have not yet been completed or achieved at the time of writing this paper. The most important among them are

> Making the financing of political parties and election campaigns transparent and establishing inspection mechanisms; determining

> the rules of political ethics compliant to the examples in developed countries; initiating administrative procedures act and laws concerning state secrets and trade secrets; revising substantively a number of legislations including the Law of Declaration of Property, Struggle Against Corruption and Bribery, Public Procurement Law, and major legislations concerning local governments; strengthening capacities of public inspection/auditing units; ensuring that investigations related to public officials are carried out efficiently; and increasing transparency of and decreasing corruption around private firms and non-governmental organizations.

It will suffice here to note that significant progress in some of those areas requires more than bureaucratic or administrative capacity. It calls for, among others, a strong will and an unwavering commitment from the ruling political cadre vis-à-vis anti-corruption, which is a commitment that has yet to be exhibited extensively and effectively.

'Transparency in the Public (Sector) Package'

On 14 January 2015, Prime Minister Davutoğlu held a press conference in Ankara to announce the so-called 'Transparency in the Public (Sector) Package'. Accompanied by five cabinet members during the event, the Prime Minister outlined a number of 'new' measures related to political financing and ethics, asset declarations involving public servants and politicians, as well as urban planning and rents.

According to the various local news reports of the day, the government intends to expand the scope of public servants who are required to file asset declarations periodically to include: the local and provincial chiefs; the central-level administrator of political parties represented in the Turkish parliament; the local, regional, and national managers of media companies; and the chiefs of high courts. The frequency of asset declarations for public servants and politicians will also be shortened from the current five-year period to every two years instead. There are also proposals involving the monitoring of donations made to political candidates for membership in the Turkish parliament and mayoral positions, and the possible tabs suggested for the amount of donations that can be made to these political candidates.

Equally important are the proposals toward making the practices involving local development, zoning, and building permit issuing processes more transparent and accountable, along with imposing kind of some new taxes/duties on these areas to ensure that some portion of the value increases stemming from changes therein will be reclaimed by the public authorities. It is sufficient to say here that when, how, and to what extent these proposals would be turned into legal mandates and concrete policies remain to be seen. In part because of the timing, content, and context of these proposals, some government critics have largely dismissed the package itself as a 'joke of the year' (Vural 2015), and a 'hidden camera trick' (Kamalak 2015). Still others have viewed the package as a step taken in the right direction, but kept criticizing it as insufficient since 'it seems that the expectations regarding transparency and accountability in politics are left for another time to be met'. (Gençkaya 2015).

Issues

In standard textbook treatments of the public policy cycle, the initial phase of public policy processes is usually described as consisting of problem definition and/or agenda setting. Further stages of a typical public policy process are preceded by a period of discussion and debate as to the existence and characteristics of a 'common' problem that may deserve the attention of society in general and policymakers specifically. In other words, there must be a 'public' problem, at least a 'widely-shared perception' about an issue before any attempts are launched to seek solutions, or to identify mechanisms dealing with it. It is in part because of such a notion of public policy that a set of questions were included in our interview protocol in order to assess whether and to what extent the study participants view corruption as a serious concern deserving (immediate/serious) attention from society and its political representatives.

Defining the Problem and Setting the Agenda amid Divergent Perspectives

The first question was worded as follows: How would you rate/place corruption in the broader context of general problems of Turkey? Briefly told, approximately 75 per cent of the participants (around 45 interviewees) chose to respond to this question. With the exception of few individuals whose views on the issue might be best described as 'no-need-for-making-fuss-out-of-it', a great majority of the participants viewed corruption either as the most important problem in the country, or among the major societal problems deserving one of the top three spots in the public policy agenda.

It is interesting to note here first that this finding from the interviews is in a stark contrast to the outcomes of the survey we conducted with 'ordinary citizens' around the same time. While the 'experts' viewed corruption as a serious concern for the country (oftentimes as the most significant problem), the 'ordinary citizens' paid almost no or little attention to it during the survey (see Graph 16.1). In fact, the views expressed by the survey participants were far more in tandem with the findings of some recent opinion surveys

Graph 16.1: Serious Problems in the Community

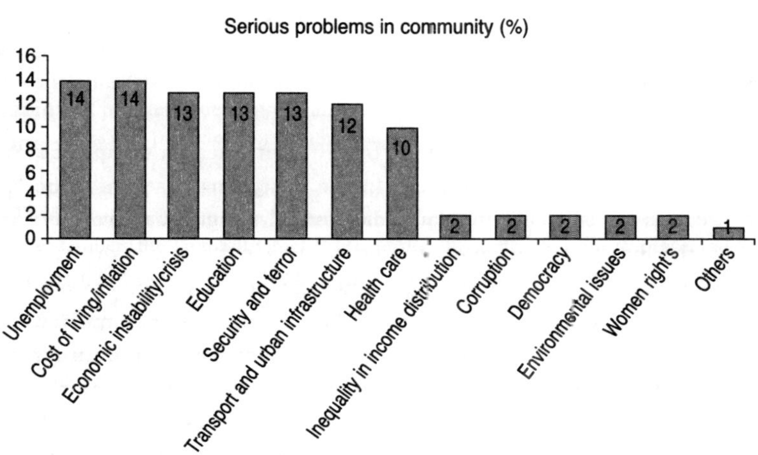

Source: Acar and Yağcı (2014: s. 16)

conducted in Turkey than those of the 'experts' involved in our field study (e.g., Adaman, Çarkoğlu and Şenatalar 2009; TEPAV 2013).

A rather easy way of interpreting the sharp difference between those two groups on the matter might be that significant differences exist in many countries between political and economic elites and rest of the society in terms of their perspectives regarding corruption (for a comparison and a bit more discussion, see Acar and Dede 2013: 622–23). Another possible explanation is related to the composition of our interview sample, which included many 'experts' who have long been investigating, studying, and/or reporting on corruption-laden issues, institutions, and/or individuals. As such, they could have become more sensitized to the main issues covered by the study than have a random sample of 'common folk'. Finally, the differences between the 'common folk' and the 'educated elites' might also be analysed within the context of petty vs. grand corruption, meaning that substantial decreases obtained in the former type of corruption over the last decade or so may have happened to make the latter form of corruption less visible/significant in the eyes of ordinary citizens. Furthermore, the 'experts' have been more knowledgeable and much vigilant about all forms of corruption, including those treated as cases of grand corruption (e.g., big-ticket construction projects, public procurement and privatization cases, and so on). Some clues about such reasoning can be found in the interview materials, as illustrated below by the excerpt taken from the interview with an NGO representative,

> In public opinion surveys done by different research companies, corruption was a big concern in the past, now it seems to be decreasing. It is because it was those small things that have been bothering the citizens most: waiting too long in the lines in the land registry offices, in the hospitals, handing out money to middlemen to get a report, document and so on.... There had been money involved everywhere. (...) Citizens are interested, involved in the things that affect them directly, if there is money stolen, let's say on the overhaul of a bridge and if the citizens' daily routines got disrupted, then they start cursing those people as corrupt. (...) Other issues are too big for them!

Corruption: Cause, Consequence or Multiplier?

An underlying theme emerging from the responses of those participants who perceive corruption as the most important problem in the country relates to conceiving the same phenomenon in a three-dimensional way: a cause (source of some societal problems), a consequence (of failures in other areas), or a multiplier (expands or augments some already existing problems). For example, one scholar told the interviewer the following, 'I would put it in first place. It comes first because it is the underlying cause of many problems Turkey has been experiencing'. A public prosecutor representing a similar line of thought offered that, 'if you have a strong state, you can solve many of those problems. Corruption inhibits this, it prevents a state from becoming a strong state, and it stands in the way of resolving other issues. Therefore, I would put corruption in first place'.

On the other hand, an illustrative example for those holding the corruption-as-consequence view that emanated from the interview with a public auditor working for one of the ministries and is worth quoting at length here:

> I consider corruption as the main problem of Turkey. Because it (corruption) puts forth shoots between all other problems, it is fed by them. If you have problems in the realm of health, then you will have corruption problem; if you are experiencing problems in justice/judiciary, then you would encounter corruption there. (...) I am very sure about it. In order for corruption to occur, there must be some adverse condition; it is fed by an anomaly or a deviation.

Finally, a representative from an NGO explains his/her view on the issue by emphasizing the role of corruption as a 'multiplier',

> Perhaps I am a bit one-sided, but I would put corruption in first place. Because, corruption is not a sole problem, it goes beyond that; it is an issue with a multiplier effect. Corruption does not just involve monetary exchange or creating a milieu for unfair competition, it is at the same time turning that into an identity. Once you start getting into that modality, when you bribe someone at the land registry

> office to complete a transaction, that profile would reflect on your private life as well, you might start defrauding your neighbor. (…) Once you wear on that modality, you might see it at the core of all the problems in the society.

Forms or Types of Corruption

To gather information and insight from the interviewees on the second issue, namely, forms of corruption, two subsequent questions were directed to them: What are the most common or prevalent forms of corruption in the country? Which of these are most costly to society? The responses to these inquiries were collected and then evaluated together.

All in all, corruption surrounding public procurement processes has been above-board as the most common and costly form of corruption in the country, followed by fraudulent actions and transactions involving urban development, local city planning/zoning, and issuing construction/occupancy permits, and favouritism concerning recruiting and rewarding public employees and bureaucrats. Bribery, legalized corruption, getting commissions out of work rendered/contracts signed, malfeasance in professional conduct, gift-taking, and embezzlement were also mentioned in the context of those two questions.

Our research finding regarding the emergence of public procurements or public purchasing as the most common or costly form of corruption in the country is indeed in line with the results obtained through a number of international and national studies on corruption in Turkey. For instance, the 2013 Enterprise Survey by the World Bank and IFC singled out public procurement as the greatest source of corruption, along with other activities such as getting a construction permit, as well as import and operating licenses. According to a report issued by SIGMA in 2013, 'criminal acts' reported to the public by the Turkish Court of Accounts frequently involve procurement issues, among others. A nationwide survey conducted among firms (Adaman et al. 2009) pointed out that perceived favouritism in public procurement increased between the years 2004 and 2008 (see Emek and Acar 2015, for more detailed information and documentation on the issue). Similarly, the corruption-prone characteristics of urban/physical development have been the focus of different studies and debates (e.g., Kılınç, Özgür and Genç 2012).

'Prevalence of the Hidden' or 'the Widely Mainstreamed' Corruption?

One of the issues our research attempted to uncover relates to the existence and extent of common practices in the country that are not commonly regarded as corrupt but might be considered as such. In other words, with the help of a carefully worded question, the participants' perspectives were sought as to whether defining a list of common practices delicately bordering along the line of 'accepted'/'legitimized' versus 'rejected'/ 'reproached' is possible or not. The following question was directed to the participants during the interviewing period of our field research: What types of common practices are not seen as corrupt while they can be considered as corrupt (at least potentially)?

Except for fourteen participants who were either not directly asked or opted not to address the question at all, study participants named at least one 'topic', while some of them threw out as many as six different 'subjects' within the context the aforementioned question. It was eventually possible to come up with some kind of clustering around most-frequently mentioned issues. Below is the list of top-ten 'common practices that are not seen as corrupt while they can be considered as corrupt' in order of frequency, ranging from 18 people mentioning the first issue, to four cites during the interviews about the last issue:

- Nepotism/favouritism in recruiting and promoting in public sector;
- Gift giving hospitality practices involving public employees and managers;
- Waste, extravagance and misuse of public resources;
- Rent-seeking activities in city planning and zoning, urban development;
- Public procurement, purchasing and privatization;

- 'Petty corruption': small bribes and 'facilitative payments';
- Using a 'middleman', 'strongman', or 'our man';
- 'Legalized corruption', misuse/abuse of 'discretionary' power;
- Influence peddling;
- Conflict of interest.

Obviously, for many study participants, the number one concern, in some cases even the single most important issue mirroring the essential elements of corruption, is related to the personnel selection and/or promotion policies and practices of public organizations. Various Turkish words, such as *iltimas* (preferential treatment, patronage); *kayırmacılık* (favouritism); *adam kayırma* (favouring your man); and *kadrolaşma* (putting cronies/political fellows into bureaucratic positions) were interchangeably used by different participants to describe the number-one 'common practice that is not seen as corrupt while it can/should be considered as corrupt'. It is interesting to note that 'favouritism in recruitment and promotion of public employees and managers' was one of the top issues identified by the study participants in two different contexts. This finding should not be treated as too surprising, however, given for instance the intensive public debate about many instances involving irregularities and nepotistic instances vis-à-vis recruitment and promotion of public servants, including the so-called *VIP torpil* (VIP favouritism) allegations widely reported in various media outlets during 2014.

To a lesser extent, many participants suggested a diverse set of behaviours or actions to be included in the list regarding common practices that are not seen as corrupt while they can be considered as corrupt, in addition to those already cited above. Among them are the following:

- Political use/abuse of social assistance programmes to manipulate the political preferences or the votes of poor people;
- Tolerating the building of many *gecekondu*s (shanty houses, slums) on public lands in and around metropolitan cities;
- Almost automated overtime payments made to some public servants regardless of whether they actually worked those extra hours;
- Frequent pardons issued by subsequent governments lifting or discounting taxes, traffic fines;

- The use/abuse of public vehicles by public employees and/or their family members for private purposes or travel;
- Imposing on private individuals or companies 'donations' to 'quasi-foundations' who are affiliated with public organizations to get a service, license, or government contract; specific versions of which involve encouraging government contractors to 'donate' to some foundations or associations preferred by politicians and bureaucrats;
- Selective enforcement of rules to sanction not-so-friendly media companies;
- Actions or transactions involving a type of favouritism wherein the actors committing to them do not get monetary or material benefits;
- 'Obligatory' donations students or parents are forced to pay during registration in public high schools and universities;
- *Bıçak parası* (knife money), which refers to extra money doctors receive from the patients when they go through a medical operation;
- Gift cards, free vacations, and other promotional benefits provided by the drug companies/distributors to medical doctors; and
- Goodies, extractions (sometimes amounting to extortions!) attached to transactions of private companies doing business with public agencies and municipalities

All in all, it is fair to say that the participants presented a strong case for the widely-shared perception concerning the existence of a set of perspectives and practices that seem to make the boundaries between corrupt and not-so-corrupt behaviours/actions much more porous and problematic. These findings can also be interpreted as the characteristics of challenges awaiting future 'anti-corruption crusaders' in describing, detecting, and deterring corruption in such a country context.

Influences

In an increasingly globalized world, it is almost impossible to imagine a public policy area not affected from the debates ensuing in and around various global or regional platforms. Corruption has been no exception for this matter. There are an ever-increasing number of forums and formats through which anti-corruption policies of different countries are critically evaluated and discussed comparatively and continuously. Perhaps more importantly, Turkey's status as candidate country vis-à-vis the EU opens its anti-corruption policies to international influences, especially to those emanating from EU institutions. Whether and to what extent those intended influences were reflected in and through the existing anti-corruption policies and practices in the country is another matter. It is important to note here that some of the issues regarding the anti-corruption policies of Turkey have consistently been pursued (and pushed) by the EU in the last decade or so. For instance, the following were listed among the short-term priorities regarding the anti-corruption policy of Turkey in the Accession Partnership:

- Develop a comprehensive anti-corruption strategy, including the fight against high-level corruption, and a central body to oversee and monitor its implementation, including through establishing statistical data. Improve coordination between all institutions involved.
- Ensure implementation of the Regulation on Principles of Ethical Behaviour for Civil Servants and extend its provisions to elected officials, judiciary, academics and military personnel.
- Limit the immunities granted to politicians and public officials in line with European best practices and improve legislation on transparency in political party and election campaign financing (EC 2008: 7).

The Strategy described and discussed in the previous section cites 'Turkish National Programme Regarding the Undertaking of European Union Acquis and various international institutions' evaluations about Turkey, among the policy documents it referenced during its preparation. In fact, the strategy, in and of itself, might be regarded as one of the outcomes of Turkey's EU accession process, since 'developing a comprehensive anti-corruption strategy' has been a recurring theme in EU policy proposals designed for Turkey from the very beginning. Nevertheless, the extent to which this and other such proposals were influential in shaping the substance and sequence of legal-institutional initiatives in the country needs further analysis and a more comprehensive debate. Fully and effectively implementing the existing framework, on the other hand, would pave the way for jumping on an array of rather complicated and contentious debates, which should be saved for another time and place.

Finally, the most recent EU Progress Report on Turkey offers, among others, the following:

> Corruption allegations played a significant part in the political debate in Turkey, particularly following the anti-corruption investigations launched in December 2013. The handling of these allegations of corruption raised serious concerns that allegations of wrongdoing would not be addressed in a non-discriminatory, transparent and impartial manner. Civil society organizations had very limited opportunities to contribute. Turkey has to decide whether it will adopt an anti-corruption strategy and action plan for the period after 2014. Greater political will and civil society involvement are needed if results are to be achieved on the ground so as to establish a track record of investigations, indictments and convictions. (EU 2014b: 14).

Views from the Field

During the interviews, the study participants were not asked any direct questions as to whether international actors and factors have played a role in defining and/or determining anti-corruption policies in Turkey. Instead, after the interviewing process and reflecting on an array of responses from the interviewees, we identified and described a set of issues. Although related responses were originally scattered in different segments of the interviews, a significant number of them were traceable to the contexts based on these two questions: a) In which sectors or fields have there been some improvements in most recent years? What has caused this decrease in corruption? b) Have you heard of successful anti-corruption initiatives? All-in-all, it was possible to collapse the majority of related responses into four different yet somewhat related subcategories.

For one, the respondents in the first group were much eager to mention international influences, those coming from actors outside the country, in shaping anti-corruption policies in the country. While international organizations such as the OECD and World Bank were also cited in the context of this question, the role of Turkey's EU candidacy (and thus the influence of EU) in triggering or accelerating anti-corruption-oriented public policies in the country was definitely most visible and frequent across many responses. For instance, a scholar working on ethics opined that

> This EU Process has been one of most influential factors in making us put things into an order, shaping up things on [the] home front... we don't do things by ourselves, unless we are held accountable toward somebody...may be someone from the outside, from the above is involved.

Similarly, a chief auditor working for an influential government organization argued that 'the principal factor triggering transparency in Turkey has been the EU, the process of adopting Acquis Communautaire'.

Finally, an inspector from one of the line ministries offered the following perspective:

> Why did those things happen? They have largely stemmed from the EU Adaptation Process; a big chunk of this whole thing comes from there. Many reforms and regulations I have alluded to early on were initiated during 2004–2005. This period has been the most dynamic one. To be frank with you, I couldn't say much about what happened after that period, since I don't know of it...I don't see too many new initiatives concerning transparency in the country after that.

The second subcategory is indeed an intriguing one in the sense that it directs our attention to the influences of the EU and other international actors seemingly similar to those mentioned in the previous subsection. It also calls for a more in-depth and critical examination of whether and how much those influences were actually reflected in the working realities of political and administrative structures of the country. In other words, some respondents were keen on assigning a key role to the EU in terms of the introduction of legal-institutional initiatives concerning anti-corruption in Turkey, while they were at the same time very sceptical when it comes to the real impact and full implementation of those policies and measures aiming at fighting corruption in the country.

For instance, one NGO representative maintains that 'our laws and regulations in general are quite progressive, yet there are problems in their implementation…There exist many legal initiatives, such as Open Government Initiative, that were crafted for the sake of adaptation to Europe…but there is this problem of transferring them into practice'. An activist from another NGO has echoed similar sentiments by saying, 'these EU treaties should not stay as mere legal papers, conventions; we should raise our voice to do otherwise, to get them implemented. Most recently legal framework was improved significantly, but there is no implementation!' A chief auditor working for a government institution argued that 'transparency seemed to be increasing due to regulatory initiatives put forward within the framework of adopting Acquis Communautaire, along with changes and improvements in the realm of technology and Internet… Nevertheless, it is more accurate to say that corruption has changed its format, the change is about its perception'. Finally, a scholar claimed that, 'we have this problem vis-à-vis the EU. We are taking their rules and regulations, but we do not have the consciousness and culture required for putting them into practice. Therefore, legislations are arriving here, but they are not implemented'.

The responses falling into the third subcategory, on the other hand, pointed to the mixing and mingling of internal and international dynamics and influences in the process of developing policies and practices related to anti-corruption in the last decade or so. Said differently, some respondents attributed the current changes and challenges associated with anti-corruption in the country to both internal and international factors and actors at once. For instance, an auditor reasoned that, 'after the crisis of 2001, many changes have been introduced into the financial system and the banking system to prevent future crises, possible corruption…Then, the EU integration process has also contributed to the initiation of new policies or the improvement of the existing rules and institutions in those areas'.

Another participant working for a government organization echoed a similar view by arguing that, 'well, some of those changes were long overdue…we should have completed them long before as our major tasks…they were done recently in part because of Turkey's obligations, commitments regarding its EU candidacy'.

Perhaps a better and more complete reflection on the theme identified in the third category emerged from the interview with one of the chief auditors working for a government institution that might be worth quoting at length here:

> In the last ten years or so, there has been significant progress in Turkey in terms of increasing transparency and reducing corruption, maybe up until mid-2011. Then, the situation has started deteriorating, it has even regressed…it has stopped progressing, consolidating the achievements, in part because the EU process has come to halt, in part because the existence of a very strong government in power, without a potential alternative to it… They (the rulers) have started thinking, 'well, the citizens love us, support us,' and then they have stopped making progress on this front… In essence, this whole progress has been a joint outcome of both the needs of the country and the acceleration of the EU process. It might be thought that Turkey couldn't have experienced this fast transformation without the EU, but it would have gone through a reform/transformation process, anyway.

The last and fourth category consists of responses taking a critical view of the EU vis-à-vis its approaches to corruption and anti-corruption in Turkey. For example, a freelance journalist criticized the EU for not paying enough attention to the issue:

> In my view, corruption has not been given its due consideration in the EU's priorities for and expectations from Turkey. For instance, the EU has not been insistent on this issue as much as it has been toward freedoms and democratization in the country. I see them as issues that are parallel to each other. A society can be a free and democratic one only if it is a society free from corruption. If you

> ignore one pillar there, if you heavily focus on one side there and not pay attention to the other, then over time any one of them brings down the other.

A parliamentarian from an opposition party also heavily criticized some international actors, including Transparency International and the EU, for not being 'objective observers', producing overly lenient, one-sided reports about corruption in Turkey, without consulting opposition parties and individuals. He kept arguing that

> A similar process went through with the EU. It has written false, not-so-true reports about the country for a long time, although they are making some corrections to them and doing a bit better in the last couple of years. Hey, what would happen to those corrupt behaviors that kept going (maybe because of) after your false, tainted reports? How would these guys (in the EU) be held accountable to their people back in their countries for those wrongly informed reports?

Slightly different versions of those types of opinions, on the other hand, have pointed out unfavourable consequences of some changes propelled by the EU. For instance, a chief auditor/inspector working for a central government organization commented on this issue as follows:

> I think there must be a good understanding of the country and society, right? Well, there has been a problem in the judiciary in Turkey. Then, some reforms have been initiated there from the perspective of EU (for the sake of adaption to the EU). Nevertheless, those judicial reforms have created another set of significant problems. Thus, there is always this possibility that if you introduce anti-corruption policies in this country without properly understanding Turkish society, then you would get different results and unexpected outcomes.

After all is said and done, the study participants were as much divided as academics and politicians as to the influence and impact of international actors and factors in defining the agenda for and shaping the outcomes of policies in Turkey. Alternatively, it is possible to suggest that all those responses grouped into four subcategories might be taken into consideration together to capture a bigger and a better picture of anti-corruption policies in the country since different perspectives point to an array of dimensions related to the whole process.

Conclusion

The paper was construed as one of the initial scholarly attempts at framing anti-corruption as a complex public policy problem in Turkey. As such, it argued for taking into consideration the interplay of major instruments, issues, and influences vis-à-vis corruption and anti-corruption in the country without presumptuously claiming to cover all the bases. It employed a methodology combining literature review and document (content) analysis with the findings from field research specially designed to obtain the perceptions and perspectives of a group of experts on a number of anti-corruption-related issues deemed important within working realities of the existing political-administrative structures in the country.

Due to time, space, and other constraints, the following points highlight the concluding remarks that have come out of the efforts so far in preparing this paper:

- Corruption as a societal problem was taken more seriously in the programme of the first AKP government than the subsequent ones in that a more comprehensive agenda for fighting it was outlined in the former, as opposed to relying on the enumeration of 'successful' reforms much visible throughout the latter.
- There exists a wide gap between the 'ordinary citizens' surveyed and the 'experts' interviewed within the scope of our field research in terms of perceptions and perspectives about the existence and extent of corruption (cf. Şarlak and Bali 2008a; 2008b). This might be due in part to the differences between the information and expertise those two groups relied on when forming their opinion and judgements about the issues involved. Beyond considering the existence of an increasingly politicized and polarized polity

in the country, serious scholarly attention should be devoted to better understand the long-adhered customs and changing values in the society vis-à-vis corruption (cf. Torsello 2014).

- There have been a number of issues constantly raised in national and international evaluations and proposals still waiting to be acted upon: establishing an almighty anti-corruption institution, political financing, conflict of interests, and so on (e.g., Emek and Acar 2008; Gençkaya 2008; GRECO 2012; EU 2014b). In addition, our relevant research findings suggest that the recruitment and promotion of public servants should also be taken seriously as one of the problematic areas to work on. All-in-all, establishing a free and fair competition in key societal areas (i.e., in economic and financial markets, in politics and public bureaucracy) seems essential in reducing the risks for corruption, including political favouritism/nepotism (cf. Acar and Emek 2009; 2008).
- Developing of a legislative-institutional framework should not be taken as a strong enough safeguard against corruption: fully and effectively implementing it should also be considered equally, if not more, important to win the fight against corruption.
- Also important to note is the need for comprehending the potentially shifting venues of risks and challenges associated with corruption in the country. The findings from our field research and some other studies (e.g., Buğra and Savaşkan 2014; Emek and Acar 2015) point out that more attention should be given to the analysis of the risks of 'grand corruption' emanating from mega-projects involving substantive public-private interactions.
- Finally, a new, comprehensive anti-corruption policy is desperately needed in the country, which in turn calls for a credible commitment from the ruling elites.

References

Acar, Muhittin and Kadir Dede. 2013. 'Bir Kamu Politikası Olarak Türkiye'de Yolsuzlukla Mücadele.' (Anti-corruption as a Public Policy in Turkey: Legal-Institutional Framework). In Mete Yıldız and M. Zahit Sobacı (eds.). *Kamu Politikası—Kuram ve Uygulama (Public Policy—Theory and Practice) (In Turkish)*. Ankara: Adres.

———., and Murat Yağcı. 2014. 'Institutional Performance and Social Values in Turkey.' http://anticorrp.eu/publications/report-on-turkey/.

———., and Uğur Emek. 2009. 'Preventing Corruption in Turkey: Issues, Instruments, and Institutions.' In *Preventing Corruption in Asia: Institutional Design and Policy Capacity.* Ting Gong and Stephen Ma (eds.). New York: Routledge.

———., 2008. 'Building a Clean Government in Turkey: Pillars, Perils, and Prospects.' *Crime, Law, and Social Change*, 49(3), 185–203.

Adaman, Fikret, Ali Çarkoğlu and Burhan Şenatalar. 2009. *Hanehalkı Gözünden Kamu Hizmetleri ve Yolsuzluk,* (Public Services and Corruption from Household Perspective). Ankara: TEPAV.

ANTICORRP. 2015. Overview. http://anticorrp.eu/project/overview/. Accessed 03 January 2015.

Başbakanlık, T.C. 2014. '62. Hükümet Programı' (62nd Government Programme) (In Turkish). http://www.basbakanlik.gov.tr/docs/KurumsalHaberler/HProgram.pdf. Accessed 01 February 2015.

———. 2003. *'58. Hükümet Acil Eylem Planı (AEP)'* (Republic of Turkey, 58th Cabinet Urgent Action Plan) (In Turkish). http://www.linux.org.tr/wp-content/uploads/2010/04/AcilEylemPlani.pdf. Accessed 01 February 2015.

Buğra, Ayşe and Osman Savaşkan. 2014. *New Capitalism in Turkey – The Relationship between Politics, Religion and Business.* Cheltenham: Edward Elgar.

Council of Ministers. 2002. 'Decree on Increasing Transparency in Turkey and Enhancing Good Governance in Public Sector.' Action Plan. No. 2002/3, 12 January 2002.

Emek, Uğur and Muhittin Acar. 2008. 'Yolsuzlukla Mücadelede Bir Temel Soru(n): Kurumsal Tekelcilik mi, Çoğulculuk mu?' (A Big Question in Anti-Corruption: Institutional Monopoly or Multi-agency Model?) (In Turkish). *İktisat, İşletme ve Finans*, 23 (September), 64–89.

———. 'Public Procurement in Infrastructure: The Case of Turkey.' In *The Anti-corruption Report, Vol. 3.* Alina Mungiu-Pippidi (ed.). Berlin: Barbara Budrich Publishers. September 2015.

European Commission. 2008. 'Council Decision of 18 February 2008 on the Principles, Priorities and Conditions Contained in the Accession Partnership with the Republic of Turkey and Repealing Decision 2006/35/EC.' http://www.abgs.gov.tr/files/AB_Iliskileri/Tur_En_Realitons/Apd/Turkey_APD_2008.pdf.

———. 2014a. 'EU Anti-corruption Report.' http://ec.europa.eu/dgs/home-affairs/e-library/documents/policies/organized-crime-and-human-trafficking/corruption/docs/acr_2014_en.pdf.

———. 2014b. Turkey Progress Report. http://ec.europa.eu/enlargement/pdf/key_documents/2014/20141008-turkey-progress-report_en.pdf.

Freedom House. 2014. 'Democracy in Crisis: Corruption, Media, and Power in Turkey—a Freedom House Special Report.' https://freedomhouse.org/sites/default/files/Turkey%20Report%20-%202-3-14.pdf.

GCB. 2010/11. 'Global Corruption Barometer 2010/11.' http://gcb.transparency.org/gcb201011/results/.

Gençkaya, Ömer Faruk. 2015. '*Kamuda Şeffaflık Paketi Ne Getirecek?*' (What is Transparency in Public Sector Package Bringing Alone?) (In Turkish). http://www.aljazeera.com.tr/gorus/kamuda-seffaflik-paketi-ne-getirecek.

———. 2008. 'Political Finance, Conflict of Interest and Accountability in Turkey: Implications for Democracy.' In Council of Europe (ed.). *Corruption and Democracy.* Strasbourg: Council of Europe Publishing.

GRECO. 2012. 'Third Evaluation Round - Compliance Report on Turkey.' http://www.coe.int/t/dghl/monitoring/greco/evaluations/round3/GrecoRC3%282012%294_Turkey_EN.pdf.

Kamalak, Mustafa. 2015. 'Kamalak's Comment on Transparency Package: Is it a Hidden Camera Trick?' http://www.aktifhaber.com/kamalaktan-seffaflik-paketiyorumu-kamera-sakasi-mi-1108428h.htm.

Kılınç, Gökçen, Hüseyin Özgür and F. Neval Genç. 2012. 'The Possible Sources of Ethical Issues in Urban/Physical Planning in Turkey.' *Turkish Studies*, 13(1), 45–65.

Ledeneva, Alena. 2011. 'Open Secrets and Knowing Smiles.' *East European Politics and Societies*, 2 (4), 720–36.

Mungiu-Pippidi, Alina. 2014. 'Why Control of Corruption Works-When it Does.' In *The Anti-corruption Frontline: The Anti-corruption Report, Vol. 2.* Alina Mungiu-Pippidi (ed.). Berlin: Barbara Budrich Publishers.

Ömürgönülşen, Uğur and Alan Doig. 2012. 'Why the Gap? Turkey, EU Accession, Corruption and Culture.' *Turkish Studies,* 13(1), 7–25.

Özhabeş, Hande. 2011. *Yolsuzlukla Mücadele Kriterleri: Yargı, Yasama ve Kamu Yönetimi Türkiye İzleme Raporu 2010.* (Anti-corruption Criteria: Turkey Follow-Up Report on Judiciary, Legislature and Public Administration) (In Turkish). İstanbul: Şeffaflık Derneği.

Persson, Anna, Bo Rothstein and Jan Teorell. 2013. 'Why Anti-corruption Reforms Fail—Systemic Corruption as a Collective Action Problem.'

Governance: An International Journal of Policy, Administration, and Institutions, Vol 26, No. 3 (July 2013), pp. 449–471.

Strateji. 2010. 'Saydamlığın *Artırılması* ve *Yolsuzlukla Mücadelenin* Güçlendirilmesi Stratejisi (2010–2014).' http://www.resmigazete.gov.tr/eskiler/2010/02/20100222-1.htm.

Sarlak, Zeynep and Bülent Besim Bali. 2007. 'Research Report Turkey: Perceptions of Corruption in Turkey—A Content Analysis of Interviews from Politics, Judiciary, Police, Media, Civil Society and Economy.' Sixth Framework Programme of the European Commission, Research Project: Crime and Culture. http://www.unikonstanz.de/crimeandculture/docs/scientificreports2007/STREP%20Crime%20and%20Culture%20Scientific%20Report%20GSU%202007.pdf.

———. 2008a. 'Corruption in Turkey: Why Cannot an Urgent Problem Be a Main Concern?' University of Konstanz Crime & Culture Discussion Paper Series, No: 14.

———. 2008b. 'Türkiye'de Siyaset Yolsuzluğa Mahkum mu? (Politics in Turkey: Condemned to Corruption?' (In Turkish). *Turkish Journal of Business Ethics*, 1(2), 27–37.

Tarhan, R. Bülent vd. 2006. 'Yolsuzlukla Mücadele – TBMM Raporu – Bir Olgu Olarak Yolsuzluk: Nedenler, Etkiler, Çözüm Önerileri.' (Struggle Against Corruption—the TGNA Report—Corruption as a Phenomenon: Causes, Impacts, Suggested Solutions) (In Turkish). Ankara: TEPAV.

TEPAV. 2013. 'Hanehalkı Gözünden Kamu Yönetimi, Kamu Hizmetleri ve Yolsuzluk.' (Household Survey on Public Administration, Public Services, and Corruption). http://www.tepav.org.tr/upload/files/haber/13850243211.Hanehalki_Gozunden_KamuYonetimi_KamuHizmetleri_ve_Yolsuzluk.pdf.

Torsello, Davide. 2014. 'Corruption as Social Exchange: the View from Anthropology.' ANTICORRP Report, University of Bergamo. http://anticorrp.eu/wp-content/uploads/2014/12/D1.1_Part5_Corruption-as-social-exchange-the-view-from-anthropology.pdf.

Transparency International. 2014. 'Corruption Perception Index 2014: Results.' http://www.transparency.org/cpi2014/results.

Vural, Oktay. 2015. 'Let's See the Transparency of the Prime Minister in Voting.' http://www.haberturk.com/gundem/haber/1031668-basbakanin-seffafligini-oylamada-gorelim.

17 Higher Education Policy in Turkey under Globalization

Mustafa Kemal Bayırbağ[1]

Father: Son, what is university?
Eren Deniz: I do not know dad (looking puzzled)
(And a few seconds later…)
Eren Deniz: It is a place where one works to become a professor.
Father: … (puzzled and saddened)[2]

Abstract

This paper concentrates on the tensions shaping the higher education policy (HEP) in Turkey during the 2000s. It is argued that the higher education scenario in Turkey has been characterized by four

[1] I am indebted to Professor Korel Göymen for organizing the *'International Workshop on "Public Policymaking" in a Globalized World'* (Istanbul Policy Center, Sabancı University, 28–29 November 2014, İstanbul), for which this work was prepared. I am grateful to the workshop participants and to Professor Eyüp Özveren for their comments and help.

[2] This is a real dialogue that came out of my curiosity about how a young child would see 'university', as I was preparing this work. I trust the conscience and senses of children. What is more, Eren Deniz – my first son, about six years old – is familiar with 'university'. He has been living on campus for the last five years, knows all my friends (mostly academic), and has met many students of mine. And being aware of his witty nature, I was expecting an element of surprise in his answer, poking a hole in my reasoning. But, his answer was plain and simple. Nothing about learning. Nothing about teaching. Nothing about students. Nothing about fun. He was speaking to a slave, at that moment, working to become a professor. And it hurt a lot… I had not been around for days, working in my office day and night, preparing this work… My job has become my life. The Higher Education system I am a part of shaped my life and brought its contradictions home (literally). So, here it is…

major tensions between related policy goals, all of which stem from globalization. These conflicting goals, it is further argued, produce a set of policy impasses that block the way to a much needed, comprehensive HE reform in Turkey. The impasses include the following: a) Promotion of social justice (via increasing public access to university education) vs promotion of competition among higher education institutions; b) Developing the research environment vs strengthening managerial control over higher education institutions; c) Increasing emphasis on the public service role of universities (mass education) vs de-politicization of the higher education institutions; d) The discourse on protection and promotion of diversity (especially in a fragmented country like Turkey) vs standardization of service provision (procedures) and product quality.

Introduction

In this paper, I argue that structural and institutional changes in a policy field that take place under the influence of globalization (imposed or adopted) tend to create gridlocks in public policymaking and implementation. This is mainly because globalization is an eclectic process full of contradictions, composed of a series of parallel (political, social, economic and cultural), intended or unintended, transformations shaking the relationship between the state and society or economy.

The thesis put forward is especially true in the field of Higher Education Policy (HEP) pursued in Turkey during the 2000s. That is not to say that HEPs adopted by different countries during the era before globalization have been immune to contradictions or stagnation. The role and place of higher education (HE) in capitalist societies/polities inevitably imbues it with a number of conflicting policy goals that are hard to resolve. The different forms of globalization, however, deepen and institutionalize the existing conflicts and problems, while introducing further uncertainty into the field of HE policymaking.

In part II of the paper, I first build the analytical framework to discuss what is meant by globalization and policymaking in a globalized world, and what this means for HEP in particular. I then discuss institutionalization of contradictions and problems and insertion of uncertainty into policymaking, and how globalization process creates a unique amalgam of elements from different HE models, blending their negative sides. Section III concentrates on the case of Turkey. I first talk about the historical roots of globalization in Turkey's HEP, and then in part II, I bring out how that amalgam came to fruition and was institutionalized, producing a very complex and ungovernable HE system. The third section wraps up the findings and focuses on the contradictions and policy deadlocks created by an HEP shaped by the globalization process.

Analytical Framework

Globalization and Policymaking

The term 'globalization' is much like the proverbial elephant in the room. Although there is a general agreement on the policy significance of globalization, depending on the context and the problem addressed, different authors might actually be referring to different processes in their usage of the term. This is also the case with studies on HEP (Dodds 2008). Depending on the normative premises employed, even contradictory conclusions might be reached regarding the impact of globalization on our lives. Despite the complications involved, why then do we continue alluding to this term? The following twofold answer also shapes the analytical basis of this study: First, the magnitude, depth, breadth and speed of social change we try to explicate have reached a level where available accounts fall short of portraying a clear big picture. These are broad, deep, and disruptive transformations that link and shake different societies across the world, mostly to increase social unrest and political uncertainty.

Second, the nation state, as the political embodiment and container of 'society', and as the natural bed of 'public authority', is not the only player in town now (Robertson and Dale 2006: 4). We witness the proliferation of public authorities established at different spatial scales, in different institutional forms. Supra-national and global public authorities now play a more central role in the public policy process., even though it is hard to argue that a truly global authority, i.e., a separate and coherent global policy field, exists in the case of higher education policy (Lingard and Rawolle 2011: 499). The 'economy' is now mainly a global construct, rather than a national one. Thus, decisions shaping the lives of ordinary citizens of a nation-state are being taken elsewhere, and mostly imposed upon policymakers held accountable. In fact, these decisions play a key role in triggering and spreading the transformations mentioned above.

As long as we are concerned with policymaking, particularly national policymaking in a globalized world, there are two distinct yet interrelated definitions of globalization, as follows:

a) Globalization as a set of external influences over the national policymakers and implementers: On the one hand, we talk of top-down pressures, largely stemming from economic concerns, on national policymakers. Management of integration with the global economy (and competition) draws the red line for other policy fields (what can or cannot be done) (cf. Robertson, 2007: 7). On the other hand, socio-economic inequalities further deepened by neoliberal policies and unpredictable ups and downs of global markets, intensify the bottom-up political pressure on policymakers. Demands for better quality education and enhanced access to higher education to promote social justice, for example, echo more deeply now. Globalization, then, only allows narrow room for manoeuver for the national policymakers (Ball 2007: 42; cf. Robertson and Dale 2006: 7, 9, 12–14; cf. Tekeli 2011: 131).
b) Globalization as a policy discourse/pretext: the term here stands for a programmatic formulation of universal reform proposals that inform the content of policy programmes implemented by the service providers (HE institutions) and their overseeing bodies. These programmes are borrowed because of the necessity to comply with emergent global policy trends. However, the more important issue is the broader policy agenda of the national policymakers (the central government + overseeing bodies + universities). The challenges of policy

complexity and uncertainty play an important role in the adoption of such readymade policy packages. Key policymakers and implementers tend to employ 'globalization as a policy discourse' to render their task simpler, and thus manageable; and/or to promote their own individual/institutional agendas (Deem and Brehony 2005; cf. Stensaker et al. 2008: 5, 9). Here, policymakers are mainly interested in expanding their room for manoeuver narrowed by globalization as a set of external influences.

To summarize, globalization increases the burden for the national policymakers. Not only do the problems become complicated, shaking the very basis of policymakers' political legitimacy, but also damage their policymaking capacity due to the narrowed room for manoeuver. Readymade policy packages adopted under the umbrella of globalization discourse seem to come to their help for the reasons listed above. Yet, these solutions, as this paper will show, serve to only deepen the problems of policymakers. This holds true particularly for the field of HEP in Turkey.

Higher Education Policy and Globalization: What is New?

Is not the nature of academic work inherently international or universal? (cf. Tekeli 2011: 134) Thus, was not the field of HEP more exposed to global developments in comparison to other fields of public policy even before globalization? And if so, should not we expect HEP field to be more accustomed to operating under the conditions of globalization? What is new here? Stensaker et al. (2008: 4) provides a clear answer, especially to the last question. Listing the differences between 'old' and 'new' (read globalization) forms of internationalization in HE policy the authors draw our attention to institutionalized, routinized, formalized, standardized and top-down nature of this 'new form'. While the old form has its roots in academic, social and cultural concerns, the new one is shaped by political and economic reasons. To quote them:

Table 17.1: Reasons for and manifestations of internationalization in higher education

Academic, social and cultural reasons often manifested in 'old' forms of internationalization	Political and economic reasons often manifested in 'new' forms of internationalization
as a responsibility for the individual student or teacher	as a responsibility for the department or institution
as a 'bottom-up' activity	as a 'top-down' activity
related to diversity	related to standardization
as a physical activity (for example through mobility)	as a more technology enhanced activity (for example through ICT)
as an informal and ad hoc activity	as a formal and routinized activity

Source: Stensaker et al. 2008: 4.

These two models stand in contrast to each other in many ways, and the most important is the clash of bottom-up and top-down logic of HEP. Organizationally speaking, today these two logics coexist in academia and create ethical and psychological dilemmas for academics (and managers in certain cases) (Nalbantoğlu 2011 [2003]; Deem and Brehony 2005; Göktürk 2011; Yılmaz Şener 2012), along with institutional challenges during transition to the new form. These dilemmas, serve to worsen the problems associated with the old form. It must be noted here that the old form is still a broad generalization, and the evolution of higher education systems across the world has thrown up different models. Nevertheless, all these models have been exposed to the influence of the new form (Dobbins et al. 2011: 665; Green 1999: 69; Deem 2001; Verger and Hermo 2010: 117).

The contradictions introduced by globalization into the field of HEP are not simply restricted to the institutional domain of service provision (internal structure and functioning of universities). The place and meaning of education in general, and HE in particular, is a field of constant contestation (Robertson and Dale 2006; cf. Robertson 2007: 6; McCarthy 2009; Uzunyayla and Ercan 2011; cf. Tekeli 2011: 123–25), where the battle is becoming fiercer under globalization. This is inevitable as 'the client base is large and heterogeneous in terms of their expectations and demands, and the service provided assumes a complex set of ideological, social and political functions' (Bayırbağ 2014: 1). For policymakers, the legitimacy issue is as important as observing the signs and commands of the global economy (cf. Robertson and Dale 2006: 12–14). This is a more urgent problem for developing countries (Bayırbağ and Penpecioğlu 2014), where state policymakers are concerned with maintaining national integrity and social cohesion (Bayırbağ 2014).

In the case of HEP, the boundary between policymaker and implementer is rather blurred. Implementers take an active part in the politics revolving around policy reforms given the nature of the task performed, which requires a certain degree of autonomy. This autonomy has both historical and practical roots. To be more specific, a) the size and complexity of the implementation apparatus (universities, schools, teachers, academics); b) the fact that street level bureaucrats dominate the implementation process; c) that they develop political affinity for their service recipients, the students in this case (1991: 350; Lipsky 1980; cf. Gitlin and Margonis 1995: 380; Croll et al. 1994); d) and that major changes in the implementation structure tend to damage the autonomy of the implementers, are the key reasons why new policies are shaped through bargaining and struggles between the policymakers and the implementers.

In this game, the higher education sector is in a relatively advantageous position – lower levels of education have less political leverage than higher ones despite the fact that the number of teachers is large (Reimers 1991: 350). For example, while the number of primary school teachers is large, because they are dispersed geographically, their mobilization capacity is lower. Moreover, the policymaking capacity of the different layers is also critical. This is especially true for universities. According to Reimers, 'The higher education sector is better equipped than other levels to fight not only real political battles in the street but also the bureaucratic battles' (1991: 351). The fact that HE institutions have political leverage, however, does not suggest that all of them are ready to take on the top-down reforms. This is for two reasons: a) HE systems have their own inner hierarchies inherited from their past and not every university enjoys the same level of bargaining power; b) HE institutions may be willing to adopt reform proposals to sort out their inner problems

(Stensaker et al. 2008: 3). Besides, certain HE institutions could well serve as the agents of change in their own system, pushing the boundaries towards globalizing it (cf. Dodds 2008: 515).

It can be concluded that globalization of higher education policy is far from a smooth process. In fact, the pace of reform and change in this field is slow when compared to other fields, such as social policy or health policy (Robertson 2007: 4; cf. van Velzen et al. 2012: 208), given its contentious nature and complex institutional structure. What is more, in both geographical and institutional terms, transition works in an uneven manner (van Velzen et al. 2012: 203–05). In other words, not every HE institution is globally connected, and even if connected, not in the same way or for the same reason. A number of factors produce this unevenness, namely the place of a particular country in the global political-economy (cf. Nalbantoğlu 2011 [2003]: 56–61); the source of global/supranational impetus (Verger and Hermo 2010: 117); the division of labor (and hierarchy) among the HE institutions within a national HE system (Stensaker et al. 2008: 7); the form a HE system takes depending on the history of relations between the state, market and civil society in a given context (namely, collegial model, state-centered model and market-oriented model) (Dobbins et al. 2011; Tekeli 2011: 134–45; cf. Gölbaşı 2011; cf. Devos et al. 2012: 5–7); and the individual culture and identity of a higher education institution (Stensaker et al. 2008: 3; cf. Özbudun 2011).

Institutionalization of Contradictions and Insertion of Uncertainty

The discussion above suggests that instead of dissolving the previous HE system, globalization puts yet another historical layer on HE policymaking (cf. Devos et al. 2012: 5–7). The main effect of globalization is the institutionalization of pre-existing contradictions, while adding further uncertainty into the system. These contradictions revolve around the question of autonomy. Generally speaking, universities are different from other public service providers (especially those operating in the field of education) in that they are not institutional extensions of a central bureaucracy. They are, rather, organized and function in the form of local governments.

This feature of universities has its roots in their history, and has always been contested due to the ceaseless concern of political authorities with establishing and protecting their legitimacy (cf. Özbudun 2011; Ünal 2011: 99), and thus their need for the consent and support coming from the learned ones. The rift between the state and the church, and the challenge posed by the Enlightenment to the idea of 'authority' (Özbudun 2011: 87–88; cf. Tekeli 2011: 137–39), ensured the persistence of these tensions. Capitalism, added yet another tension, given its need for operational knowledge and trained labour (cf. Özveren 2012: 258) that could be translated into profit. While, apparently, there was a need for solemn solitude and a childish curiosity for a scholar to produce and invent (cf. Nalbantoğlu 2011 [2003]), this creative effort had to be directed towards a strictly-defined and pragmatic purpose. Academy was not a place to waste time on fruitless endeavours, which, ironically, are needed to nourish the creativity required by a capitalist funder (cf. Özveren 2012: 261–63).

These tensions shaped the institutional structure of universities and the working environment of academics throughout history. Broadly speaking, the relations between the state and society in different countries resulted in the emergence of three different models of HE (ideal types) (Dobbins et al. 2011: 669–73): a) the collegial model, where the university emerged as an autonomous community of scholars observing a certain distance from the world outside (the state and the market) (cf. Tekeli 2011: 135–37), 'self-governance' defining its mode of management (Dobbins et al. 2011: 671–72); b) the market-oriented model, where a rather eclectic and diverse (cf. Balaban 2012) set of administrative practices and institutional forms emerged. The dominant feature of these institutions has been their corporate form of organization, and the entrepreneurial orientation of their management (Dobbins et al. 2011: 672–73; Birler 2012); c) the state-centred model, where the state (its central bureaucracy) formally sits atop the HE system. Universities serve as rational instruments of national policies. Uniformity of their organizational structure (and legislation), a strong emphasis on standards and standardization, state's oversight on the content of education and research are the key characteristics of this model (Dobbins et al. 2011: 670–71).

To reiterate, these models are ideal types. Different countries might contain elements from all these models, even though the features of a certain model are dominant. The process of globalization exposes all these models to the same set of influences, promoting similarities across different cases (not to the degree of convergence all the time, though). To understand better how these models are articulated, and how the process of globalization institutionalizes their contradictions, we need to discuss how the 'autonomy' is configured in each case. Slightly reworking and interpreting the comparative framework developed by Dobbins et al. (2011: 673–79) to empirically observe and measure the degree of autonomy enjoyed by HE institutions in these three models, I will concentrate on the following dimensions: a) administrative autonomy (institutional balance of power of the university system); b) financial autonomy (financial governance + personnel autonomy); c) Academic freedom of individual members (substantive autonomy: research and teaching).

The collegial model is jealous about protection of academic and intellectual freedoms. Since it is a scholarly community, self-governance is essential to protect its freedom. University administrators are elected by members of the community, and scholarly merit is a key factor in the selection. The scholarly hierarchy among the community members also translates into its administrative structure. This hierarchy, however, could well create castes and cults (also fed by a culture of master-apprentice), creating glass ceilings for new members of academia, while also reducing its accessibility to a potentially larger pool of aspirants. This high degree of selectivity and the pride in being a special group of individuals with a sense of mission (Prometheus) may also foster a conservative, exclusive and elitist culture. The funding pattern, depending on the context, might have different consequences for this model: if funded by students (self-financed), it would turn into an elite private college or university only accessible to students from privileged segments of society. If (indirect) public funding is also part of the scheme, depending on the academic merits of that university, we could expect emergence of a strict hierarchy of universities, according to the academic profile of its students. In an ideal type, financial support from the market might not be seen to be desirable by the members of the community.

The market-oriented model, depending on the political balances in the country, might well enjoy a certain degree of academic freedom, at least in political terms. This is partly because its administration is relatively insulated from the likely pressures of political circles and the state. Importantly, this freedom is also needed to pursue academic excellence (product quality), as the institution's positive image and popularity ensure a constant demand for its services (despite its high student fees), and thus secure a continuous flow of funds. Yet, depending on its financial structure, the limits to intellectual freedom would be determined by the concern to keep the (market) sponsors close. In this model, performance (productivity and the value for money) would be a key factor in employing or firing the academic personnel. With reduced prospects for job security, the academic personnel are overworked, while the competitive pressure for more publication and research threaten the quality of outputs, in contrast with the collegial model (Özveren 2012: 264–65). Under such conditions, the divide between successful personnel and the underdogs is sharpened. The divide between the skilled and under-skilled labour in capitalist enterprises inevitably translates into a divide between tenured, well-paid researchers (white collar) academics and temporary, underpaid teachers. In this scheme, the hierarchy between decision-makers (the board + the provost + senior academics) and service providers (the rest) is sharp, unquestionable, and visible, unlike the former model where power relations producing administrative hierarchies are more subtle, refined, and covert.

The state-centred model is more likely to enjoy public support in comparison to the other two models, especially if it offers increased access for the citizens to higher education. In developing countries, using resources more efficiently, this model might help build a HE system. For developing states, a state-controlled HE system might also serve to implement national development plans more effectively (such as creation of a labour force in line with development priorities). This model, in its purest form, could insulate the researchers from market pressure and pragmatism. The price paid, however, is exposure to the political wishes, caprices, and threats of the highest authority, who could be the national government or ministry and/or an overseeing public body. Non-compliance with the research priorities determined by the state or expression of political dissent might result in losing one's job. This model does not necessarily guarantee a relatively stable academic environment. Things could get worse if the central government changes hands frequently. Constant uncertainty and political polarization within the academic circles in a university or among universities could emerge as a key characteristic of such systems. University administrators are appointed mainly on the basis of their political affiliations rather than their academic merit. The academic success and productivity of an HE institution ultimately depends on the vision and character of the president as the one-and-only decision-maker. Given that political affiliation is the key criterion here, national champions will be luckier. To keep the national profile high, these institutions have to be given more significance. For the rest, the prospects for institutional development and success will not be that bright. Thus, depending on the division of labour among the universities, a strict hierarchy of universities is likely to emerge reproducing the internal divide of the market-oriented model at the national scale.

These models are not found in their purest forms, as already noted. The evolution process of an HE system determines how different features of these models come together to form a pattern peculiar to a country. But I think processes of globalization (as a set of external influences) tend to promote a new configuration, combining the negative features of all these three models, and thus destabilizing the HE education systems across the world. This is especially true for countries like Turkey, which are policymakers under globalization. To be more specific, the following features are inserted into and/or intensified in HE systems under globalization: intellectual and scholarly hierarchy among colleagues and conservatism based upon elitism (the collegial model); right to manage and loss of job security (the market-oriented model); and political control, both through vertical public pressure and horizontal market pressure (Dobbins et al. 2011: 672–73) and polarization within the HE system (cf. Stensaker 2008: 7; Kitagawa and Oba 2010). Below, I will discuss the case of Turkey to illustrate how this configuration has come into being, and has created a policy gridlock during the 2000s under globalization.

The Case of Turkey

Historical Roots of Globalization in the HE Policy

Recent debates on HE reform in Turkey revolve around the core issue of autonomy, especially the tensions between the state and academia; and rightly point out the role played by globalization via neoliberalization of HE in harming the institution called the university (Ercan and Korkusuz Kurt 2011; OED 2011; 2012; 2014; *Eğitim, Bilim, Toplum* 2013 (42); Ateş 1999; and İnal and Özkaymak 2012). Most of the arguments implicitly suggest that the current development represents a state of decay from a rather ideal past model, where the university as an institution had been relatively well-protected from political interventions. This relative autonomy previously enjoyed by HE institutions truly served public interest, assuming that to serve the public interest had always been seen as the core concern for all, and it was interpreted by all academics/universities in the same progressive manner. Admittedly, the pre-1980 HE system in Turkey was formally more autonomous, and the political weight of universities and academics was much more significant than today. Yet, the state interventions into the HE system had equally been conflict-ridden earlier. This has to do with the fact that, in Turkey, the institution called the university in the modern sense is a product of the state (established, designed and closely monitored by the state in every respect) (for detailed accounts see: Tekeli 2010; 2011: Chapter 3; Girgin Sağın 2011; Ateş 1999: 60–72).

In many ways, the case of Turkey fits into the state-centred model. The initial Ottoman example was followed by the young republic established in 1923. The system was designed after the state-centred model, while tensions between the political authorities and academics and universities had never ceased to exist. The law passed in 1933 had been pretty strict in that regard. The law passed in 1946 (No. 4936), soon after Turkey joined the post-World War II Western bloc, relieved the tensions created by the past law. It introduced the 'Professors Council' as the decision making organ of faculties (with legal personality), and deans or presidents were to be elected by academics. This autonomy, however, was not fully enjoyed during the decade to come (cf. Ateş 1999: 68–71). Following the coup d'état of 1960, the academic and administrative autonomy characteristic of the collegial model was constitutionally inserted into the system (financial autonomy based on collection of student fees, for example, was not an issue). Hence, we could take 1960 as a definitive moment in the introduction of the collegial model into the system. Universities and university professors acted as agents of change, and this change brought yet another feature of the collegial model under political spotlight, 'academic elitism', something that is still a source of mainly right wing populist criticism against universities.

By 1960, there were only seven universities in Turkey. Four were established by the Democratic Party a few years before the coup. In practice, there were three universities in Turkey, aside from the military colleges, that dominated the scene (see Table 17.2). These universities had contributed to the creation of the country's civilian intellectual elite. The condition for academic elitism, characteristic of the collegial model, was already there. This feature, thus, did not stem from the emergence of university as an independent community of (religious or enlightenment) scholars, as in the ideal collegial model.

In fact, university professors and students subscribing to the ideals of Kemalism inherited from a state-centred past, its leftist interpretation in particular), played an important role in the opposition movement to the Democratic Party. The party had been seen as an anti-Kemalist (right wing). Student uprisings of the late 1950s helped pave the way for the coup d'état of 1960. Thus, the autonomy gained by the universities afterwards had much to do with the influence of the university professors on civilian (their ex-students) and military bureaucrats, as well as on their students. These professors also played a key role in drafting the new constitution of 1961.

Table 17.2: The expansion process of the HE system in Turkey since 1923 (inception of the republic)

Period established	Public	Private (foundation)	Total
Republican (1923–50)	3	0	3
Democratic Party (1950–60)	4 (Regional universities + Internationalization starts: connection with the West)	0	4
Keynesian Period (1960–80) – Mainly post transition period	13 (real expansion starts in 1970s, after the Military Memorandum of 1971 + 1 university established in 1979 is actually located in Cyprus, and not part of the political struggles in Turkey)	0 (Private Academies opened – and closed later, to join public universities)	13
Military coup transition (1980–83)	8	0	8
Motherland Party Period (1984–91)	1 (Neoliberal Roll-Back Period)	1	2
Coalition Parties (1991–01)	25 (Populism comes back)	23	48
Justice and Development Party (2002 – Present)	52 (2 colleges) (Neoliberal roll-out period + populism)	51 (8 colleges – 2 years education)	103

Source: The list of universities (active) currently operating under the supervision of the Higher Education Council (Yükseköğretim Kurulu – the YÖK) is available on: YÖK (2014a) https://istatistik.yok.gov.tr/ (Birim istatistikleri). For the logic behind the periodization, see Bayırbağ 2013a.

It is interesting to note here that despite the formalized autonomy and increased political weight of universities, the HE system in Turkey did not expand for almost another decade (except for Hacettepe University, established in 1967) (see Table 17.2). This despite the fact that the economic development model post-1960 was Keynesian, and expansion of the HE system is necessary for such a model, promoting industrial development (requiring trained labour), concerned with the negative consequences of uneven development in a rapidly urbanizing country. So, the exclusive character of the collegial model remained for a decade.

The first wave of expansion came soon after the military memorandum of 12 March 1971, as shown in the table. The post-memorandum changes to the HE system involved introduction of Law No. 1750 – 20 June 1973 – on HE (and the HE personnel Law No. 1765), and establishment of 11 new universities in Turkey. The laws passed aimed to contain political activism in universities, which peaked during the late 1960s, also thanks to their newly gained autonomy (Tekeli 2010: 175; cf. Ateş 1999: 171). Apparently, the sense of mission inherited from the state-centred past (as Prometheus) was there. Yet, this sense of mission rooted in a Kantian elitism, further nourished by the collegial model, was not interpreted in the same way by all universities or students (right vs left oriented universities and students) (See the minutes of the speech by Ertuğrul Kürkçü, quoted in Hürriyet 2012: 71–72). At any rate, the intellectual and political diversity of the universities, as well as the heterogeneous landscape of their institutional structures, had to be tamed (YÖK 1988). Universities were founded by separate, individual laws, such as Law No. 7307 of the Middle East Technical University.

Rules, procedures, and standards about how to establish a university (in organizational terms) and introduction of the Higher Education Council (the YÖK) to ensure coordination across the HE system (and to facilitate state control) were critical developments in the above regard. Introduction of a central examination centre and a national university entrance exam in 1974 (http://www.osym.gov.tr/belge/1-2706/tarihsel-gelisme.html) was also a part of this scheme, stripping the universities of their right to choose their own students. While the first YÖK had later been cancelled by the constitutional court, the logic behind it was the harbinger of the developments to come, the second YÖK of the neoliberal era, (see the comments by the first president of post-1980 YÖK, İhsan Doğramacı in YÖK 1988). At any rate, those legal interventions were not as effective as expected (Ateş 1999: 71), thanks to the bargaining power enjoyed by the universities (see Section III).

The second pillar of the post-1971 intervention was about the expansion of the higher education system via introduction of 11 new universities throughout the decade. Unlike the early republican universities in Ankara and Istanbul, they were established mostly in more prominent cities and provinces of Anatolia. As the locations of these new universities were determined, the expansion strategy pursued by the Democratic Party (four regional universities had been established) was also adopted by the post-Memorandum governments (Kavili Arap 2010: 12–14). This was also a remarkable step towards introducing mass education into the HE system, diffusing it to Anatolia (the non-metropolitan, relatively underdeveloped regions). The number of universities had almost tripled in a decade, during a decade marked by political-economic instability (11 different governments formed by rival/different parties/coalitions and/or technocrats). That almost all governments pursued this expansion strategy, despite deep party-political disagreements in many other policy issues and fields, also suggests that there was a strong bottom-up pressure coming from the broader public in that direction (cf. Tekeli 2010: 175–76).

Emerging Amalgam: Institutional Base of the Current HE System

The decade of 1970s ended with yet another coup d'état (12 September 1980). Universities, this time, were among the major enemies of the Junta. Seen as 'nests of disorder and anarchy', universities had to be tamed and brought under state control. The second coming of the YÖK was ground-shaking (see Tekeli 2010: 204–36). Law No. 2547, still in effect, stripped the universities of their administrative and academic autonomy. The institutional logic of this reform was underlined by the principle of hierarchy; articles 6 to 18 of the law are critical in that regard. The Higher Education Council (the HEC) was given the task of regulating higher education and directing HE institutions in the country (article 6). The article states that the council is autonomous, but this is only true in administrative terms. The composition of the council is determined by three different organs: the President of the Republic appoints one third of its members (senior professors); the cabinet appoints another one third, this time high profile/ranking public servants (still active or retired) and the inter-university board, a component of the HEC, sends the last one-third. In other words, the political balances in the country are directly reflected into council membership.

The rector constitutes the second rank in this hierarchy. The person to fill this post is determined through a complicated procedure which almost entirely silences the voice of academics in the decision-making process (article 13). This article, along with article 6, dealt the deadliest blow to autonomy in the collegial sense. First, at the end of the fourth year of service, an election is held. Only those academic staff with the title of assistant professor or upwards in the academic ranking can vote. Teaching staff with a PhD, and yet not holding a professorial position, and research and teaching assistants are left out. A list of six candidates with the highest vote rates is submitted to the YÖK, where a shortlist of three candidates is determined. Finally, the president of the republic appoints one of these names as the rector. Apparently, the election process is a pretty tough one and is open to covert and open political disputes. In most cases, the figures are politically biased, depending on the political balances in the country. The same story repeats in the case of deans, officially leaving no room for faculty members to determine the person to fill the post. While in practice, in certain universities a similar election process takes place under the label 'opinion poll' (also for department chairs), though this is not a general rule. According to article 16, the dean is appointed by the YÖK, from among a list of three candidates suggested by the rector, and the figure to fill this post could also be a professor from another university. The faculty board is the only elected organ. Yet, even there, not all members are elected. Election takes place on the basis of academic titles, with posts to be filled in a descending order (three posts for professors, two posts for associate professors, and one for assistant professors). A similar procedure is run for department chairs, this time appointed by deans (article 21).

The scheme outline above is quite close to the logic of a bureaucratic organization. This particular bureaucratic organization tends to privilege the highest academic rank, full professor, in administrative terms. The way in which academic titles are incorporated into the intra-university decision-making mechanisms is reminiscent of the academic elitism characteristic of the collegial model. What we see here is formalization of intra-academic hierarchies inherited from the collegial model of the 1960s and 1970s. This hierarchy is also reflected into the new tenure system. Articles 23 (assistant professors), 31 (teaching staff with or without PhD – Öğretim Görevlisi), 32 (teaching staff without PhD – Okutman), and especially the infamous article 51, limiting the terms of appointment and giving a strong hand to the university administration. This employment regime, which favors associate and full professors, immensely increases the university administration's control over its academic personnel (Ersoy and Keskinok 2014), leaving 86.94 per cent of the public universities' academic workforce (YÖK 2014b) at their mercy.

To summarize, the formalization process facilitates administrative control (Ersoy and Keskinok 2012: 67), helping the rector run the affairs smoothly as the top manager. What we see here is the 'right to manage' principle in flesh and bones. The top manager is a rather political figure equipped with the legal power and administrative means that will help in the running of administrative affairs as desired. This institutional feature of the public universities prepares the ground for implementation of a 'market-oriented' HE agenda. The three decades that passed since Law No. 2547 testify to the claim that this has actually been the case. Political meddling in academic affairs (state-centred model), academic elitism (collegial model), the right to manage, and job insecurity principles (market-oriented model) existed even before the start of the globalization process of the HE system in Turkey. In fact, these features facilitated the transition process.

The transition process, however, has not been easy, and it has created more problems to complicate matters. The most visible evidence of this is the number of changes the law has gone through. It did not take long before the amendment process started. According to Tekeli, there are two possible explanations, both of which, I think, make sense: the law was not that well prepared; and that the political authorities did not hesitate to bring the law even more in line with their priorities, whenever necessary (2010: 222–26). Between the years of 1982 and 2011, the law has gone through 66 amendments (see the Law's text, pages 5394, 5394-1 and 5394-2), leaving very few articles untouched. Initially, the law had 66 original articles. There are now 28 additional and 68 provisional articles. The following figures from Ersoy and Keskinok (2014) indicate that this process gained speed during the 12 years (2003–14), under the hegemony of a neoliberal Justice and Development Party. While the Law No. 2547 has gone through 29 amendments, the HE personnel law has been amended twice. The Law No. 2809 on organization of HE institutions has been modified 31 times. It is not surprising to see that despite the frequency of changes in institutional or organizational matters, personnel issues have not received much attention. It looks like the current employment regime in public HE institutions is in a state with which the party in power is rather content.

Dynamics of Institutional Expansion: Neoliberalism and Globalization

A third reason behind this incremental style of policymaking is the expansion and diversification of the HE system in Turkey under the influence of globalization (the bottom-up and top-down pressures on the policymakers). The process of institutional expansion of the HE system has gained speed during the post-1980 period, also characterized by neoliberalization of the policymaking process and the country's integration with global economy. The magnitude of this expansion, and the subsequent institutional diversity, renders a bureaucratic and centralized policymaking scheme increasingly helpless. To give an idea, the increase in the number of the HE institutions has been nine-fold (from 20 public universities of the pre-1980 period to over 180 HE institutions – coming up in every corner and province, with more than one third of them being 'private' universities/colleges) (see YÖK 2014a; 2014b). The increase in the number of students enrolled in these institutions has been more than twentyfold: from 266,877 students (1979–80) to 5,449,961 students (2013–14). A similar trend can be observed in the number of the academic staff: growing from a total of 20,699 (1979–80) to

141,674 (2013–14), almost sevenfold (see Tekeli 2010: 280–81; YÖK 2014b). These numbers also tell us that educational responsibilities have increased significantly. In the midst of the increasing pressures on publication and research during the last three decades, the teaching burden on the academic staff in particular has more than doubled. Of course, these numbers are totals. Once they are broken into categories such as public vs private, old vs new universities, the picture gets much worse and uneven.

Now let's take a closer look at the dynamics of expansion. For this purpose, I have constructed Figures 17.1 and 17.2. They offer a timeline of the expansion on the basis of the type of university (public vs foundation universities).

Figure 17.1: Expansion process of the HE system in Turkey – Public Universities

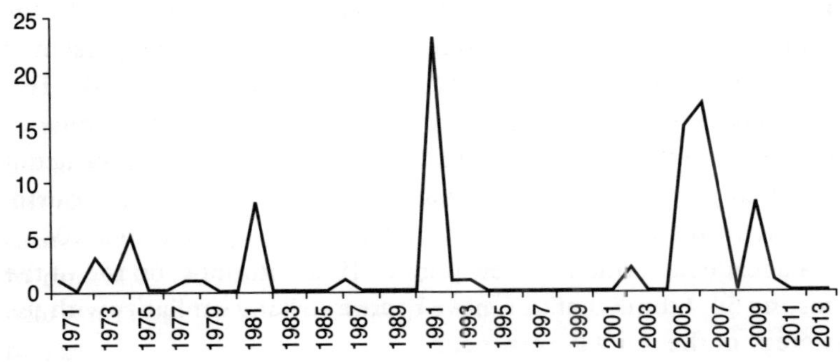

Source: See Appendix 1.

Figure 1 indicates that evolution of the public side in the HE system works through waves of aggressive expansion to be followed by a period of stability. It is not surprising to see that these waves coincide with the political upheavals in the country's history. It is interesting to observe that an openly anti-academy junta government, which also paved the way to the neoliberal policies to come (see Table 2), took the first step in that direction. Why might have this been so? One possible explanation has to do with a concern to balance the power of old universities, and to introduce 'their own universities' to tame the HE system (cf. Serbest 2011: 128). A strong anti-elitist

Figure 17.2: Expansion process of the HE system in Turkey – Foundation Universities

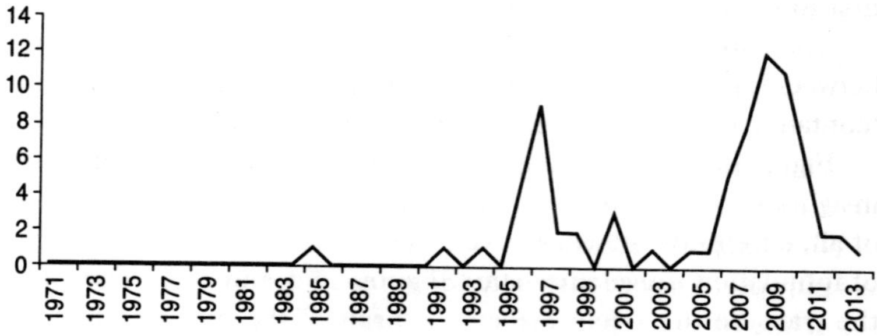

Source: See Appendix 1.

discourse underlined this strategy. Tekeli (2010) notes that elitism of universities and professors constituted a major axis of criticism by the leader of the junta, Kenan Evren. The new universities represented an anti-elitist challenge to the old system, by introducing 'mass HE', while also building the legitimacy of the coup. It is interesting to note that the third wave of 2006–07 (and 2010) was the product of a political party, again, subscribing to a strong anti-elitism discourse. In fact, the Justice and Development Party era (in power since 2002), in a decade has added 52 new public HE institutions, on top of the existing 54. I think that this move bears a striking similarity with the strategy of the junta government.

Turgut Özal's Motherland Party, which facilitated the transition to neoliberalism and initiated the integration process with the global economy, however, was not active at all in that regard. Yet, as we will see, the period of the Motherland Party rule has been characterized by another sort of intervention, of cleaning up the legal ground for the new HE system (see Figure 17.3).

The second wave of expansion (1992) was a product of the True Path Party (Doğru Yol Partisi) and the Social Democratic Populist Party (Sosyal Demokrat Halkçı Parti) government. Widespread public discontent with the austerity and rollback measures of the Motherland Party brought the coalition to power. Apparently, negative consequences of the first generation neoliberal policies in

Turkey were translated into a populist move for enhancing public access to HE. In other words, bottom-up pressures created by the first round of neoliberal globalization triggered this second move.

The third wave of the JDP, however, aimed to contain the tension between two conflicting aims, 'furthering neoliberal policies' and 'containing its negative consequences', through populist moves.

Figure 2, when read in relation to Figure 1, offers a set of further insights about the evolution of the system under globalization. First of all, except for Bilkent University (1985), the wave of expansion of foundation universities started about more than a decade after the transition to neoliberalism. Therefore, we can conclude that introduction of the market oriented model into Turkey's HE system did not start through marketization of HE services and creation of an HE market in line with global policy pressures. Rather, the first stage of the transition to the market model started with institutional transformation of the existing public universities. Another important point to be underlined is that a public expansion is immediately followed by yet another wave of foundation universities. Hence, it might be argued that the public investment process into the field of education encourages the private sector to step in. Birler notes that certain changes made to the regulations about prerequisites to establish a university also played a key role in this expansion process. This is especially true for the post-2008 period. In 2008, the prerequisite of having faculties of 'sciences' and 'humanities' was lifted (two no-profit fields) (Birler 2012: 146–47).

The last observation is about the influence of the global policy developments on the expansion of foundation universities, especially during the second expansion process under the rule of the JDP. The top-down pressure on the national policymakers has become institutionalized during the 2000s, thanks to the Bologna Process (Özgün 2011: 392–400; Gümüş and Kurul 2011: 44–60). In fact that the expansion process accelerated during the 2000s is not a coincidence. Birler argues that this development has much to do with the expansion of external public funding opportunities, which are both supranational (EU Framework Programs) and national (The Scientific and Technological Research Council of Turkey) (2012: 147; Balaban and Karahanoğulları 2013: 74–75). Here it should be noted that expansion of the national public resources is a component of the integration process with the Bologna Program.

Conclusion

In a mind-expanding exegesis of Veblen's works on 'Higher Learning', Özveren notes that:

> … what was important for him [Veblen] was to recognize how this process [intrusion of business as an outside force into the university] diverts the university from the pursuit of long-term goals to a myopic concern with short-term usefulness. This is a more general diagnosis and applies equally well when the external 'yoke' comes not from business interests but from governments, or local communities that provide public funds in return for extracting short-term services or benefit from these institutions of higher learning that fell prey to their utilitarian ends (2012: 267).

Especially, when market oriented reforms are implemented by a state-centred HE system, the systemic myopia worsens, leading to inevitable policy-myopia and paralysis in HE. In that regard, 'Higher learning as the iron cage from within' (ibid.: 268–72), also translates into an 'iron cage from without', that of polarization in the HE system of Turkey.

Under the influence of globalization (in terms of bottom-up and top-down pressures), the HE system in Turkey has become increasingly complex, and the contradictions it was built upon have become deeper. A striking feature of the current system is polarization among the HE institutions. The waves of expansion discussed above contributed to this polarization, which also corresponds to the socio-spatial injustices in the country (cf. Özuğurlu 2014). There are five axes of differentiation behind this iron cage of polarization, which are continuously reproduced in the policy discourse through the university entrance exam results, research and publication based rankings, competitive funding procedures and ideological debates: a) public universities vs foundation universities (ownership); b) older universities vs new universities (generation/level of institutional maturity); c) metropolitan universities vs non-metropolitan universities (geographical); d) research vs teaching (performance); e) pro-government vs anti-government (political).

The polarization process has become more and more visible during the JDP era (2002 onwards), when Turkey's integration with global economy (and global policymakers) has reached a point of no return, in a time when neoliberal policy reforms have reached their apex. For example, currently public universities have 5,089,291 students (including 1,609,528 open university – distant education students), while foundation universities have 350,999 students (and + 9,671 students in eight colleges). Hence, despite the remarkable expansion, foundation universities are far from sharing the burden of the public universities in mass education. This is also reflected in the institutional size of the universities. A public university, on average, has about 129 departments (13,478/104), whereas a private university has 34 departments (average student per teaching staff is close in both category, 20 and 18 respectively). Apparently, private universities are quite selective in opening an academic department, in comparison to public universities, given their profitability concerns (for the figures, see YÖK 2014b, Table 17.1).

Generational polarization could easily be read from the preference rankings of the universities or departments in the central national university entrance exam, reflecting the public's perception of the quality and popularity of universities. These rankings have remained almost unchanged throughout the last three decades. In fact, the logic of the preference procedure is pretty similar to the market pricing mechanism where the university or department averages reflect the socially determined price of the institution (Bayırbağ 2013b). Similar reports available on the YÖK website (YÖK 2014b) as well as the international auditing reports (research performance) also reproduce the same perception. In fact, the generational dimension coincides with geographical differentiation, given the logic of expansion in the public sector (cf. Kavili Arap 2013), and is further deepened by increasing selectivity, and the uneven distribution of public resources among the public universities (cf. Oruç et al. 2011: 24–25). This selectivity has much to do with the fact that the public purse is now overstretched given the magnitude of expansion (cf. Ulutürk and Dane

2011: 424). The story told so far is also true for the differentiation among the foundation universities (metropolitan first generation – 1990s vs non-metropolitan second generation – 2000s) (Birler 2012).

As for the performance-based polarization, this is a blurred area, especially as second generation public universities (those established in the 1990s) have been catching up with the first generation in terms of research and publication (Tekeli 2010). The research and publication orientation of the first generation foundation universities is remarkable, which draws the first generation public universities into competition in that regard. Yet, it is hard to argue that this observation is valid for the second-generation foundation universities, for two reasons: a) Targeting the job market, and to train their students accordingly, comes forth as a key strategy (Birler 2012). In fact, private profession-oriented college, as a phenomenon, is a product of the last period (2002–present), and they constitute about 16 per cent of the private HE institutions established during that period; b) The pace of expansion of the academic workforce could not match the pace of expansion of both public and private sectors. This is especially true for scholars with strong credentials. Hence, in the private sector, the race to attract and keep such scholars is likely to get fiercer given the shortage. In this race, apparently, the first generation private universities enjoy a clear advantage. The third generation public universities (post mid-2000s) are not in the game. They are still in the process of forming their cadres, mostly through a scholarly breeding programme operating under the supervision of the YÖK. Nevertheless, these newly established universities are already in the teaching business due to the impatience of the JDP (and the YÖK) about expanding mass education. As such, the young academics joining newly established small departments find themselves in the middle of an unbearable teaching load, without much time and energy left for research and publication.

Political polarization is both an inter-university and intra-university phenomenon. Foundation universities, depending on the political views or backgrounds of their founders, could either choose a side, especially if established by a religious foundation, or adopt an apolitical stance. As for the public universities, those whose top decision-makers are not under the political yoke of the party in power are very few. The media outlets are full of news about investigations started by university administrations that target the academics with a critical stance in political matters. A good example of inter-university polarization is a recent public declaration undersigned by more than 30 rectors (mostly from public universities), condemning the Middle East Technical University and its students. A student protest erupted soon after the then Prime Minister's visit to the university campus on 18 December 2012. The intervention of the police force resulted in a snowball reaction, turning the campus into a battle zone. Already portrayed as the devil's nest (given its leftist past) by the politicians from the party in power and their media people, the rectors rushed to attack this scapegoat to fortify their relations with the PM.

Given its state-centred character and its firmly centralized policymaking structure – heavily promoting standardization, furthered by the Bologna Process (Ercan 2011; Yönden 2013) – one would normally expect the formation of a rather homogeneous HE system, which is relatively easy to govern. However, we have an opposite result. Introduction of 'managerialism' (characteristic of the market oriented model) into the system to fortify the state control and to catch up with the global trends in the field of HE policy (see YÖK 1988), and the recent global policy programmes such as the Bologna Process, constituted the top-down influences contributing towards this complexity. The popular demand for mass education and the political parties/authorities concern with building/protecting their own legitimacy could be seen as the bottom-up influences shaping the evolution of the HE system in Turkey. These bottom-up pressures are unintended products of the neoliberal policy schemes implemented by consecutive government programmes.

The demand for mass education stems from concerns with social justice, via increasing public access to university education (Robertson and Dale 2006: 13; Robertson 2007: 2; Robertson et al. 2002: 491–93; cf. Tekeli 2011: 212–13). It should be noted that socio-spatial injustice in the country has been deepening during the last three decades, thanks to the increasing speed of integration with the global economy (Bayırbağ and Penpecioğlu 2014). In fact, the masses reaction to the injustices and economic crises induced by the first round of neoliberalism brought the JDP to power. The party, however, had to meet two conflicting targets: to address the injustices inherited from the previous neoliberal governments; and to galvanize support for a broader post-crisis policy reform programme to accelerate Turkey's integration process with the global economy, and to consummate the neoliberalization process (Bayırbağ 2013a). The party's aggressive expansion policy in the field of HE (mass education), deepening and spreading the logic of central examination (objectivity and equal opportunity for all) and its anti-elitist discourse towards universities could be understood in that regard.[3]

The policies pursued under globalization have created a complex HE system shaped by a set of contradictions, which could be listed as follows: a) promotion of social justice, via increasing public access to university education, vs promotion of competition among higher education institutions; b) development of research environment vs strengthening of managerial control over higher education institutions; c) increasing emphasis on the public service role of universities (mass education) vs de-politicization of the higher education institutions; d) the discourse on protection and promotion of diversity, especially in a fragmented country like Turkey, vs standardization of service provision (procedures) and product quality.

It is very hard for a single authority to handle this complexity, and to implement a radical policy reform to tidy up the house. The history of amendments to the Law No. 2547 testifies this. To give a closer view of this difficulty I have constructed Figure 17.3, which brings together the overall expansion of the system and the history of amendments (cumulative increase in the number of amendments).

Apparently, a constant expansion process has turned amendments into a necessity: run the bike faster so as not to fall. Yet, this incremental approach, at certain points in history, falls behind the developments. These are moments of rapid expansion, which almost choke the system. Hence, it should come as no surprise that reform proposals and intense debates tend to come soon before or after these radical

[3] Nevertheless, the policy measures aiming to address this social justice issue (including central exams) tend to create new inequalities, while also extending the period of unemployment for university graduates (see Bora 2011; Gürbüz 2011: 80; Bayırbağ 2013b). Besides, access to the HE system is still a luxury for the first two layers (20%) of the income stratification scheme (Bayırbağ 2014).

changes. For example, following the wave in 1992, came a report by the TÜSİAD (the big bosses' businessmen association in Turkey) in 1994. An unsuccessful draft law of 2003 came towards the end of the post-1992 expansion. Soon after the third wave started in 2006, the strategy report of YÖK came in 2007. Following the establishment of a set of new universities, almost reaching the current numbers, the most recent reform attempt of the YÖK came in 2012 (for the pre-2012 reports, see Tekeli 2010; Serbest 2011). Nevertheless, there has been no success. Ironically, most of these reform proposals, especially the last one[4] seem to have internalized the globalization discourse. The report is filled with references to the term globalization, and contains contradictory policy proposals, which would formalize and worsen the current polarization within the system.[5]

Figure 17.3: The post-1980 expansion of the HE system in Turkey and the incrementalism in policymaking

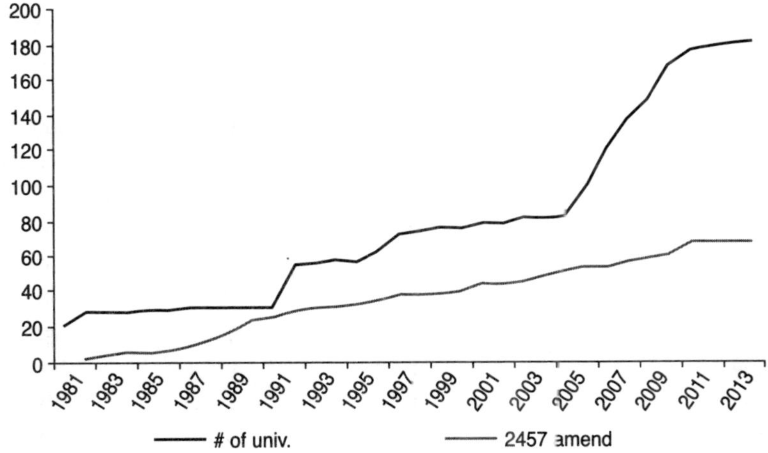

Source: Appendix 1 and Appendix 2.

[4] For a rich critical exposé of the content of the proposal see the issue 42 of the journal *Eğitim, Bilim, Toplum*.

[5] For instance, while decentralization of university administrations are proposed so as to relieve the political pressure coming from the central government, the proposed 'administrative board' system (the mayor, provincial governor, top tax payers, etc. being among its members) would further strip the academics of their research/teaching autonomy.

APPENDIX 1: YÖK universities by their years of establishment and status

YEAR	Public	Foundation	TOTAL
1971	1	0	1
1972	0	0	0
1973	3	0	3
1974	1	0	1
1975	5	0	5
1976	0	0	0
1977	0	0	0
1978	1	0	1
1979	1	0	1
1980	0	0	0
1981	0	0	0
1982	8	0	8
1983	0	0	0
1984	0	0	0
1985	0	1	1
1986	0	0	0
1987	1	0	1
1988	0	0	0
1989	0	0	0
1990	0	0	0
1991	0	0	0
1992	23	1	24
1993	1	0	1
1994	1	1	2
1995	0	0	0
1996	0	5	5
1997	0	9	9
1998	0	2	2
1999	0	2	2
2000	0	0	0
2001	0	3	3

(Continued)

(Appendix 1 continued.)

YEAR	Public	Foundation	TOTAL
2002	0	0	0
2003	2	1	3
2004	0	0	0
2005	0	1	1
2006	15	1	16
2007	17	5	22
2008	9	8	17
2009	0	12	12
2010	8	11	19
2011	1	7	8
2012	0	2	2
2013	0	2	2
2014	0	1	1

Source: YÖK 2014a.

APPENDIX 2: Timeline of amendments to the Law No. 2547

YEAR	Number of legal changes made to Law No. 2547
1982	2
1983	1
1984	2
1985	0
1986	2
1987	2
1988	3
1989	5
1990	6
1991	2
1992	3
1993	2
1994	1
1995	1

(Continued)

(Appendix 2 continued.)

YEAR	Number of legal changes made to Law No. 2547
1996	2
1997	3
1998	0
1999	1
2000	1
2001	5
2002	0
2003	1
2004	3
2005	3
2006	2
2007	0
2008	3
2009	2
2010	2
2011	6
2012	0
2013	0
2014	0

Source: The Law's text, pages 5394, 5394-1 and 5394-2.
http://www.yok.gov.tr/documents/10279/29816/2547+say%C4%B1l%C4%B1%20Y%C3%BCksek%C3%B6%C4%9Fretim+Kanunu/f439f90b-7786-464a-a48f-9d9299ba8895

References

Ateş, T. 1999. *Üniversiteler: Bitmeyen Şarkı*. Ankara: Ümit Yayıncılık.

Balaban, U. 2012. 'Türkiye'de Yükseköğretim Reformu ve ABD'de Endüstri-Üniversite İlişkisinin Tarihi.' *Ankara Üniversitesi SBF Dergisi,* 67(4), pp. 25–61.

———., and Y. Karahanoğulları. 2013. 'Yükseköğretim Kanunu Taslağı'nın Mali Boyutu.' *Eğitim, Bilim, Toplum* (42), pp. 65–93.

Ball, S.K. 2007. 'Big Policies/Small World: An Introduction to International Perspectives in Education Policy.' In *The Routledge Falmer Reader in Education Policy and Politics*. B. Lingard and J. Ozga. London and New York: Routledge. pp. 36–47.

Bayırbağ, M.K. 2013a. 'Continuity and Change in Public Policy: Redistribution, Exclusion and State Rescaling in Turkey.' *International Journal of Urban and Regional Research,* 37(4), pp. 1123–146.

———. 2013b. 'Is There a Job After College?: Higher Education's Impact on Transition from School to Work. *METU Studies in Development,* 40(3), pp. 465–92.

———. 2014. 'Dynamics of Post-crisis Reform in Public Policy: The Case of Education Policy in Turkey.' In *Public Administration and Policy in the Middle East.* A.R. Dawoody. New York: Springer. Forthcoming.

———., and M. Penpecioğlu. 2014. 'Urban Geography of Contestation: Dispossession, Exploitation, Commons and Representation in the Eastern/Southern Cities.' Conference Paper. Paris: City Futures Conference 2014.

Birler, Ö. 2012. 'Neoliberalization and Foundation Universities in Turkey.' In *Neoliberal Transformation of Education in Turkey.* K. İnal and G. Akkaymak. New York: Palgrave Macmillan. pp. 139–50.

Bora, T. 2011. 'KPSS'ye Sığındım': İşsizler, Seçme Sınavları, Stres ve Adalet Duygusu.' In *'Boşuna mı Okuduk?': Türkiye'de Beyaz Yakalı İşsizliği.* T. Bora, A. Bora, N. Erdoğan and İ. Üstün. İstanbul: İletişim Yayınları. pp. 259–74.

Croll, P., D. Abbott, P. Broadfoot, M. Osborn and A. Pollard. 1994. 'Teachers and Education Policy: Roles and Models.' *British Journal of Educational Studies,* 42(4), pp. 333–47.

Deem, R. 2001. 'Globalisation, New Managerialism, Academic Capitalism and Entrepreneurialism in Universities: Is the Local Dimension Still Important?' *Comparative Education,* 37(1), pp. 7–20.

———, and K.J. Brehony. 2005. 'Management as Ideology: The Case of "New Managerialism" in Higher Education.' *Oxford Review of Education,* 31(2), pp. 217–35.

Devos, G., M. Ekholm, K. Kofod, K. Seashore Louis, L. Moos, M. Schratz and B. van Velzen. 2012. 'Political Culture and Educational Reform.' In *Educational Policy in an International Context: Political Culture and its Effects.* K. Seashore, Louis and B. van Velzen. New York: Palgrave Macmillan. pp. 5–27.

Dobbins, M., C. Knill and E.M. Vögtle. 2011. 'An Analytical Framework for the Cross-Country Comparison of Higher Education Governance.' *Higher Education,* 62, pp. 665–83.

Dodds, A. 2008. 'How Does Globalisation Interact with Higher Education: The Continuing Lack of Consensus.' *Comparative Education,* 44(4), 505–17.

Ercan, F. 2011. 'Ölçerim, Ölçebilmek İçin Biçimlendiririm, Biçimlendiğine Standartlaşmışsındır, Standartlaştığında Yönetirim, Ölçemediğimi Yönetemem O Zaman Cezalandırır Dışlarım.' In *Metalaşma ve İktidarın Baskısındaki Üniversite*. F. Ercan and S. Korkusuz Kurt. İstanbul: SAV Sosyal Araştırmalar Vakfı. pp. 361–88.

———., and S. Korkusuz Kurt. 2011. In *Metalaşma ve İktidarın Baskısındaki Üniversite*. F. Ercan and S. Korkusuz Kurt (eds.). İstanbul: SAV Sosyal Araştırmalar Vakfı.

Ersoy, M. and Ç. Keskinok. 2011. 'YÖK'ün Üniversitelere İlişkin Gelişme Politikalarının Tarihsel Değerlendirilmesi.' In Ç. Keskinok, *5. Üniversite Kurultayı*. Ankara: OED (Orta Doğu Öğretim Elemanları Derneği). pp. 65–74.

———. 2014. AKP İktidarı Döneminde YÖK Politikaları Ne Yönde Evrildi? *Bilim ve Üniversite Sempozyumu 18 Nisan 2014*. Ankara: OED. http://www.oed.org.tr/oed/wp-content/uploads/2014/06/BilimveUniversiteSempozyumu.pdf.

Girgin Sağın, F. 2011. 'Darülfunun'dan Günümüze Universiteleşme Sancımız.' In *5. Üniversite Kurultayı*. Ç. Keskinok. Ankara: OED (Orta Doğu Öğretim Elemanları Derneği). pp. 41–46.

Gitlin, A., and F. Margonis. 1995. 'The Political Aspect of Reform: Teacher Resistance as Good Sense.' *American Journal of Education*, 103, pp. 377–405.

Göktürk, A. 2011. 'Üniversite…! mi? Yoksa Akademisyen Romantizmi mi?' In *Metalaşma ve İktidarın Baskısındaki Üniversite*. F. Ercan and S. Korkusuz Kurt. İstanbul: SAV Sosyal Araştırmalar Vakfı. pp. 223–38.

Gölbaşı, Ş. 2011. 'Düzenlemeden Yeniden Düzenlemeye: Bildiğimiz Üniversitenin Sonu.' In *Metalaşma ve İktidarın Baskısındaki Üniversite*. F. Ercan and S. Korkusuz Kurt. İstanbul: SAV Sosyal Araştırmalar Vakfı. pp. 523–54.

Green, A. 1999. Education and Globalization in Europe and East Asia: Convergent and Divergent Trends. *Journal of Education Policy*, 14(1), pp. 55–71.

Gümüş, A., and N. Kurul. 2011. *Üniversitelerde Bologna Süreci Neye Hizmet Ediyor?* Ankara: Eğitim Sen Yayınları.

Gürbüz, B. 2011. 'Türkiye'de Yüksek Eğitimden Yararlanan Kesimler ve Bologna Süreci.' In *Bologna Süreci Sorgulanıyor*. N. E. Önal. İstanbul: Yazılama. pp. 73–88.

Hürriyet. 2012. '*12 Mart 1971 Muhtırası Araştırma Raporu.*' http://dosyalar.hurriyet.com.tr/haber_resim_3/12_mart_raporu.pdf.

İnal, K., and G. Akkaymak. 2012. In *Neoliberal Transformation of Education in Turkey*. K. İnal and G. Akkaymak (eds.). New York: Palgrave Macmillan.

Kavili Arap, S. 2010. 'Türkiye Yeni Üniversitelerine Kavuşurken: Türkiye'de Yeni Üniversiteler ve Kuruluş Gerekçeleri.' *Ankara Üniversitesi SBF Dergisi*, 65(1), pp. 1–29.

Kitagawa, F., and J. Oba. 2010. 'Managing Differentiation of Higher Education System in Japan: Connecting Excellence and Diversity.' *Higher Education*, 59, pp. 507–24.

Law #2547. 1981. '*2547 Sayılı Yükseköğretim Kanunu.*' http://www.yok.gov.tr/documents/10279/29816/2547+say%C4%B11%C4%B1%20Y%C3%BCsek%C3%B6%C4%9Fretim+Kanunu/f439f90b-7786-464a-a48f-9d9299ba8895.

Lingard, B., and S. Rawolle. 2011. 'New Scalar Politics: Implications for Education Policy.' *Comparative Education*, 47(4), pp. 489–502.

Lipsky, M. 1980. *Street-Level Bureaucracy: Dilemmas of Individuals in Public Service*. New York: Russell Sage Foundation.

McCarthy, M. 2009. 'Commentary: Research on Actors and Institutions Involved in Education Policy: Themes, Tensions, and Topics to Explore.' In *Handbook of Education Policy Research*. G. Sykes, B. Schneider, D.N. Plank and T. Ford. New York and London: Routledge. pp. 842–47.

Nalbantoğlu, H.Ü. 2011. 'Üniversite A.Ş.'de Bir "Homo Academicus": "Ersatz" Yuppie Akademisyen.' In *Metalaşma ve İktidarın Baskısındaki Üniversite*. F. Ercan and S. Korkusuz Kurt. İstanbul: SAV Sosyal Araştırmalar Vakfı. pp. 21–74.

OED. 2011. *5. Üniversite Kurultayı*. Ç. Keskinok (ed.). Ankara: OED (Orta Doğu Öğretim Elemanları Derneği).

———. 2012. 'Hocam Forum Var (7 Kasım 2012).' *Transcriptions of Forum Discussions*. Ankara: OED (Orta Doğu Öğretim Elemanları Derneği).

———. 2014. *Bilim ve Üniversite Sempozyumu (18 Nisan 2014)*. http://www.oed.org.tr/oed/wpcontent/uploads/2014/06/BilimveUniversiteSempozyumu.pdf.

Oruç, K.O., E. Çekin, A.E. Tenderis and H. İ. Özmen. 2011. 'Yükseköğretimde Kaynak Dağılımı Üzerine Bir Değerlendirme: Türkiye'deki Devlet Üniversitelerinin Cari Hizmet Ödenekleri.' *Süleyman Demirel Üniversitesi Vizyoner Dergisi*, *3*(4), pp. 19–34.

ÖSYM. 2014. *Tarihsel Gelişme*. http://www.osym.gov.tr/belge/1-2706/tarihsel-gelisme.html.

Özbudun, S. 2011. 'Üniversitelerde "Başkalaşım" ve Aydınlar.' In *Metalaşma ve İktidarın Baskısındaki Üniversite*. F. Ercan and S. Korkusuz Kurt. İstanbul: SAV Sosyal Araştırmalar Vakfı. pp. 87–92.

Özgün, Y. 2011. 'Bologna Süreci Derken?' In *Metalaşma ve İktidarın Baskısındaki Üniversite*. F. Ercan and S. Korkusuz Kurt. İstanbul: SAV Sosyal Araştırmalar Vakfı. pp. 389–412.

Özuğurlu, M. 2011. 'YÖK ve Üniversite Üzerine Kısa Notlar.' In *Metalaşma ve İktidarın Baskısındaki Üniversite*. F. Ercan and S. Korkusuz Kurt. İstanbul: SAV Sosyal Araştırmalar Vakfı. pp. 253–60.

Özveren, E. 2012. 'Veblen's "Higher Learning": The Scientist as Sisyphus in the Iron Cage of a University.' In *Thorstein Veblen: Economics for an Age of Crises*. E.S. Reinert and F.L. Viano. London and New York: Anthem Press. pp. 257–79.

Reimers, F. 1991. 'The Impact of Economic Stabilisation and Adjustment on Education in Latin
America.' *Comparative Education Review*, 35(2), pp. 319–53.

Robertson, S.L. 2007. 'Globalisation, Rescaling National Education Systems and Citizenship Regimes.' On-Line Papers. Centre for Globalisation, Education and Societies, University of Bristol. http://www.bris.ac.uk/education/people/academicStaff/edslr/publications/06slr/.

———., and R. Dale. 2006. 'Changing Geographies of Power in Education: The Politics of Rescaling and its Contradictions.' On-Line Papers. Centre for Globalisation, Education and Societies, University of Bristol.
http://www.bris.ac.uk/education/people/academicStaff/edslr/publications/03slr/.

———., X. Bonal, and R. Dale, R. 2002. 'GATS and the Education Service Industry: The Politics of Scale and Global Reterritorialization.' *Comparative Education Review*, 46(4), pp. 472–96.

Serbest, H. 2011. '2547 Sayılı Yasa Yerine Son Yıllarda Önerilen Yeni Yasa Taslaklarının Karşılaştırılması ve Üniversite Yönetim Modeli Üzerine Öneriler.' In *5. Üniversite Kurultayı*. Ç. Keskinok. Ankara: OED (Orta Doğu Öğretim Elemanları Derneği). pp. 125–42.

Stensaker, B., N. Frolich, A. Gornitzka and P. Maassen. 2008. 'Internationalisation of Higher Education: The Gap Between National Policymaking and Institutional Needs.' *Globalisation, Societies and Education*, 6(1), pp. 1–11.

Tekeli, İ. 2010. *Tarihsel Bağlamı İçinde Türkiye'de Yükseköğretimin ve YÖK'ün Tarihi*. İstanbul: Tarih Vakfı Yurt Yayınları.

———. 2011. *Türkiye İçin Eğitim Yazıları*. İstanbul: Tarih Vakfı Yurt Yayınları.

Ulutürk, S., and K. Dane. 2011. 'Yükseköğretimin Finansmanı: Neoliberal Dönüşüm ve Türkiye.' In *Metalaşma ve İktidarın Baskısındaki Üniversite*. F. Ercan and S. Korkusuz Kurt. İstanbul: SAV Sosyal Araştırmalar Vakfı. pp. 413–38.

Uzunyayla, F., and F. Ercan. 2011. 'Türkiye'de Eğitim Sistemine Yönelik Yeni Talepler ve Yeni Aktörlere Sınıfsal Bir Bakış.' In *Metalaşma ve İktidarın Baskısındaki Üniversite*. F. Ercan and S. Korkusuz Kurt. İstanbul: SAV Sosyal Araştırmalar Vakfı. pp. 197–222.

Ünal, I.L. 2011. 'Yükseköğretim Finansmanı: Neoliberal "Çözüm" ve Tehditler.' In *Metalaşma ve İktidarın Baskısındaki Üniversite*. F. Ercan and S. Korkusuz Kurt. İstanbul: SAV Sosyal Araştırmalar Vakfı. pp. 93–120.

van Velzen, B., K. Louis Seashore, G. Devos, M. Ekholm, K. Kofod, L. Moos and M. Schratz. 2012. 'Wer Vorwarts Kommen Will, Muss Auch Mal Rückwarts Denken.' Reflections on the Case Studies. In *Educational Policy in an International Context: Political Culture and its Effects*. K. Seashore Louis and B. van Velzen. New York: Palgrave Macmillan. pp. 193–211.

Verger, A., and J.P. Hermo. 2010. 'The Governance of Higher Education Regionalisation: Comparative Analysis of the Bologna Process and MERCUSOR-Educativo.' *Globalisation, Societies and Education*, 8(1), 105–20.

Yılmaz Şener, M. 2012. 'Turkish Academics as Neoliberal Subjects?' *Journal of Developing Societies*, 28(3), pp. 299–322.

YÖK. 1988. '*Kasım 1981 - Kasım 1988 Döneminde Yükseköğretimdeki Gelişmeler.*' https://www.yok.gov.tr/documents/10279/30217/KASIM+1981KASIM+1988+D%C3%96NEM%C4%B0NDE+Y%C3%9CKSEK%C3%96%C4%9ERET%C%B0MDEK%C4%B0%20GEL%C4%B0%C5%9EMELER.pdf/45642fc7-e2ec-4b9c-bd4305fcadde6a3c.

———. 2014a. Birim İstatistikleri: https://istatistik.yok.gov.tr/.

———. 2014b. Yükseköğretim Temel Göstergeleri: https://istatistik.yok.gov.tr/.

Yönden, E. 2013. 'Yükseköğretim Müfredat Denetimi ve Akıl Tutulması.' *Redaksiyon (EK)*, pp. 2–4.

18 An Analysis of Policy Transfer
The Policy on Protecting Women against Domestic Violence in Turkey

A. Argun Akdoğan, Mete Yıldız and Can Umut Çiner

Abstract

This paper is one of the first outputs of the research handling the policy formulation process of a case study about the Law No. 6284 Protection of the Family and Prevention of Violence against Women, within the scope of the Public Policy Formulation Project by the authors. The aim of the research is to determine how public policies are placed on the agenda and the impact of pressure groups, and to develop advice by putting forward the similarities and differences between the policy formulation processes of Turkey and other countries. Firstly, in this paper, concepts like policy transfer, policy diffusion, and policy learning are described in a detailed manner by exemplifying and relating them to the case at hand. Secondly, the emphasis is put on the role of the policy transfer in the policy formulation and ongoing debates about the prevention of violence against women. Finally, the paper discusses the findings evaluating the success of policy transfer.

Introduction

This paper reflects the partial findings of a research project financed by the Turkish Ministry of Development regarding the nature, actors and development of public policymaking in Turkey. Preventing domestic violence against women was selected as the topic of a demonstrative case to study the process of public policymaking.

The data are collected by conducting in-depth interviews with (i) members of the parliament (MPs) who are also members of the parliamentary committees that deal with violence against women (The Justice Committee and the Committee of the Equality of Opportunity between Men and Women); (ii) the parliamentary staff that aid these MPs; (iii) mid- and high-level bureaucrats in the Ministry of Family and Social Policies, which is the main policy actor in the bureaucracy, as well as other high-level bureaucrats who take part in the making and shaping of policy within the Turkish Prime Ministry, the Ministry of Justice, and the Ministry of Interior (and the Police Force); and finally (iv) the directors and members of the women's rights non-governmental organizations (NGOs) with different ideological positions and varying ideological and political distance from the governing party.

Within this framework, the main objective of this study is to analyse the policy process in Turkey on the basis of the 'Law on The Prevention of Violence against Women and The Protection of the Family' (Law Numbered 6284) enacted by the Turkish Grand National Assembly on 8 March 2012. This law sets forth basic arrangements to combat violence against women, which stipulates specific protective and preventive orders. Thus, the essence of Law No. 6284 is to prevent violence against women and protect actual and potential victims of violence.

Enacting this law was directly related with the topic of policy transfer. The law in question was introduced to the Parliament shortly after Turkey signed the Istanbul Treaty in 2011, a document drafted by the Council of Europe for the main purpose of motivating European countries to take measures to prevent violence against women. Since the treaty was adopted in Istanbul, the Turkish government saw an opportunity to prepare a law in line with the treaty. Furthermore, the fact that during the preparation of the law, members of the Ministry of Family and Social Policies and the Parliamentary Committee on the Equality of Opportunity between Men and Women organized visits to European countries deemed successful in protecting women against violence, such as Spain and Ireland, is also indicative of policy transfer. For instance, the use of electronic cuffs for men who can potentially commit violence to their wives is inspired by Spain.

During the study, it became increasingly clear that policy transfer on policy regarding domestic violence has had certain limitations. Despite mimicking technical aspects that are common in some European countries, the Turkish government was reluctant to adapt the European discourse on preventing domestic violence. For example, as the title makes it clear, the law seeks to protect women against violence and at the same time to preserve the unity of the family. These dual objectives were considered to be contradictory by most of the representatives of the women's associations working in the field. During our interviews, the members of the Parliament from the governing party specifically indicated that they do not wish to increase the rate of divorce as an indirect and unintended result of trying to protect women against the violence of their husbands and other family members, such as fathers and brothers.

Within this framework, this article seeks to focus on the role of policy transfer in the process of policy formulation in the area of violence against women, and to highlight tensions in transferring similar policy measures implemented in some European countries to Turkey. We discuss what motivated the government to transfer some aspects of European practice on this matter. We will then argue that while the government officials adopted technical aspects of combatting violence committed against women, they were much more cautious against the transfer of the European discourse and terminology on this issue. We will further argue and conclude that the conservative and Islamic sensibilities of the government officials could be influential for this selective transfer.

Policy Transfer: A Brief Conceptual Review and Findings

This article examines the concept of public policy transfer, which deals with the question of how to utilize the different policy formulations and implementations of different geographical entities to solve problems encountered in various stages of public policy analysis. In this respect, this paper handles policy transfer as a generic concept and further associates sub-categories such as policy diffusion, policy learning and policy convergence with descriptive models. This paper then analyses these sub-categories with examples and data gathered in this study. The final section presents some interpretations regarding the measurement of successful policy transfer regarding the issue and time period in question.

Policy transfer, which focuses on the ideas, policies, and the change of policy instruments, is a relatively new field in the discipline of public policy. The analysis of policy transfer covers the external factors creating changes in public policies, policy actors, and the factors motivating these actors and transfer processes of the policies. Concepts of policy transfer first appeared in studies about the way ideas, policies, and policy instruments were disseminated among the states of federal systems such as the US. The interactions in the policy production process among the states and between the state- and federal-level governments aroused academic interest. This mobility of ideas and applications in federal systems were found increasingly similar to the multi-level governance implementations within the European Union (EU). Therefore, the focus of interest in policy transfer studies shifted from transfers within federal systems to interactions between nation states (Bulmer, Dolowitz, Humphreys and Padgett 2007: 4–5).

Policy transfer can occur within a spectrum, one end of which may be marked as policy convergence, with policy divergence at the other end. Intellectual roots of policy convergence may be traced to political economy. In this respect, policy convergence is thought to be guided by factors like liberalization, information technologies, and the growth of international markets. The role of national policymakers in this global system is the determination of public policies in accordance with sector-focused solutions and market signals of such solutions designed for policy problems. Such a determination of national policies minimizes the differences among them (Bulmer et al. 2007: 4).

It is doubtful how much we can distinguish policy transfer and policy formulation from other steps of the policy process (Hill 2005: 136). Even though analysing public policy processes in steps may be perceived as an oversimplification of the complex nature of public policies, there is no doubt that this eases the analysis by dividing it into more manageable sections. Still, Jann and Weigrich (2007: 51) believe that there is no meaningful separation between policy transfer and the other steps in the policymaking process. Similarly, policy learning or lesson-drawing concepts strongly resemble the rational model of decision making (James and Lodge, 2003; quoted by Jann and Weigrich 2007: 51).

Drawing attention to the presence of a similar problem between the agenda setting and policy formulation stages, Hill (2005: 136), states that nation states only declare war when they are completely ready, and thus he questions how much one can separate these two stages. He also advocates that in some cases that the stages of policy formulation and policy implementation are very much intertwined (Hill 2005: 134, 175).

The policy transfer literature analyses the importance and role of ideas and their communication in public policy circles. Today, the rapid transmission of knowledge and ideas via improving information and communication technologies increases the significance and ease of policy transfer. While nation states developing public policies are searching for when and which certain solutions are developed and put to use in other countries, at the same time international institutions such as the United Nations, the World Bank, and the Organisation for Economic Co-operation and Development (OECD) present prescriptions, which are different manifestations of policy transfer (Hill 2005: 88).

Think tanks, with their increasing presence, should also be listed among the important actors of policy transfer at the global scale (Stone 2004). In this sense, the basic question when analysing the presence or absence of policy transfer is whether there really exists a comprehensive literature that analyses the transfer process, its actors, causes, and consequences. Answering in the affirmative is indeed very doubtful (Hill 2005: 88).

As a complex process, there are many dimensions of policy transfer – the first being time. For example, recently developing East Asian countries may adopt the economic policies of developed countries by transferring these policies after fine-tuning them according to the experiences and particularly to the failures in these countries (Hill 2005: 98). That is, the time gap will enable the developing countries to transfer corrected and better-adapted public policies.

Another dimension of policy transfer is the way in which the transfer is conducted. Researchers investigating both policy transfer and policy learning processes make use of organization theory in general, while utilizing normative, coercive, and mimetic types within the institutional isomorphism concept (Di Maggio and Powell 1983) in particular to examine and explain the similarities and differences of different transfer experiences (Jann and Weigrich 2007: 51).

With such a variety, policy transfer is described on a wide spectrum starting from policy dissatisfaction and ending with policy enforcement (Dolowitz and March 2000). International agreements and actors play important roles in different points along this spectrum, which is described in detail in the following pages. For instance, international agreements, relations, and processes had important influences in making policies regarding violence against women in Turkey and Turkey's subsequent participation in the Committee on the Elimination of Discrimination against Women (CEDAW). Primary among the other factors affecting these policies is the attendance at the Parliamentary Committees on the elimination of violence against women and Turkey's Programme for Alignment with the EU Acquis.

In a similar manner, the European Parliament's reports prescribed the creation of a new committee, the Committee on the Equality of Opportunity between Men and Women in the Turkish Parliament and the foundation of the Ministry of Family and Social Policies as important developments (European Parliament 2012: 3–4). A member of the Turkish Parliament, who was interviewed by the researchers, emphasized the importance of international influence on the establishment of the Equal Opportunity Commission as follows (emphasis belongs to the author):

> This commission concerning women, the gender equality Commission and the commission of Elimination of Violence Against women, such commissions are introduced into our agenda as a result of influences stronger than just advices of the international community. ... There is a demand from international organizations, from the EU... and none of these are mentioned in the newspapers, only civil society organizations are told to have such a demand. I

> have no idea about how this news was produced. Someday someone told that we would talk about a law proposal about the elimination of violence against women. Where? In the Justice Commission as the main commission and in the Equal Opportunity Commission and Health Commission as secondary commissions… Proposal had been forwarded to five commissions, while only three responded. It is handled in Equal Opportunity Commission at the end, because this commission is established by international demand.

Related Concepts: Policy Diffusion, Policy Learning and Policy Convergence

The following section explains the three concepts of policy diffusion, policy learning, and policy convergence, which are closely related to policy transfer and sometimes confused with it or used as a synonym for policy transfer.

Policy Diffusion

Policy diffusion studies are mostly interested in examining and explaining the reasons and impacts of the diffusion of certain policies among federal systems of government, such as the United States, as well as the process of diffusion itself, together with the actors playing important parts in these processes. For example, Berry and Berry (1999: 169) argue that if a policy is traced back in time long enough, one can almost always find a non-incremental policy decision that can be attributed to policy diffusion.

Modern policy diffusion research can be traced back to research conducted by Berry and Berry, who first studied the diffusion of policy ideas among states in the US during the 1970s (Berry and Berry 1999). These studies showed that there are two main reasons as to why a state embraces a new policy idea. The first reason is the factors that are related to the nature of the state in question, such as political, economic, and/or social characteristics. The second reason is the functioning of policy diffusion models, which will be explained in detail below.

The concepts of diffusion are explained as the communication of an innovation among the members of a social system in time (Rogers

1983: 5, quoted by Berry and Berry 1999: 171). The literature on diffusion first examined the diffusion of ideas and technologies. Then came the studies as mentioned above, which examined the diffusion of public policies among the states in the US. Although these findings are the results of studies that examined state-level governments in the US, we believe that they are equally applicable to nation-states, such as Turkey and its relationships with the EU, as they pertain to policy diffusion. The results of these studies uncovered three reasons regarding why the states influence each other in adopting public policies (Berry and Berry 1999: 171–72).

First, policy ideas that are deemed successful in states are adopted by other states. In other words, states were using shortcut solutions for similar problems, the effectiveness of which were proven in other states. For example, our study shows that the research trips of the members of the Equal Opportunity Commission's to the EU countries such as Spain and Ireland were specifically aimed at determining and if possible adopting certain remedies for decreasing domestic violence. The mimicking of the use of electronic bracelets for the abuser spouses in Spain is a case in point.

A second reason for the diffusion of public policies among states is the rivalry and competition between the states. Even though states have a certain level of autonomy in a federal system of government, there are still regional and national standards that they need to adhere to. The pressure to conform to these standards helps the diffusion of public policies. In addition to such pressures, states want to gain competitive advantage by applying new ideas and refrain from being left behind by the successful policy adoption of other states. In our study, an interesting example of being subject to such standardization pressures and seeking competitive advantage is the adoption of the Istanbul Convention on violence against women. By being the initiator and the first signatory of this international agreement, Turkey strongly signalled to the international community its intention to deal with the problem of violence against women and conform to international standards in this policy area.

The third reason for the diffusion of public policies among states is the citizens' demand for certain polices that they witness being successfully implemented in other states, and thus pressure their elected officials to adopt similar policies. The media outlets, who share successful implementation stories with the world, have a very important/critical role in the creation and communication of such civic pressures. The European Parliament acknowledges the importance of all media outlets such as newspapers and TV series in creating awareness about violence against women and its solutions, as well as identifying and popularizing positive role models in Turkey (2012: 15–16). Since Turkish TV soap operas have become extremely popular in the Middle East, the Balkans, and in some Turkic republics of Central Asia in recent years (Buccianti 2010), such awareness about and popularization of model violence against women may have effects reaching far beyond the borders of Turkey.

In our study, not the citizens, but effective members of the civil society organizations helped elected officials such as ministers to adopt a close translation of the Austrian law for violence against women. The result was the adoption of the Law numbered 4320 in 1998 as the first law in Turkey that set up a comprehensive system to counter violence against women. In another example, members of a women's rights-oriented NGO, Mor Çatı, seemed to be strongly effective in pushing members of the Equal Opportunity Commission for the adoption of electronic bracelets/cuffs.

These studies and their models that explain why and how public policies diffuse among American states show that geographical proximity between states is an important determinant in policy diffusion. The models also determined some states as leaders and some as followers at regional or national levels (Berry and Berry 1999: 175–77). The results of our study show that although Turkey generally uses European examples for policy diffusion about violence against women, there is no leading country that dominates this process.

Policy diffusion not only happens horizontally among states, but it also includes vertical diffusion between federal and state governments in either direction (Berry and Berry 1999: 177). Such vertical policy diffusion is not limited to federal systems of government, but is possible in unitary systems of government as well.

The study of policy diffusion processes, models and actors in American states also uncovered the limitations of such models (Berry and Berry 1999: 192). First, the models present quite simple causal models. However, public policy processes operate in a much more complicated world. Secondly, these explanatory models fail to take into account many policy actors and channels of communication and leverage at local, regional, national, and international levels.

Policy Learning

Policy learning or policy-oriented learning is a process that is born out of experience and useful for realizing policy goals or changing these goals as needed, and has relatively lasting impacts on intentions, thoughts, and behaviours of policy actors (Birkland 2001: 190–91, quoting Sabatier, 1986). Jann and Weigrich (2007: 51) prefer to call this phenomenon 'lesson-drawing' instead of policy learning, arguing that this is only one of the presentations or patterns of different types of policy transfer.

One can link policy learning to policy failure. From this perspective, policy learning is critical analysis of and lesson-drawing from policy failures for the explicit purpose of changing the ongoing policy for a better one (Birkland 2001: 190). Policy failure, in this respect, can be failure of process and or outcomes. For example, in our research, failure to come up with a new and comprehensive law about violence against women before 2012 partly shows a policy failure of both the (political and legal) process (of producing a new law) and outcome (the inability to create a legal environment in which less and less women become subject to violence). Such policy failures in turn created fertile ground for policy learning from countries, which managed the policy process and outcome(s) in ways that Turkey could not.

The main issue in the policy learning literature is the identity of the policy actor that actually learns something. Sabatier (1986) hints that organizations cannot actually learn: it is the individuals who learn policy lessons. Even though individuals learn, it is the groups that act upon what is being learned (Birkland 2001: 191).

This begs the question whether people or organizations learn. If it is the organizations that learn, then the evaluations of the implementation of various policies can be used as an invaluable source for learning. If it is the persons that learn, key employees with high experience that hold much of organizational memory are the main actors of policy learning. In the middle of these two extremes is the argument that information management systems are the real units of policy learning, which both hold and distribute critical policy information as needed for policy decisions (Birkland 2001: 190).

Policy Convergence

A final concept that is related to policy transfer is policy convergence. In its essence, policy convergence is the development of similar remedies/policies by countries which experience similar problems but different initial policy implementations. Conversely, policy divergence is the increasing difference between countries which come up with increasingly differing policy ideas so as to solve a similar policy problem. Actors of policy convergence can be listed as government agencies, local governments, nation states and international or supra-national organizations. Processes through which policy convergence emerges are quite similar to those of policy transfer: imitation, effects of international policy networks, standardization and penetration (Gupta 2012).

Conclusion: The Success of Policy Transfer

According to Dolowitz and Marsh (1996: 10–11), there are three processes that can influence the success of policy transfer. The first one is the institutional context in which the policy is transferred. The second is policy transfer without sufficient information and knowledge about the policy area, which may in turn result in policy failure. The lack of enough knowledge about the policy that is transferred could also result in incomplete transfer. The third process, which may result with policy failure, is inadequate transfer when a policy is attempted to be adopted in a different context.

Some members of the Equality between Men and Women Committee of the Turkish Grand National Assembly visited Spain and Ireland on November and December of 2009. The programme and evaluation of these visits was made public through reports published on the committee's website (KEFEK 2009a; 2009b).

Officials from the UNDP joined both visits. While there were two UNDP representatives among nine members of the delegation in the visit to Ireland, three representatives were present in the visit to Spain. The presence of UN representatives within the Turkish parliamentary delegation shows the role of international organizations in policy transfer.

The second important factor to dwell on is the reason for choosing Spain and Ireland as examples to be inspired for preventing violence against women in Turkey. The Catholic religion is quite influential in both countries and these countries are not among the top countries in Europe in the field of equality between men and women. Both countries use a considerable amount from the European Social Fund to implement policies preventing violence against women (KEFEK 2009b: 4).

Thirdly, the issue of equality between men and women is a relatively new policy field in these countries. For example, until 1983, violence against women was not legally considered as a felony in Spain. A law specifically on preventing violence against women was only enacted in Spain in 2004, six years after the introduction of the first Turkish law specifically on the same issue. The parliamentary committee in Spain on this issue was established in 2007, just two years before the establishment of a similar committee in Turkey (KEFEK 2009b: 1, 3). It seems that in both countries legal and organizational measures for preventing violence against women were considered as obligatory for harmonizing EU Acquis Communautaire, rather than the will of the dominant political party (KEFEK 2009a: 5).

Despite these similarities, the Turkish government's approach to the issue is divergent from that of Spain in terms of language. For example, while the name of committee in Spain on this matter is the Commission on Social Equality, in Turkey it is called the Equality of Opportunity between Men and Women Committee. The name of the Ministry in Spain is the Ministry Responsible for Women, though in Turkey it is called the Ministry of Family and Social Policies (KEFEK 2009b: 1–2). The discourse on this issue varies from the discourse used in most European countries. The conservative government of Turkey is concerned that protecting women against violence may result in more women divorcing their husbands. As the government highly values keeping the family together and increasing the average birth rate, the issue of family unity becomes as important as, and maybe sometimes more important than, preventing violence against women.

Apart from the rejection of transferring the discourse, some processes and organizations that are in place in Spain and Ireland have not been adopted in Turkey. In Spain, courts specializing in violence against women were established and 94 judges gained their expertise on this issue. With the support of relevant public organizations, 160,000 complaints are received by these specialized courts (KEFEK 2009b: 4). Even though the Turkish parliamentary delegation has examined some prevention methods used in Spain such as electronic cuffs and panic buttons, the use of both has not been fully accepted in Turkey. The panic button option is currently tried in some provinces of Turkey: when a woman presses the button, her location and her call for help is received by the '155' police emergency line and the closest police units are dispatched to her location (Bayhan and Vural 2013: 272). One expert in the Turkish parliament told us that there are organizational problems in implementing the panic button system in Turkey.

> ... this tracking device belongs to the police. 155 receives the call but it is ŞÖNİM (Violence Prevention and Tracking Centers of the Ministry of Family and Social Policies) that she has to reach. If a problem arises on the device, the woman has to get in touch with ŞÖNİM, then she has to go the police. Police gets in touch with Avea (GSM Company) and Avea replies back to ŞÖNİM.

A representative of a women's organization claimed there are problems regarding the implementation of the panic button. She elaborated by saying: "The ministry will be in trouble in the future as it does not have enough personnel. There is no technical unit that can help a woman who pushes the button".

In Spain, the system for sheltering women has three steps. In the first step, the women are hosted by emergency centres, where women make their complaints and stay for two or three days. In the second step, women are accommodated in the shelter houses and can stay anywhere from three to eighteen months. In the last phase, women are placed in private apartments. The locations of these apartments are not disclosed. This sheltering system has not been adopted by Turkey (KEFEK 2009b: 5–6).

The importance of systematic data gathering and processing on the women's problems is one of the underlying outcomes of both visits. For example, in Spain the first initiative of the legislative committee was to gather statistical data on violence committed against women (KEFEK 2009b: 4). Systemic gathering of data on social gender became critical to develop Ireland's National Strategy on Women (KEFEK 2009a: 5). In Turkey, the authorities accept that current and standardized data cannot be gathered. The Ministry (2012a: 3) announced that pilot studies have begun to compile a database on this issue.

In conclusion, in the Turkish case that we examined, continuous administrative reorganization in the Ministry (the last one being in 2011), which is responsible from the policy area that we have examined resulted in low levels of expertise and organizational memory. This was due to continuous personnel transfer/loss to international organizations and women's NGOs, mostly due to high levels of politicization of government agencies, coupled with the lack of comprehensive and longitudinal collection of data about violence against women in organizational databases of public agencies. This, in turn, negatively affected the systematic analysis of this policy domain as well as successful learning from policy success and/or failure in this domain in the past in Turkey or elsewhere. The result was that the lessons which can be drawn from relative policy successes and policy failures are kept hidden in the memories of the members of women's organizations or retired experts of government agencies, some of whom currently work in the NGO sector. One of the main objectives of the public policy analyses such as ours is to collect, cultivate and analyse this kind of implicit knowledge about policy transfer, failure and learning, and make it explicit in reports such as this one. At this time, we can conclude that in the policy domain that we study, it is persons that learn about policy failures, not the organizations. These policy experts inside and around government agencies have recently become less effective in policy transfer and learning as political appointees and legal advisors have become increasingly influential in the processes of policy transfer, learning and making. As the policy learning and transfer process is dominated by political appointees and legal experts, the political and legal character of policy learning has become more pronounced as well.

In our study, we conclude that the policy ideas that have been put into effect before and between the enactment and implementation of two subsequent laws in 1998 and 2012 incrementally increased the similarity of the policies of violence against women to those of the international organizations in general and the EU in particular. Therefore, there is evidence for policy convergence with international standards, laws and practices in the Turkish case. However, cultural factors such as the presence of a male-dominated culture, and conservative and Islamic sensibilities of the government officials as well as of most of the politicians (who happen to be men), has at times slowed down or even reversed policy transfer and convergence, especially in the area of policy implementation.

References

Bayhan, K., and E. Vural. 2013. '6284 Sayılı Kanun Çerçevesinde Aile İçi Şiddetle Mücadelede Kolluğun Rolü.' Serdar Kenan Gül (Der.). *Aile İçi Şiddet ve Polis*. Ankara: Polis Akademisi Yayınları.

Berry, F.S., and W.D. Berry. 1999. 'Innovation and Diffusion Models in Policy Research.' In *Theories of the Policy Process*. Paul A. Sabatier (ed.). Boulder: Westview Press. pp. 169–200.

Birkland, T.A. 2001. *An Introduction to the Policy Process*. Armonk: M.E. Sharp.

Buccianti, A. 2010. 'Dubbed Turkish soap operas conquering the Arab world: social liberation or cultural alienation?' *Arab Media and Society*. http://arabmediasociety.com/articles/downloads/20100330130359_Buccianti_-_for_PDF.pdf.

Bulmer, S., D. Dolowitz, P. Humphreys and S. Padgett. 2007. *Policy Transfer in EU Governance* London: Routledge.

Di Maggio, P.J., and W.W. Powell. 1983. 'Iron cage revisited: Institutional isomorphism and collective rationality in organizational fields.' *American Sociological Review*, 48: 147–60.

Dolowitz, D.P., and D. Marsh. 1996. 'Who Learns What from Whom? A Review of the Policy Transfer Literature.' *Political Studies*, 44(2): 343–57.

———. 2000. 'Learning from Abroad: The Role of Policy Transfer in Contemporary Policymaking.' *Governance: An International Journal of Policy and Administration.* 13(1): 5–23.

European Parliament. 2012. 'Report on a 2020 Perspective for Women in Turkey (2011/2066(INI)).' Committee on Women's Rights and Gender Equality, 04/12/2012. http://www.europarl.europa.eu/sides/getDoc.do?pubRef=-//EP//NONSGML+REPORT+A7-2012-0138+0+DOC+PDF+V0//EN.

Gupta, K. 2012. 'Comparative Public Policy: Using the Comparative Method to Advance Our Understanding of the Policy Process.' *The Policy Studies Journal,* 40(1): 11–26.

Hill, M. 2005. *The Public Policy Process.* Harlow: Person-Longman, 4th Edition.

James, O., and M. Lodge. 2003. 'The Limitations of "Policy Transfer" and "Lesson Drawing" for Contemporary Public Policy Research.' *Political Studies Review,* 1, 179–93.

Jann, W., and K. Weigrich. 2007. 'Theories of the Policy Cycle.' In Frank Fischer, Gerald J. Miller and Mara S. Sidney (eds.). *Handbook of Public Policy Analysis: Theory, Politics and Methods.* New York: CRC Press. pp. 43–62.

KEFEK. 2009a. '*Kadın Erkek Fırsat Eşitliği Komitesi (KEFEK) İrlanda Raporu.*' (Turkish Parliament Equality of Opportunity Commission Ireland Report). http://www.tbmm.gov.tr/komisyon/kefe/docs/irlanda_raporu_son.pdf.

———. 2009b. '*Kadın Erkek Fırsat Eşitliği Komitesi (KEFEK) İspanya Raporu.*' (Turkish Parliament Equality of Opportunity Commission Spain Report). http://www.tbmm.gov.tr/komisyon/kefe/docs/ispanya_raporu_son.pdf.

Rogers, E.M. 1983. *Diffusion of Innovations,* New York: Free Press.

Sabatier, P.A. 1986. 'Top-Down and Bottom-Up Approaches in Implementation Research: A Critical Analysis and Suggested Synthesis.' *Journal of Public Policy,* 6(1): 21–48.

Stone, D. 2004. 'Transfer Agents and Global Networks in the "Transnationalisation" of Policy.' *Journal of European Public Policy,* 11(3): 545–66.

Bibliography

Adler, T., and M. Oelofse. 1996. 'The housing subsidy scheme.' In K. Rust & S. Rubenstein (eds.). *A Mandate to Build: Developing Consensus around a National Housing Policy in South Africa.* Johannesburg: National Housing Forum. pp. 109–37.

African National Congress (ANC). 1994. *The Reconstruction and Development Programme: A Policy Framework.* Johannesburg: Umanyano Publications.

Anonymous (a). nd. Housing and the Urban Poor. http://www.dialogue.org.za/Documents/Outside%20Docs/.

Appadurai, A. 2002. 'Deep democracy: urban governmentality and the horizon of politics.' *Public Culture*, 14:1, pp. 21–47.

Baumann, T., and J. Bolnick. 2001. 'Out of the Frying Pan into the Fire: The Limits of Loan Finance in a Capital Subsidy Context.' *Environment & Urbanisation*, 13:2, pp. 103–15.

Bay Research and Consultancy Services (BRCS). 2001a. Review of Department of Housing Policy Document. Prepared by BCRS for *People's Dialogue* (e-mailed to writer by Ted Baumann on 1 June 2001).

———. 2001b. 'The South Alliance.' A Report Prepared for the Homeless International. Cape Town.

———. 2002. 'Delivering the Housing Subsidy in a People's Housing Process Context: Challenges, Experiences and Options.' Cape Town.

———. 2003. 'The People's Housing Process in South Africa.' Review for the People's Housing Partnership Trust. Cape Town.

Berry, M. 2014. 'Neoliberalism and the City: Or the Failure of Market Fundamentalism.' *Housing, Theory and Society*, 31:3, pp.1–18

Bond, P. 2000. *Cities of Gold, Townships of Coal: Essays on South Africa's New Urban Crisis.* Trenton: Africa World Press.

———. 2000a. *Elite Transition: From Apartheid to Neoliberalism in South Africa.* South Africa: Pluto Press & University of Natal Press.

———., 2006. 'Neoliberal Urban Policy: Are Those Planact Fingerprints.' Paper presented at the Conference on NGOs as Innovators and Agents of Change: A history interpreted by development practitioners. University of Witwatersrand, Johannesburg. 5 August.

———., 2014. '"Talk Left, Walk Right" in South African Social Policy. Tokenistic Extension of State Welfare versus Bottom-up Commoning of Services.' (Personal copy).

———., M. Mayekiso, D. Miller and M. Swilling. 1996. 'Response to Government's Draft Urban Strategy Document II.' *Urban Forum,* 7:1, pp. 101–20.

Buroway, M. 1997. 'Neoliberal Pitfalls – South Africa Through a Russian Lens.' Paper presented at the Harold Wolpe Memorial Trust Inaugural Conference, 1–2 April.

Calhoun, C., R. Sennett and H. Shapira. 2013. '*Poiesis* Means Making.' *Public Culture,* 25:2, pp. 195–200.

Council for Scientific and Industrial Research (CSIR). 1999. 'The State of Human Settlements South Africa 1994–1998.' Draft report for comment, prepared by the CSIR for the Department of Housing.

Cronin, J. 2014. 'Rethinking the South African Crisis: Nationalism, Populism, Hegemony – Review of Gillian Hart.' *New Agenda,* 54, Second Quarter, pp. 54–56. (Book review).

d'Cruz, C., and D. Satterthwaite. 2005. 'Building homes, changing official approaches: The work of urban poor organizations and their federations and their contributions to meeting the Millennium Development Goals in urban areas.' Human Settlements Programme. IIED Poverty Reduction in Urban Areas Series Working Paper 16, London.

De Loor, J.H. 1992. 'Housing in South Africa: Proposals on a Policy and Strategy.' The Task Group on National Housing Policy and Strategy of the South African Housing Advisory Council. Pretoria.

Dean, M. 2002. 'Liberal government and authoritarianism.' *Economy and Society,* 31:1, pp. 37–61.

Development Works. 2002. 'Cities Alliance Project on a pro-poor slum upgrading framework for South Africa for submission to the Cities Alliance/United Nations Centre for Human Settlements.' Report prepared by Development Works for People's Dialogue, Johannesburg.

Dolowitz, D., and D. Marsh. 1996. 'Who learns what from whom: a review of the policy transfer literature?' *Political Studies*, XLIV, pp. 343–57.

Fine, B., and Z. Rustomjee. 1996. *The political economy of South Africa: from minerals-energy complex to industrialisation.* Johannesburg: Witwatersrand University Press.

Fine, B. 2001. Fine, B. 1999. 'Transition and the political economy of South Africa.' Revised version of paper presented to African Studies Association of Australasia & the Pacific, Perth, Australia, November.

Fischer, F. and J. Forester. 1993. Editor's Introduction. In F. Fischer & J. Forester (eds.). *The Argumentative Turn in Policy Analysis and Planning.* Durham & London: Duke University Press. pp. 1–17.

Foucault, M. 1983. Social security [Interview]. In L.D. Kritzman (ed.). 1988. *Michael Foucault: Politics Philosophy Culture: Interviews and Other Writings 1977–1984.* London: Routledge. pp. 159–77.

Freund, B. 2010. 'Is there such a thing as a post-apartheid city?' *Urban Forum,* 21, pp. 283–98.

Isaacs, G. 2014. 'The Myth of "Neutrality" and the Rhetoric of "Stability": Macroeconomic Policy in Democratic South Africa.' Working Paper 1 for the Political Economy of Restructuring in South Africa. (Personal copy).

Gilbert, A. 2002. '"Scan Globally; Reinvent Locally": Reflecting on the Origins of South Africa's Capital Housing Subsidy Policy." *Urban Studies,* 39:10, pp. 1911–33.

———., 2002a. 'Power, Ideology and the Washington Consensus: The development and spread of the Chilean housing policy.' *Housing Studies,* 17, pp. 305–24.

———., 2004a. 'Learning from others: the spread of capital housing subsidies.' *International Planning Studies,* 9:2/3, pp. 197–216.

———., 2004b. 'Helping the poor through housing subsidies: lessons from Chile, Colombia and South Africa.' *Habitat International,* 28, pp. 13–40.

Goodlad, R. 1996. 'The housing challenge in South Africa.' *Urban Studies,* 33:9, pp. 1629–45.

Habib, A. 1998. *Structural constraints, resources and decision-making: a study of South Africa's transition to democracy.* Department of Politics, City University of New York (unpublished PhD).

———., and V. Padayachee. 2000. 'Economic Policy and Power Relations in South Africa's Transition to Democracy.' *World Development,* 28:2, pp. 245–63.

———., D. Pillay and A. Desai. 1998. 'South Africa and the global order: the structural conditioning of a transition to democracy.' *Journal of Contemporary African Studies,* 16:1, pp. 95–115.

———., 2013. *South Africa's Suspended Revolution: Hopes and Prospects.* Johannesburg: Wits University Press

Hajer, M.A. 1993. 'Discourse Coalitions and the Institutionalization of Practice: The Case of Acid Rain in Britain.' In F. Fischer & J. Forester (eds.). *The Argumentative Turn in Policy Analysis and Planning.* Durham & London: Duke University Press. pp. 43–76.

Harris, R. 2003. 'Learning from the Past: International Housing Policy Since 1945 – An Introduction.' *Habitat International,* 27, pp. 163–66.

Hart, G. 2013. *Rethinking the South African Crisis: Nationalism, Populism, Hegemony.* Scottsville: University of KwaZulu-Natal Press.

Hervé, F. 2009. Integrating Poor Populations in South African Cities: A Challenge for Government Authorities. *Study produced under the supervision of Thierry Conzalez.* Agence Francaise de Dévelopment Research Department (France).

Huchzermeyer, M. 2001. 'Housing for the Poor? Negotiated Housing Policy in South Africa.' *Habitat International,* 25, 3, pp. 303–31.

———., 2001a. 'Consent and Contradiction: Scholarly Responses to the Capital Subsidy Model for Informal Settlement Intervention in South Africa.' *Urban Forum,* 12, 1, pp. 71–106.

Institute for Democratic Alternatives in South Africa. (IDASA). 1999. 'Executive Policymaking in the New South Africa: Policymaking in the Department of Housing.' (Unpublished, available from IDASA Resource Centre in Cape Town).

Jenkins, P. 1999. 'The Role of Civil Society in the Development of Housing Policy: Some Lessons from Southern Africa.' *Third World Planning Review,* 21:2, pp. 177–99.

———, 1999a. 'Difficulties Encountered in Community Involvement in Delivery Under the New South African Housing Policy.' *Habitat International,* 23:4, pp. 431–46.

———., and H. Smith. 2001a. 'An Institutional Approach to Analysis of State Capacity in Housing Systems in the Developing World: Case Studies in South Africa and Costa Rica.' *Housing Studies,* 16:4, pp. 485–507.

Jessop, B. 2001. 'Institutional (Re)turns and the Strategic-relational Approach.' *Environment and Planning A,* 33, pp. 1213–35.

Johnson, K. 2003. 'Liberal or Liberation Framework? The Contradictions of ANC Rule in South Africa.' In H. Melber (ed.). *Limits to liberation in Southern Africa: The Unfinished Business of Democratic Consolidation.* Cape Town: HSRC Press. pp. 200–23.

Jones, G.A., and K. Datta. 2000. 'Enabling Markets to Work? Housing Policy in the "New" South Africa.' *International Planning Studies,* 5:3, pp. 393–416.

Kanbur, R. 2011. 'Structural Inequalities and the New Growth Path: A Response to Jeremy Cronin.' Deputy Minister of Transport, Republic of South Africa, 24 March. http://www.kanbur.dyson.cornell.edu.

Khan, F. 1997. 'Democracy, Forums, Social Compacts and the Fuzzy Relationship between Conflict and Development: A Reflection on the

Cato Manor Experience.' In Urban Sector Network (ed.). *Best Practices of Developmental Local Government*, Johannesburg: USN (Unpublished).

———. 2004. 'The City and its Future? The Eternal Question.' *Development Update: Special Edition – The City and its Future*, 5:1, pp. 5–52.

———. 2013. 'Poverty, Grants, Revolution and "Real Utopias": Society Must be Defended By Any and All Means Necessary!' *Review of African Political Economy*, 40, 138, pp. 572–88.

———., and S. Mohamed. 2014. 'From the MEC to the Green Economy Conglomerate: Wiring a Green Economy-Green Society-Developmental State Circuit.' *New Agenda: South African Journal of Social and Economic Policy*, no. 56: 47–53.

Lalloo, K. 1999. 'Areas of Contested Citizenship: Housing Policy in South Africa.' *Habitat International*, 23:1, pp. 35–47.

Leftwich, A. 1994. 'Governance, the State and the Politics of Development.' *Development and Change*, 25:2, pp. 363–86.

Leroke, W. 1996. 'Development as a Post-modern Condition: Towards a Post-modern Development.' In J.K. Coetzee & J. Graff (ed.). *Reconstruction, Development and People*. South Africa: International Thomson Publishing Southern Africa (Pty) Ltd. pp. 222–45.

Lester, A., E. Nel and T. Binns. 2000. 'South Africa's Current Transition in Temporal and Spatial Context.' *Antipode*, 32:2, pp. 135–51.

Lupton, M., and S. Murphy. 1995. 'Housing and Urban Reconstruction in South Africa.' In A. Lemon (ed.). *The Geography of Change in South Africa*. New York: John Wiley & Sons. pp. 143–68.

Mabin, A. 2000. Urban development, urban policy and state action (mimeo)

Mackay, C.J. 1999. 'Housing Policy in South Africa: The Challenge of Delivery.' *Housing Studies*, 14: 3, pp. 387–99.

Macroeconomic Research Group (MERG). 1993. *Making Democracy Work: A Framework for Macroeconomic Policy in South Africa*. Bellville (Cape Town): Centre for Development Studies.

Makgetla, N.S. 2004. 'The Post-Apartheid Economy.' *Review of African Political Economy*, 100, pp. 263–81.

Napier, M. 2003. 'Supporting the People's Housing Process.' In F. Khan & P. Thring (eds.). *Housing Policy and Practice in Post-Apartheid South Africa*. Sandown: Heinemann. pp. 321–62.

Ocampo, J.S. 2006. 'Foreword: Some Reflections on the Links Between Social Knowledge and Policy.' In P. Utting (ed.). *Reclaiming Development Agendas: Knowledge, Power and International Policymaking*. New York: Palgrave, pp. viii-xiv.

Pieterse, E. 2009. 'Post-Apartheid Geographies in South Africa: Why are Urban Divides so Persistent?' Paper presented at Interdisciplinary

Debates on Development and Cultures: Cities in Development – Spaces, Conflicts and Agency, Leuven University, 15 December.

Rodrik, D. 2000. 'Institutions for high-quality growth: what they are and how to acquire them.' Draft paper prepared for the International Monetary Fund Conference on Second-Generation Reforms. No. w7540. National Bureau of Economic Research.

Rolnik, R. 2009. 'Report of the Special Rapporteur on Adequate Housing as a Component of the Right to an Adequate Standard of Living, and on the Right to Non-discrimination in this Context.' United Nations General Assembly. http://daccess-dds-ny.un.org/doc/UNDOC/GEN/G09/106/32/PDF/G0910632.pdf?OpenElement.

Rust, K. 2002. 'No Short-cuts: Implementing the South African Housing Policy.' Paper prepared for the Institute for Housing of South Africa.

Saul, J.S. 2005. 'South Africa: Debating the Transition.' *South Africa: The Post-Apartheid Denouement.* (Emailed to writer on 17 May 2005).

Sheridan, A. 1980. *The Will to Truth.* London and New York: Tavistock Publications.

Simon, D. 2001. 'Trading Spaces: Imagining and Positioning the "New" South Africa within the Regional and Global Economies.' *International Affairs,* 77:2, pp. 377–405.

Sisulu, L. 2008. Speech by L.N. Sisulu Minister of Housing at the Occasion of the Budget Vote of 2008/09 for the Department of Housing (RSA). http://www.pmg.org.za/briefing/20080528-housing-ministers-budget-speech.

Smit, D. 1999. 'Housing in South Africa: Significant Government Achievement based on Public-Private Partnership.' *CDE Focus,* November.

Swilling, M. 1998. 'Rival Futures.' In H. Judin & I. Vladislavic. (eds.). *Blank: Architecture, Apartheid and After.* Rotterdam: NAI Publishers. pp. 285–99.

———. 1999. 'Changing Conceptions of Governance.' *Africanus: Journal of Development Administration – Special Issue on Administrative Culture,* 29:2, pp. 20–40.

———. 2005. 'Thoughts and Notes' (Unpublished).

Tomlinson, M. 1998. 'South Africa's Housing Policy: An Assessment of the First Two Years, 1994–1996.' *International Journal of Urban and Regional Research,* 22, pp. 137–46

———. 1999. 'South Africa's Housing Policy: Lessons from Four Years of the New Housing Subsidy Scheme.' *Third World Planning Review,* 21, pp. 283–95.

———. 2002. 'Efforts and Errors: South Africa's Search to Extend Housing Finance to Low-Income Households.' *Housing Finance International,* XVII, pp. 8–14.

———. 2002. 'International Best Practice, Enabling Frameworks and the Policy Process: A South African Case Study.' *International Journal of Urban and Regional Research,* 26:2, pp. 377–88. (Version used in the article e-mailed by author to writer, 1–14).

Treasury. 2003. Briefing Notes on Housing and Urban Development. Prepared by Sharon Lewis for the Director-General and Minister of Finance, July.

UN-Habitat. 2010. *The State of African Cities 2010: Governance, Inequality and Urban Land Markets.* London: Earthscan.

Utting, P. 2006. 'Introduction: Reclaiming Development Agendas.' In P. Utting (ed.). *Reclaiming Development Agendas: Knowledge, Power and International Policymaking.* New York: Palgrave. pp. 1–24.

Vale, P. 2014. 'Introduction – The New South Africa at Twenty: Some Brechtian Whispers.' In P. Vale & E.H. Prinsloo (eds.). *The New South Africa at Twenty*. Pietermaritzburg: University of KwaZulu-Natal Press. pp. 1–18.

Vawda, A. 2003. Address to the National Housing Policy and Strategy Workshop. Department of Housing. (Available from author).

———. 2012. 'Altering Path Dependencies: Sketching Contours of the Built Environment: A Sector's Response to Climate Change.' http://www.gsdpp.uct.ac.za/course-materials/viewcategory/42-wednesday-7-march-2012.html.

Vattimo, G., and S. Zabala. 2011. *Hermeneutic Communism: From Heidegger to Marx.* New York: Colombia University Press.

Watson, V., and B. Agbola. 2013. 'Who will Plan Africa's Cities?' *Counterpoints,* September. London: African Research Institute.

Watson, V. 2006. 'Deep Difference: Diversity, Planning and Ethics.' *Planning Theory,* 5:1, pp. 31–50.

Wilkinson, P. 1998. 'Housing Policy in South Africa.' *Habitat International,* 22:3, pp. 215–29.

Wilson, P.A., and C. Lowery. 2003. 'Building Deep Democracy: The Story of a Grassroots Learning Organization in South Africa.' *Planning Forum,* 9, pp. 47–64.

Wolpe, H. 1995. 'The Uneven Transition from Apartheid in South Africa.' *Transformation,* 27, pp. 88–102.

World Bank. 1993. 'Housing: Enabling Markets to Work.' World Bank Policy Paper. Washington, DC: World Bank.